The Eloquent Screen

THE ELOQUENT SCREEN

A Rhetoric of Film

Gilberto Perez

Foreword by James Harvey

University of Minnesota Press

Minneapolis

London

The publication of this book was assisted by a bequest from Josiah H. Chase to honor his parents, Ellen Rankin Chase and Josiah Hook Chase, Minnesota territorial pioneers.

Published by the University of Minnesota Press
111 Third Avenue South, Suite 290
Minneapolis, MN 55401-2520
http://www.upress.umn.edu

Printed in the United States of America on acid-free paper

The University of Minnesota is an equal-opportunity educator and employer.

25 24 23 22 21 20 19   10 9 8 7 6 5 4 3 2 1

Library of Congress Cataloging-in-Publication Data
Perez, Gilberto, author.
The eloquent screen : a rhetoric of film / Gilberto Perez.
Minneapolis : University of Minnesota Press, 2019. | Includes bibliographical references and index.
Identifiers: LCCN 2018046160 | ISBN 978-0-8166-4132-1 (hc) |
ISBN 978-0-8166-4133-8 (pb)
Subjects: LCSH: Motion pictures—Philosophy. | Subjectivity in motion pictures. | Metaphor in motion pictures. | Motion picture plays—History and criticism.
Classification: LCC PN1995 .P3965 2019 | DDC 791.4301/5—dc23
LC record available at https://lccn.loc.gov/2018046160

CONTENTS

Introduction: John Ford's Rhetoric

I. Cinematic Tropes

II. Melodrama and Film Technique

PUBLISHER'S NOTE

At the time of his untimely death in January 2015, Gilberto Perez had completed the manuscript for his second book, *The Eloquent Screen*, save for a planned brief preface and acknowledgments. Several of the writings included in the manuscript were originally published in the *Yale Review*, *London Review of Books*, *Senses of Cinema*, and elsewhere. The preface that now opens this volume has been drawn from his earlier statements about his intentions for the work. The University of Minnesota Press gratefully acknowledges the help of the author's partner, Diane Stevenson, in finalizing the text and of his former student, Malia Haines-Stewart, in preparing it for production.

FOREWORD

James Harvey

"The rhetoric of film," answered my friend Gil when I asked him what his new book (*this* one, as it turned out) was going to be about. And the truth is that my heart sank a little at his answer. Not my kind of book, I thought. But then, as I also thought, I could have had the same fear ahead of time about his earlier one, *The Material Ghost: Films and Their Medium*, a book I had been rereading and learning from almost since the first time I opened it—so full as it was of fresh illuminations and brilliant writing about films and filmmakers that I loved as much as the writer did. Never mind the intermittent academic film theory that was also in it. I read those passages a little faster, I suppose, than the others. "I am as drawn to film theory," said the author in his Introduction, "as I was drawn to theoretical physics." Fair enough warning, for a reader like me. But none of that had mattered in the end to my love of the book itself. And now, soon it seemed, I would be reading its successor.

So I hoped. But soon turned out to be a long way off. My friend Gil died the next morning—suddenly, shockingly, utterly without warning of any sort—from a heart attack at the airport meeting his wife's plane. Four years ago now. By that time we had been friends—growing to be close ones—for almost twenty years.

Memories, as we know, can be deceptive. My own stubbornly insist on placing that exchange about his work-in-progress on the last night we saw each other: on that Monday in January, in that restaurant we liked, after that particular movie (*Inherent Vice*, which we both disliked). Surely I would have asked him that question about his book long before, in all the times we talked and hung out? But maybe not, after all. Gil in those days was regularly publishing his criticism in places like *Raritan* and *London Review,* pieces I was often reading in manuscripts beforehand. If I never asked about the "new" book, it was not only that (as Diane, his wife, now confirms) he never wanted to talk about it, it was also because his writing then was ongoing and alive. In fact—as I now understand—it was this remarkable book taking shape in those pieces all along.

The first time I met Gil—before I knew of his writing or even his name—I was flacking my own book *Romantic Comedy in Hollywood* at Lincoln Center's Walter Reade Theater, appearing there with a movie. I was told just before things began that there was someone who wanted to meet me waiting in the manager's office: Gil, of course, who had read and admired my book. I don't recall what we talked about in that brief office meeting, but I do remember the impact of the Gil smile on that first encounter: someone you could laugh a lot with, was what I thought. As turned out to be the case. That was 1999.

No question: professor-like as we both were, Gil had his own brand of star quality. Wearing his favorite Mexican serape, smoking one of his thin black cigars, he could have been a lead out of a Sergio Leone western. Ordinarily, with his mischievously inflected affability, his openness and warmth, he had the kind of presence that made him, among other good things, a much beloved teacher.

From the start I was in awe of his brilliance, and of the broad and deep learning that undergirded it. So when he asked me early on who I thought was the greater American filmmaker, John Ford or Preston Sturges—knowing that Sturges was a personal favorite for me, just as I knew Ford was for him—I was both pleased and flattered. "Ford, of course," I said. With no hesitation—but with a certain pang nonetheless, which Gil—the consummate gent I was getting to know—could have picked up on, even sympathized with at the time. We were both happier for the exchange: I knew the question had meant a lot to him—and *that* meant a lot to me, I found. It was like a pact for going forward.

We went to lots of New York events during school semesters over the years—Gil driving in from Sarah Lawrence, me coming from Brooklyn, sometimes walking over the Bridge if we were meeting in the Village. But mostly (almost every other weekend in the latter years) we went to the movies. And to a restaurant afterward to talk about them (as we did on his last night). Mostly we agreed. No surprise, to either of us. That consonance of taste and temperament had kicked in between us from the very beginning, flourishing over the years, especially in those late-night postmovie dialogues, at places where we knew the wait staff and they us. (They remembered him, most of them.)

Because it was our movie life that mattered to us as friends. *That* for us was the *personal* one. Much less so the sort of details and life stories we could have shared yet rarely did. Like Pauline Kael—the critic we cited in conversation more than any other, probably—who was famously said never to ask first how you were but instead what you'd seen lately and what you'd thought of it.

Now the last book is here. So is Gil, again, in this stunning final accomplishment. The range alone is breathtaking—from Griffith's *Way Down East* to Capra's *It Happened One Night,* from Ernie Gehr's *Serene Velocity* to Malick's *Tree of Life,* and much more. More films and filmmakers, more breadth and depth, more original insights and penetrating writing, all of it successfully controlled and developed within the conceptual frame—the rhetoric of film—that he named to me when I asked, on our last postmovie night.

More theory, then—much more. As it turns out, film theory organizes *The Eloquent Screen,* while the book itself, also and at the same time, transcends it. Something you discover—however bumblingly, as in my case—by following its controlling (and impersonal) theoretic pathway to where you find that it regularly goes, over and over again: to the author's humanist depth and richness.

Gil was a philosopher—and a historiographer. In his writing he calls our own secular and postmodernist-ironic time an age of mystery—in contrast to the long-gone ones, so called, of faith and reason. And he's in synch with mystery, so called—with something beyond human limits, something closer to Wittgenstein's "wonder at the existence of the world." Gil was not religious. But he was attuned to spirituality and the possibility of grace—even when it's not the "amazing" kind. At any rate, it's a topic (and a word) that recurs in this movie book almost as often and as centrally as romantic love does. And *that* too in these pages is something spiritually fraught: "divine and dangerous" in an Ophuls film (*La signora di tutti*); imperiled by casual adulterers in a Wong Kar-wai movie (*In the Mood for Love*); linked to grace itself by the dancing heroine in Terrence Malick's *To the Wonder.*

He and I saw that Malick movie together in 2012 when it was new. And neither of us knew anyone besides ourselves who saw it and liked it—or read any reviewers who did. But it was Gil who wrote about it back then, for the *London Review.* And now in his book, in the Malick chapter (the most illuminating I've found anywhere so far), where he wonders (regarding the relation between film and audience)

if the dissenting critics had been embarrassed to see love depicted so
"earnestly," let alone connected to "a sense of the divine," to "religious devotion." (That dancing heroine, for example.) Maybe so. But
how does *that* work in the movie itself?

It has to do, among other things, with the available natural light
("the documentary light") that Malick films in (as Godard also
does)—and its "singular beauty," as Gil calls it. The *real* light—
coming straight from the sky, through the window's stained glass.
"Feel it," urges the Oklahoma church's white-haired black janitor.
"Touch it!" They both put their hands on the glass. "That's spiritual,
you know," says the janitor (who also speaks in tongues—in another
scene). And as Gil says, Malick wants us to feel that this is so in this
film. Then, following this: "What is this love that loves us? That
comes from nowhere, from all around?" asks the heroine in a voice-
over to a lyrical succession of broadly and serenely flowing waters, in
overhead close shots, shining in the sun, beautiful yet oil-polluted.
"Not just the wonder but the difficulty of love is the theme of *To the
Wonder*," writes Gil—"the light of love" somehow shining still, and
"despite all doubts," in and upon "a fallen world."

One of the movies that he specially celebrates in his book
("It's a wonderful film," he writes) is the Iranian filmmaker Abbas
Kiarostami's *Where Is the Friend's House?* A simple, fable-like film,
based on a Persian poem, about a little boy whose confused search
for a schoolmate turns into a journey—for him and for us (we share
his perspective)—of discovery of the world, of its revelations and of
its mysteries. "This is a film about wonder," says Gil: "The wonder
of seeing things with fresh eyes, the wonder from which philosophy
is born."

And this book—amazing and multifaceted as it is—is finally about
the same thing. And it too is wonderful, as you will find.

ON GIL PEREZ

Diane Stevenson

At first, I wasn't sure I could write this essay. Gil's death was too new. I was too sad. Time passed. Now I am sitting down to try.

Besides the grief, I was inhibited by a worry that in writing about Gil I'd put too much of my own slant on his work. Of course, as in any long marriage, Gil and I agreed about a great many things. But I was more pell-mell, more strident; Gil was more polite. I didn't want to compromise the good etiquette of his arguments, his keen and delicate sense of things, his eloquence and equipoise. Still, I wanted to set out what seemed to me habits of mind that tie this last book *The Eloquent Screen: A Rhetoric of Film* (finished two days before he died) to the first, *The Material Ghost: Films and Their Medium*.

The Material Ghost is exactly what its subtitle says it is, an exploration of film as a medium. What makes a movie a movie? What makes movies distinct from other arts? What do movies do compared to other crafted media, theater, painting, photography, the novel, architecture? What don't they do? These were natural questions for him. To an unusual degree, Gil acquainted himself with all the arts. He thought deeply and critically about them all. But because film was his great love, it was film he tackled.

What constitutes the medium we call film? What sets film apart? What qualities are implicit in its technological innovation? Still photography is cousin to film. Both innovations belong to the nineteenth century, yet there are unmistakable differences. Gil describes how, with movies, what remains outside the picture is implied; you are aware of a world beyond. Not so a photograph. As in theater, as on a stage, time and space are marked off, without the same extensive implication of film (Gil would state this better than I do). Unlike a movie, then, what's there is all there is. This is the sort of formal sorting Gil does in his criticism. Yet Gil was never formalist in any reductive sense, as his foray here into rhetoric decisively shows.

Gil's first book explores film as a set of distinct, bounded formal habits. The second, broadening the investigation, looks at movies in relation to an audience. How do films persuade? What qualities characterize these persuasions? What gives film its persuasive power? Two key terms inform *The Material Ghost*: "narrative" and "drama." The key term organizing *The Eloquent Screen* is "identification," pretty much as Kenneth Burke defines it. In fact, Gil came late to that philosopher's work, but all along the compatibility was there (Burke is nothing if not dialectical). And now, taking my own cue from Burke, I'd like to observe that *The Eloquent Screen* follows on *The Material Ghost* much as Kenneth Burke's *A Rhetoric of Motives* follows on *A Grammar of Motive*. Grammar, rhetoric: a logic of progression that's Gil's own.

Gil investigated the conventional. He looked at habits, developing over time, that would come to define film as a medium and how, with particular filmmakers in particular concrete circumstances, these habits impact and sway audiences: conventions of editing, for example, the close-up, crosscutting, ellipses, and other kinds of visual convention, like metaphor, like metonymy.

Conventions aren't set in stone. Innovation breaks in. Rules are made to be broken. Yet, continuities persist. Both interested Gil: the formally autonomous and the historically dynamic; the coherence of movie making over time and the way it is ever renewing. He had a stout regard for history. He appreciated that from concrete social circumstance the new emerges. In the broadest sense Gil's intellect, his sensibility, was dialectical.

The terms I've mentioned as key, "narrative" and "drama," are presented in *The Material Ghost* as opposing terminological guideposts. In *The Eloquent Screen,* the same is true for "metaphor" and "metonymy." Careful to steer clear of a stasis inherent in such oppositions, Gil regards what is dynamic instead. It's wonderful to follow him worrying the contradictions. Neither end term is exclusive; neither is terminal; neither cuts out the possibilities of its opposite number. His bias is dialectical. This means Gil's dichotomies never get bogged down in simple contrast. Key terms interact. They refuse isolation. Each interrogates the other; they deflect and reflect each other. They leak.

What emerges from Gil's binary scales is subtlety. By definition, polarities exist in unstable equilibrium, artifacts of the argument they find themselves in. They're artificial. They're tools; nothing is really so black and white, so clearly right or wrong. In this regard, Gil is canny. He knows tools intervene. He knows tools impose a logic of their own—their own ripples of consequence. He knows that the setup matters—in scientific measurement, in philosophy, in film criticism—so he sets out his argument with contending terms only to transcend the contention. (Perhaps he has a lesson for us during this strange, disconcerting, contentious time in our national life.)

In short, Gil understood convention. He understood "ideology," the word we use to indicate the broadest sort of social consensus. He understood that we are all shapers of ideology and that we are all shaped by it, himself included. He knew his own bias. He knew the ground he stood on. This means he was less susceptible to the imperatives of critical fashion. His critical self-consciousness gave Gil a critical edge.

Gil's advantage was the advantage of a scientific background. He ended as a film critic and historian, but he started as a physicist. He studied at M.I.T. and Princeton. He was used to dealing with knowledge patterned into paradigm, and he appreciated its vagaries. Theories, he knew, come and go. He knew that no one floats above theory, above convention, above ideology, above history. Each of us is grounded in a time and a place. Gil's experience told him that. A Cuban, he came to the United States for college, then stayed. He moved from one country to another, from one language to another, from one set of cultural etiquettes to another, from one set of political outlooks to another. (Gil experienced the Cuban Missile Crisis from his end of the Cold War scheme; in Mississippi, I experienced it from mine.) He knew, from two national sides, the multiple insecurities of social and political stricture. He knew the permeabilities.

Of course, we all talk the talk of such intellectual relativism, but not many of us walk it with Gil's canniness. Dialectical habits of mind are actually pretty rare. Plus, Gil's own dialectical reckonings were stout. The movie makers he admired most were the hard-reckoning and stout-hearted ones, open to possibility, to a hope that possibility itself makes possible the possible. Thus, he was modernist in instigation. Modernism was the mood of the aesthetic community he grew up in, and he never repudiated this first utopian, and at the same time skeptical, loyalty. His was a life-long, open-ended, critical interrogation of the movies. Modernism was a ground for him, a point of view, not a piety. Gil's intellectual agility persisted throughout.

Gil delighted in our long-standing human habit of bringing into rational focus our irrational and chaotic everyday experience, our human habit of codifying what we observe, of giving order to disorder, of settling observation into clear-cut category, of turning particulars into generals, facts into speculation, and speculation into rules—law, convention, thesis, theory. He knew the give and take of human speculation; he knew the profound wonder and weirdness of it all. Gil approached with delight and humor and humility the job he chose of interpreting the bigger world through the smaller world of film. It was a delight living with his delight, and I miss him.

December 2018

PREFACE

It is time that we develop a rhetoric of film. In an era that mistrusts certainties and embraces differences, rhetoric, the study of argument and persuasion, of different points of view that can be taken and different ways of expressing them and influencing others, is much called for. Film theory nowadays is in a contested and confused state, and rhetoric is a form of theory that may be particularly useful and welcome at this point. Rhetoric stands between poetics and reception studies. Whereas poetics looks at the work and its construction, and the study of reception looks at the audience and its response, rhetoric looks at the way construction elicits response and the way the work works on the audience. We have had various attempts at a poetics of film—Eisenstein's montage poetics, Bazin's realist poetics, Brakhage's visionary poetics, Metz's semiotic poetics, among others—and we have had several studies of the reception of films. Although poetics and reception studies often touch on rhetorical matters—boundaries are not hard and fast—we have not had any sustained attempt at a rhetoric of film. This book is such an attempt. It seeks to develop a film rhetoric that provides a meeting place for aesthetic and social concerns, the pursuit of theory and the examination of practice, scrutiny of the work and attention to historical circumstance.

Around the turn of the nineteenth century, at that pivotal juncture of the Enlightenment and Romanticism, the classical tradition of rhetoric came to an end. Neither the Enlightenment, with its belief in reason, nor Romanticism, with its embrace of emotion, could accept a discipline that combined reason and emotion in the service of persuasion. We are the heirs of that juncture and by and large have inherited its repudiation of rhetoric ("Oratory is the art of playing for one's own purpose upon the weaknesses of men, and merits no respect whatever," said Kant).[1] Nobody in American public life would have a good word to say about rhetoric; "spin" is our current derogatory term for it. Yet rhetoric is all around us: you decry rhetoric in your opponent while using it yourself, not least when you decry it in someone else. Moreover, it seems that intellectually, rhetoric in recent decades has been making a comeback. This is not exactly a return to classical rhetoric: "The idea of reviving its code in order to apply it to our literature would be a sterile anachronism," Gérard Genette notes in the process of contributing to our rhetorical reawakening. What we have been witnessing is not a revival but an endeavor of renewal, a striving to devise an art of argumentation and figuration, a discipline of persuasion, suitable to our time. It is as a discipline of persuasion, as a transaction between the artist's work and the beholder's share, that E. H. Gombrich, for example, discusses art and illusion in his well-known book of that title. From Gombrich to Genette, from Kenneth Burke to Wayne Booth, from Roman Jakobson to Mikhail Bakhtin to Roland Barthes, from Stanley Fish to Paul de Man to Terry Eagleton, from Hayden White to Judith Butler to Dave Hickey to Jacqueline Lichtenstein—there have been various ways of undertaking the endeavor of rhetoric in our time.

Film being very much an art of our time, this book undertakes a rhetoric of film in light of these efforts toward a modern rhetoric. Classical heritage is brought to bear when pertinent, but the main concern is with understanding how movies work on their audiences. Classical rhetoric recognizes the importance of emotion to persuasion— the rhetorical principle of *movere*, moving the audience—as well as the importance of identification in arousing emotion: "As the human countenance smiles on those who smile, so does it sympathize with those who weep," writes Horace in the *Ars Poetica*. "If you would have me weep you must first express the passion of grief yourself; then . . . your misfortunes hurt me."[2] Although much discussed, our identification with the characters in a film, so that we feel what they feel, smile when they smile, and weep when they weep, remains insufficiently understood. Surely we don't feel exactly the same thing that a character feels; some even deny that such an identification exists. In *A Rhetoric of Motives*, Kenneth Burke reconceives the notion of identification, making it central to the workings of rhetoric. Broadening the notion beyond personal or psychological identification—in international politics, for example, the United States rhetorically identifies its interests with the cause of democracy, as the USSR used to identify its interests with the cause of the workers—Burke argues that all persuasion rests on identification. His enlarged conception of identification is one of the principles of a modern rhetoric that will be adopted in this book and applied to the workings of film. Roman Jakobson's influential reformulation of the rhetorical tropes and figures around the poles of metaphor and metonymy is another move of modern rhetoric that we will apply to film, though we will not follow Jakobson to the extent of accepting that all figures can be subsumed under these two master tropes. Nor will we follow those such as Paul de Man who give primacy to figuration over persuasion in rhetorical studies. We will study the figures at some length, but always as they enter into the workings of persuasion.

Much of our discussion will be devoted to the means and forms of film, but with emphasis on their effect on the spectator and their transaction with the audience. Take the shot/reverse shot, for example—the common technique of cutting back and forth between two characters facing each other, each shown in turn from the other's side. What is the difference between studying the shot/reverse shot as technique, which has been done many times, and studying it as rhetoric, as we propose to do? Studying it as rhetoric—as a figure of rhetoric, not a trope but what we will call a figure of arrangement—brings forward what the shot/reverse shot does to the audience, where it puts us, how it orients us, what it makes us feel. Studying it as rhetoric makes clear, for one thing, that the exchange between shot and reverse shot creates an identification not just with one or the other but also with both characters in the exchange—though not necessarily with both to the same degree or in the same way. How much we identify with each character, and in what way, will depend on the specifics of the shot/reverse shot in question: the distance, the angle, the duration may be significantly different in shot and reverse shot, and they may change as the exchange unfolds. Our response will also depend, of course, on the specifics of story and characterization, what has been happening so far in the film, and what we expect to happen. The specifics of the spectator must be reckoned as well: what the shot/reverse shot does to us will depend on what we bring to it. Rhetoric deals in specifics. It is a theory of practice. Its generalizations particularize.

The Eloquent Screen

INTRODUCTION

JOHN FORD'S RHETORIC

Judge Priest's Rhetoric

In *Judge Priest* (1934), the second of three movies he made with John Ford, Will Rogers is the title character, William Priest, a judge in a small Kentucky town some years after the Civil War. At one point in the movie, he is discussing with a friend the challenge he faces in the upcoming election. "He's a spellbinder and a silver tongue from way back," says the judge about his opponent. "I'm just a, well, an old country jake who's kind of a baby kisser. [They laugh.] I ain't got much to offer the boys in the . . . in the way of rhetoric." "I understand he doesn't approve of your grammar," says the friend. "My grammar?" replies the judge. "First thing I learned in politics was when to say 'ain't.'"

Knowing when to say "ain't," the judge says he "ain't got much to offer . . . in the way of rhetoric." His opponent, the spellbinder with the silver tongue, is of the florid, orotund school, and of that kind of rhetoric, it is true, the judge hasn't much to offer. But he is master of another rhetoric, and knowing when to say "ain't" is part of that mastery. It's clear the judge will beat his opponent in the election, as he beats him in the courtroom in the central action of the movie. He wins because he's the better rhetorician. His is the kind of rhetoric that pretends not to be rhetoric, the kind that is all the more persuasive for seeming not to be trying to persuade. When he tells his friend

1

that saying "ain't" is not a matter of grammar but of political savvy, the judge is in effect admitting to that other kind of rhetoric, acknowledging that his plainness of speech and colloquial manner are something calculated to have an effect. And Ford's movie lets us know all along that this rhetoric that seems not to be trying is indeed a highly effective form of persuasion, that it's not innocent but calculated, that in pretending not to be rhetoric it's being cunningly rhetorical.

The judge's political opponent is the prosecutor of a case in which he alleges the judge is biased: "I call upon you, Judge Priest, to vacate the bench during this trial and yield your place to a qualified judge." Judge Priest is visibly shaken. After all these years, he's being deemed unqualified to sit on the bench. He takes out his handkerchief, fumbles with his pipe, wipes the sweat off his face. He is at a loss for words. At length he rises, walks toward a portrait of Robert E. Lee hanging on the wall, and haltingly recalls how, after fighting in the Civil War "for what we thought was right," he returned to his hometown, put up his shingle, and before long was sitting on that bench. "Maybe I did have a hankering for the spirit of the law . . . not the letter . . . but as far as I know nobody ever found cause to complain . . . till now." Gradually we come to recognize that this man whose feelings have been hurt is turning those hurt feelings into rhetoric. He's giving a performance. He instructs the jury to "forget everything that I've said . . . my feelings have no place in the . . . in the records of . . . of this trial"—which of course only serves to impress those feelings more firmly in the minds of the jury. Those hurt feelings are by no means false. Judge Priest is being quite sincere, but at the same time he's being quite rhetorical. He's all choked up with emotion when he asks another judge to "come up here . . . and take . . . take my p . . . my place on . . . on the bench." We scarcely know whether to cry or cheer—cry over the genuine emotion or cheer the consummate performance. Ford is asking us to admire the judge as a man of feeling, and to admire him all the more because he knows how to make those feelings effective in a public situation.

In *Judge Priest*, two kinds of rhetoric, the judge's and his opponent's, are set in contrast. The contrast is not merely between plainness and verbosity, or between colloquial and high-flown language. Rhetoric, the film makes clear, is not merely a matter of language. The judge's pauses, his hesitations and repetitions, are as eloquent as his words. Rhetoric is not only language but also gesture, movement, action. Rhetoric is performance. And like all performance, it's addressed to an audience. Judge Priest is a great rhetorician because he knows his audience, and he knows how to play to that audience.

The judge is made to step down from the bench during the trial of Bob Gillis, a man we know is innocent. But the testimony of three—three who ganged up on him and are now accusing him of assault—goes against him, as does the fact that Gillis keeps to himself and has few friends in town. Moreover, he doesn't say much at the trial in his own defense; he refuses to give testimony that would be likely to exculpate him because he doesn't want to involve a nice young woman named Ellie May. The judge is fond of Ellie May and has been encouraging her romance with his nephew, Rome—short for Jerome—against the objections of Rome's mother, who disapproves of a young woman whose father is unknown. Rome, fresh out of law school, is Gillis's defender at the trial. This is a small town; neither the number of lawyers nor the circle of relationships is large. As much as a story about justice, this is also a story about family, about a community not very much larger than a family, about the ties of blood that bind a community of that size.

Things are looking bad for Gillis at the trial—only the summations remain—when Judge Priest receives a visit at home from Reverend Ashby Brand (Henry B. Walthall, who played beside Lillian Gish in *The Birth of a Nation*). The reverend has something to tell him about Gillis that leads the judge to intervene in the case. He writes an anonymous letter to the prosecutor and entrusts Jeff Poindexter (Stepin Fetchit), a black man he has brought into his service, to deliver it without revealing its provenance. The letter discloses that Gillis was once convicted of murder and sentenced to life imprisonment—a fact that the prosecutor naturally wants to bring to the attention of the jury, so the next day he reopens the case and calls Gillis back to the witness stand. This gives Judge Priest his chance. He comes forward and announces himself to the sitting judge as associate counsel for the defense. He has no questions to ask Gillis, but he has tricked the prosecutor into allowing him to call Reverend Brand as a witness. The reverend now tells the story of Gillis's release from a chain gang to join the depleted Confederate army, and of his fighting with truly exceptional courage in the last days of the Civil War. Meanwhile Judge Priest has arranged for Jeff Poindexter to play "Dixie" right outside the courtroom, so that everyone can hear it as a rousing background to the story of Gillis's bravery. The reverend also makes known that Gillis is Ellie May's father and has been secretly providing for her. Of course Gillis is acquitted—and not only acquitted but welcomed into the community as a hero of the lost Southern cause.

To be sure, what Gillis did in the war has nothing to do with the case being tried. The judge wins the case not by evidence or by argument but by staging a performance. This time as director more than as actor, he puts on a show, complete with stirring musical accompaniment—a shameless manipulation of the allegiances and emotions of his audience. When I showed *Judge Priest* to a class, the students

liked the movie but objected to this rhetorical manipulation. They had
expected the judge would unearth some decisive piece of evidence or
significant judicial precedent, or maybe bring forward an expert or a
key eyewitness whose testimony clears up the facts, which is what
lawyer heroes usually do in courtroom dramas. The students expected
the judge's rhetoric to address the facts of the case; instead, it engages
the feelings of the audience. It would have been easy enough for Ford
and his scriptwriters to contrive the finding of evidence or the enlisting of factual testimony that would have made the judge a more conventional lawyer hero. But they chose not to do that. They chose not
to make the judge into a detective, which is what the lawyer hero is
most of the time—a digger into evidence, a finder of facts, the hero
of a positivist ideology. Nor did they make him into a philosopher, an
upholder of abstract principles, a manager of reason aimed at a universal humanity, the hero of an idealist ideology. Rather, they made
Judge Priest into a hero of rhetoric. Rhetoric is most effective—which
is to say, most rhetorical—neither when it merely adduces facts that
presumably speak for themselves nor when it merely invokes principles that presumably speak in the same way to everyone everywhere.
Rather, it is most effective when it speaks in the terms of a concrete
social situation to the particular human beings living in that situation
and belonging to that society.

Plato and Cicero

Plato condemned rhetoric as deception. He similarly condemned
poetry and painting, but many who balk at that nonetheless go
along with his condemnation of rhetoric. In the *Poetics* and the *Rhetoric*, Aristotle came to the defense of those arts, but this was primarily a defense of them as arts of language—of tragedy as the art of the
poet, not the actor, of rhetoric as a matter of discourse, of the content
and form of words, and only secondarily of their delivery before an
audience. Aristotle would not have thought so well of Judge Priest's
rhetoric because it depends too much on performance. But just as
the proof of the pudding is in the eating, the test of rhetoric is in the
audience. Rhetoric as such is not to be judged by principles but only
by effects.

In *The Eloquence of Color*, her book on rhetoric and painting in the
French seventeenth century, Jacqueline Lichtenstein puts forward
Cicero, the great orator of republican Rome, as the classical defender,
not only against Plato's condemnation but against Aristotle's conde-
scension, of rhetoric as an art of performance. Delivery (*actio*) was for
Cicero the most important thing in oratory; he liked to cite another

famous orator, Demosthenes, who, when asked about the parts of oratory, is said to have answered that delivery comes first, second, and third.[1] "Delivery, or action, which includes an audible and a visible aspect, since it consists of voice and gesture, derives not from a rhetoric of discourse," Lichtenstein comments, "but from an eloquence of speech in which the body participates with all its expressive forms."[2] She contrasts Cicero's bodily rhetoric with Plato's disembodied philosophy:

> Plato tried to rid philosophy of the risk from the body and from images, from all the effective and affective forces set off by speech. . . . The emotive body reduced to silence by philosophy, the direct and physical relation to the other ruled out by the mediations of writing, and the theatrical expressivity annihilated by the abstractions of a disincarnated theory—these are elements that Ciceronian rhetoric tries to bring back into speech. In the Ciceronian oratorical art the various modalities of physical expression like bodily gesture and tone of voice can finally regain their claims to wisdom and dignity.[3]

Plato divides truth from eloquence, but Cicero stresses the truth of eloquence:

> Because it passes beyond traditional distinctions of nature and artifice, of reality and illusion, of being and appearing, Ciceronian eloquence brings us to a universe of tangible representation in which the staging of the body and of discourse has sincerity as its condition and real emotion for effect. No one can make another believe a cause to be just without sharing the belief, at least during the speech. Through many examples and varied formulations, Cicero never ceases to repeat it: the orator must not only be *actor* but also *auctor*; he must himself feel the effects of the passion whose gestures he imitates in order to make its effects felt by his audience.[4]

Cicero has a point when he argues that by valuing only principles and discounting effects, philosophy becomes ineffectual; it renders itself impotent by renouncing the power of eloquence. Even if eloquence requires sincerity, however, and even if one grants Cicero's contention that the effective orator must feel what he would have his audience feel and believe what he would have his audience believe, this may yield real emotion but not necessarily justice or truth. Plato had a point too.

The term "Ciceronian" customarily refers to a style that is profuse, flowing, Latinate, ornamental. A tourist guide is called a cicerone, my dictionary tells me, "from the usual loquacity of guides." *Ciceronian* would not seem to be the term for Judge Priest—it's much more like his verbose opponent. Yet the judge's rhetoric is no less ornamental than his opponent's, and if it seems otherwise, it's only because the judge makes a more effective use of ornament. Although his language may be plain and colloquial, not what we would call Ciceronian, it comes with all the ornament of his pauses, his gestures, his inflections of voice, all the embellishment of delivery he's master of. The judge is Ciceronian in his rhetoric of performance. I may not be doing him a favor by calling him that. *Ciceronian* isn't exactly a term of praise—but then neither is *rhetorical* usually a term of praise. If *Ciceronian* means ornamental, so does *rhetorical* mean ornamental. Plato likens rhetoric to cosmetics. Rhetorically, he is disparaging rhetoric. The comparison has behind it the breach he posits between appearance and reality. Cicero calls that breach into question, but by and large the philosopher has prevailed. To this day, rhetoric is suspect as ornament is suspect. One may dispute Plato's metaphysics and one may dispute his disparagement, but he is not wrong to make the comparison. The fates of rhetoric and ornament are fittingly bound up together. A defense of rhetoric must also be a defense of ornament.

When the judge turns into rhetoric his hurt feelings over vacating the bench, it's real emotion he communicates to his audience, bearing out Cicero's claims for the truth of eloquence. We sympathize with the judge and feel that his opponent is treating him badly. However, his opponent is right to maintain that the judge has a bias in this case. This doesn't mean that the judge wouldn't have been able to rise above that bias and conduct the trial fairly, but his opponent has reason to ask him to step down. The judge's hurt feelings do not speak to the issue of his vacating the bench. They are real emotion, but they are not the truth of the matter. The feelings of a corrupt judge might have been just as hurt. The real emotion is an embellishment.

It's the same with the reverend's testimony. The reverend speaks with sincerity, with real emotion, and he arouses real emotion in the audience. He's speaking the truth, the truth about Gillis's bravery in the war, but that truth does not speak to the issue of Gillis's innocence or guilt in the charge of assault. It's not the truth of the matter but an embellishment, just as the musical accompaniment of "Dixie" is also flagrantly an embellishment. We know that Gillis is innocent and that all this embellishment is in the service of a just cause. We know the judge is a good man. But what if Gillis were not innocent? What if the judge were not a good man? Couldn't the same embellishment, the same manipulation of the audience, be put in the service of injustice? If Judge Priest is a hero of rhetoric, what kind of hero is this, winning not by principles but by effects, not by truth but by ornament?

Rhetoric and Comedy

Judge Priest is a hero of comedy. Rome and Ellie May, young lovers meeting with opposition from the older generation, are the stuff of New Comedy. New Comedy is very old—it was new in ancient Greece—but has endured through the centuries, from Plautus and Terence to Shakespeare and Molière to the romantic comedies of the screen. As Northrop Frye notes, "New Comedy normally presents an erotic intrigue between a young man and a young woman which is blocked by some kind of opposition, usually paternal, and resolved by a twist in the plot . . . a discovery in which the hero becomes wealthy or the heroine respectable."[5] In *Judge Priest*, we have the young lovers, we have the blocking parental figures—not only Rome's mother but also, more indirectly, the judge's opponent, who is prosecuting Ellie May's father and whose daughter is the woman Rome's mother would like her son to marry—and we have the twist in the plot, the discovery that makes the young woman respectable and happily resolves the situation. That the hero is the judge, the older man rather than the young lover, isn't so much of a departure from a genre whose young lovers, as Frye remarks, are often not very interesting and pale beside other, more vivid characters. *Judge Priest* is of course a courtroom drama as well as a comedy, but the action of comedy, as Frye notes, is a social contest "not unlike the action of a lawsuit, in which plaintiff and defendant construct different versions of the same situation, one finally being judged as real and the other as illusory. This resemblance of the rhetoric of comedy to the rhetoric of jurisprudence has been recognized from earliest times."[6] Gillis's trial fits nicely into the plot of the comedy. It leads to his acquittal and social vindication, and at the same time to the revelation that he is Ellie May's father, which enables the young lovers to come together with the blessing of the community.

What may be more of a departure from the configuration of New Comedy is the governing role the judge plays in his society. As the chief representative of the older generation, not only is he not a blocking figure, but he also sides with the young lovers not from the sidelines but from the center, from a position of power in the society they are up against. At the end of Molière's *Tartuffe*, the king intervenes to set things right, but the judge is setting things right in *Judge Priest* from the very beginning—not that he assumes the position of a king or lord; his authority has the democratic cast of a man of the people. As Frye outlines, the plot of New Comedy begins with blocking figures in control of society, figures of undesirable authority such as the *senex iratus* (heavy father) and the *miles gloriosus* (braggart warrior, a type found in *Judge Priest* among the Confederate veterans telling war stories); it ends with the formation of a new society around the triumphant young lovers. Judge Priest, however, is in control at the end as he was at the beginning, a benevolent authority presiding over the world of the movie. He may be seen as a figure out of romance, a wise old man like Prospero in *The Tempest*. But the old Kentucky town depicted in *Judge Priest*, though invested with a bygone sweet-ness, is a human society with its share of imperfections and limita-tions, prejudices and problems—not the idyllic and enchanted land of romance. The judge, unlike Prospero, has nothing arcane or occult about him, nothing of the magician. His skills are worldly skills, his power worldly power. His only magic wand is the least otherworldly, the most thoroughly implicated in actual human society: his rheto-ric. Will Rogers comes up in Frye as a type of satirist, the rustic who exposes the pretensions of society; the society in *Judge Priest* is rural rather than urban, and the judge is a leader rather than an outsider, but he still subjects its ways to comic puncturing. If Judge Priest is a Prospero, the wise old man of romance, he is a Prospero brought down to the domain of comedy.[7]

According to Frye, "the movement of comedy is usually a move-ment from one kind of society to another."[8] That doesn't happen in *Judge Priest*. But I would argue that comedy—and we're talking about New Comedy—is more accepting and less subversive than it sounds in Frye's account. Though often irreverent or unruly, it is seldom revolutionary. What happens in *Judge Priest* is in my view what more usually happens in comedy—not the formation of a new society but merely a renewal of the existing one. Take a classic boy-meets-girl comedy, *It Happened One Night*, made the same year as *Judge Priest*. It begins with the heroine's overbearing rich father as a *senex iratus*, but as the plot develops, the old man is shown to have been right about the phony his daughter wanted for a husband, and in the end he's the one who sets things right between her and the hero. Rather than the old man's antagonist, the hero is his chosen successor, a young version of himself who will perpetuate his lineage. *It Happened One Night* seems to me typical of New Comedy in the way it leads not to the overthrowing of a social order but to its rejuvenation. New Comedy pits a young couple against the dictates of convention, but the conflict is conventionally resolved. The community is disturbed but not disrupted, and its values are revitalized by the disturbance and reaffirmed at the happy ending. Youth wins, but its victory only strengthens the social fabric and ensures its continuation. That's what happens in *Judge Priest* under the judge's benevolent manipu-lation. The very instrument that serves him to revitalize his society relies on its established ways and notions and becomes part of the comedy: *Judge Priest* is a comedy of rhetoric.

The comedy of rhetoric may be most evident in the exaggerated verbosity of the judge's opponent (played by Berton Churchill, who a few years later plays the thieving banker in *Stagecoach*, another pompous upstanding citizen coming in for Ford's scorn), whose oratory during the trial is repeatedly punctured by the spitting of a drunken juror (Francis Ford, the director's brother) into a spittoon that keeps being moved out of his reach and that he keeps managing to hit with a resounding noise. But the humor isn't solely at the opponent's expense; it takes in the judge's own rhetoric too. I have called the judge Ciceronian in his rhetoric of performance, but the way we are made aware—and aware that he's aware—of his rhetoric as a performance, involving not just a flowing sincerity but a certain feigning, a matter not merely of real emotions but of calculated effects, undercuts the Ciceronian truth of eloquence. The reverend's testimony is Ciceronian in its earnestness, but the judge's use of the reverend's testimony is a knowing manipulation of an audience—not outright deception, but surely a bit of a cheat. The comedy of the judge's rhetoric comes from our amused awareness of this. It was for cheating that Plato earnestly condemns rhetoric, and it was in terms no less earnest that Cicero defends it. In the terms of comedy, Ford acknowledges that rhetoric cheats and asks us to recognize the need for that cheating in society. Gillis went to trial with the community prejudiced against him. It's hard to argue a community out of a prejudice. Had he attempted that, the judge would have been right, but he would have lost the case. Instead, he played to another prejudice of the community, and won the case. We approve of his ends and smile at his means in this comedy of rhetoric.

Both the rhetoric and the comedy reach a high point with the playing of "Dixie." Wearing an elegant raccoon coat and a vest given to him by the judge in compensation for his musical services, Jeff Poindexter steals a bass drum from the Confederate band getting ready to play on Memorial Day—which happens to be the last day of Gillis's trial—and sets himself up outside the courthouse with the drum and a tambourine, by a large window so that his playing carries inside and can be heard loud and clear. At the right moment in the reverend's testimony, the judge signals to Jeff that the music is to start. Jeff is joined by other black musicians, one playing a banjo and another a fiddle, as the sound of "Dixie" rises into the courtroom. The joke here is not on the blacks playing the music of the Southern Confederacy. The joke is on the white Southerners whose sentiments are being swayed by this music, by this performance the judge has arranged and that Jeff has orchestrated in behalf of Gillis. Two decades later, in *The Sun Shines Bright* (1953), Ford returns to the character of Judge Priest. Will Rogers was long since dead, and Charles Winninger now plays the part. Beside this different judge—"little Billy Priest," one character calls him, which no one would call Will Rogers—Stepin Fetchit is again Jeff Poindexter. When a young black man fond of playing the banjo is brought before the judge on charges of vagrancy, Jeff gets him to play "Dixie" on his banjo to sway the judge in his favor—the same rhetorical ploy used by Judge Priest in the earlier movie. This time, the joke is on the judge.

Will Rogers and Stepin Fetchit

Stepin Fetchit is an actor who has been maligned for his portrayal of a type that some find demeaning to his race. Some find all types demeaning and think that people should be portrayed as individuals. But types are a representation of people in society, of individuals as part of a group. Comedy especially calls for types in its rendering of the human accommodation to society—an accommodation not without its troubles, but the troubles allow for laughter when seen as something shared. To be against types is to be against comedy. Still, it cannot be denied that some types are objectionable. What about Stepin Fetchit? He is alleged to portray black people as dumb and lazy. But in *Judge Priest*, his character is neither dumb nor exactly lazy. In the white supremacist society in which he lives, he must play dumb—or else he would be seen as surly or insolent—in order to get away with doing what he wants to do as much as he does. His dumbness is a mask that Fetchit subtly lets us see through so we can glimpse the intelligence beneath. And as for his being lazy, in that regard Jeff Poindexter is at one with Judge Priest. They are both easygoing Southern types. Their relaxed quality, which matches Ford's own directorial style, is construed positively. Neither Jeff nor the judge subscribes to the work ethic, which doesn't mean they don't work, only that they value other things in life and see no reason to drive themselves too hard. At the beginning of *Judge Priest*, Jeff is brought before the judge and falls asleep in the courtroom as the prosecutor carries on. "Sheriff, wake him up there," says the judge, who has been reading the comic pages of a newspaper. "If anybody's going to sleep in this court it'll be me." After his appearance in court, Jeff goes fishing with the judge.

Across the differences that divide them, Jeff and the judge are akin. One black and the other white, one low and the other high in the hierarchy of their society, the two are counterparts, doubles of each other. When a suitor comes to visit Ellie May, the judge, who lives next door and is hidden behind some bushes, stages a dialogue between Jeff and himself designed to scare the suitor, to trick him into running away so that Rome can take his place by Ellie May's side. In a gesture of complicity, Ford's camera moves to reveal that we have been hearing the judge alone playing both parts in this dialogue, taking turns as himself and his imitation of Jeff—which conveys a sense of his identification with Jeff. Far from being dumb, Jeff Poindexter is a variant of that traditional figure of comedy, the clever servant, the *dolosus servus* or tricky slave of Roman comedy, Harlequin in the commedia dell'arte, or Figaro in *The Barber of Seville*—except that Jeff is paired with his master, the judge, who is himself something of a Harlequin or Figaro scheming in behalf of the young couple and something of a trickster giving the affairs of society a turn for the better. At the same time that he represents the law, the judge partakes of the resistance to the law, the incipient anarchy, represented by Jeff. It's that dash of anarchy that makes the judge's rhetoric successful. His opponent's is a rhetoric shackled by decorum and convention. The judge's is a rhetoric that takes liberties, that doesn't break the law but doesn't play strictly by the rules. It's the rhetoric of a trickster.

Will Rogers and Stepin Fetchit are good together, both in *Judge Priest* and in their next film with Ford, *Steamboat Round the Bend* (1935), which was made just before Rogers's death in a plane crash. With the room to improvise they enjoyed under Ford's direction, the two actors palpably had a good time playing off each other—surprising each other, as Fetchit said in a newspaper interview at the time.[9] More than "a remarkable harmony of acting styles," as Joseph McBride wrote,[10] the rapport between Fetchit and Rogers—who was himself part Cherokee and proud of it—represents a rapport between the races, a harmony bringing black and white together, albeit within a hierarchy that places white above black.

The harmony may be all very well, but the hierarchy is not, and the harmony may be taken as a justification of the hierarchy. *Judge Priest* could be seen as an apology for a society that, while relegating blacks to an inferior position, allows individuals of different races to get along together and even develop a warm rapport with one another. In *The Defiant Ones* (1958), Stanley Kramer's liberal drama of the civil rights era, two escaped convicts chained together, one white (Tony Curtis) and the other black (Sidney Poitier), start out hating each other but end up forming a bond of human fellowship. *Judge Priest* starts where *The Defiant Ones* ends: the judge and Jeff form a bond of human fellowship when they go fishing together. Ford shows happening naturally within society what Kramer can only imagine happening in extreme circumstances outside society. Kramer removes his characters from society so that the racial problem can be solved by their coming to terms with each other as individuals. Like other liberals, he assumes that racism is nothing but the belief that persons of another race are humanly inferior, and he supposes that a personal recognition of common humanity is enough to dispel it. Tony Curtis's racist in *The Defiant Ones* is Southern white trash. Judge Priest is a better type of Southerner, yet he is not exempt from the racism of his milieu. His privilege and authority as a white man rest on racist premises he never questions. This is not to damn him but to describe him, not to impugn him personally but to understand him socially. Being an admirable man, he makes a revealing portrayal of racism, which isn't confined to the obviously reprehensible. (Nor, of course, is it confined to the South; none of us is exempt from the racism of our milieu.) Judge Priest is no bigot—he doesn't believe that blacks are humanly inferior. He has an easy human affinity with them. As individuals, he and Jeff have no problem, but they cannot solve the racial problem as individuals. The problem is plain to see: on account of their race, blacks are socially inferior. The judge relates to them as a good master relates to his servants. The problem is social, and removing the characters from society is not a way of solving it but of avoiding it. If *Judge Priest* is an apology for a racist society, then it's an apology that doesn't dissemble the racism of the society. It puts its finger on the problem even though it leaves it unsolved.

Judge Priest contained a scene in which the judge saves Jeff from a lynching—a triumph of rhetoric against force, bearing out Cicero's claims for the civilizing power of eloquence—but the studio (Fox) cut out the scene for fear of displeasing audiences in the South. All that remains is one mention of it the judge makes to Jeff. Planning his strategy for the last day of Gillis's trial, the judge asks Jeff if he can play "Dixie" on his harmonica. Jeff says yes and adds that he can also play "Marching through Georgia." He's taunting the judge with "Marching through Georgia," which, as Jeff well knows, is a tune of liberation for blacks but a reminder to Southern whites of defeat and devastation by Sherman's invading army. "I got you out of one lynching," says the judge as the scene fades out. "Catch you playing 'Marching through Georgia,' I'll join the lynching." This exchange shows that Jeff is no fool. He doesn't need to be told what playing "Dixie" means any more than the judge needs to be told what playing "Marching through Georgia" means. The two understand each other perfectly. Both of them know, and each knows the other knows, that they are alluding to something very serious. Yet their exchange is humorous. Comedy helps to live in a world where Jeff could be lynched to the tune of "Dixie" for playing "Marching through Georgia." Not that comedy can do away with the world's wrongs, but it serves to ameliorate and conciliate. Not that it can erase the difference between white master and black servant, but it makes possible a certain parity between the two. It's the wisdom of comedy the two of them share—the wisdom of humility, of accommodation to necessity—that enables the harmony they enjoy together.

Identification

Will Rogers was one of the most popular Americans of his time. More than an actor, a top box-office attraction in the movies, he was a figure on the national scene, heard on the radio and read in the daily newspapers, even talked about as a presidential candidate. Many people identified themselves with him—or he identified himself with them; he was popular as a populist, homespun and down to earth, an image of the common man speaking common sense. In *A Rhetoric of Motives*, Kenneth Burke argues that identification is key to the workings of rhetoric, as when a politician says to an audience of farmers, "I was a farm boy myself."[11] We may think of identification as personal affinity, putting ourselves in another's place, as when we identify with a character in a movie. But we never simply identify with a character; we identify with an action, a situation, an emotion, a motive, an interest, a point of view, something the character represents. Our identification with a character usually works together with other identifications that precede it, accompany it, modify it, complicate it. Like the politician speaking to farmers, Will Rogers identified with his audience before his audience identified with him. And *Judge Priest*, beginning with its title—as well as a shot before the titles, a head-on view of the judge looking right at us, pounding his gavel and calling the court to order—identifies itself with its protagonist judge before we identify ourselves with him.

There are different degrees and kinds of identification. We side with the hero against the villain, but if we didn't in some way identify with the villain also, the conflict between the two wouldn't have much dramatic force. Every movie star elicits identification from many in the audience, but when we identify ourselves with Greta Garbo or Cary Grant, we reach for an ideal of glamour and beauty, which is not how we relate to the engaging ordinariness of Will Rogers. With the Rogers character in *Judge Priest*, Ford makes a special kind of identification—I don't mean Ford the actual person but Ford the implied author, the governing intelligence we sense behind the camera.[12] More than the protagonist, Rogers's Judge Priest is a governing intelligence dramatized in front of the camera: the way he presides over the movie identifies him with the author or director.

To the rhetoric of a film or play, the effect of drama on its audience, the actors are always important. In this film, Will Rogers is singularly so. When the judge vacates the bench under pressure from the prosecutor, the rhetoric of hurt feelings he addresses to his audience in the courtroom is the film's rhetoric as well, addressed to us through the actor commanding our attention. After asking another judge to take his place, our protagonist leaves the courtroom, and we see him in long shot from behind, darkly framed by the door as he puts on his hat and goes down the steps toward the sunlit town square in the background. It's a lovely shot sustained on the screen in a felt gesture of sympathy for the judge. With as much sincerity as the judge exhibited in the courtroom performance this brings to a conclusion, the film's visual rhetoric is here identified with the judge's rhetoric. This identification with Judge Priest isn't subjective. It's not an identification with his individual point of view. Rather, we see him from the collective viewpoint of his audience in the courtroom, turning to look at him as he departs. We are identified with that audience, are as moved by his performance as they are, and share their lingering last look at the judge we and they feel shouldn't be departing. The emphasis isn't so much on how the judge himself feels as on how he has made his audience feel. It's an identification with the judge's rhetoric fittingly assuming the perspective of those he has affected.

In another scene, the film makes a more subjective identification with its presiding figure. After the feigned dialogue with Jeff succeeds in scaring away Ellie May's suitor, the judge goes up alone to his darkened bedroom and looks out the window, and in a point-of-view shot through his eyes, we see Rome and Ellie May down in the garden. The sight of the young couple he has contrived to bring together reminds the judge of his own youth, and when again he looks out the window and again we see through his eyes, a ghostly image from the past takes over the present. In Rome and Ellie May's place, we see an apparition of the judge as a young man beside the young woman he married. The judge lights a candle that illuminates the portrait of his dead wife and children on his bedroom wall, and his reflection appears on the glass over the portrait, like a ghost from the present over the imprinted image of the past, as he starts talking to his wife: "It's been a long time, honey, since . . . you and the . . . babies . . . went away." This may be the most moving of the several scenes in Ford's films enacting a conversation with the dead. Will Rogers is wonderful. With barely contained emotion—emotion made more affecting by the attempt to contain it—the judge tells his dead wife about his nephew's return and points out that Rome is just the same age their son would have been: "I guess it's . . . Rome coming home . . . what makes it seem more lonesome than . . . ever around here." Not wanting to show himself in this mood in front of his wife, he changes the subject. Gazing with a smile at the portrait on the wall, he tells her that the fellow who "enlarged that tintype . . . sure did a pretty job. . . . I wish you could see it, honey." Noticing a blemish in the oval frame, he disparages the fellow who "put that gilt on there" and promises to "get that fixed" as he blows out the candle and leaves the room to continue the conversation in the cemetery.

In a move of identification with the character, sentiment in this scene is allowed to take over from comedy—the judge's personal, private sentiment, which the film enters into and shares with us. When his feelings are getting too personal, too painful for him in the privacy of his bedroom, the judge moves to the more public space of the cemetery. There, sitting by his wife's grave, he still has a private conversation with her, but about more public matters: "People are funny, honey . . . always got their eyes set on something"—Rome on Ellie May, Rome's mother on the prosecutor's daughter she wants for her son, the prosecutor on the judge's job—"some of them are going to be disappointed." The judge puffs on his pipe and talks about the honeysuckle he smells. Then the film cuts to a more distant view, and from behind a tree at screen center, near the wife's grave, Bob Gillis appears carrying a bouquet of flowers, the camera panning with him as he walks toward another grave. Cut to a frontal view of Gillis as he reaches the grave he came to visit and stands over it; cut to an analogous frontal view of the judge watching and reporting to his wife, whose grave from this angle seems to blend with the tree rising beside it, now at the edge of the screen framing the view like an outgrowth of her spirit. Cut back to Gillis, who bends down with his offering of flowers; cut back to the judge, who informs his wife as the scene fades out—and informs us, like a narrator entrusted by the film to fill us in—that the grave Gillis came to visit is Ellie May's mother's. An identification is made here between the judge and Gillis. Two men each visiting a woman's grave, the loner Gillis and the lonesome judge, are joined together in the community of their privacy. In the bedroom, the film's identification with the judge brought us into community with his privacy. In the more public space of the cemetery, the judge's privacy connects with another's, the identification with the judge opens out into an identification between him and Gillis, and the community of privacy links up with the life of the community.

The judge's personal story harbors sadness, yet out in the community, he's a hero of comedy. The comedy is shaded by the sadness, by the recognition that all's not quite well even though it ends well enough. Nowhere is the film's identification with its protagonist more evident than in the way the judge arranges the happy ending. The reverend's testimony to the accompaniment of "Dixie" that wins the day in court and wraps up the plot is a "spectacle," as McBride writes, "stage-managed by Judge Priest, serving as the director's on-screen surrogate."[13] Here as previously in the film, Judge Priest concurs with Demosthenes and Cicero that in rhetoric, what counts the most is delivery, the speaker's performance before an audience—except that previously the judge was the speaker, the performer of his rhetoric, and here he's the director of the performance. Allowed by the sitting judge to talk without interruption, the reverend becomes the narrator of a flashback illustrating in images the story he tells, with his face superimposed as a vignette, an unusual device that enhances our identification with the audience in the courtroom; we see the face before them and at the same time see the images he evokes in their minds. More than they, however, we're aware that behind the reverend as narrator stands the judge as director, whose arranging hand in these proceedings we're better placed to recognize. We may be swayed as they are by the judge's rhetoric, but our response is qualified by the irony that comes from seeing it as rhetoric—seeing the judge giving Jeff the cue to start the music, seeing the black ensemble playing "Dixie" out in the street—and as the amused irony of undeceived comedy. The crowning touch of the judge's rhetoric, "Dixie" accompanies not only the reverend's words in the courtroom but also the images rendering his narrative on the screen. It becomes part of the film's own rhetoric, identified with the judge's and acknowledged like the judge's to be a manipulation. The film's close identification with the judge and what he represents—the good and the not so good, the humaneness of his character and the racism of his milieu—is combined with the distance of comedy.

Comedy and Hierarchy

Every society has its hierarchy. A society pledged to equality—such as the United States or the old Soviet Union—may want to deny or dissemble this, but a hierarchy is nonetheless in place. Comedy disturbs hierarchy. It brings down the high and gives play to the low. It recognizes the injustices of hierarchy and holds them up to laughter. Jeff and his fellow blacks playing "Dixie" at the climax of *Judge Priest* humorously declare the injustice of their situation, the fact that the Confederate glory whose tune they sing for their supper rests on the backs of their race. But the laughter of comedy carries another recognition: the recognition of limits. Comedy knows that there are things wrong with society but also limits to what can be done to right them. Its laughter is both a mockery and an acceptance—sometimes more of a mockery, sometimes more of an acceptance. Comedy is about living in the world. While it may contest the way things are and move toward change—and in the hands of someone like Brecht, even toward revolution—it remains aware that society admits improvement only up to a point, and that beyond that, its wrongs can only be lived with. The endings of comedy may be happy, but the reconciliation they bring about is always in some measure a reconciliation to injustice.

Judge Priest is a figure of tolerance. We're able to appreciate this despite being unable to see what must have been his finest moment: the rescue of a black man from a lynch mob, omitted by a studio as timorous as the judge is courageous. He succeeds in overcoming the social prejudice against Ellie May and against the loner, Gillis, who turns out to be her father. He has a kinship with Jeff and a genuine sense of fellowship with the blacks in the community. But he does not attempt—there is nothing he could do within the terms of his society—to change the racial hierarchy that keeps blacks in an inferior position. He is reconciled to that injustice. We of course are not, and we may object to a comedy proposing such a reconciliation. But let's not indulge in that easiest of self-congratulations, a feeling of superiority toward the past. How many films can we put beside *Judge Priest* that have given us such a vivid portrayal of an interracial community and of blacks as integral to that community? *Do the Right Thing* (1989) comes to mind as one, but I can't think of many others. The blacks in *Judge Priest* are inferior socially but not humanly, and they're not token individuals but part of a living texture of social interrelationships. They are, it is true, at the bottom of a racist hierarchy. The film knows that as well as we do, even though, like its judge protagonist, it takes no stand against it. *Judge Priest* sees the flaws of the society it depicts, and if it asks us to accept them, it's not because it approves but because it also sees that under the circumstances, there is nothing else to be done. Such is the spirit of comedy, its accommodation to the world. Under changed circumstances, it may be a different story. The happy endings of comedy promise a better society, and the change for the better that concludes *Judge Priest* leaves open the possibility that further changes for the better may come about in the future.

After Gillis's acquittal and the ensuing cheer and anarchy in the courtroom, Jeff and the other musicians gathered around him, the blacks who from their position outside have played the tune and set the tone for the proceedings, stride down the street and go on playing. They move toward the camera, which moves with them, and their little parade dissolves into the bigger one: the Memorial Day celebration that brings the film to a close. There are no blacks marching in this parade of Confederate veterans, which Gillis joins as a now honored hero of the South, yet the advancing black musicians trigger the transition into it as if they were setting in motion the whole communal ceremony. So smooth and seamless is the transition that they seem to be taking part in a celebration that excludes them, and even to be leading it. Ford not only includes them but puts them first—the last shall be first. This is one of his fondly staged ceremonies of community, often supposed to express nostalgia for a romanticized past. But like the dance at the unfinished church in *My Darling Clementine* (1946), the parade at the end of *Judge Priest*, the little black parade together with the large white one, celebrates a community to come. It looks forward to an envisaged future in which blacks will rise from their inferiority in the social hierarchy and assume their rightful place in the community.

Plato condemns rhetoric in terms of an ideal society where truth and reason would prevail and embellishment could only get in the way. Politics would be banished from such a society, along with rhetoric and poetry. Cicero defends rhetoric in terms of practical politics, but he still idealizes the truth of eloquence. Ford shares neither idealism. His comedy of rhetoric takes place in the realm of the imperfect. It recognizes that society has flaws and that rhetoric must work with the flaws of society. Its laughter both exposes and accepts those flaws. We laugh at the discrepancy between rhetoric and truth at the same time that we cheer rhetoric's ability to help the cause of truth. Things are not perfect, but within the limits of the possible, they turn out well. Like politics, rhetoric is the art of the possible. It must build its persuasions on the beliefs of society, which it may bend to its purposes but cannot afford to break, or else it may succeed as reason but will fail as rhetoric. Knowing the limits the world sets, comedy is glad to see that things can get better, even if not as much as we would wish. Cynicism about politics—and about rhetoric—is widespread in our society. Ford's comedy of rhetoric—and of politics—is not cynical. Its undeceived appreciation of the possible, the change for the better that negotiates an imperfect situation for the best, counters a cynicism that by disdaining politics lets things remain unchanged.

Larger Than Life

On the screenplay of *Judge Priest*, built around a character from stories by Irvin S. Cobb, two writers who often worked with Ford collaborated, Dudley Nichols and Lamar Trotti. Trotti also wrote *Young Mr. Lincoln* for Ford to direct (1939, with Henry Fonda as Lincoln), the character taken from history, the screenplay taking the liberties of fiction. The two pictures, each a courtroom drama with a

populist lawyer hero who upholds justice through cunning rhetoric—
and who in *Young Mr. Lincoln* actually gets to stop a lynching—have
much in common.

Like Judge Priest, young Lincoln is at the center of almost every
scene. But if Judge Priest is an author figure, a character whose governing role in the fiction identifies him with the author, young Lincoln is both less and more than that—less because he's young and
unsettled, of humble origins, a frontiersman who has yet to prove
himself and rise to a governing position in society, and more because
he's Lincoln, who we know—and the film keeps reminding us—will
rise to the highest position in the history of his country. As the editors of *Cahiers du cinéma* observed in a collective text that used to be
required reading for film theoreticians, *Young Mr. Lincoln* in effect uses
the future perfect tense, what will have been.[14] It enacts the young
lawyer's story as if it were happening before our eyes yet invests it
with the hindsight of history, what will have happened, a perspective
in which the future president looms larger than life. In Frye's terms,
the film manages to combine the low mimetic mode, where the hero
is one of us, and the high mimetic mode, where the hero is superior
to the rest of us. Thus it portrays Lincoln as both a man of the people,
a democratic hero, and a man destined to tower above the people, a
hero incipiently larger than life.

For the *Cahiers* editors, this is an ideological sleight of hand, a
way of mystifying Lincoln, but Lincoln is already mystified in American hagiography, and Ford can be seen as doing just the opposite:
bringing Lincoln down to earth. In a film where the *Cahiers* editors
see a repression of politics in the name of morality, what most struck
me on my first viewing was not being given a saintly Lincoln but a
crafty politician. Geoffrey O'Brien, who finds the *Cahiers* text "by now
scarcely readable," writes, "In trying to pin down the meanings of
Ford's art . . . *Cahiers du cinéma* missed his mercurial—and, admittedly,
sometimes infuriating—ability to be in two places at once. If Ford's
Lincoln exhibits at once a radiant sincerity and the devious subtlety
of a trickster, he is to that extent the director's mirror image."[15] That
better describes *Judge Priest*, though. There the character and the
director meet as equals, but in *Young Mr. Lincoln*, the director looks
up to the character even as he brings him down to our level. As the
critic says, two places at once.

Young Mr. Lincoln opens in 1832, when Andrew Jackson was running for his second presidential term and Lincoln was with the opposition, a local candidate making his first political try.[16] Introduced by
an orotund politician, Lincoln stands before a small rural audience
and speaks: "I presume you all know who I am—I'm plain Abraham
Lincoln." Plain versus orotund: a contrast of rhetorical styles recalling

Judge Priest. In frontal view, isolating him from his audience inside the movie, Lincoln seems to be addressing us, who certainly know who he is—or rather, this fledgling politician seems already to be standing before the eyes of history. Ford regards him with affection and a certain awe, a figure that from the start transcends the frame of the movie depicting him and assumes a commanding place in the long perspective.

The River and the Dance

We start with our hero's first bid for public office, presented as the dawn of a great political career. There is no repression of politics here: Lincoln's electoral defeat in 1832 is skipped but clearly implied, and the omission of that early setback keeps the emphasis on the future of a young hero who has still a lot to learn. He isn't yet a lawyer but rather is a rural shopkeeper who accepts some old books in payment from a family in a covered wagon. Among those books is one he avidly reads, a law book that initiates him in the profession. He learns law in the midst of nature: he reads the book by the Sangamon River, his long legs up a tree and his head on the ground. This suggests the law has roots in nature, as his getting the book from a humble family suggests the law stems from the people. Yet his upside-down posture—which Ford's camera accents by "reversing to give us the same posture from opposite angles," as O'Brien points out, "before Lincoln himself reverses his position"[17]—strikes a qualifying note. "Trouble is, Ann," the riverbank reader explains to a young woman who arrives on the scene, "when I'm standing up, my mind's lying down, when I'm lying down, my mind's standing up." This contrary orientation may be taken to indicate that no ready harmony, no simple equivalence, obtains between nature and the law. Lincoln the budding lawyer seems both at ease in nature and at odds with it.

The young woman he talks to is Ann Rutledge, his legendary true love. She flirts demurely with this young man hesitant about what to do with his life—torn between the river and the law, you might say, between staying close to nature and striking out in the world—and encourages him to become a lawyer. She is thus identified with the law. But she is also identified with the river by which Lincoln meets her—the frozen river the scene dissolves into as a symbol of her death, the river by which she lies buried, with Lincoln talking to her grave as the ice starts to thaw with the coming of spring. These are not the simple identities—woman = law, woman = nature, law =

nature—posited by the *Cahiers* editors. Ford's play of identifications is more complex than they recognize, and more dialectical. *Young Mr. Lincoln* has a kinship to his Western, a genre in which the woman typically stands for culture, for civilization—the schoolteacher from the East, Clementine in *My Darling Clementine*—and the man for nature, for the wilderness he roams. And in Ford's Westerns, the encounter between civilization and the wilderness is not a static opposition but a dynamic transaction, a dialectic of culture and nature. To equate culture and nature is for the *Cahiers* editors bourgeois ideology, but it is *their* ideology to keep the two apart. Ford does not equate them. He enacts a give-and-take between them, so that in identifying Ann Rutledge with both the law and the river, he brings together two different things reaching for a synthesis: the law coming to terms with nature. Lincoln's romance with Ann Rutledge, like Wyatt Earp's (also played by Henry Fonda) with Clementine, represents the civilizing of a frontiersman. But Ann dies, and Lincoln is left with her memory and with the ideal she embodied: the law she wanted him to pursue while keeping faith with nature.

Years pass, Lincoln is practicing law, and his success at facing down a lynch mob is the talk of the town, so Mary Todd, his future wife, invites him to a dance. Chief among Ford's ceremonies of community are dance scenes. Wyatt Earp and Clementine dance together in the unfinished church, the man of the West and the woman from the East joining a frontier community in the process of formation. At Mary Todd's party, however, a community is in place, a posh society to which the rough-edged Lincoln is an outsider. Normally such a scene would either treat the outsider as oafish and vulgar, the butt of comedy, or the society as puffed up and snobbish, the target of satire. Ford does neither. He presents the society as gracious and the outsider as sympathetic, making gentle fun of Lincoln in just the way Lincoln makes fun of himself, taking the hero's side without enmity toward the other side. When Lincoln arrives at the party, the camera moves forward to the circling dancers and shows him in the background, outside their circle. Yet as the camera movement suggests, this is a circle he must enter, a society he must negotiate, if he is to fulfill his worldly aspirations—which we know he will, as we know he will marry Mary Todd. She asks him to dance, and he does, though so stiffly and awkwardly—a bit of comedy perfectly balanced with affection—that she proposes they go to the balcony and talk instead. But out on the balcony he falls silent and stares at the Sangamon River in the distance. The river makes him think of Ann Rutledge. It's not, however, just a personal matter, the remembered lost love pulling him away from the woman beside him. Personal matters in

Ford are always bound up with social matters. The river, the memory of Ann Rutledge, represents the nexus of nature and the law, nature as something Lincoln mustn't leave behind in his dealings with the world, the law as an ideal he must reconcile with the demands of actual society.

Politics and Principle

In an admiring essay on *Young Mr. Lincoln* that begins by declaring it the one American film he wished he had made, Sergei Eisenstein describes a scene: "Here's a tug-of-war, with a rope stretched across a well-prepared mud puddle, into which the group at each end of the rope is trying to pull the other. At the last minute . . . a gaunt and gawky youngster, just stepped from a gallery of daguerreotype portraits of American country youths . . . comes very close to cheating."[18] Seeing that his group is losing, Lincoln ties the rope to a horse-drawn wagon, which drags the group at the other end straight into the mud. Cheating indeed. Eisenstein condones it ("his absolutely innocent look bespeaks only resourcefulness in a moment of decision"),[19] others would take it as all in fun, but the *Cahiers* editors are stern: "Law represented by its ideal figure has every right."[20] But even if you believe in the law's right to cheat, would you make its cheating so evident? The whole *Cahiers* argument rests on the assumption that the film intends to idealize Lincoln to the full and that such things as his cheating at tug-of-war unintentionally belie the ideal. But there's nothing unintentional about his cheating, either on his part or Ford's. As I see it, the figure of ideal law is Ann Rutledge, Lincoln is a politician both staunchly principled and shrewdly practical, and Ford is quite aware of the contradictions involved. True, the moralizing pretense to stand above politics is all too common among American politicians, but Ford is the wrong filmmaker to pin that on.

At the country fair that includes the tug-of-war, another event is a pie contest with Lincoln as judge. He takes a bite out of an apple pie, then a bite out of a peach pie, back and forth, each time thinking that the pie he has just tasted is the best and reaching no decision that we see. This, according to the *Cahiers* editors, "censor[s] the moment of choice,"[21] but the point is that Lincoln can't choose between the apple and the peach, which plainly symbolize the North and the South. He loves them both. This is Lincoln the unifier, the savior of the Union, not so much the Lincoln who waged war against the South. If the film's ideology may be found anywhere, it may be in its portrayal of a Lincoln who in one scene even plays "Dixie"—catchy tune, he says, unable to name it but playing it on his Jew's harp as he rides along the river. This is a Lincoln that, like Judge Priest, fits in with Franklin Roosevelt's New Deal and his embrace of the South in his winning Democratic coalition.

Lincoln saves two brothers from a lynching—the now grown children, as it happens, of the family from which he acquired the law book. They're accused of murder, and he's defending them. Each of them thinks the other did it, and for the other's sake, each takes the blame, while their mother keeps silent, refusing to pick one over the other. Lamar Trotti drew on an actual case from his youth for this situation: "When Trotti was a reporter in Georgia he had covered the trial of two young men accused of murder at which their mother, the only witness, would not tell which son had committed the crime. Both were hanged."[22] Just as Lincoln, comically, can't choose between two pies, so the mother, tragically, won't choose between two sons—who in the movie, with Lincoln as their lawyer, are not hanged but acquitted. The comedy of the equally good pies has a parallel in the near tragedy of the equally good brothers, who can also be construed as North and South, and their family as the people Lincoln preserved as one nation.

The New Deal in many ways descended from the Populism of the 1890s, which also arose at a time of economic depression. That Populism gained special strength in the South and may have nourished the Southerner Trotti. "Perhaps the most remarkable aspect of the whole Populist movement," historian C. Vann Woodward writes,

> was the resistance its leaders in the South put up against racism and racist propaganda and the determined effort they made against incredible odds to win back political rights for the Negroes, defend those rights against brutal aggression, and create among their normally anti-Negro following, even temporarily, a spirit of tolerance in which the two races of the South could work together in one party for the achievement of common ends. These efforts included not only the defense of the Negro's right to vote but also his right to hold office, serve on juries, receive justice in the courts and defense against lynchers. The Populists failed, and some of them turned bitterly against the Negro as the cause of their failure. But in the efforts they made for racial justice and political rights they went further toward extending the Negro political fellowship, recognition, and equality than any native white political movement has ever gone before or since in the South.[23]

This neglected chapter of history, not just Southern but American history, is worth recalling in connection with *Judge Priest* and *Young Mr. Lincoln*, one set in the South, the other with an eye on it, and both populist films from a time of renewed populism, even if not with a capital P.

Young Lincoln is of the people and for the people, as represented by the family whose case he takes up and wins. Theirs is the law book, theirs also the farmer's almanac (derived from one similarly used by Lincoln in an actual case) that plays a decisive role in the trial by telling when the moon set on the night of the murder. The film's populism extends even to the lynch mob, which would usually be rendered as a bunch of subhuman savages—look at Fritz Lang's misanthropic *Fury* (1936)—but which Ford portrays as misguided ordinary people, capable of brutality yet amenable to persuasion, responsive to the civilizing power of Lincoln's rhetoric. That must have been how he portrayed the lynch mob in the scene deleted from *Judge Priest*—not as nasty and brutish beyond words, but as human beings who can be reached by an appeal to their humanity. In *The Sun Shines Bright*, his later Judge Priest movie, the Tornado boys kept by the judge from lynching an innocent black man end up repentantly voting for the judge and deciding the election in his favor. Ford does not exclude from the community anyone who can be brought into it.

The way Lincoln pitches his appeal to the mob about to lynch the two brothers exhibits a rhetorical mastery comparable to Judge Priest's. At first he says he's not going to make any speeches but can lick any man there hands down. The alarmed *Cahiers* editors speak of "his castrating violence."[24] He is a large man, but they miss his braggadocio, which smacks of Southwest humor.[25] His readiness to fight is a rhetorical ploy. He engages the crowd at their level, establishes common ground with them as rhetoric requires, and at the same time, by daring any one of them to come forward, he begins to split up the crowd into individuals who wouldn't do on their own what they're doing collectively. Then he switches to self-belittling humor, the other side of braggadocio: the two brothers, he jokes, are sure to be hanged anyway, with him as their lawyer. Only at the appropriate moment does he move to the higher moral ground. By the roundabout route of politics, he gets to principle; beginning there would have gotten him nowhere. About one thing, though, the *Cahiers* editors aren't wrong. While laced with humor—Lincoln was famous for telling jokes—his rhetoric, unlike Judge Priest's, has an edge of violence. At the trial, for example, he doesn't just present the almanac's evidence; he surprises the culprit with it and uses it aggressively, like a weapon, to break him down and make him confess. Force starts where rhetoric ends, and behind political rhetoric there often lies the potential use of force. That edge of violence in Lincoln's rhetoric bespeaks the leader who will have waged war.

Like the man nearly lynched in *Fury*, the two brothers in *Young Mr. Lincoln* are white. In the 1930s, several movies dealt with lynching, which in the United States had been distressingly on the increase, but Hollywood, reluctant to take on the issue of race, usually made the victims white. Still, young Lincoln stopping a lynching would have put audiences in mind of blacks, who everybody knew were often the victims, as everybody knew he was to be the president who brought slavery to a stop. It is significant, however, that not only in the lynching scene but throughout the movie (aside from one brief mention) race and slavery, even if implied, are left unspoken. This confirms the *Cahiers* editors in their view of the film as disowning politics: "With the total suppression of Lincoln's political dimension, his main historico-political characteristic disappears . . . his struggle against the Slaver States."[26] This may be the suppression of a political issue, but surely not in the name of morality, for no higher moral issue attaches to the figure of Lincoln, no loftier principle is invoked by those who would idealize him above politics, than the liberation of the slaves. Liberty and equality are of course both political and moral values, and for their substantiation, one wants to remind the *Cahiers* editors, politics looks to nature, to the natural rights of man, as Lincoln looks to the river in Ford's film.

The historical Lincoln was personally against slavery but politically cautious in his handling of a divisive issue—too cautious, some would say. Although others appreciate his moderation and astuteness in a thorny situation, abolitionists at the time thought him insufficiently principled, and to this day he has come under similar criticism. In presenting him chiefly as the unifier, and leaving race and slavery implicit, the film can be seen as true to the Lincoln of history, who himself stressed the preservation of the Union rather than the abolition of slavery. The film also reflects the politics of its own time, when the New Deal sought an alliance of North and South and tended to skirt the issue of race so as not to antagonize the South. You could say that Roosevelt played "Dixie" like the Lincoln of the film.

A lawyer for the railroad, a president who, whatever else he accomplished, furthered the interests of the corporate industrial North, the historical Lincoln was not exactly a populist. The triumph of the North in the Civil War brought in its wake—though Lincoln may not be to blame for that—the plutocracy of the Gilded Age, which the Populists reacted against. But if the patrician Roosevelt could assume the mantle of populism, Lincoln, a man of the people even if not always for the people, lent himself well to it. Enlisting on your side an enshrined American hero makes good rhetorical sense, and so the movie, here again reflecting the politics of the New Deal, gives us a populist young Lincoln. The more radical Populism, however—the Populism that fought racism in the South—waned after the Populists joined forces with the Democrats and supported William Jennings Bryan for president in 1896. Roosevelt was heir to that weakened populism. *Young Mr. Lincoln* leaves the fight against racism to the vagaries of implication. Populism, a movement of the common people working together across their differences toward common ends, has always been a difficult proposition in racially divided America.

For all its humor, *Young Mr. Lincoln*, unlike *Judge Priest*, is not a comedy. Lincoln may crack more jokes than Judge Priest, but comedy does not live by jokes alone. Comedy, the comedy of Judge Priest's rhetoric, presupposes a society stable enough to absorb quarrel and disturbance, the reconcilable quarrels, the resolvable disturbances of comedy. On the horizon of young Lincoln's society the Civil War impends, symbolized by a thunderstorm at the close and in our consciousness all along as something that will have happened, a bloody conflict irreconcilable and irresolvable within the action of a movie poised between comedy and the tragic future weighing on its hero. Although, like Judge Priest, young Lincoln happily wins the case on trial, for him, that's not the end of the story: we're not allowed to forget that far more momentous trials await the future president.

Twice in the film, at the outset and near the conclusion, Lincoln stands in sustained frontal view before an audience off screen, which in effect removes him from the present moment in the story and places him on the stage of history. Ford knows where to put the camera. Neither frontal view is a close-up of Lincoln, which would have been too intimate, too much about an individual's thoughts and feelings. This is an individual standing before a public, taking on a political, historical role, and the camera isolates him from his public of the moment, only to situate him in our minds before an immeasurably larger public. Facing the camera, Lincoln seems to be facing his compound personal and public destiny. These two frontal views at each end of the film aren't quite symmetrical, however; his countenance at the finish has discernibly changed. In the opening scene, the first-time candidate, who has "just stepped from a gallery of daguerreotype portraits of American country youths," looks ingenuous and unaware that the eyes of history are on him. After the acquittal of the wrongly accused brothers, a happy ending but a barely averted tragedy, one perceives in the young lawyer who has won his first case something like a somber awareness, a tragic sense of history and his place in it.

"I'm so glad you won," Mary Todd tells Lincoln after the trial, and Stephen Douglas, his future political adversary, congratulates him. He bids them good day and is about to leave through a door when, directly across, another door opens and throws light on him like a spotlight on a stage. "Hurry up, Abe," someone says, "the town's waiting." A crowd we never get to see has gathered outside, and as Lincoln turns and starts moving toward the opened door, a ninety-degree cut gives us the final frontal view. The movie could have ended with this extraordinary shot—an ending as well as a beginning, a conclusion to the story and at the same time an arresting image of the hero's emergence from obscurity into the light of history. At first Lincoln appears veiled in shadow against the light cast by the opened door on the wall behind him, a kind of screen within the screen, a reminder that we are watching a movie and that, like the light of the screen, the arena of politics is a space of performance. Frontality connotes theatricality. This scene, the *Cahiers* editors remark, has "a very specifically theatrical dimension: congratulations backstage after the performance, recall to the stage of the primadonna."[27] But Lincoln is no prima donna eager for the spotlight. Slowly, unsmilingly, his arms hanging down awkwardly, the trouble that lies ahead perhaps on his mind, he comes forward into the light and does not wave or speak to the cheering crowd outside the door. He shyly takes off his tall hat as his only gesture toward the audience before him, and that includes us. If in the initial frontal view he was on the stage of history without knowing it, here he responds to the call of history with a certain grave reticence in the face of what will have been.

Politics is often seen as theater, and for many this depreciates politics: theater as opposed to principle. But Ford recognizes the value of theater, rhetoric, performance before an audience, as a political means by which principle can be put into practice and actually have effect in the world. His Lincoln carries conviction both as a man of principle and as a successful politician.

Myth and Truth

Of the great directors of classic Hollywood, John Ford was the most political and remains the most controversial. Was he conservative or liberal, on the right or on the left? Both sides have claimed him, and both have found fault with him. If Richard Nixon decorated him, the conservative critic Vernon Young denigrated him.[28] If the *Cahiers* editors criticize him from the left, the leftist film modernist Jean-Marie Straub, of the European school influenced by Bertolt Brecht's epic theater and its alienation effect, praise him as the most Brechtian of filmmakers.

John Ford Brechtian? What's he to do with modernist self-consciousness and the calculated estrangement of the audience? Brechtian, Straub explained, "because he shows things that make people think."[29] Recall what O'Brien says about his subtlety and cunning, and ability to be in two places at once. Straub points to the ending of *Fort Apache* (1948), when the good soldier knowingly assumes the mantle of the falsely glorified bad soldier he had opposed.[30] Ford describes this film, the first of his cavalry trilogy, as "a variation inspired by Custer's last battle. We changed the tribe and the topography."[31] The bad soldier is a Custer figure, Colonel Thursday (Henry Fonda), an ambitious martinet who seeks glory by vanquishing the Apaches he disdains but little knows; the good soldier is Captain York (John Wayne), a friend of the Apaches who recognizes the justice of their cause and negotiates a truce with them. Thursday breaks the truce and marches against the Apaches; sure of victory, he succumbs to an enemy he has badly misjudged and dies, along with his whole regiment. As the dust settles, the action is construed as heroic by politicians and the press, and comes to be widely admired around the country. A painting in Washington grandly memorializes it, and York, talking to reporters as the fort's new commanding officer, pronounces the painting "correct in every detail."

Thursday's ill-advised last stand ironically gains him the glory he was after. "He's become almost a legend already," one of the reporters says. "He's the hero of every schoolboy in America." This has an alienation effect on us: we are astonished that the bad soldier has become a legend, a national hero, with the blessing of the good soldier who has been our hero and, better than anyone else, knows the legend is a lie. York's loyalty to the cavalry and to the men who fell in combat may explain his public endorsement of the legend. But then, as he goes into battle with his regiment, York puts on the distinctive hooded cap that Thursday wore. That cap is a striking touch and another alienation effect: we realize with a shock that the good soldier doesn't just honor the memory but turns into the continuation of the bad soldier.

The painting in Washington is never shown, only talked about, which puts the emphasis on the response of its viewers, the political consequence of its visual rhetoric. It isn't just that pictures can lie, whether in Washington or on the screen, but that lies, when acted on, can become fact. The rhetoric of Thursday's legend fuels the fires of war—a false legend yet a real war. York doesn't personally believe in the legend, but he says publicly that he does and he acts militarily as if he did—so in effect he does, in every way that counts socially and politically. Although he wanted peace, he now fights the war that Thursday wanted and, being a good soldier, he fights it better than the bad soldier ever could. That's something to make people think.

In an interview with Ford, Peter Bogdanovich brings up this ending in connection with a much-cited line from *The Man Who Shot*

Liberty Valance (1962): "The end of *Fort Apache* anticipates the newspaper editor's line in *Liberty Valance*, 'When the legend becomes fact, print the legend.' Do you agree with that? 'Yes," the director replied, "because I think it's good for the country."[32] "Really?" Tag Gallagher asks. "How come, then, that in both movies Ford 'prints' the facts, while exploding (and explaining) the legends?"[33] But if Ford tells the truth, he also sees the rhetorical value, the social function of myth in shaping the imagination of a people and holding a polity together. He knows that myth persuades and that truth, in order to persuade, has need of something like the images and stories of myth. He knows that discredited myth does not give way to plain truth but to myth of another sort. He tells the truth not merely to debunk the myth but as a reflective mythmaker.

John Ford made Westerns, a genre that enacts the myth of the frontier. It is a scenic genre, not just on account of the scenery, the landscape and the horses, the dust and the buttes and the sky, but because it is chiefly characterized by the scene in Kenneth Burke's sense: the background comes to the fore, and the setting determines the meaning.[34] Its scene is the frontier; it tells the story of the frontier as the story of the United States. But the frontier has been imagined in different ways. Historian Frederick Jackson Turner sees the frontier, or rather the successive frontiers in the national movement westward, as the scene of a transaction between the civilization coming from the East and the wilderness out West, a dialectic of culture and nature, order and freedom, authority and equality, which brought about on one frontier after another a renewal of American democracy.[35] Beginning with *Stagecoach* (1939), his first Western in sound, Ford reconceived the genre along the dialectical and democratic lines of Turner's frontier thesis. The double protagonist of *Fort Apache*, with Thursday standing for the East and York for the West, dramatizes the meeting of East and West on the frontier. In *My Darling Clementine*, with Doc Holliday and Wyatt Earp, Ford similarly doubles the protagonist to represent East and West. He does that again in *The Man Who Shot Liberty Valance*, a late and self-aware work that is also a reflection on the myth of the frontier and the conventions of the Western.

Monument Valley as an icon of the frontier was Ford's creation; no maker of Westerns has done more with the landscape of the West, the scene of this scenic genre. Yet *Liberty Valance* mostly does without natural scenery. This strikes us right off when Senator Ransom Stoddard (James Stewart) begins relating the story of his early days in the West and we go into a past that, as William S. Pechter notes, "to strange effect, is recognizably a set."[36] The studio landscape is surely intended to remind us that this picture of the old West is a fabrication. And the alienation effect is compounded by the fact that the lead actors,

Stewart as a young lawyer gone West to seek his fortune and John
Wayne as the rugged Westerner Tom Doniphon—plus Andy Devine
as the fat, frightened sheriff—are visibly too old for the parts they
play, figures from the movie past no longer credible as incarnations
of the frontier past ("the sight of a barrel-bellied, fifty-five-year-old
John Wayne heaving himself onto a horse" is for Pechter "hopelessly
destructive . . . of any suspension of disbelief"[37]). We don't go to Hollywood movies for realism; rather than the illusion of reality, their
business has been to give us the conviction of fantasy. We know that
the West depicted in Westerns never actually existed, but *The Man
Who Shot Liberty Valance* does not let us forget it.

Ransom Stoddard is the East and Tom Doniphon the West, doubles of each other. In the persons of Doc Holliday and Colonel Thurs-
day, the East dies in *My Darling Clementine* and *Fort Apache*, while the
West personified by Wyatt Earp and Captain York lives on, a West
that, for better or worse, has gained qualities of the East—better when
Wyatt Earp grows civilized and dances with Clementine, worse when
Captain York becomes the enemy of the Apaches he had befriended.
But in *Liberty Valance*, it is the West that dies and the East that lives
on. Senator Stoddard has come with his wife, Hallie (Vera Miles), to
Shinbone, the small Western town of their youth, for the funeral of
their old friend, Tom Doniphon. The East that lives on seems to have
mostly lost any qualities it gained from the West. If Wyatt Earp's
romance with darling Clementine represents the winning of the West,
her reciprocal affection for him signifies the winning of the East to a
new beginning on the frontier, and their dance together proposes a
happy synthesis of West and East. The synthesis reached when York
takes on Thursday's qualities at the end of *Fort Apache* isn't so happy.
In *Liberty Valance*, Ranse Stoddard is what Clementine was, the schoolteacher from the East, and Hallie, his first pupil, is what Wyatt Earp
was, the Westerner drawn to the civilizing East. Ranse's winning
Hallie away from Tom, who had been courting her—and offered her
the flower of the West, the cactus rose—represents the winning of
the West. This is done without much of a reciprocal winning of the
East. Though Ranse goes West as a young man, he goes back East
with Hallie, and only in their old age does he talk to her about settling in the West, which anyway is now a transformed place. *The Man
Who Shot Liberty Valance* is truly about the conquest of the West, with
wilderness vanquished and vanished; it is an elegy to the dead West,
or, as Pechter says, "an elegy to the cactus rose,"[38] which Hallie places
on Tom's coffin.

I have been giving an allegorical reading: Clementine and Ranse
as the East, Wyatt Earp and Hallie and Tom as the West, are figures
of allegory. The Western allegorizes history through the myth of the

frontier; it deals with social and political issues not realistically but allegorically. And in *The Man Who Shot Liberty Valance*, the allegory, usually implicit, becomes fully conscious, even self-conscious. It is above all an allegory of violence—the violence of the wilderness and the violence of civilization, the violence that society must suppress and the violence that society must use.[39] The vicious bandit Liberty Valance (Lee Marvin) personifies savage violence, which the Western counters with the hero's measured, civilized violence. Such is the legend of Ransom Stoddard as the man who shot Liberty Valance. But the senator tells the true story: when he bravely faced the bandit on the main street of town—which is where the Western characteristically situates the showdown between hero and villain, no mere personal fight but an affair of the community—he would have been killed had Tom not furtively intervened and shot Liberty Valance in cold blood under cover of darkness. The hero's violence was actually Tom's rather than Ranse's, and savage rather than civilized violence.

A hero with something of the villain in him, Tom is the shadow of savagery that lurks behind law and order. He has another double besides the gentler Ranse in the rougher and wilder Liberty Valance. The hero's violence, usually represented in Westerns not only as a means to civilized order but also as an epitome of justice and poise, a prototype of the law, can hardly be distinguished here from the villain's lawlessness. A number of thinkers (Walter Benjamin, Carl Schmitt, Hannah Arendt, Frantz Fanon, Giorgio Agamben, Jacques Derrida) have examined the question of law and violence, the foundation of law in violence, the problematic distinction between legitimate and illegitimate violence. That is the question Ford raises in this movie.

At the time, Ranse, like everybody else, thought he had shot Liberty Valance, and at the statehood convention, amid flowery oratory and overbearing spectacle—a broad comedy of political rhetoric—he is nominated to represent the territory as "a lawyer, teacher, but more important . . . a champion of law and order"—that is, as the man who shot Liberty Valance. He's displeased and walks out of the hall; it goes against his principles to use an act of violence as a political slogan. Enter Tom, who looks like he has a hangover, a Western hero uncharacteristically worn down, bitter, troubled—but then, he not only murdered a man and lost a woman, but he also allegorically lost the West to the East. He takes Ranse aside and tells him what really happened—in a flashback within the flashback, we return to the showdown from Tom's point of view—and Ranse goes back into the hall and accepts the nomination that gets his political career underway.

If he wouldn't run when he believed he had done the deed, why is he now willing to run under false pretenses? His running as the man who shot Liberty Valance is a matter of rhetoric, and Ford, even as he pokes fun at political rhetoric—on both sides, the proponents who call Ranse a champion of law and order and the opponents who say he has blood on his hands—makes clear that in politics, rhetoric is indispensable. Ranse objects to violence on principle, but he must avail himself of rhetoric to succeed politically and do something for the country ("Hallie is your girl now," Tom barks at him. "You taught her how to read and write, now give her something to read and write about"), and the best rhetorical card he can play is the act of violence that has won him fame. When he finds out that it is Tom, not he, who has blood on his hands, murderous blood, he realizes that he too must get his hands dirty, rhetorically dirty.

Rhetoric and force, like diplomacy and war, work hand in hand. Rhetoric can prevent the use of force, as Cicero said—no need for aggression when persuasion serves—but as the legend of Thursday's last stand shows, rhetoric can also provoke the use of force. The legend of the man who shot Liberty Valance turns force into forceful rhetoric. Ranse the lawyer, the man of rhetoric, and Tom the Westerner, the man of force, dramatize in a double protagonist the duality of rhetoric and force. They also bring out the flaws, the dangers, of both force and rhetoric: Tom's force amounts to murder, Ranse's rhetoric to a lie. Perhaps Ford would say that the murder and the lie are good for the country, but he makes us see that even a good man's violence and even a good man's deceit carry a risk. The partnership of force and rhetoric works out well for Ranse but not for Tom, whose force Ranse steals for his rhetoric in behalf of the East conquering the West. Ford calls into question Tom's violence against Liberty Valance as earlier he did not the violence against villains like the Clantons in *My Darling Clementine* or the Cleggs in *Wagon Master* (1950); and he calls into question Ranse's rhetoric as earlier he did not the rhetoric of protagonists like Lincoln (another young frontier lawyer with a future in politics) or Judge Priest. *The Man Who Shot Liberty Valance* is a work of reckoning.

The flashback that comprises most of the movie enacts the story the senator tells the local newspaper, whose editor insists on the public's right to know about the little-known man the senator and his wife have come to bury. But after the editor hears the story, he decides not to publish it: "When the legend becomes fact, print the legend." So much for the public's right to know. Is Ford saying that we should let men like the editor of the *Shinbone Star* decide for us what we are and are not to know? Plato bans the poets from the Republic because they tell lies, but he gives the leaders, the guardians of the Republic—men like the editor of the *Shinbone Star*—license to lie to the people when they saw fit. Whether or not Plato, the inventor of dialectics, really means to forbid poetic and sanction official lies, that position—the position of those who think that the few know better and should rule over the many unfit to know—has a long history. But it's not Ford's position. As we see in the flashback, the first editor of the *Shinbone Star*, Dutton Peabody (Edmond O'Brien), published the truth about Liberty Valance and was brutally beaten and almost killed for it. Plato proposes that myths entrusted to the guardians, not the poets, would be good for the people. Ford is a popular poet who publishes the myth and the truth side by side for everyone's benefit; he is a mythmaker who takes the view that myths can be good for the people but that the people should decide.

How can the people, once apprised of the truth, decide in favor of the myth? It's impossible to go on believing in a legend that has been exposed as false: "You can't make yourself believe something," Robert Pippin argues, just because you believe that it's good for the country to believe it.[40] You can, however, find Tom guilty of murder and Ranse of mendacity and still think they did the right thing for the country, which is the real issue at stake—the national rather than the individual story. Some suppose that the Western, for years the most popular genre of American movies, fell into disfavor when audiences found out that the myths it propagated are not the historical truth. But did people ever take the legend for fact, myth for truth? Surely they always knew that Westerns are a fiction, and they loved them as a fiction. Plato knows that the hierarchical myth of gold, silver, bronze, and iron souls recounted in the *Republic* is a fiction, and though he may not have wanted the people to know, surely they would have. They may still have accepted the myth, but as an allegorical rather than a literal truth, as a fiction that seemed to accord with and make sense of their reality. Thus the legend becomes fact. But in Plato's republic, the people are to accept what has been decided for them. In Ford's movie, the people have decided by voting for the man who shot Liberty Valance. Now, after the fact, after the legend has become fact—and even printing the truth in the *Shinbone Star* wouldn't change that fact—the people are to decide whether that was the right decision.

Rhetoric of Genre

The hero of the *Toy Story* trilogy is a toy cowboy. When in *Toy Story 3* (2010) the toys belonging to Andy, now about to leave for college, find themselves at a day care center, and a kind-mannered bear welcomes them into a community of toys freed from their owners, the cowboy alone stays loyal to Andy; and when the toy bear turns out to be a dictator worse than any owner, the cowboy never persuaded by the rhetoric of toy solidarity is proved right. This Pixar animation for children seems to be a political fable. The day care center may be taken to represent the public realm, the polity, and Andy the private realm, the family; the cowboy is the hero because he stands for family values. But why make the hero a cowboy? Boys may still play with toy cowboys, but the Western has lost the popularity it enjoyed in the past. The idea must have been that family values are old-fashioned like the cowboy hero—though the cowboy riding off alone into the sunset was never exactly a paragon of family values. This is an example of the rhetoric of genre. *Toy Story 3* is of course not a Western, but it invokes the Western rhetorically; it enlists for its purposes the generic expectations that the cowboy hero reliably summons up.

As a boy in the 1950s, during the heyday of a genre that half a century later would claim his attention as a professor of philosophy, Robert Pippin grew up steeped in Westerns. He watched them both on television (his favorite show was *Have Gun—Will Travel*) and "all day Saturdays at the movies (10 in the morning until 6 at night) . . . one Western after another."[41] Growing up in Havana around the same time, I saw no cowboys on television but plenty on the movie screen, from the Lone Ranger and Tonto to John Wayne, and I still have a picture of myself as a little boy in a cowboy outfit with a hat, chaps, and toy pistols. It's a small indication of how deeply influenced Cubans were by our mighty neighbor to the north, and how the fiction of the frontier, which was not our fiction, held us in its sway.

What's special about the Western? The cowboy hero, as Robert Warshow notes in his essay on the genre, carries a gun but uses it only when he must. The Western doesn't just tell violent stories, it tells stories about the meaning and management of violence, about the establishment of social order and political authority. As *Toy Story 3* recognizes, the cowboy hero is a political figure of some kind. "Being an American is essentially a *political* identification," Pippin maintains. "Political ideals are all that hold us together as a nation . . . without a common long tradition on the same territory."[42] In his book on the Western, he brings three movies under sustained scrutiny—*Red River*, *Liberty Valance*, and *The Searchers*—and ponders the political dimension of a genre that portrays the move into new territory as the American national story.

Pippin first examines *Stagecoach*, which he considers—and I agree with him—the first great Western. I also agree that the central political issue in *Stagecoach* is equality, which for Jacques Rancière is *the* political issue, and that, because the film begins in a frontier town already hardened into hierarchy and intolerance, here equality is not imagined as something inherent or simply achievable in a "Jeffersonian idealization of frontier or yeoman democracy."[43] A prostitute, Dallas, thrown out of town by the Law and Order League, and an outlaw, Ringo, are the two main characters. They are the lowest in the social hierarchy and the highest in our esteem. Sharing the stagecoach with them are several other travelers given almost as much importance in the movie. There is social inequality but dramatic equality among the characters in this group portrait.

Thomas Schatz, author of *The Genius of the System* and no advocate of the auteur theory, deems *Stagecoach* "altogether exceptional" under the Hollywood studio system as a director's film ("Ford orchestrated virtually every phase of its development and production") and comments on the "paradox" that it is also a dyed-in-the-wool genre film, as conventional as it is original, as "audience-friendly" as it is "socially astute" and "formally accomplished."[44] It gives proof, if proof is needed, of how well a genre can serve an artist. It brings into play both the Indian attack and the gunfight showdown, the two climactic scenes most typical of the Western—though by setting them back to back, resolving one thing only to move on to another, it suspends narrative closure and instead conveys a sense of unceasing evolvement on the open frontier. Its characters are generic types—the tough sheriff, the alcoholic doctor, the shady gambler, the gallant outlaw, the good-hearted saloon girl—but generic with a difference. Ringo is not a loner in the wilderness but has ties to frontier society and wishes to regain a place in it. And Dallas departs even more from type. The typical whore with a heart of gold endears herself to us, but she usually dies to spare us the embarrassment of her irredeemability. This saloon girl doesn't die in the hero's arms after taking a bullet meant for him. She rides off by his side at the end, a fellow pioneer of better things, a fallen woman not merely good but as good as anyone.[45]

Nor should Dallas and Ringo be seen as natural aristocrats even if they are the best people in the film, the best hope for the future, they are still very much of the common people. David O. Selznick wouldn't take on *Stagecoach* as producer because he saw it as "just another Western" with no big stars, and he would have wanted Marlene Dietrich and Gary Cooper in the leads. But Ford insisted on Claire Trevor and John Wayne (who wasn't a star until this movie made him one). Dietrich and Cooper would have turned Dallas and Ringo into the natural aristocrats that Ford didn't want. Trevor and the young Wayne bring to their roles a plebeian nobility assuming no superiority. The aristocrat in the movie is Lucy, a Southern army wife who disdains Dallas but whose baby, born at a way station, Dallas takes care of when Lucy is unwell—the saloon girl as apt mother. Though grateful to Dallas, Lucy still keeps her distance, and some viewers are disappointed to find no class reconciliation, no personal acknowledgment on Lucy's part of Dallas as her equal. But *Stagecoach* does enact a break in hierarchy, an opening toward equality on the frontier. It is not resigned to inequality but knows that equality is difficult to secure.

"The frontier is the outer edge of the wave—the meeting point between savagery and civilization," writes Frederick Jackson Turner.[46] Pippin seems uneasy with Turner's frontier thesis and objects to the opposition between savagery and civilization. But it is enough for Turner's argument that the encounter with so-called savagery disturbs the order of so-called civilization—Rancière gives it another name, the order of the police—and opens it to the prospect of greater liberty and equality. "For politics to occur," Rancière says, "there must be a meeting point between police logic and egalitarian logic."[47] Turner's—and Ford's—frontier is such a meeting point.

Howard Hawks's *Red River* (1948) is not about equality but authority. It is a tale of two leaders: Tom Dunson (John Wayne), who organizes a massive cattle drive starting from southwest Texas, and his adopted son, Matt Garth (Montgomery Clift), who takes over along the trail and brings the cattle to the railroad in Kansas. The kinder and gentler Matt assumes leadership when the cowhands grow unhappy with Dunson's increasingly tyrannical rule, and Dunson vows to kill his disloyal son. He catches up with him in Kansas and through a sea of cattle advances to confront him. Even a young gunfighter from the trail who pulls out his pistol scarcely breaks Dunson's stride, his irresistible forward movement, which prompts the camera to move with him as if itself unable to stop him. But when father and son come face-to-face, Matt refuses to draw his gun, and the ensuing fistfight is interrupted by a young woman, Tess Millay (Joanne Dru), who has fallen in love with Matt and who reminds Dunson of his own lost love. "Anybody with half a mind would know you two love each other," she tells the two men we had thought would fight to the death. As Diane Stevenson has discussed, Hawks is adept at mixing genres, and here he shifts from epic and tragedy to comedy.[48] Love conquers the conquerors in the comedic happy ending.

This ending, this final break with the expectations of epic, has met with much criticism. Borden Chase, the scriptwriter, says that the original intention was to have Dunson killed by the young gunfighter, who would in turn be killed by Matt, but that Hawks got angry and dropped the idea when John Ireland, who plays the gunfighter, started fooling around with the director's girlfriend. Whether or not this bit of gossip is true, that ending would have fitted the epic sweep of the movie. But James Harvey finds the happy ending a relief ("*Sensible* people don't kill or maim each other for revenge or honor or empty matters of pride"⁴⁹) and *Red River* an admirably sensible Western. For Pippin, the happy ending fits because the film was not really an epic to begin with: Dunson's cattle drive, despite the titular allusion to the Red Sea, is not at all comparable to the biblical exodus but a mere commercial undertaking, a bringing of cattle to market. This seems to mean that there can be no bourgeois epic and that epic belongs to a warrior class, never to a merchant class. But isn't the cowboy hero a warrior of the merchant or middle or peasant class? I'm not convinced by Pippin's argument that *Red River* qualifies its epic mode by imputing it to Dunson's—or to Texan, or to American—self-aggrandizement. The ending aside, the film achieves an epic grandeur unsurpassed among Westerns.

Red River is a capitalist epic. The railroad, which in populist Westerns is usually the enemy, the corporation dispossessing the farmers, is in *Red River* a business partner. Hawks draws a parallel between the cattle crossing the river—a scene that memorably conveys the epic sense of vast natural energies harnessed to human enterprise—and the cattle arriving in Kansas and crossing the railroad track. Why, then, after depicting the enterprise of frontier capitalism so grandly does the film resolve the issue of authority comedically? It seems to be a matter of great moment, the transition from "an autocratic, charismatic, largely pre-modern or feudal form of authority to a much more humanistic, consensus-oriented, prudent, more recognizably modern mode of rule and civil order," as Pippin describes it. But he accurately points out that "this transition of power from Dunson to Matt *is not inherently revolutionary*. It does not require an eruption of violence and death."⁵⁰ Matt's consensual democracy is not the antithesis but the continuation of Dunson's feudal autocracy. Father and son stand for the same thing—the rule of capitalism—and the son manages democratically to hold on to the power that the people were going to take away from the autocratic father. That's why it all comes down to comedy in the end.

The shift into comedy carries the recognition that Matt finishes what Dunson started, that the rival leaders actually join forces in business. It does not diminish the epic magnitude of the cattle drive, but it does cut the heroes down to size. More precisely, a woman cuts them down to size, which bears out Pippin's claim that the Western identifies civilized order with femininity and bourgeois domesticity. In *Red River*, comedy brings civilization, sensible comedy taming heroic epic. By contrast, in *Liberty Valance*, Ford's wintry remembrance of springtime, civilization brings tragedy—the tragedy of the West that was won. The Western is first of all an epic genre, but it does not abide by the rules of classical decorum that would keep genres separate, each in its own domain with its own conventions. The Western epic can shade into tragedy or turn into comedy or incorporate melo-drama or even the musical.

Aristotle distinguishes between epic, which is narrated, whether by the poet or one of the characters, and tragedy, which is performed by actors on a stage. We may think of the movie camera, or the intelligence we sense behind it, as a sort of narrator leading us through the story, but narrative in film comes mixed with drama, with actors moving and talking on the screen. A character whose path the camera follows or whose perspective it adopts is not thereby relating the story; only by voice-over narration can a character actually narrate a movie. Beginning with Ford's *How Green Was My Valley* (1941), voice-over became popular in the 1940s and 1950s, when the Western was riding high, but Westerns use it infrequently. We call them epic not because they are narrated—except in the way that the camera may be said to narrate—but because they tell stories too ample for any stage and assume a perspective too encompassing to be attributed to any individual.

Isn't Ranse the narrator of *Liberty Valance*? Pippin takes for granted that he is and finds him unreliable as such. But the film uses voice-over narration solely to introduce the flashback into the frontier past. It's a movie convention for a character to begin telling a story that then proceeds in dramatized form. No further voice-over confirms Ranse as narrator, and the story he tells is enacted in images only loosely attributed to his individual recollection. Consider two images of Hallie that intimate her growing preference—not just a personal but a socially motivated preference—for Ranse over Tom, East over West. In one image, she stands at the door, lit from behind as Tom goes out into the night. She watches him go as if they were parting for good. In another image, she pensively stands alone in the empty classroom where Ranse has been giving civics lessons and teaching her and others to read and write. Each of these images shows us something the presumed narrator couldn't have seen and tells us something crucial to the story. Ranse is neither exactly the narrator nor unreliable.

Pippin's concern with what he calls "political psychology"—the "assessment and understanding of human motives and reasons in political situations"[51]—leads him into sometimes reading Westerns too psychologically. He surmises that Ranse and Hallie have a bad marriage and that she grieves for Tom not just as a dear friend but as the love of her life. He supposes that her marriage is childless—which we have no way of knowing—and conjectures that Hallie may be "thinking about what a life with Tom on the ranch, perhaps with children, would have been." He finds "no sign that she knows at all that the Valance myth is a lie."[52] But when the newspaper editor presses the senator to talk about the friend he and his wife have come to bury, Hallie looks at her husband and indicates her approval. Ford is a subtle filmmaker, and that look is an unmistakable sign that Hallie knows the truth and wants Ranse to let it be known. At the end of the movie, on the train leaving Shinbone, Hallie tells Ranse that her heart is there. She doesn't mean that she has always loved Tom rather than the husband she rejected him for: she means that she enduringly loves the West, the West of her youth, the dead West. *Liberty Valance* isn't the psychological story of a love triangle; it is a national allegory.

As much as in Gothic stories, the double in Westerns—Tom and Ranse, Dunson and Matt, Wyatt Earp and Doc Holliday—is a fixture of the genre, a figure central to its rhetoric. *My Darling Clementine*, made right after the war that led the United States out of the Depression and into world ascendancy, may be Ford's sunniest Western; *Liberty Valance* may be his darkest. If Clementine, in turning her romantic attention from Doc Holliday to Wyatt Earp, is the East facing West, Hallie is the West facing East and forsaking the West. If Wyatt Earp and Clementine look forward to the marriage of East and West, Ranse and Hallie are the marriage of East and West looking back in sorrow.

The twinned heroes of *Liberty Valance* are a murderer and a liar. Pippin exculpates the murderer ("He does what needs to be done silently and selflessly, disappearing into history, not honored in any legend, not mythologized, not even remembered"), but he cannot forgive the liar, the man "willing, without much visible struggling with his conscience, to build his life on a lie. In a simple word, this is dishonorable, and there is no question that Ford wants us to see that it is dishonorable."[53] I don't see it—and don't think Ford wants us to see it—that way. He does expose the hypocrisy of a civilization that dissembles its violence in the guise of law and order. But Tom sacrifices himself for that civilization, and Ranse would have been priggish and foolish to disown the act of violence that saved his life and served to uphold his values. What should trouble Ranse's conscience is not the lie he has lived with—not the fact that he wasn't the man who pulled the trigger—but that the law and order he eloquently advocated entailed the violence that killed the West; so that, in effect, he was the man who shot Liberty Valance.

House of Miscegenation

Westerns wouldn't be so American if they weren't racist. When I played cowboys and Indians as a child, the cowboys were of course the good guys and the Indians the bad guys. Although Indians in Westerns are often good guys, and from Chingachgook and

Natty Bumppo to Tonto and the Lone Ranger, they have been paired with white frontiersmen as kindred spirits, the racial divide in the genre can't be denied. In a letter to his old friend Truffaut, Godard calls him a liar but adds that he means it as a criticism, not an insult, and though Truffaut felt insulted all the same, this is a distinction worth making.[54] When you insult someone by calling him a racist, you exempt yourself from racism, as when racist whites accuse blacks of racism against whites to deflect the charge away from themselves. You insult someone else, but you can criticize yourself, and no American should claim exemption from the racial and ethnic rifts of an immigrant nation founded on slavery and the conquest of the West. Let us then criticize without insulting. The protagonist of Ford's most complex Western, *The Searchers* (1956), is racist to an astonishing degree. Liberals who disapprove of Westerns without knowing them well take this protagonist as typical and his racism as endemic to the genre. But *The Searchers* is a critique, troubled and troubling, incisive yet constructive, of the racism endemic to American society.

John Wayne, the greatest cowboy hero, plays the film's racist hero, Ethan, an unreconstructed Confederate in the wake of the Civil War and a probable mercenary and robber. He crazily slaughters buffalo so that Indians will have nothing to eat, shoots out a dead Indian's eyes so that the man's soul will "wander forever between the winds" in accordance with Indian belief, and goes on an extended search for Debbie (Natalie Wood), his niece in Indian captivity, fully intending to kill her because he deems her unworthy of rescue. As Pippin remarks, having John Wayne in the role invites us into an identification with the character that is then stopped short and turned against us.[55] Hateful though he is, Ethan is not a villain, and we don't simply hate him as we would if he were played by a villainous actor. We have to come to terms with him, a terribly flawed hero but still a hero, still John Wayne, still a commanding figure we identify with as a paradigmatic American. When we identify with John Wayne as a good guy, we feel good about ourselves, but in *The Searchers*, our identification with him makes us feel uneasy and question ourselves.

Though a singular case, Ethan is not an aberration. Martin (Jeffrey Hunter), part Indian and derided by Ethan for it, and Laurie (Vera Miles), a blonde of Nordic ancestry, are supposed to get married, but Martin joins Ethan on the search for Debbie and aims to bring her back home, and Laurie, after years of waiting for Martin, finally blows up at him: "Fetch what home? The leavings of Comanche bucks, sold time and again to the highest bidder, with savage brats of her own? Do you know what Ethan will do if he has a chance? He'll put a bullet in her brain!" Pippin finds this the most shocking moment in the film. But Laurie is not a villain. Even a nice young woman impatient for her own mixed-race marriage shares Ethan's racism. It was for such ironic contradictions that Straub called Ford Brechtian.

The Searchers opens with a woman, Martha, opening the door of her frontier home, which frames a view of the desert. The camera is identified at the start with the view-framing Martha, a figure of civilization facing the wilderness, and moves out with her onto the porch, where she, her husband, and her three children welcome the arriving Ethan, her brother-in-law. Majestically choreographed, proceeding like a tribal ceremony, this inaugural homecoming establishes Ethan as the stuff of legend. It feels like part of the homecoming ritual that the first thing the prodigal uncle does in his brother's house is to pick up little Debbie, the youngest of the family, and lift her high above his head. Between Martha and Ethan an amorous attraction is subtly suggested, and though this movie has been so much talked about that the unspoken love between wife and brother-in-law has come to seem obvious, what the director chose not to spell out, we shouldn't feel free to embellish. (Some have even proposed that Debbie is Ethan's daughter.) Ford's subtlety, his mastery of the picture worth a thousand words, calls not for speculation on what we don't know but for reflection on what we do know. That Ethan desires his brother's wife tells us that he's disruptive of the family, the burgeoning social order, and at the same time that he's drawn to the family, as his avuncular gesture of lifting Debbie also tells us.

Comanches threaten the settlers in the region, and Ethan joins the posse of Texas Rangers organized against them. When it becomes apparent that a raid on his brother's house is likely, the posse is too far away to get there in time. From Ethan's somber countenance as he pauses to ponder what awaits his family, we cut to the house at sunset as the Indians are about to attack. In its eerie portent of violence, this is the film's most expressionistic sequence, almost like a horror movie; indeed, Peter Stowell has suggested that we see not the actual scene but the frightful vision in Ethan's mind.[56] Expressionism invests dramatic action with a quality of anxious subjective narration; *The Cabinet of Dr. Caligari* (1920) brings a madman's story to enacted life. But if *Caligari* dramatizes a first-person account, then the raid scene in *The Searchers* is more like a third-person account with language belonging to a character entering into the author's narration as free indirect speech. While Ford's images express something of Ethan's imagination, and while they have a coloring of it, they don't depict a fantasy but rather a reality subjectively shaded.

Ethan returns to find that the Indians have killed his brother, his nephew, and Martha, whose raped and dead body is the sight that affects him the most. The older of her two daughters suffers the same fate before long. Debbie, attempting to escape, meets the

Comanche chief, Scar, in the family graveyard. His shadow falls on her, and when she looks at him, we see that his eyes are blue—not, as may be supposed, because Hollywood Indians are played by white actors, but for a good reason, as Diane Stevenson has argued: Scar's eyes are blue on purpose, and they tell us that the Comanche chief is part white, as was the historical Quanah Parker, a famous Comanche chief of the period who was the son of an abducted white woman.[57] Ford does not explain; he shows. Scar's blue eyes are meant to give us pause, to make us think. *The Searchers* is a movie about race and about miscegenation.

Ethan is the frontiersman who has more in common with the Indians than with white civilization. Yet he hates the Indians he resembles; we may surmise that he hates himself.[58] Scar as much as Debbie is the object of his obsessive search. Ethan and Scar are doubles of each other, Natty Bumppo and Chingachgook turned into mortal enemies. In the end, however, it's not Ethan but Martin who kills Scar, and it's not Martin but Ethan who rescues Debbie—another ironic reversal, which implies that the vindictive Ethan and the humane Martin are in it together, that the whole white community is in it together. They are together in the violence against the Indians and together in bringing the captive woman back into white society.

Critics have debated at length why Ethan ends up rescuing Debbie instead of killing her. After a brutal raid on the Indians by white soldiers, Ethan, on his horse and apparently with murderous intent, chases Debbie as she runs away. Martin can't stop him. But then Ford cuts to a view looking out at the action from inside a cave. When I first saw the film, many years ago, I knew at that moment that Ethan was going to rescue Debbie. The view from inside looking out through a door—the inside–outside shot, as Pippin calls it—opens and recurrently punctuates the movie. Initially it was a view associated with Martha, and you could perhaps say that her spirit, summoned in this shot, keeps Ethan from killing her daughter. However, I didn't think of Martha; I thought of the family, of the civilization, that Martha represents. Now the uncle picks up his niece and lifts her above him, repeating the gesture he performed on arriving at his brother's house: "Let's go home, Debbie." Once more, Ford declines to explain. He cut out the explanation in the script, which had Ethan changing his mind on the point of shooting Debbie, softening when they look at each other and saying to her, "You sure favor your mother."

What difference does it make that the connection to Martha, spelled out in the script, is left implied in the finished movie? As Stevenson notes, the movie doesn't suggest that Ethan changes or that he undergoes a conversion. Avuncular at the end as he was at the beginning, he gives us no reason to think he has suddenly become any less racist than he has been all along. Skipping the transition from nasty to caring, truculent to affectionate, Ford sharpens the sense that such contraries dwell in Ethan side by side: the nice uncle rescues Debbie, but the man full of racial hatred is not gone.

The Searchers ends as it began, with a homecoming, and it closes as it opened, with the inside–outside shot. It is Debbie's homecoming this time, and again it has a ceremonial quality. The house that welcomes her is not her mother's—it belongs to Laurie's parents—but it is again the house of white civilization. Ethan brings Debbie to the porch, but he does not go inside the house. Laurie goes out to welcome Martin, and the two come inside, past Ethan, whom we watch through the door until finally he turns and goes away. You could say that Ethan is excluded because his racism is inadmissible, but nobody tells him to go, and Laurie is not excluded. This is her house, and her racism isn't exceptional; it is part of the house and part of society. Here we have a generic ending—the cowboy hero riding off alone into the sunset—invested with a new significance. We watch Ethan leave from our vantage point inside the house, receiving in its midst the niece he saved above all from himself, and even if he hasn't changed, the house has. The Debbie that comes home brings with her if not Indian blood then an experience of Indian life, an admixture of Indian culture, a tolerance of difference; and Laurie and Martin will marry and consummate their mixture of races. American society hasn't overcome its racism, but it now lives in the house of miscegenation.

Road to the Promised Land

The heyday of the Western roughly coincided with that of film noir, and since that time, film noir has risen in popularity while the Western has fallen, maybe because our outlook has darkened. If the Western is a genre of optimistic beginnings, film noir is a genre of pessimistic endings. (Though film noir tempers its doom and gloom with a certain humor or wit, evident in its hard-boiled style of dialogue and voice-over narration.) The Searchers and The Man Who Shot Liberty Valance are the two darkest and most troubling of Ford's Westerns and the two most often discussed—it seems to be assumed that Westerns get more interesting the more questioning, the more brooding they are, the more like film noir—but not necessarily the two best. Let me end this chapter with the wonderful, luminous Wagon Master, a low-budget movie Ford made between the second and third installments of his cavalry trilogy and a work that, as Pechter writes, "in its dispensing with an individual hero for a communal one and with a dramatic structure for the more open, epic form of narrative, spectacle, dance and song, has been characterized by Lindsay Anderson as an avant-garde Western."[59]

No doubt that was meant as an oxymoron, but the elite art of the avant-garde and the popular genre of the Western are in a fundamental way akin: they share in common a regard for the pioneering spirit, a conviction that breaking new ground, venturing into new territory, is intrinsically something to be valued. Never resting content with its innovations, the avant-garde forges ahead and keeps on making them—this has been called the tradition of the new—just like the advancing wave of the frontier as Turner theorizes it and as Ford portrays it, the repeated encounter with the new giving rise to American democracy. Ford portrays the emergence of democracy on the frontier nowhere more resonantly than in *Wagon Master*, and the formal qualities motivating a comparison to the avant-garde do much to enhance the film's social and political resonance.

If the outlaw, the whore, and the drunken doctor are the most sympathetic characters in *Stagecoach*, then *Wagon Master* has a whole cast of outcasts: Mormons made to leave town in their covered wagons, horse traders they enlist as guides on their westward journey, traveling entertainers, outlaws, Navajo Indians coming across their path. This is truly the film without stars that Ford wanted *Stagecoach* to be. None of its actors—Ben Johnson as Travis the horse trader; Harry Carey Jr. as his partner, Sandy; Ward Bond as Elder Wiggs; Joanne Dru as Denver, the young woman with the traveling medicine show—became a star like John Wayne. And none of its characters stands out from the group like Ringo and Dallas in *Stagecoach*. *Wagon Master* is a communal story, a film pledged to equality, through and through.

Initially Travis and Sandy refuse the job of wagon masters on the Mormon caravan, but on the point of leaving town, Elder Wiggs asks that the ritual horn be blown once more, and we dissolve to the horse traders responding to its call. The geometry here is worth noting. Two fences meet at right angles, and Travis and Sandy ride along one fence toward the wagon train departing along the other fence, on which they proceed to sit. We cut closer to them as Sandy waves his hat to a young Mormon woman he likes, and before long the horse traders start singing a song that means they're throwing in their lot with the Mormons. Then Sandy goes in one direction to collect their horses and Travis goes in another to catch up with Wiggs; Sandy rides along one fence, away from the wagon train and nearly parallel to the bottom edge of the screen, and Travis rides along the other fence into the distance, alongside the wagon train and eventually exactly parallel to the right edge of the screen. At right angles and away from each other, the two move toward a common goal: movement on the frontier calls for a new orientation. We cut to the elder on his horse as Travis jumps over the fence separating them and tells him that to find water, the caravan must turn west. Fences, straight lines, signify boundaries, established patterns, lines of enclosure from which the Mormons and their new wagon masters are breaking free. Now we dissolve to the caravan crossing a river. The pioneers and their covered wagons and attendant horses form an ample, graceful curve in the water, with the camera panning with a wagon as it climbs up the riverbank, then cutting to the next wagon and again panning with its onward movement, then cutting and panning yet again, like a wave of freedom advancing on the open frontier.

Class differences, which in *Stagecoach* linger amid the wilderness, dividing the doctor from the banker, the peasant outlaw from the patrician gambler, the saloon girl from the Southern lady, have in *Wagon Master* mostly been left behind. On the wagon train, there are no characters with any claim to a higher class. But there are differences nevertheless; there are group, even if not class, divisions, as well as harbored prejudices. The Mormons frown on the loose morals of the show people, who in turn view them as rigid and unrefined, and the Mormons wouldn't have allowed the show people to join their wagon train had it not been for Travis, who has his eye on Denver. It's not that the differences between people are erased in the pioneer experience. Equality doesn't mean sameness; nor does democracy require that people like each other, only that they tolerate each other, and that's what Ford shows happening on the frontier—people coming to find their differences mutually acceptable.

The show people bring a civilized touch to the wagon train. Their leader, Dr. A. Locksley Hall (Alan Mowbray, in a role similar to his traveling actor in *My Darling Clementine*), never goes without a shave, and even when water is scarce, he helps himself to some from the Mormons. But Travis explains that water can't be wasted on shaving and returns it to the Mormons, who now deem it tainted and throw it away. As Travis brings back the show doctor's empty pail, water suddenly pours out of the troupe's covered wagon and falls on the cowboy and his horse, which goes wild and bucks him off. Denver looks on and smiles; this is the water from a bath she has just taken. She promises Travis she won't take any more baths until she has his permission. "Looks like you got yourself an admirer, Denver," an older woman in the troupe tells her, and doesn't stay for the delayed response: "That rube?"

Water is a necessity of life. The show people had no water when the wagon train found them in the desert; they had been drinking liquor for days. But now water becomes a civilized amenity, something you shave or take a bath with, as well as something you throw away because you want nothing to do with people of loose morals. Water plays a part in the frontier transaction between nature and culture. The cowboy endeavoring to safeguard natural water for the caravan's survival is struck by the outpouring of cultural water from a pretty woman's bath. Like Wyatt Earp in *My Darling Clementine*, Travis is a rube, a frontiersman drawn to the civilized woman, though unlike Clementine, and like Dallas in *Stagecoach*, Denver is a fallen woman. "That rube?" expresses not merely snobbery but a poignant insecurity. In a way Denver may feel superior to Travis, but in another way she feels unworthy of him. Compared to the romance between Ringo and Dallas, that between Travis and Denver is an unfinished sketch, a suggestion rather than a fulfillment. We surmise they will get married, but no love scenes are enacted between them, and the last time we see the two of them together, she runs away from him after he proposes to her. Sketch, suggestion, vivid impression rather than dramatic development—this is the avant-garde method of *Wagon Master*. Had the romance between Travis and Denver been more developed, their story would have stood out from the communal story like that of Ringo and Dallas.

Dance and song: there are two dances in *Wagon Master*, and on the soundtrack, over images of covered wagons crossing water or pushing forward in the desert, of trekkers doggedly advancing on foot in the sun and the dust, we hear the Sons of the Pioneers singing several songs. If the dance in *My Darling Clementine* takes place in an unfinished church, in *Wagon Master* there is not even that, only an improvised dance floor of wooden planks on the desert sand. Elder Wiggs asks the older show woman to dance, Travis asks Denver, Sandy the Mormon woman he fancies, and they all join in a spirited square dance on wobbly planks, a happy occasion stopped short by the arrival of the Cleggs. Interrupting a dance is a bad sign in a Ford movie, a sign of discordance with the community, and the Cleggs, a family of outlaws we saw rob a store and kill a man in the precredit sequence, are the bad guys. They find the wagon train "providential" as a place to hide from the law.

In *Stagecoach* the Apaches are the enemy; in *Wagon Master* the Navajos are friendly to the Mormons, who are "not big thieves like most white men, just little thieves," and they invite the Mormons and their fellow travelers to a ceremonial gathering. Indians and their white guests dance together in a circle around a fire until the Cleggs interrupt this dance too, this time with an act of violence. One of the outlaws rapes an Indian woman, and the Mormons promptly have him whipped to avoid a worse conflict with the Navajos. However, the Cleggs have not only committed a crime but they also take rancorous exception to a punishment lenient for the crime and necessary for the common good. Outcasts like the other characters, the Cleggs are truculently antisocial, incapable of entering into a community beyond their own ingrown family. They are, like the Earps and the Clantons in *My Darling Clementine*, a frontier family of men without women, but the Earps broaden and transform their family values into social values, while the Clantons and the Cleggs do nothing of the kind, which sets them at odds with the emergent democracy and makes them villains. Because they do not tolerate others, they cannot be tolerated themselves.

The Mormons bring with them a wagon full of grain seed for planting when they get to the San Juan River, which they believe to be their promised land. But when they are almost there, and about to drive the precious seed wagon on a precarious trail across a mountain to their fertile destination on the other side, the Cleggs, in revenge for a whipping they haven't forgotten, pull out their guns, kill the driver, and threaten the elder. The Mormons have no guns—violence is against their principles—and the horse traders have been disarmed. Yet a hidden gun inherited from a man who later converted to the faith turns up among the Mormons—providential is the word—and Travis and Sandy take the Cleggs by surprise and manage to kill them all. "While reaching the very summit of Ford's optimism," Joseph McBride notes,

> *Wagon Master* acknowledges the bitter, real-world irony that even a utopian community cannot survive without occasional recourse to violence in self-defense. Delegating the job of killing the Cleggs to the two "horse traders," the Mormons commit an act of moral compromise that enables their community to survive and reach their "promised land" while at the same time calling into question the viability of their own principles.[60]

I see no irony here. Strict pacifism is not a tenet of the Mormon faith. Portraying the Mormons as peaceful sets them far apart from the brutal Cleggs and serves to heighten the difference, central to the Western, between civilizing and antisocial violence. These Mormons do not break their principles—they refrain from any violence of their own—and in any case the principles that count in *Wagon Master* are not theirs but the more inclusive ones of a democratic society that embraces them and the horse traders and the show people. Ford scarcely goes into the beliefs and mores particular to the Mormons; his concern is with the incipient American polity. That, and not the Mormons alone, is here the utopian community.

The narrative structure of *Wagon Master* is loose, episodic, epic. By contrast, *High Noon* (1952, written by Carl Foreman, produced by

Stanley Kramer, directed by Fred Zinnemann) is tightly organized dramatically. It even adheres to the classical unity of time: as it keeps reminding us with recurrent looks at the clock, the movie lasts exactly as long as the drama it unfolds, which begins with the marriage of Marshal Will Kane (Gary Cooper) to Amy (Grace Kelly) and ends with the couple leaving town after an extended gunfight. The central situation can be found in many Westerns since Owen Wister's 1902 novel *The Virginian* (in whose 1929 film version the young Gary Cooper starred): the hero fights the villain against the wishes of the woman he loves, and she comes to see that he was right. Taking a generic situation and modifying it so that a new meaning plays off an old one—the rhetoric of genre often works that way. Amy in *High Noon* is a Quaker who, like the Mormons in *Wagon Master*, objects to violence on principle, and not only she but virtually the entire town wants Kane to back away from the fight. He cleaned up the town, made it a civilized place, but now the bad guys are returning and the townspeople won't help him fight them, for motives amounting to self-interest and lack of communal spirit. This is a society of selfish, alienated individuals. The marshal feels let down by them and fights the bad guys single-handed—and in the event with help from Amy, who breaks her principles to such an extent that she shoots one of the bad guys in the back. Travis and Sandy resort to violence for the common good, but Kane and Amy kill in their own behalf and in spite of an alienated community from which they are themselves alienated. Ford's Westerns portray individuals forming a society and being formed by it. *High Noon*, while critical of a townspeople grown selfish and bourgeois, shares the bourgeois assumption of a split between the individual and society, a split no less marked in the self-pitying hero than in the uncaring others.[61]

After the Mormon caravan accomplishes the difficult passage over the final mountain, the pioneers stare awestruck at the promised land they have reached, but we get just a glimpse of it, and *Wagon Master* closes with a retrospective look at their journey. McBride describes this as a "'curtain call' reprise of characters" similar to the conclusion of *How Green Was My Valley*, in which "Ford intended . . . a cinematic equivalent of a curtain call [and] shows Huw, his parents, and his siblings reunited in memory images that even more pointedly resemble a vision of life after death."[62] *How Green Was My Valley* is narrated by Huw in first-person voice-over, and its closing images evoke his mind's eye. But *Wagon Master* has no narrator, no character looking back whose memory or vision the "curtain call" images evoke, and though they may refresh our memory of the movie we've been watching, they don't exactly reprise images we have seen. First we go back to the square dance, which this time seems a little more orderly, the planks less wobbly; certainly no villains bring it to a halt. Then we see and hear the horse traders singing the same song ("I left my gal in old Virginny") they sang when they decided to join the wagon train, but this time they are on horseback, and the elder is riding and singing along with them. Then, after an extreme long shot of the covered wagons making their way across the vast landscape, we see Sandy riding in a wagon with his Mormon sweetheart and kissing her. Is he converting to her faith to marry her, or is she giving it up to marry him? Not to worry; this image doesn't represent a reality but a fantasy, or a desire. The same can be said of the image of Travis and Denver together in a wagon that soon follows. This retrospective look at the journey is just as much prospective.

The mythmaker acknowledges the myth: the coda to *Wagon Master* heightens the idealizing stylization of the preceding movie and thereby declares that it has all been a fiction. But what is it a fiction of? What is the point of the myth? It is not a myth of the promised land; the movie does not end with the Mormons cultivating the land of their dreams come true. It is the journey, the road to the promised land, that Ford idealizes, the frontier road to democracy. Last, the coda returns to the river crossing at the journey's beginning, and the final image, which goes on past the end titles, pans with a young colt trying its legs and striding up the riverbank.

I

CINEMATIC TROPES

Metonymy

Meet John Doe (1941) begins with a trope. On a carved plaque by the entrance to a building, we read the name of a newspaper, *The Bulletin*, and its motto, "A free press means a free people." A man with a jackhammer comes into view and starts chipping away the words inscribed in stone—the words that seemed so solid with their reinforcing shadows. We dissolve to a close-up of the "free" in "free press" as the tip of the jackhammer chips the letters away one by one, after which we pan to "press" as the jackhammer turns to clear off the next word. Then we dissolve to the plaque with its entire inscription wiped out except for a faint trace, whereupon two men install a new plaque on top of it. In clean slanted letters, this metal plaque bears the name *The New Bulletin* and the motto, "A streamlined newspaper for a streamlined era."

You don't have to know what to call it to know this is a trope. Everyone understands what it means, and everyone recognizes that its meaning is not literal but figurative—or rather, that the literal meaning, the fact that the old plaque is cleared off and replaced with a new one, is a vehicle for another, more significant meaning, a point being made in this figurative way. Everyone gets the point, and everyone sees the trope—the figurative way of making the point.

A trope that everyone sees gives everyone a sense of the author implied by the trope. It's not that the director of *Meet John Doe*, Frank

Capra, or the writer, Robert Riskin, is necessarily called to the audience's mind, only that what is plainly a trope is plainly a way of making meaning, so that a maker is called to mind—a maker that has us in mind. A trope exhibits artifice in which we discern an artificer; it bespeaks someone speaking to us, an author addressing us more directly than usual, coming forward to our notice instead of remaining hidden behind the actors and the story. That's part of its rhetorical effect.

The trope at the beginning of *Meet John Doe* tells a story. The change from the old plaque to a new one tells us that the newspaper is undergoing change; a new management is making it over. And the trope comments on the story; it tells us that the change is for the worse, that the new management, under guise of streamlined modernization, is destroying the solid old principle of freedom of the press. This trope might be called a synecdoche, the part for the whole. The plaque here stands for the whole newspaper, the new plaque for the new management. But the plaque isn't exactly part of the newspaper; it's an identifying sign outside the building. A sign standing for the thing signified—as when we say allegiance to the flag, meaning the country signified by the flag—is a classic type of metonymy. Indeed, metonymy would be a better term for this trope. Not only does a plaque bearing the name of a newspaper stand for the newspaper—a sign for the thing signified—but the words "free press" stand for the free press they signify, the solidity of their inscription in stone stands for the solidity of the principle they signify, and their obliteration by jackhammer stands for the forcible destruction of that old principle by the paper's new management.

Tropes and Figures

In classical rhetoric, synecdoche is a trope that substitutes a part for the whole ("Give me a hand") or the whole for a part ("The police arrived"), species for genus (cutthroat for killer) or genus for species (vehicle for car). Metonymy is a trope that for one thing substitutes another related to it or associated with it (head for reason, heart for emotion, gold for wealth), including the sign for the thing signified, the container for the thing contained (as when you say you drink a glass or eat a dish), the place for what comes from there or is located there (Bordeaux for the wine, Wall Street for finance), the material for the thing made out of it (plastic for credit card), the tool for what it serves to do ("The pen is mightier than the sword"), the author for the work ("Do you like Brahms?"), cause for effect ("holding your tongue" for keeping quiet, "hit" for the result of hitting the ball in a baseball game) or effect for cause (sweat for toil, tears for grief, laughter for joy).

Tropes alter the meaning of words. When you say you drink a glass, you don't mean a glass but the liquid inside it; when you say you like Brahms, you don't mean Brahms but the music he composed. "Theorists have differed in defining this term," Richard A. Lanham writes in the entry on trope in his *Handlist of Rhetorical Terms*. "Such consensus as there is wants trope to mean a figure that changes the meaning of a word or words, rather than simply arranging them in a pattern of some sort."[1] This distinction mustn't be too strict—arranging words in a pattern will likely affect their meaning. Still, we may think of tropes as giving words a turn from their ordinary meaning (*trope* in Greek signifies "turn") and distinguish them from figures of speech that mainly have to do with the arrangement of words. There are many such figures: *antithesis*, which brings contraries together, or *periphrasis*, which expresses something in an intentionally protracted and roundabout manner, or *aposiopesis*, which breaks off a sentence with a thought left dangling, or the various figures involving repetition or reordering, to mention a few. This has application to the rhetoric of film. As words in a trope mean something other than what they literally say, so the old carved plaque being wiped out at the start of *Meet John Doe* and the metallic new one taking its place are images that mean something other than what they literally show. We may likewise distinguish film tropes such as this one, which alter the meaning of images, from figures of arrangement such as crosscutting or the reverse angle.

Metaphor

In *Once Upon a Time in Anatolia* (2011, directed by Nuri Bilge Ceylan), a group of men in two cars and a jeep—including a prosecutor, a doctor, policemen, soldiers, gravediggers, and two apprehended homicide suspects—are searching for the buried body of a murdered man. All the places look the same in the desolate rural night. The suspect who confessed to the murder and supposedly knows where the body is buried is having trouble finding it; he says he was drunk on the night of the crime and doesn't exactly remember, but perhaps he means to mislead. The police chief is losing patience; the men have been at this for hours and are getting tired and hungry. One of them shakes a tree, and several apples fall to the ground. The camera follows the course of one of the apples as it rolls down hills and flows down a stream until it eventually joins other apples that have come to a stop and are beginning to rot. It seemed like an adventurous apple, one that was going places, and it surprises us to find that it has taken the same path as the others, a path concluding in death.

This is a metaphor. Metaphor is the queen of tropes; any trope, anything that represents something else, may be called a metaphor. But more precisely a metaphor works by a significant—and rhetorically better if surprising—similarity between one thing and another. Here the apple in its meandering course toward death represents the course of human life, the way we may think we are going places but all end up in the same place. It is a simple metaphor but a reverberant one in this film about death.

The Unraveled Underwear

In *City Lights* (1931), Chaplin's tramp falls in love with a blind flower girl he encounters on the street. She mistakes him for a rich man, and he decides to keep up the pretense of being what she imagines him to be. This comically exaggerates a common situation: haven't we all tried to impress others, to gain their approval or win their affection, by pretending in some way to be something we are not? We then assume, or hope, that the other person can't see who we really are—which is what the girl's blindness metaphorically represents.

The tramp pretending to be rich visits the poor blind girl. He brings her food and the news that a Viennese doctor has a cure for blindness. "Wonderful!" she cries out. "Then I'll be able to see you." He smiles with her but casts a brief glance toward us, signaling his awareness that her being able to see him may not be an unmixed blessing. He is a sweet impostor, though, and there's nothing he won't do—in the end he steals from a real rich man and goes to jail for it—to make possible the miraculous eye operation. For the moment he extends her a peculiar courtesy. She asks him to help her roll up her knitting yarn, and she accidentally catches a loose thread from his underwear, which he then lets her unravel in its entirety.

Chaplin's tramp is a man of feeling and cultivation, "like an aristocrat fallen on hard times," as Robert Warshow describes him, "for what he attempted in all his behavior was to maintain certain standards of refinement and humanity, to keep life dignified and make it emotionally and aesthetically satisfying."[2] But it's the business of comedy to bring such lofty-mindedness down to earth. Chaplin's gentlemanly character is still a tramp scraping by, capable of deceit, dishonesty, even violence; he may reach for higher things but is never far from the gutter, and his big flat feet are liable to trip. A creature of contradictions, he mingles the smooth and the rough, the elevated and the low. His refinement is in a way genuine yet in another way feigned; you can see him as a hard-up aristocrat or as a bum putting on airs. He tries to rise above vulgarity but can never quite escape it—which is why he is comical.

Warshow appreciates the tramp's gallantry in allowing the blind girl to unravel his underwear: "The delicacy of feeling is wonderful, all right—who else could have conceived the need for this particular kindness?"[3] But the delicacy gets comically mixed up with indelicacy. The gallantry bumps against a coarse sexual joke: the unknowing girl touches the tramp intimately, and (as Walter Kerr puts it) "he writhes under the threads that are slithering and knotting against his skin."[4] He looks toward us—Chaplin often plays directly to the audience— and his alarmed expression seems to be asking us if this isn't going too far. Yet the joke is not merely coarse: the way the girl touches him intimately goes deeper than sexual titillation. More than his skin, she touches his heart. This is a joke on the pretender who doesn't want to be seen for what he really is yet finds himself affected in his inner-most being. If the heart is a metonymy for the emotions, then here the unraveled underwear is a metonymy for the inside—not just the sexual but the sentimental inside, the inside that would be dissem-bled but becomes exposed in the very act of dissembling.

The Broken Necklace

Boris Barnet's *By the Bluest of Seas* (1936), a Soviet comedy about romantic love and collective work, begins with shots of a turbu-lent sea, briskly edited telephoto shots that seem to plunge us into the unruly waves. Two shipwrecked sailors, Yussuf (Lev Sverdlin) and Alyosha (Nikolai Kryuchkov), are rescued by a fishing boat and brought ashore on a calm island in the southern Caspian Sea, where they join a fishing collective as if that had been their intended des-tination. Excited, chaotic nature gives way to the organized culture of a communist kolkhoz. But as soon as Yussuf and Alyosha set foot on the island, romantic feelings are aroused when the two friends lay eyes on a beautiful woman, Masha (Yelena Kuzmina), who smiles at them and walks away singing a song about her absent sweetheart, the camera following her and cutting back to the smitten young men side by side in two-shot.

Having two characters fall in love with the same person sets them in comparison, makes them doubles of each other. Alyosha is a mechanic, and Masha shows him the motorboat that needs his ser-vices, but as he flirts with her, he breaks her necklace and the beads fall into the sea. She asks him to dive after them, and Yussuf, who has been watching, enters the scene and pushes his friend into the water, telling Masha not to worry, Alyosha is a fine swimmer sure to retrieve the beads—which of course can't be retrieved from the sea. Now Yussuf gains the advantage in the pursuit of Masha. One day, however, Alyosha sings a song about the woman he dreams of, "clad in ribbons, earrings, lace," tells the others he's sick at heart, and lets them go fishing by sail, without him and without the motorboat he alone knows how to run, which he then takes by himself to get flowers and a new necklace for Masha. But fishing goes much worse without the motorboat, and before the assembled group, Yussuf accuses his friend of selfishly appropriating what belongs to the collective. That personal rivalry and jealousy have a part in motivating his social accusation is only human and not too much to be held against him, as it is only human and not too much to be held against Alyosha that he forgets his social responsibilities for love of Masha. These are comic doubles treated with equal sympathy, not one good and the other bad but both under a sway as natural and as potent as the waves in the sea.

Rising to defend himself before the group he has wronged, Alyosha looks at Masha, and we see her upset face in close-up. She no longer wants the new necklace he has given her, and it breaks as she takes it off, the beads falling in slow motion all around her pretty face and dropping to the floor like big crystal tears she seems to be shedding. It is an extraordinary image. Her falling beads are a metaphor for tears of sorrow and shame—sorrow over the cost to the group of Alyosha's romantic gesture, and shame over her own complicity in that gesture and potential betrayal of her absent sweetheart. And the beads are also a synecdoche, a significant part of her flirtation with Alyosha, and a metonymy too, a motivating cause of his taking the motorboat by himself to the detriment of the collective. The broken necklace eloquently cries for her in an arresting mix of tropes.

Metaphor and Metonymy

In "Two Aspects of Language and Two Types of Aphasic Disturbances," Roman Jakobson brings to the figures of rhetoric the perspective of structural linguistics.[5] The two aspects of language are selection and combination. The speaker selects each word from a set of available possibilities, "linked by various degrees of *similarity* which fluctuate between the equivalence of synonyms and the common core of antonyms," and combines words into sentences that give them an order and a context "in a state of *contiguity*."[6] The two types of aphasic disturbances are the "similarity disorder," in which the speaker has a "selection deficiency" and, for example, will point to something because unable to think of its name; and the "contiguity disorder," in which the speaker can name things but has difficulty putting sentences together. Corresponding to the "twofold character of language" and the two types of speech disorder are two figures of speech Jakobson posits as rhetorically sovereign, as dividing between them the field of figuration and indeed of signification, one a figure of similarity and the other a figure of contiguity: metaphor and metonymy. Jakobson gives these tropes a turn—so much of a turn that, in his conception of them, metaphor and metonymy are no longer tropes but something grander, lines of association, ways of making the connections of meaning: the way of similarity and the way of contiguity.

When, in *The Man with a Movie Camera* (1929), Dziga Vertov cuts between a woman washing her face in the morning and street cleaners washing the city, he's making a connection of similarity, a metaphor in Jakobson's sense. But classical rhetoric wouldn't call this a metaphor. It's merely a comparison between similar things set side by side. A metaphor, strictly speaking, is a substitution of one thing for another on the basis of a similarity that becomes an identity—hence the trope, the turn of meaning—because one thing stands in for the other as if they were the same thing. In the terms introduced by I. A. Richards, the thing that stands in is the vehicle, and the other, the thing referred to, is the tenor.[7] A metaphor in the strictest sense leaves the tenor implicit and gives us the vehicle alone, but when the tenor is explicit, we can still, in a somewhat looser sense, have a metaphor: "those boughs which shake against the cold, / Bare ruin'd choirs, where late the sweet birds sang" (Shakespeare, sonnet 73). Here the vehicle, the bare ruined choirs, without standing in nonetheless stands for the tenor, the boughs in winter, and takes its place in the mind.

In *The Man with a Movie Camera*, neither the woman washing nor the washing of the city stands for the other. Do we want to call this a simile? A simile is traditionally distinguished from a metaphor by its use of a linking word such as *like* or *as*: "When the poet says of Achilles that he 'Leapt on the foe as a lion,' this is a simile; when he says of him 'the lion leapt,' it is a metaphor."[8] Film, however, unless it uses words, has no such linking particles with a set meaning, and so, at least with regard to the film image, we may leave that distinction aside and subsume simile under metaphor, as Jakobson does.[9] Moreover, like a metaphor, a simile ("My love is like a red, red rose") has its vehicle (the red rose) and its tenor (my love). In a simile, as in a metaphor, the comparison is asymmetrical, irreversible: the vehicle carries the comparison and tells us something about the tenor, not the other way around. But Vertov's comparison is quite symmetrical, quite reversible; neither of the two washings is a vehicle for the other; each tells us something about the other. The point is not that the woman is like the city (the city as vehicle for the woman) or that the city is like the woman (the woman as vehicle for the city) but that, in a perfect equality of washing, the woman and the city are alike.

The Man with a Movie Camera is a celebration of the machine. Vertov takes the machine he knows best, the camera, and shows off all its techniques not for their own sake but as part of the encompassing Soviet modernization. The camera is the star of this movie. It acts as a synecdoche for all the machines working together in the vast machinery of the city. Since the onset of the industrial revolution, there has been an opposition between the organic and the mechanical, and proponents of the organic have generally been opponents of the mechanical. Is Vertov, proponent of the mechanical, then an opponent of the organic? The equality between the woman washing and the washing of the city tells otherwise. The woman is not mechanical like the city any more than the city is organic like the woman. Vertov transcends the opposition between the organic and the mechanical. He envisions their happy marriage under socialism. His synecdoche involves not just the machine that is the camera but also the man operating that machine—the man with a movie camera.[10]

Jakobson's broader conception of metaphor is useful in dealing with a case such as Vertov's evenly compared washings, not a metaphor (or a simile) in the classical sense but still a metaphoric connection, of a kind made possible, or at least made easier, by film technique, by the straight juncture of things across a cut setting them side by side without slanting the comparison one way or the other. Though derived from language, Jakobson's twofold rhetorical scheme of metaphor and metonymy applies beyond language to other means for making connections—connections of similarity and connections of contiguity.

Traditionalists have objected. Regarding metonymy, Brian Vickers contends that

> Jakobson is using the term "contiguity" in a loose, indeed metaphorical way, to describe how aphasics, unable to recall the proper word, substitute the *next* best, or the *nearest* word they can think of. But in rhetoric . . . metonymy involves the substitution of a "related" term (where *propinquis* does not mean literally "next to") according to fixed transitions or tropings within a category on different levels, such as putting the container for the thing contained, or the sign for the thing signified.[11]

Jakobson is called to task both for being overly metaphorical—the classical use of propinquity to define metonymy is surely no less metaphorical—and for being overly literal. The real issue is that Jakobson takes liberties with rhetorical tradition, and Vickers wants to limit the permissible connections of propinquity or contiguity to those fixed long ago. But at that time the realistic novel didn't exist, and Jakobson, through his broader conception of metonymy, elucidates the rhetoric of realism, the way of making connections metonymically that he finds to be characteristic of the novel. "Following the path of contiguous relationships," he writes, "the Realist author metonymically digresses from the plot to the atmosphere and from the characters to the setting in space and time. He is fond of synecdochic details."[12]

Metonymy in this sense subsumes synecdoche. (Note, however, that Jakobson tacitly distinguishes between the two by using synecdoche for details and metonymy for setting and atmosphere.) In this sense, synecdoche and metonymy are not exactly tropes but, as Jakobson says, paths of relationship between the narrative and its synecdochic details, between the characters and incidents and their metonymic circumstances—paths taken by the novel in its pursuit of meaning in the detail and circumstance of social existence.

Besides the attention to detail and circumstance typical of the novel, another metonymic move characteristic of narrative is the linking of things by cause and effect. Narrative does not, as some suppose, necessarily proceed by causality, but it often does, and realistic narrative takes the path of causal connections particularly often.

If, in this twofold scheme, metonymy prevails in the novel, then metaphor has primacy in lyric poetry. From literature Jakobson goes on to painting and cinema:

> A salient example from the history of painting is the manifestly metonymical orientation of Cubism, where the object is transformed into a set of synecdoches; the Surrealist painters responded with a patently metaphorical attitude. Ever since the productions of D. W. Griffith, the art of the cinema, with its highly developed capacity for changing the angle, perspective, and focus of shots, has broken with the tradition of the theater and ranged an unprecedented variety of synecdochic close-ups and metonymic set-ups.[13]

In cinema it isn't close-ups alone that may be called synecdochic: whether a closer or a more distant view, every shot is a detail, a piece of a larger space that extends beyond the frame. A painting is a whole and a theater stage is a whole, but every shot in a film is merely a part of a whole. A novel may speak in general ("It was the best of times, it was the worst of times"), but film images must always depict something in particular. Synecdoche is the figure that moves from the particular to the general.

Synecdoche

The part for the whole, the general in the particular: synecdoche is too important a figure to be subsumed under metonymy. Particulars, which are all the camera knows, are synecdochic inasmuch as they have a meaning, which is always something general. Film is a medium of particulars invested with meaning as parts of a whole. Each image on the screen shows something in particular, but something that has a place in a construction of the general. Out of the bits and pieces the camera renders, a film puts together an inclusive picture. Synecdoche is the figure of inclusion. Each piece of appearances a film brings into view is one chosen and arranged to fit in with all the rest. When a film breaks down a scene into shots, each shot in turn implies the rest of the scene; when different scenes are cut together (a wife at home calling for help, her husband in town reached by telephone—to cite an early instance of crosscutting from Griffith's 1909 *Lonely Villa*), each bears on the other, and each in turn implies the other. A part fitting into and implying an encompassing whole is in that way a synecdoche for that whole. As the images of a film succeed one another in time, so the particular thing now in view may be said to stand, synecdochically, for the succession of things that are the plot: this being the part that unfolds the plot at this moment, for the moment, it represents the whole plot being unfolded. Synecdoche can claim to be the chief figure of expression in this medium of details that film is.

Giambattista Vico gives primacy to four tropes: metaphor, metonymy, synecdoche, and irony.[14] These are the same ones put forward by Kenneth Burke two centuries later as "four master tropes."[15] Irony finds no place in Jakobson's binary scheme. Something like his broadening of metaphor and metonymy had already been done to irony, which at least since the Romantics has acquired an ampler sense than the classical saying one thing and meaning the opposite. Synecdoche, a form of metonymy in Jakobson's scheme, calls for a similar broadening in its own right. Like other rhetoricians, Vico and Burke recognize that synecdoche and metonymy are akin and at times hard to tell apart. (Burke is more inclined to treat metonymy as a form of synecdoche than the other way around.) But they don't confound the two, and they also note a kinship between synecdoche and metaphor, since a part representing a whole will often in some way resemble it or typify it or become identified with it. Vico: "Synecdoche developed into metaphor as particulars were elevated into universals or parts united with the other parts together with which they make up their wholes."[16] Burke:

> The "noblest synecdoche," the perfect paradigm or prototype for all lesser usages, is found in metaphysical doctrines proclaiming the identity of "microcosm" and "macrocosm." In such doctrines, where the individual is treated as a replica of the universe, and vice versa, we have the ideal synecdoche, since microcosm is related to macrocosm as part to whole, and either the whole can represent the part or the part can represent the whole. (For "represent" here we could substitute "be identified with.")[17]

Microcosm is related to macrocosm both as part to whole and by virtue of a similarity amounting to an identity. Burke's "ideal synecdoche" is a metaphor as well.

Here it may be relevant to bring up those two modes of dream figuration theorized by Freud: condensation, the symbolic composite of related things, and displacement, the allusive, associative shift from one thing to another. Both "are based on contiguity," Jakobson says, "metonymic 'displacement' and synecdochic 'condensation.'"[18] Jacques Lacan, however, in his application of Jakobson's scheme to psychoanalysis, agrees on displacement as metonymic, but he views condensation as metaphoric rather than synecdochic. Condensation exemplifies the kinship between synecdoche and metaphor. As a condensation of figures of authority, a policeman in a dream is synecdochic, a part standing for authority as a whole, and at the same time metaphoric, an authority figure resembling all the others.

Jean Vigo's *Zero for Conduct* (1933), which surreally combines the dreamlike and the bodily real, was banned in France as subversive. Why would the censors have felt threatened by a film about a bunch of schoolboys making trouble? Because they took the film's figurative dimension seriously. They saw the school as a microcosm of society, a synecdoche and a metaphor. They saw the schoolboys as the people and saw themselves and all other authorities in the teachers the boys rebel against. They saw the boys' revolt microcosmically as both synecdoche and metaphor for revolution.

Taking the four tropes beyond "their purely figurative usage," Burke looks into "their rôle in the discovery and description of 'the truth'" and proposes that

For *metaphor* we could substitute *perspective;*
For *metonymy* we could substitute *reduction;*
For *synecdoche* we could substitute *representation;*
For *irony* we could substitute *dialectic.*[19]

Of the four, the most important one, it seems to Burke, is synecdoche:
"The more I examine both the structure of poetry and the structure
of human relations outside of poetry, the more I become convinced
that this is the 'basic' figure of speech, and that it occurs in many
modes besides that of the formal trope." After quoting this in his
Handlist entry on synecdoche, Lanham comments on the centrality
of this figure to "postmodern aesthetics" and on the "similarity of
part to whole, self-similarity as it is called," and the role it plays in
chaos theory.[20]

"I feel it to be no mere accident of language," Burke continues, "that we use the same word for sensory, artistic, and political
representation"[21]—the word he couples with synecdoche. Wherever
a part represents a whole, figuratively or in reality, we can say we
have a synecdoche: "artistic representation is synecdochic, in that certain relations within the medium 'stand for' corresponding relations
outside it"; and so is "political representation, where some part of
the social body (either traditionally established, or elected, or coming into authority by revolution) is held to be 'representative' of the
society as a whole."[22] Whether or not Louis XIV actually said what
legend ascribes to him, *l'état c'est moi* (the state is me), he assumed
during his reign, as Peter Burke observes, the role of synecdoche for
the French nation, "Louis being the part that stands for the whole,
with the achievements of ministers, generals and even armies being
attributed to the king in person."[23]

The Hands, the Bootie, the Sandals

A close-up shows us something and also, by synecdoche, tells us
something. Siegfried Kracauer underlines the importance of what
a close-up shows us as opposed to what it tells us, what it signifies
as a part referring us to a whole. He cites a "famous Griffith close-up:
Mae Marsh's clasped hands in the trial episode of *Intolerance*" (1916),
which "help establish the whole of her being in a dramatic interest . . . illustrating eloquently her anguish at the most crucial moment
of the trial." But beyond that, he argues, "this close-up contributes
something momentous and unique—it reveals how her hands behave
under the impact of utter despair. . . . To Griffith such huge images
of small material phenomena are . . . disclosures of new aspects of

physical reality. . . . Isolated from the rest of the body and greatly enlarged, the hands we know will change into unknown organisms quivering with a life of their own."[24] It's in the revealed part, not the signified whole, that Kracauer finds the special power of the close-up. But those anguished hands are a telling detail, a part animated with the life of a whole. What the close-up shows us serves to render more vivid what it tells us. At such revelatory proximity, the young woman's hands perform all the better as a dramatic synecdoche for her feelings, a trope enhanced rather than diminished by our concrete perception of the hands themselves.

Let's look at another close-up from *Intolerance*. Deemed an unfit mother by the Uplifters—whom Griffith portrays as meddling upper-class women out to control the life of the working class—the Mae Marsh character, called the Dear One, has her baby forcibly taken away from her. As she lies on the floor, her resistance overpowered, her baby gone, a close-up shows us her hand tenderly, despondently grasping her child's bootie. This is a synecdoche both for her loving motherhood and for its defeat by the Uplifters, the bootie representing both the baby and its loss. The bootie belongs to the baby, but the baby is no longer there to wear it, a remnant part desolately apprehended in the absence of the whole. Griffith may not have invented the close-up, but he used it in his dramatic rhetoric of images as no one had before him and few have since.

The ancient rhetorician Quintilian notes that synecdoche goes together with ellipsis, the figure of omission. Whenever a part stands in for a whole, everything but that part is omitted. As a thoroughly synecdochic medium—what we see on the screen is always only a detail, a part of a whole—the movies are at the same time thoroughly elliptical: what the image contains is always seen in relation to what it leaves out, what lies implied in the space off screen. The part before our eyes at the moment takes the place of a whole omitted from view and left to our imagination. When we see the Dear One's clasped hands at the trial, the rest of her, the rest of the courtroom scene, is omitted and implied. In the close-up of her hand with her child's bootie, however, the baby isn't just omitted and implied but gone. The synecdoche and concomitant ellipsis thereby acquire special poignancy.

Kenji Mizoguchi's *Ugetsu* (1953) tells the parallel stories of two men driven by ambition and the wives they leave behind. One of the wives, Ohama (Mitsuko Mito), whose peasant husband wants to be a samurai, is wandering alone by the waterside when brigands roaming the war-torn land seize her, take her into an empty temple, and jointly rape her. An ellipsis spares us the rape, and instead we see Ohama's sandals abandoned in the sand. This is a resonant trope, a metaphor for her abandonment, a synecdoche for her abduction and rape, a symbol of her lost place in the world. Her forlorn sandals signify that she is no longer in her own shoes, no longer herself, no longer where she belongs. And animal bones lying nearby in the sand allude to death. The brigands throw her some coins after raping her, and the peasant wife now becomes a prostitute. Only her sandals remain on the ground from which she has been violently displaced. Like the bootie, the sandals don't merely refer to an absent person but also convey a sense of absence. Like the Dear One's baby, the woman Ohama was until now is gone.

Faces

In a legendary experiment performed by Lev Kuleshov around 1920 and reported by V. I. Pudovkin in *Film Technique and Film Acting*, close-ups of an actor's blank face were joined with shots of a plate of soup on a table, a dead woman lying in a coffin, and a little girl playing with a toy bear, so that in each case, by sleight of montage, viewers were induced to see a different expression—hunger, sorrow, fun—on a face with no expression at all.[25] Was that face a synecdoche? It was not a meaningful detail; by itself it meant nothing in particular. All its meaning came from its context—food, death, child's play. Bearing in mind the distinction, tacit in Jakobson, between synecdoche as detail and metonymy as context, we can say that metonymy was at work here—metonymy fabricated by montage.

The Kuleshov experiment relied on the device known as the point-of-view shot. We see a character looking off screen. We cut to the object of the look, then back to the character. The camera's perspective, which is also ours, is identified with the character's, and usually we are led to identify ourselves not only with the character's perspective but also with the emotion expressed on his or her face. In the Kuleshov experiment, the face expressed no emotion, but the audience supplied it: they projected onto the face the emotion elicited in them by the object of attention they and the character shared. Instead of identifying with the character's emotion, they identified their emotion with the character. In most point-of-view shots, we do some of both, whether we know it or not. To varying degrees, we identify with the character's perceived response, and we identify our response with the character.

In the Kuleshov experiment, the face acquired meaning from the adjoining images, the surrounding space. Yet Béla Balázs holds the view that "the expression and significance of the face has no relation to space and no connection with it. Facing an isolated face takes us

out of space, our consciousness of space is cut out and we find ourselves in another dimension . . . when we see, not a figure of flesh and
bone, but an expression, or in other words when we see emotions,
moods, intentions and thoughts."[26] In her study of the face on the
screen, Noa Steimatsky proposes a dichotomy between Kuleshov and
Balázs, between the face as a subordinate part and as an autonomous
whole—the face read in terms external to it, and the face apprehended
in its interiority and individuality.[27] For Balázs, the close-up enables
the face to express itself eloquently in its own terms. Steimatsky
thinks that the face gains autonomy and interiority to the extent that
it is opaque—that it neither expresses nor can be assigned a clear
meaning.

With neither Kuleshov nor Balázs is the face exactly a synecdoche,
but with both it is a metonymy, with Kuleshov a cause for an effect
and with Balázs an effect for a cause. With Kuleshov the cause is
visible and leads the viewer to imagine that the effect shows on the
character's face. With Balázs the face is the mirror of the soul—that
is, we take the facial expression as the effect of a cause in the character's mind, a smile being the effect of pleasure, a frown the effect of
anger, a tear the effect of sorrow. We don't see emotions and thoughts
on a face, only the expression they cause. With Balázs the effect is
visible, and we infer an invisible cause beneath the surface—which
is why an opaque face can give us the sense of depths unplumbed.
With most facial close-ups, we do some of both, cause for effect and
effect for cause: we read the face in relation to the adjoining images,
in terms of its environment, and we read it in its own terms, construe
its expression as a sign of its inner dimension.

Kuleshov didn't just use anybody's blank face in his experiment.
He used the face of a Russian movie star, Ivan Mozzhukhin, a face
with a special allure, a capacity for arresting the attention and engaging the imagination. The expression viewers saw on that face wasn't
wholly conjured up by montage; there was something there that
allowed the audience to imagine there was something there. For an
epitome of that kind of countenance, look at the final shot of *Queen
Christina* (1933) and the way the camera seems to want to hold on
forever to the expressively inexpressive face of Greta Garbo.

Abbas Kiarostami's *Shirin* (2008) is entirely composed of close-
ups of women, young and old. They're all looking toward us, though
not at us. They're all watching what seems to be a movie. We see
nothing—we only hear the sounds—of the movie we're watching
them watch. *Shirin* is a movie about the audience at a movie, and so
it is about us. The men we glimpse in the background of the close-
ups serve to make clear that women are here the principal audience.
We are to see our likeness in these female viewers, to respond to the

response we see on their faces. The movie they are viewing, a version of a classic Persian tale, centers on Shirin, an Armenian princess abidingly in love with the Persian king Khosrow, who loves her too—she does not lack for the love of men—but never at the right moment, never in the right fashion. Shirin personifies love and the way it is bound to turn out sadly. Hers is a story of tears, but also of thrills and smiles; there is even an unseen nude scene when the princess bathes in a pond and, as we hear watery sounds and her voice asking the water to caress her like a lover, we see delight on the faces of the audience. "We get an encyclopedia of expressions—neutral, alert, concentrated, bemused, amused, pained, anxious," David Bordwell writes. He goes on to say, "Kiarostami has been busy reinventing the Kuleshov effect."[28] Which is it, the encyclopedia of expressions or their projection onto inexpressiveness? While the heard words, music, and sound effects of the unseen movie help pinpoint expressions in themselves more or less elusive, these are not blank faces. Kiarostami, who has almost always worked with nonprofessional actors, here hired more than a hundred trained Iranian actresses (plus Juliette Binoche) to play the part of the audience.

Our reading of the faces in *Shirin* takes cause for effect (the sounds pinpointing the expression) and effect for cause in the usual way (the expression for the emotion behind it) and in another way as well: the response of the audience we're watching for its imagined cause in the movie they're watching. We strive to imagine that movie, to see it in these faces; that's what makes this movie riveting. Instead of characters in action, we watch faces in reaction. You could say that the action here is the reaction, the feelings evoked in these spectators identified with us and in turn evoked in us as we identify with them. Feeling is all, and its site is the face. If Lacanian theory posits the screen as an imaginary mirror where we see ourselves reflected, *Shirin* makes the screen into a true mirror reflecting back to us viewers like ourselves. And yet even as we identify with their identification with Shirin and her story, the very mirroring, the exact similarity between their situation and ours, brings out their difference from us and leads us to reflect on the reflection. Feeling may be all, but we stand back and think.

The Stolen Necklace

Satyajit Ray's *Pather Panchali* (1955) tells the story of an impoverished Brahmin family living in a Bengali village in the early twentieth century. It opens with little Durga, the family's only child as yet, stealing from a neighbor's garden a guava she brings home for her dear old aunt and hides in a bowl under some bananas. Then she steps toward a clay jar, and as she looks into it and reaches to pull three kittens out of it, we get a close-up of the little girl's smiling face, viewed from inside the jar and darkly framed by its round opening. In this film, done in a naturalistic style that conveys the sense of watching things as they might look to an observer in real life, the camera placement inside the jar stands out as a breach, an impossible perspective for any imaginable human observer. The breach seems to me deliberate, calculated to impress on our minds the circular close-up of Durga's moment of pleasure in the little kittens she's pulling out of the jar, as if it were a womb from which they are being born, as if it were a womb giving birth to the little girl herself. This initial image of emergent life will find its counterpart near the end in another circular image, one of sinking and death.

Let me briefly summarize what happens in between. *Pather Panchali* gives a ruminative account of everyday village life over several years. A baby boy, Apu, is born to the family. Durga admires the beads that the better-off neighbor's daughter is stringing into a necklace; when the necklace disappears, the neighbor accuses Durga of stealing it. Apu thinks his sister may be guilty and signals her to stay clear of her accuser, but her mother confronts her, and Durga denies the theft. It's one thing to steal a guava, a fruit of nature, the mother says, but a bead necklace is private property. The aunt dies alone in the woods while the two children watch a train crossing a field: the old passes on as the new passes by. The father goes away, hoping to make some money somewhere. Durga playfully immerses herself in a rainstorm and gets sick; the doctor warns against further exposure to the elements, but the house, fallen into disrepair for want of money, cannot adequately shelter her when another storm comes, and she dies in her bed. Though far apart in age, the young girl and the old aunt have a special affinity, a certain complicity—each is something of a rebel, a rogue—and the film further pairs them as the two deaths in the family, each from natural causes aggravated by impoverished circumstances. Belatedly, the father returns with money for house repairs and gifts for the family, including a sari for the daughter he doesn't know is dead, and after he finds out about her death, he decides to quit his ancestral village and move his family to the city.

As the family is preparing to leave, Apu accidentally knocks over a small bowl that a spider crawls out of, and in the bowl, where it had been hidden all along, he discovers the bead necklace. His sister had stolen it and lied about it. In order to preserve her good name, Apu takes the necklace and throws it into a nearby pond. It sinks into the water, opening a hole in the weeds on the surface of the pond, a circular hole that, as Apu watches, gets smaller and smaller until it almost vanishes. The necklace is a synecdoche, or metonymy, for Durga, for her endearing delinquency, which her loving little brother is covering up in homage to her memory. But ultimately, as the necklace sinks out of sight and the circular hole it makes diminishes into nothing, this image is a metaphor for her death. No one will know she stole the necklace; no trace is left of it, and soon no trace will be left of her existence. No evidence of her theft will tarnish her memory; before long there will be no memory to tarnish. The circle is the womb and also the grave.

Rosebud

Perhaps the most famous synecdoche in the movies is Rosebud, the sled in Orson Welles's *Citizen Kane* (1941). "Rosebud" is Charles Foster Kane's last word and the first word we hear in the film, his lips in tight close-up as he utters it before dying in his palatial Xanadu. No one knows what it means. We only find out at the very end, when we see that it's the name of a sled from Kane's lost childhood. It is being thrown into the fire along with the accumulated junk of a lifetime and is singled out by the camera for our attention. The film begins with the newspaper tycoon's death, then shows a newsreel of his life being put together by a group of reporters whose chief feels they need to account for the man's last word, which he assumes must have key significance. And so he sends one of the reporters, Thompson, on a quest for Rosebud, the missing part they hope will serve to explain the whole.

The quest for Rosebud leads us into the retrospective, prismatic plot of *Citizen Kane*. If any part of a plot synecdochically implies the whole, Rosebud is the beginning that gets the plot going, the thread we follow through the labyrinthine middle, and the goal we reach at the end. Rosebud is a synecdoche not just for the path the story takes but also for the kind of story it is. The newsreel of Kane's life tells one kind of story—the story of the public man, the Kane everyone knows; but the film wants to tell another story, one hidden in obscurity, the story of a man no one really got to know, just as no one knows what Rosebud is. Shadows take over from the public light of day; the newsreel gives way to an expressionist chiaroscuro that remains in place through the various recollections of Kane as a fitting style for telling his story. Rosebud signifies that the real story is to be found in the dark recesses of the personal life.

Kane dies holding a glass paperweight, a little replica of a log cabin with attendant snowflakes, which falls out of his hand and crashes on the floor as he says, "Rosebud." This is a metaphor for his death and for his final remembrance of childhood. Early on in the film we see him as a little boy playing with his sled in the snow outside his home, where his mother is preparing to send him away for good. When Rosebud comes to be identified as that sled, we are led to conclude that it represents the childhood home, the maternal love, whose loss Kane never got over. Is Rosebud, then, the key to Kane's character that Thompson has been seeking? For some it's a cheap Freudian gimmick. Welles himself once said as much; he repudiated Rosebud and attributed everything about it to Herman Mankiewicz, his collaborator on the screenplay. But to disown Rosebud is to disown the part on which the whole movie hinges. *Citizen Kane* indeed tells a Freudian story that looks back to the early years for the determinant factors of a life. But this doesn't mean that Rosebud should be taken as the answer to all our questions about Kane. Rather, I would take it merely as an indication of where to look for the answer, which lies buried in the snows of childhood.

"Rosebud, dead or alive. It may turn out to be a very simple thing," says the chief reporter as he sends Thompson on his quest. The next thing we see is a poster, illuminated by lightning, of Kane's second wife, Susan Alexander, featured as a singer in a nightclub.[29] This is a false start—Susan drunkenly refuses to speak to Thompson at this point—but her insertion here suggests that she may hold the answer to what Rosebud is. Later we see the first meeting between Kane and Susan, which took place when, as he tells her, "I was on my way to the Western Manhattan Warehouse, in search of my youth." In that warehouse, among his mother's stored possessions, he would have found Rosebud, and on his way there he found Susan. Among the things she has in her apartment is the snowy glass paperweight. The butler at Xanadu heard Kane say "Rosebud" twice, just before his death and right after Susan left him, each time with her glass paperweight in his hand. If Rosebud isn't just a simple thing but a symbol—a synecdoche—for the simple things in life, then Susan likewise represents simplicity, the sweetness of the ordinary. That's why Kane is drawn to her and feels at ease in her company as nowhere else in the movie. But his simple life with Susan doesn't last. Not content with enjoying her singing in private, he strives to impose it on the public and pushes her into an operatic career that can only come to failure, as does their marriage. If by sending him away from home his mother ruined Rosebud for him, then the second chance at Rosebud that Susan represents he ruins himself. Kane's longing for the simple life he lost—which he could have had with Susan had he not willfully complicated it—provides no simple explanation for his character.

Kane's lawyer and friend, Bernstein, thinks Rosebud might have been "some girl," and when Thompson doubts it, Bernstein recounts a memory of his own:

> Well, you're pretty young, Mr.—er—Mr. Thompson. A fellow will remember a lot of things you wouldn't think he'd remember. . . . You take me. One day back in 1896, I was crossing over to Jersey on the ferry, and as we pulled out, there was another ferry pulling in, and on it there was a girl waiting to get off. A white dress she had on. She was carrying a white parasol. I only saw her for one second. She didn't see me at all, but I bet a month hasn't gone by since, that I haven't thought of that girl.[30]

James Harvey comments:

> For me, it's not lost mother love or remembered innocence or other such plausible generalities, not even what we saw early on of Kane's boyhood, that the Rosebud ending evokes most strongly and inevitably: rather, it's this story of Bernstein's about this girl on the ferry whom he never knew or saw again or forgot. The kind of memory, like Kane's Rosebud, that we all have, negligible but inexpungible: the kind that seems to "make no sense," and that makes up much of our conscious lives. A memory that's important, even intelligible sometimes, to *us*—but being incommunicable in the end (who cares anyway?), only confirms our final aloneness.[31]

In Harvey's persuasive reading, Rosebud is the kind of memory so particular to each of us that we cannot share it with others. Yet Rosebud is still a synecdoche taking us from the particular to the general: this is the kind of memory we all have. So Rosebud, the incommunicable final memory of a man who died alone, nonetheless connects with his friend Bernstein's memory of the girl on the ferry, one of the most memorable things in the movie. "Kane is unknowable," Harvey asserts,[32] but the man is knowable enough in his obscurity to connect with all our personal obscurities. Rosebud symbolizes both the knowable and the unknowable about Kane, the communicable and the incommunicable, the explicable and the inexplicable.

At the end, when Rosebud is identified for us, we see in vivid close-up the sled being consumed by the fire. This, Andrew Sarris feels, is the closest we come to Kane himself:

> "Rosebud" reverberates with familial echoes as it passes through the snows of childhood [*les neiges d'antan*] into the fire, ashes, and smoke of death. Indeed, the burning of "Rosebud" in Xanadu's furnace

represents the only instance in which the soul of Kane can be seen subjectively by the audience. It is as if his mind and memory were being cremated before our eyes and we were helpless to intervene and incompetent to judge.[33]

Synecdoche often shades into metaphor, and here the burning sled is construed as a metaphor for the man identified with it.

Havana Stories

Fernando Pérez's *Suite Habana* (2003) is a documentary of sorts. Its scenes may have been staged, but its characters are real people playing themselves as they go about their daily lives. It's also something of a silent film; it has music and other sounds, but few spoken words. It has been compared to such silent documentaries as Walter Ruttmann's *Berlin, the Symphony of a Great City* (1927) and Vertov's *Man with a Movie Camera*. But those "city symphonies" depicted collective life, whereas *Suite Habana* focuses on individuals, none of them for very long at a stretch, but each with his or her own story, a dozen or so inhabitants of Havana. We are given their first names and ages—the youngest, Francisquito, is ten, and the oldest, Natividad, is ninety-seven—and without any other background information, we watch interwoven bits and pieces of their lives through the course of a day.

Sometimes a film will show us a detail we can't identify until a cut or camera movement pulls back to a wider view. Although an unidentified detail isn't exactly a synecdoche, the move it motivates from a part to a more inclusive perspective is a synecdochic figure—not a trope but a figure of arrangement—a manner of arousing and satisfying our curiosity about the scene being visually described. We see a part of something, we wonder what it is, and then it is revealed to us.[34] The first thing we see in *Suite Habana* is a shining light, an unfamiliar close view of what a moment later we recognize from farther away as the most familiar sight in the city, the first thing we would see when arriving by boat, the Morro lighthouse at the entrance to the bay. Synecdochic moves of that kind are frequent in this film. They are used not just descriptively but also narratively. We watch snippets of everyday life, we wonder how they will come together as stories, and at length we find out. This is narrative as discovery. While always synecdochic, a succession of parts implying and unfolding a whole, narrative usually proceeds not as discovery but as design, the parts all planned out to fit into the whole they compose (the gun brought to our notice in the first act is there to be fired in the third), so that the end of the story feels inevitable—maybe not predictable, but in store from the start. No such feeling of inevitability is conveyed in *Suite Habana*, no such sense that the story pieces are predetermined parts of a designed whole. Instead, we get the documentary sense that these are pieces of ongoing life, parts yet to find their place in a whole. Every movie is synecdochic and elliptical, a succession of details and omissions. The unusual thing about *Suite Habana* is its way of leaving its details as dangling fragments, its omissions as unfilled gaps.

Havana has seen better days. Before the 1959 revolution, the capital city had enjoyed a disproportionate share of the country's wealth. Attempts to redress that imbalance, compounded with the general worsening of the Cuban economy after the break with the United States—a worsening alleviated by support from the Soviet Union and grown acute after its fall—led to the city's deterioration and impoverishment. If the city symphonies of the 1920s briskly orchestrated the energies of modernity, then *Suite Habana* conveys the sadness of a run-down city and its reduced possibilities of life. If Vertov looked forward to the future from the standpoint of confident revolution, then Pérez inspects the straitened present of Havana well after the revolution, and the people he portrays may seem to be merely surviving, getting by as best they can under the circumstances. Yet as we come to discover, they all have their dreams. (Only Amanda, who at age seventy-nine sells peanuts on the street in traditional thin paper cones, has no dreams anymore, as we're told at the conclusion. And who can tell what goes on inside the head of the decrepit Natividad as she sits fixedly in front of the TV?) Each of these intertwined Havana stories holds a surprise for us—not a contrived turn of plot but a genuine surprise such as incalculable life will bring. Pérez may not be confident about the future, but his way of telling these stories leads us to recognize that the future is always open.

Riding his bicycle to work in the morning, Iván, age thirty, stops at a cobbler's shop and drops off a pair of woman's shoes with very high stacked heels—a detail left unexplained, a part of a whole not disclosed until much later, when Iván, a launderer at a hospital during the day, in the evening felicitously performs in drag. The shoes dropped off for mending are also a part of a day in the life of the cobbler, Julio, age sixty-seven, who after the day's work also transforms himself in the evening, when he dresses up and goes out dancing at a club where they call him El Elegante and where he comes into his own with his graceful step and natty dress. Dressing up, performing, dancing—such aesthetic pursuits, which some would deem frivolous, Pérez appreciates as the embodiment of human aspirations. In the evening, in the warm Havana night, the time for dreaming (Iván dreams of acting on a great stage, Julio of wearing a different suit every evening), a number of the film's characters surprise us with what they want to be, what they have the capacity for being. The city may have seen better days, but its nights harbor dreams of what can be. Francisquito was born with Down syndrome, and after his mother died, his father, Francisco, fifty-five, gave up his job as an architect to take care of the boy and now works as a contractor. If this devoted father relinquished one dream, it was to embrace another, a dream shared by father and son, who at night climb up on the rooftops to look at the moon (which chimes in with the lighthouse).

These Havana stories are all personal rather than political. Even when Jorge Luis, forty-two, takes a flight to Miami, he is not, as we might suppose, leaving Cuba for political reasons. He went into exile for love of a woman, as we learn at the end, and now he has been back to visit his family, which he dreams of reuniting (whether in Havana or Miami may perhaps not matter to him). But if the stories unfold separately, they often intersect metonymically, just as the stories of Iván and Julio intersect in the detail of the shoes, or the stories of Francisquito and Amanda intersect when the boy buys from the old vendor two cones of peanuts for himself and his father; the parallel, piecemeal style of narrative metaphorically draws numerous correspondences among the stories. As the story pieces come together into individual stories, so the individual stories are connected together into the ensemble story of a city. And as each individual story has an unexpected, by and large hopeful, turn, so too, the film suggests, the story of the city, the political story, may unforeseeably turn for the better.

The Dancing Women

Jean Vigo made his first film, the documentary *À propos de Nice* (1930), in collaboration with the cameraman who worked with him throughout his brief career, Boris Kaufman, the younger brother of Dziga Vertov and Mikhail Kaufman (who was the man with a movie camera in Vertov's film of that title). *À propos de Nice* can be compared to *The Man with a Movie Camera* as a city symphony that keeps shifting from one thing to another and often proceeds by cutting from like to like or like to unlike—metaphorical montage. But *À propos de Nice* is an irreverent, mocking, satirical symphony. While Vertov's quick cutting and mobile camera celebrate the rhythms of the dynamic socialist city (a composite of Moscow, Odessa, and Kiev), Vigo's swift editing, panning, and tilting playfully deprecate the playground for tourists and the bourgeoisie that Nice is.

If in *Zero for Conduct* the school and the rebellious schoolboys are

a microcosm, a synecdoche, and a metaphor, so is the carnival in À
propos de Nice: a part of the life of the city that stands for the whole and
offers as well an image of it. Within this representative part and image
are other such parts and images—the carnival effigies, the big masks
and puppets, which we see being prepared from the start and which
represent the masquerade, and the outsize puppet show, which the
city's whole life is seen to be—its life and its death too. The ornate
statues in the cemetery, intercut with the carnival, are seen as carnival
effigies made of stone instead of papier-mâché.

Women dancing on a high platform with unashamed verve and
abandon, viewed from below and after a while in slow motion, are
another representative part and image, a synecdoche for the carnival
and for the city—an image so striking and so often recurring that it
becomes central to the film. P. E. Salles Gomes tells us that Vigo, finding this to be the best image of the Nice carnival that he and Boris
Kaufman were able to get under the circumstances of documentary
filming, and having shot a funeral in fast motion after the Dada manner of *Entr'acte*, wanted to juxtapose a solemn occasion made grotesque by fast motion with a grotesque occasion made solemn by slow
motion. But according to Salles Gomes, a "quite fortuitous element—
the eroticism of the images of the dancing women—prevented him
from doing so. . . . The vulgarity of this eroticism was an invitation to
satire."[35] Erotic and vulgar these women blatantly are, but the image
of their dancing affects us in a way that goes well beyond satire. For
one thing, they look neither touristy nor bourgeois. They are local,
working-class women having a good time—not a fitting target for the
film's leftist satire. For another, they're clearly aware of being filmed.
They are putting themselves on display, knowingly defying propriety.
And the slow motion lends their dance a strange solemnity, turning it into a haunting carnal ceremony. Whatever Vigo and Kaufman
may have intended, these dancing women are a part and image transcending the Nice documentary, a microcosm of the life of the flesh
asserting itself in its moment of pleasure against the strictures of
convention, of morality, of death.

The Guillotine

Jacques Becker's *Casque d'or* (1952) ends with the guillotine. From
a high window across the street, Marie (Simone Signoret) watches
her lover, Manda (Serge Reggiani), being put to death in the prison
courtyard. Death as inexorable as a descending blade and as swift:
the guillotine is an image (a metonymy, a cause for its effect) of the
very moment of death.

Casque d'or is a film of arresting moments. Moments of love: the face of Marie looking at Manda, awakening him from a riverside nap with a smile ready for love, her *casque* of golden hair radiant in the sun; Marie drinking a bowl of coffee Manda brings her the next morning, a detail summing up all the tenderness of their night together. And moments of death: a twisted arm letting go of a knife promptly seized by Manda to finish off his duel with the gangster claiming Marie as his moll; the irate, resolute face of Manda shooting the dastardly gang leader Leca, a villain getting his just deserts to our amazed satisfaction. Having confessed to one killing and escaped afterward, Manda pursues Leca back into the police station and kills him right there, well knowing that this inescapably means the guillotine. He freely accepts his own death, and Marie does not flinch from it. Their story ends sadly, but it is their own—they are no mere pawns of cruel fate. There is no fatalism for them, only recognized necessity.

Becker was assistant director to Jean Renoir in the 1930s and learned much from him. But while Renoir favored long takes, allowing movement in unbounded space and unbroken time, Becker cuts much more often (like Stroheim, whom they both admired) and puts the focus on the telling detail, the encapsulating synecdoche, the kind of moment that gives time pause. Usually we think of death as the final destination of life's passage, the point at which time stops and eternity starts. But in *Casque d'or*, the moments of love have a quality of bringing time to a standstill, of touching on the eternal. Marie watching Manda at the guillotine is a moment of death that is also a moment of love. It is aptly followed by the concluding dreamlike image of the two lovers dancing together into the distance, into eternity.

Stories of love and death are about the death of love. *Romeo and Juliet* is the story of an adolescent love that can only be short-lived; Romeo and Juliet die because their love is bound to die. If their story were a comedy ending in marriage, their love would after all fit in with the social order; but it is a love too intense for society, which is why it could never last long and why their story is a tragedy. Marie and Manda's love is like that, only they're not so young. Theirs is a story of love at thirty—love no less intense than at twenty, but more aware of what it's up against. Marie watching Manda's death with open eyes represents that awareness. Stories of love and death are about love as a moment soon gone, but she apprehends death as a moment, just like love. If the camera had traveled with Manda along the path to his execution, that would have suggested the movement of inevitability and furnished a metaphor for his passage through life toward death. But instead Becker gives us a series of precise, discrete details, each sharp like the culminant guillotine. He pins down the moment of death, as fleeting as the moment of love and as enduring.

Freedom and Predestination

Robert Bresson's *A Man Escaped* (1956) begins with a close-up of hands. Hands can have as much of an expression as faces—more of an expression with Bresson, who famously liked his actors inexpressive, "models" rather than performers. Open, ready to act, these hands in close-up are free hands expressing appreciation of their freedom. Only in a situation of confinement would hands cherish a freedom of action taken for granted under normal circumstances. The man whose hands these are, Fontaine, is riding in the backseat of a car, and the camera follows his left hand as it reaches for the door handle but holds back, waiting for the right moment to turn the handle and open the door through which he hopes to break out. The camera moves up to his face, then sideways to a stern-faced man with a mustache who sits beside him, then downward to let us see the handcuffs binding the mustachioed man to someone sitting on the other side. No wonder Fontaine's hands are glad to be free. This is Lyon under the Nazi occupation, and these men riding in the backseat of the car are prisoners of the Germans.

The opening close-up of Fontaine's hands develops as a mobile close-up of hands, faces, handcuffs, the door handle, details succinctly establishing a situation without recourse to conventional establishing long shots. As P. Adams Sitney has observed, close-ups are usually momentary insertions placed in a context of wider views, but Bresson often has his close-ups stand on their own, stripped of visible context and sustained on the screen.[36] In comparison with the usual movie, his focus is more precise, his selectivity more pronounced, his omissions more noticeable; he renders the parts more partial and leaves the wholes more wholly implied. His style distills with peculiar intensity the synecdochic and elliptical language of cinema.

The camera stays inside the car, giving us no views wider than those afforded by a small space, all through the opening sequence of *A Man Escaped*. It looks at the street outside from the perspective of Fontaine as he tries to decide when to make his dash for freedom. And when he makes his dash, the camera remains in the backseat of the car, holding a close view of the impassive mustachioed man and the empty place Fontaine occupied. Through the rear window, we glimpse another car stopping behind, we see men getting out and going after the escaped prisoner, and we hear gunshots. But the camera doesn't budge. It waits until Fontaine is returned to his place in the backseat.

It knows that his attempt to escape will result in failure. It lets us know that it knows by declining to move out to the wider space where Fontaine runs away and is captured. This sustained synecdoche and its concomitant ellipsis tell us that we don't need to see anything else; the outcome is a foregone conclusion. Fontaine is brought back to the car and handcuffed. As a German starts to beat him up with a pistol, a dissolve ends the scene elliptically.

Fontaine is imprisoned and condemned to death. But in his cell, with a pin that another prisoner obtains for him, he frees his hands from their handcuffs. And with his free hands, a synecdoche for his indomitable free will, he sets about escaping from prison. First, with a spoon as a tool, he chips away at the door to his cell and succeeds in dislodging three of its oak boards, which he can take out and put back in; he has as yet no idea how to break out of the prison, but at least he's able to get out of his cell. He laboriously proceeds step by step, one thing at a time, and to each thing in turn, each detail advancing his endeavor of escape, he devotes his full attention. Nothing else matters, neither to him nor to the film: each detail precisely falls into place in his reaching for freedom—the spoon, the lantern frame that serves him to make hooks, a parcel of clothes he receives and tears up straightaway in order to make ropes—and each detail precisely falls into place in the film's narrative. The synecdochic character of narrative, its linear progression of parts building up a whole piece by piece, one thing after another, Bresson takes to an extreme. This is an extreme of narrative as design: just as the camera waits in the backseat of the car knowing that Fontaine will be captured, so at each point in the film the camera picks out a detail knowing exactly how it fits, not only into the situation at hand but into what is to come.

We know from the start that Fontaine will escape: the film's title, *Un Condamné à mort s'est échappé*, already tells us that, and its alternative, biblical title, *Le Vent souffle où il veut* (The wind bloweth where it listeth), suggests the workings of divine grace. If Fontaine embodies free will, the steadfast will to freedom, Bresson's style of narrative represents inexorable predestination, and his film reconciles the philosophical opposition between the two as only a work of art can.

The Puncture and the Veil

It Happened One Night was the sleeper of 1934 (like *Meet John Doe*, it was written by Robert Riskin and directed by Frank Capra) and endures as a wonderful romantic comedy. It tells the story of a fugitive heiress, Ellie (Claudette Colbert), who on a bus she takes in Miami, headed for New York and the man her father doesn't want her to marry, meets a reporter down on his luck, Peter (Clark Gable), whom she comes to appreciate is the man she really wants to marry. Close to New York, in a motel room where this couple brought together on the road are spending the night, with a blanket they have dubbed "the walls of Jericho" hung between their separate beds, Ellie crosses that barrier and throws herself at Peter, telling him she loves him. Unprepared for this outburst of affection, he sends her back to her bed, and she cries and falls asleep. But he loves her too, and with a mind to earn quickly the money he feels he must have for their marriage, he takes off in the little dilapidated car they picked up on the road, intending to be back before she awakens. It's the classic cross-purposes of comedy. Peter drives to New York and writes up their story for a newspaper that pays him well for it, but in the meantime Ellie, risen from her sleep and feeling abandoned, calls her father in the city, and the old man, who has withdrawn his objection to the society fop she had chosen for a husband, now comes with him to fetch her at the motel in a motorcade with a police escort.

As Peter drives back from New York, singing happily and expecting to find Ellie where he left her, the motorcade overtakes his little car and pulls ahead. But he doesn't realize what's going on until he encounters the motorcade again, crossing paths with him on its return with Ellie, and he gets a glimpse of his beloved being driven away in another man's arms. He turns around and makes an attempt to catch up with her, but as we see from his point of view, the motorcade swiftly recedes from him on the road ahead, his little car hopelessly unequal to the task. Here the faltering little car and the fancy motorcade, and the widening distance between them, are a synecdoche for the difference in class and in clout between the reporter and the heiress and her rich father. Then the film cuts to the puncture of one of the little car's tires, which deflates as the scene concludes. This is a metaphor for the puncturing and deflation of Peter's romantic dreams. It is a synecdochic metaphor, a metaphor derived from the synecdoche of the little car and the motorcade, a metaphor that is part of the situation and therefore carries greater dramatic force. With this metaphor the author comments on the story but stays inside it rather than stepping aside; the flat tire is a trope that the man in the little car could himself have come up with.

Peter and Ellie eventually surmount their class difference and reach a happy ending of romantic fruition bound up with class reconciliation. The blocking figure is the society fop Ellie nearly marries. Her father, who rose in life by his own efforts and has no liking for the idle rich, intervenes in behalf of the young lovers. When he senses his daughter's discontent and sees that Peter loves her, the old man arranges at the last minute for Ellie to back out of her wedding to a phony and go to her true love. A movie that began with Ellie running away from her father—diving into the water off his yacht in Florida—ends with her running away from the husband she no longer wants and marrying Peter. Her escape is in both cases a gesture of defiant spontaneity, nature breaking free from the constraints of society, but at the end it is a gesture sanctioned by her father as a representative of society. It was in a setting of nature—nature invested with a quality of magic, what Northrop Frye calls "the green world"[37]—that it happened one night, that Ellie and Peter fell in love. On a moonlit night they spent out of doors on the road to New York, when he carried her on his back across a sparkling stream ("a body of water," as Stanley Cavell describes it, "so brilliant with reflected skylight that there seems no break between the earth and the heavens")[38] and they gazed into each other's eyes and almost kissed on a bed of hay, their romance blossomed, unspoken yet manifest. And out of doors, in a setting of nature—rather than in a church—is where her wedding to the fop is to take place and where she shakes her head, refuses to take the vows, and runs away.

This is a lovely image, an image whose beauty sings the praises of what we behold: the bride in her white wedding dress running across a green field, her long white veil streaming behind her, buoyant in the open air like an auspicious cloud attending her flight. A wedding veil is a synecdoche for a wedding, and here the flowing, floating veil symbolizes both the wedding that didn't take place and the one that soon will, in happy accordance with nature. A wedding is of course a social act, a wedding veil a social ornament. Ellie's running away from a wedding that would have been wrong for her is a natural impulse. But she's running toward another wedding, one that will be right for her, and one in which not only she and Peter but also nature and society are to be married. Her wedding veil, in the way it rises in response to her movement and seems to partake of nature, of her nature, is a synecdoche for that upcoming marriage of nature and society.

The Train Whistles and the Hunk of Blue

Man's Castle (1933, directed by Frank Borzage) is another Depression romance, though not exactly a comedy. Comedy deals with love in society; the lovers may go into a "green world," but they return to society and in their reconciliation with it find their happy ending. The lovers in *Man's Castle* are on their own. She is a waif named Trina (Loretta Young) who has nothing in the world until she meets Bill (Spencer Tracy). He has nothing either, but he likes it that way; he enjoys a life unencumbered by possessions and responsibilities. The two set up house together in a shantytown on the Hudson River; this movie, made before the Hollywood Production Code went into effect, is untroubled by the fact that they're not married. Their love flourishes on the margins of society, and they reach their happy ending on the run from it.

Bill loves Trina, but he cherishes his freedom, his sense of himself as a man with no attachments. When he first brings her to the shantytown, they hear the whistle of a train going by. "That's what I like the best, them train whistles," he exclaims. "They remind you of other places . . . like a long-distance call." The sound of train whistles, which she finds "scary, kind of," continues to be heard throughout the film as a synecdoche for moving on, getting away, the freedom to go anywhere. It's not just the film's but the characters' synecdoche: the train whistles represent what Bill and Trina take them to represent, an exciting prospect for the man who doesn't want to be tied down, a threat to the woman who wants him to stay with her. A trope calls attention to the implied author behind a work, and by sharing a trope with the characters, the author makes a gesture of identification with them, like a god coming down to earth rather than assigning meaning from above.

Over Bill and Trina's bed in their shantytown home, a window opens to the sky. "That's Bill's idea," she explains. "He can't stand to sleep under a roof." A roof confines; the sky symbolizes freedom from confinement. When we say, "The sky is the limit!" we mean that there is no limit. The sky as a figure of freedom is both a metaphor and a metonymy—a metaphor in that it translates freedom into boundless space (*translatio* is another term for metaphor), but such space can be looked upon as the site or the environment of freedom and thus a metonymy for it (as the heart is a metonymy for the emotions or the White House for the presidency). In *Man's Castle*, the sky is represented by the piece of it framed by the window above Bill and Trina's bed. It is a synecdoche for the metaphor or metonymy for freedom, and a figure that, like the train whistles, is the characters' as well as the author's.

Synecdoche not only reaches from the particular to the general but also grounds the general in the particular. The synecdochic piece of sky set up by Bill above the bed he shares with Trina grounds the metaphor or metonymy of the sky as freedom in the couple's situation. "Why do you always keep looking through that hole for, why?" Trina asks Bill as he, having just heard the sound of a train whistle, lies down on the bed and looks up at the sky, which we see out the window from both his point of view and hers. "When you're dead you get a hunk of earth," he replies. "When you're alive you want to hang on to your hunk of blue. That's all I got in the world, that's all anybody's got, is that hunk of blue." Yet that blue up in the sky is also right beside him. As she puts it to him, "There couldn't be any heaven much better than this, could there? I mean when it's quiet all around and we're close like now." "You know, I never noticed it before," he says with a smile, looking at her, "but your eyes are sky color, sort of." He's coming to recognize that the hunk of blue he wants to hang on to lies with her. He's revising the trope, a symbolic action that makes a real difference. He's rethinking his notion of what freedom is, and beginning to see that she represents his true freedom—not the freedom to roam, but the freedom to attain his best potential.

Bill is a sweetheart, and he assures her he has known no woman nicer than she, but his notion of manhood prompts him to disclaim binding ties and adopt a gruff noncommittal posture. "You're O.K., you suit me fine now," he tells her as she lies beside him on the bed. "But maybe you won't tomorrow, see. . . . Suppose I wake up some morning with a taste like wet hen feathers in my mouth. . . . I'm just as apt to give you a good push in the face and take a stroll for myself as not." Another train whistle is heard, and she, valor outshining fear in her sky-colored eyes, discloses that she is pregnant. "You can never leave me now, Bill, never. Even if you go away I've got you now." But he gets up and goes all the same, and as he hops a freight, for the first time in the movie we actually see one of the trains whose whistles we've been hearing.

As if this were a picture in her mind, we cut back and forth between Bill going away on the train and Trina tearfully looking up from the bed at the piece of sky, where birds in flight symbolize the fleeing Bill. The effect is curiously dreamlike, surreal in the way reality and the mind's eye seem to interpenetrate, as if this couldn't really be happening but is only being imagined, as if tropes, symbols, constructions of the mind—the train whistles, the hunk of blue, the birds that are a metaphor—were being made real. The birds and the freight train, the sky and the things taking place on the ground, alike seem to reside in her eyes, the large clear eyes of Loretta Young, which have a celestial quality as well as a capacity to pull the world into them.

As if recalled by Trina's gaze, Bill jumps off the train before he gets very far. Although he still wants his freedom, he goes back and marries her in a makeshift ceremony; although he still hankers to get away, he feels he must first provide enough money for her and the baby to be taken care of after he leaves. He resorts to crime and becomes involved in an attempt to rob a toy factory, but the toys make him think of the baby and distract him. Here two metonymies—the toys for the baby, the robbery for his wish to be free—signify his attachment to Trina and the child she's expecting. The robbery fails, and the police are after him. Yet now that he has no choice but to get

away, he wants to stay with her. When a friend in the shantytown
points out that he has the choice to take her with him, Trina and Bill
together hop the next freight.

Trina might seem like "a helpless little thing" (as one character describes her), but she proves stronger and braver than Bill. "I
wouldn't have taken that money anyway, I'd have given it back," she
tells him while tending the wound he suffered in the attempted robbery. "How do you expect to get along? It takes money to have a kid,
don't it?" he asks. "For a strong husky man you're awful afraid of a
little thing that ain't even born yet," she replies. "I didn't know you
were such a coward, darling." "Coward?" "Sure. Afraid of a baby.
Why, it's the most natural thing in the world, you big fool. They're
born all the time, and if they happen to be men kids they just never
grow up, they just keep reaching for the clouds and listening to train
whistles."

The conclusion of *Man's Castle* takes place inside a trope, you
might say, a symbol made real, a reality made symbolic. Trina and
Bill are runaways in a freight train such as has all along been a figure for freedom. This is the realization of his dream to be free, but
his freedom is with her; his hunk of blue is in her eyes. And it is her
eyes that are open, her eyes that look up, as he lies beside her in the
freight car with his arms around her and his head on her shoulder.
The camera, watching them from above, performs a closing upward
movement identified with her upward gaze, a movement that seems
to be rising with her eyes toward the kindred sky, reaching for clouds
unseen yet better founded in reality than any he contemplated.

Documentary, Repetition, Representation

Claude Lanzmann has insisted that *Shoah* (1985), his imposing
two-part film about the Holocaust, is not a documentary. Documentary films looking into the past usually rely on the selection and
arrangement of newsreel footage, old photographs, visual evidence
provided by cameras that were there at the time. *Shoah* contains no
such images from the past. That was what Leon Wieseltier meant
by "not a single frame of documentary footage"[39] and what Timothy
Garton Ash means when he writes that "*Shoah* is not a documentary.
It has none of those familiar black and white sequences: hysterical
crowd chanting 'Sieg Heil' CUT to pile of corpses at Bergen-Belsen.
No Hitler, no corpses. Instead we have nine and a half hours of interviews with surviving Jewish victims, German executioners, and Polish witnesses . . . long, harrowing, astonishing interviews."[40] But of
course interviews are a documentary method as familiar as old news

images pieced together. For Lanzmann, however, documentary is "the registering, or the recording, or the filming of a preexisting reality," which is not what he did in *Shoah*: "There was nothing to film. I had to invent everything."[41] He sees himself as an artist rather than a documenter. He notes that he harbored a wish to destroy the footage he shot (some 350 hours) but did not use in the finished film: "This, at least, would prove that *Shoah* is not a documentary."[42] (What ends up on the cutting-room floor simply ceases to exist in the world of a fiction film, whereas a documentary could be defined as the kind of film whose unused footage still belongs in the world depicted.) Gertrud Koch stressed the aesthetic qualities of *Shoah* and "the fact that long stretches of the film are not 'documentary' at all."[43] But surely the aesthetic and the documentary, the work of art and the record of reality, are not mutually exclusive.

Long stretches of *Shoah*, it is true, are staged for the camera. But interviews are always staged, set up for the purpose of asking questions and getting answers—and not just interviews. Other scenes in documentaries are often to some extent staged or in any case arranged to construct a meaning and have an effect on the audience. In Robert Flaherty's *Nanook of the North* (1922), sometimes considered the founding work of documentary film as art, Nanook builds an igloo expressly for the movie. When he is done, he smiles through a window he carved out and gazes straight into the camera. Is this fiction or documentary? It is a staged scene, and the smile at the audience acknowledges it, but Nanook is a real Inuit really building an igloo to demonstrate for us how igloos are built. Documentary, one may think, captures the unrepeatable particularities of actuality, but Flaherty, in this and other movies, focuses on actions often performed that can be repeated one more time before the camera and thus documenting even while being staged.

"No one can describe it. No one can recreate what happened here. Impossible! And no one can understand it." Simon Srebnik makes this statement at the beginning of *Shoah* as he returns to Chelmno, Poland, where the Nazis exterminated 400,000 Jews and only he and one other survived. Lanzmann tells us in a preface that Srebnik was a boy of thirteen and a half when he was sent to Chelmno, and it helped keep him alive that he could sing so well: everyone in the village knew the boy who would row up the river in a flat-bottomed boat and sing Polish folk tunes and Prussian military songs he learned from the German guards. Near the end of the war, two days before the Red Army got there, the Nazis killed with a bullet in the head all the remaining Jews in the extermination camp, but Srebnik miraculously lived. Lanzmann found him in Israel and persuaded him to return with him to Chelmno for the making of the film. "The first time I saw Srebnik," Lanzmann recalls, "he gave me an account that was so extraordinarily confused that I understood nothing at all. He had lived through so much horror that it had destroyed him."[44] We never see him interviewed in the film, though we hear him speak. In the heartbreaking opening, the survivor of Chelmno once again travels on the village river in a flat-bottomed boat and sings.

Lanzmann staged this scene, and for him and others that disqualifies it as documentary. But he did not stage it as the sort of dramatization in which a boy actor would play Srebnik and re-create what he did as a boy. Rather than a re-created past, this is a memory enacted, an embodied recollection. Doing again before our eyes and ears the same thing he would do as a boy, the middle-aged Srebnik brings an action back as a memory is brought back, by a reaching into the past that never erases the distance between then and now, between the boy singer of Chelmno and the survivor recalling him many years later. Lanzmann doesn't see it that way, though. "The film is not made out of memories," he says. "Memory horrifies me; recollections are weak. The film is the abolition of all distance between past and present; I relive this history in the present."[45] The past made present: that sounds like the aim of a conventional dramatization. Recollections are weak insofar as they recede into the long since gone; old images have a similar recessive tendency, which is why Lanzmann does without them. What is made present in *Shoah*, however, what comes alive on the screen when the returned survivor sings again on the village river, is not the past but the act of recalling it, the transaction between past and present that takes place in remembrance. What I find especially moving about the scene is the way it identifies the man with the boy he once was while keeping them distinct, the way it palpably bridges the distance between present and past without abolishing it. Call it a documentary of memory.

Memories are metonymies, in Jakobson's sense: we have a connection of contiguity with the things we recollect because we were there when they happened, and we also have a connection of contiguity with our former selves, who experienced what we remember. It is above all the metonymic connection between the boy singer and the middle-aged man shown on the screen that gives Lanzmann's staged scene the quality and conviction of documentary. Documentary is hard to define, but it depends on the direct connection, peculiar to the photographic image, between the camera and the things it reproduces—a connection of contiguity, a metonymic connection. The camera has a metonymic connection with the middle-aged Srebnik as the middle-aged Srebnik has a metonymic connection with the boy singer.

Charles Sanders Peirce, a philosopher Jakobson admired, had an appreciable influence on his thinking. Two of the three basic kinds of sign in Peirce's semiotics relate to Jakobson's scheme of metaphor and metonymy. Peirce's icon, which signifies by its resemblance to its object, relates to Jakobson's metaphor, which connects by similarity; and Peirce's index, which signifies by virtue of having an actual, existential link to its object—the link between a footprint and a foot, or between a weather vane and the wind, or between a knock on the door and someone at the door—relates to Jakobson's metonymy, which connects by contiguity. (Peirce's third kind of sign, the symbol, signifies by convention, by our agreement that a red traffic light means stop or that the word "tree" means a tree, and it has no counterpart in Jakobson's binary scheme, though metaphor and metonymy are a matter of words to begin with.) Not all metonymies are indices—the words on the plaques at the beginning of *Meet John Doe* are symbols in Peirce's sense—but all indices make a metonymic connection. Some would define documentary in terms of the index, but the photographic image is both an index and an icon, and while it gains a special documentary quality from the index—from the fact that the things depicted had to have been there in front of the camera, that they leave in the image an imprint of their light, just as a foot leaves its imprint in the sand it steps on—if it weren't for the icon, the recognizable likeness of things, the image wouldn't be much of a document.

To say that memories are metonymies is equivalent to saying that they are indices, or more precisely traces. Memories are traces of the past, just like photographic images, which in turn are vehicles of remembrance, as when we look at pictures in a family album. But memories are also icons, likenesses of the past we keep in our heads, visual, verbal, aural, tactile, olfactory, gustative likenesses, and if they weren't also icons, they wouldn't be memories but merely entries in some mental account book. The sight and sound of the returned Srebnik singing as he once sang wouldn't so movingly incarnate a memory—a memory together with the act of recalling it, its living enactment on the screen by the man who carries it imprinted in his mind—if this sight and this sound were only an index, a metonymy, and not also an icon, a likeness, a metaphor.

"If it has proven notoriously difficult to define documentary by reference to its constantly shifting stylistic practices," Dai Vaughan writes, "it is because the term 'documentary' properly describes not a style or a method or a genre of filmmaking but a mode of response to film material: a mode of response founded upon the acknowledgement that every photograph is a portrait signed by its sitter. Stated at its simplest: the documentary response is one in which the image is perceived as signifying what it appears to record."[46] We recognize the image of Srebnik singing on the river as a portrait signed by its sitter, and we respond to it as an image signifying what it appears to record: the middle-aged man back at the tragic site of his youth. In a fiction film, the image of an actor playing a character signifies the character rather than the actor. Lanzmann isn't wrong to maintain that "in a certain way" the people portrayed in *Shoah* are "transformed into actors."[47] But even if they are actors, they signify themselves, and the film is a documentary of their performance as themselves testifying to their own history before the camera recording their image. No actor except himself could so affectingly play Srebnik recalling his former self: his performance uniquely conveys the feeling of truth peculiar to documentary.

Like Flaherty photographing Nanook, or—to mention another documentary pioneer—Dziga Vertov photographing workers and machines at work, Lanzmann has repeatable actions repeated before the camera. He has Abraham Bomba, a retired barber, cut hair again while being interviewed about his experience as a prisoner at Treblinka, where he was assigned to cut the hair of women about to be killed in the gas chamber. The image of Bomba cutting hair may be a staged fiction performed for the camera, but it is a performance of what he actually used to do, what he was made to do on the threshold of extermination, and though he tries to give a dispassionate account, the point comes when he cannot hold back his tears. He almost stops the interview, but Lanzmann presses him to continue his painful recollection of that terrible experience as he repeats an action that was part of it. The action is real, and the pain is real. The image is a physical embodiment, a documentary of an unspeakable memory.

Repetition is a rhetorical means of emphasis and a way to impress something on the mind. *Shoah* proceeds slowly and repetitively. It has the form not just of endeavoring to remember but of committing to memory by repetition. The eyewitness testimonies are of course recountings, verbal repetitions of what took place. Lanzmann is a persistent interviewer who often repeats his questions and wants the answers repeated. When he interviews someone who speaks a language he doesn't know, the questions and answers are repeated in unabridged translation. A question asked in French will go through an interpreter into Polish, will then be answered in Polish, and then the answer will be translated into French. And the film abounds in visual repetitions. The camera keeps returning to the memorial stones at Treblinka. It moves around Auschwitz as if retracing Filip Müller's steps, as if we were looking at that site of death through the recollecting eyes of this *Sonderkommando* survivor whose voice we hear recounting for us what he suffered and witnessed there. Trains and railroad tracks recur in *Shoah* like a refrain. "The locomotive at

Treblinka is *my* locomotive. I rented it at Polish Railways," Lanzmann says. "The first time I went to Treblinka, I did not yet have in my head a conception of the film. . . . I discovered that there was a train station and a village called Treblinka. The sign for 'Treblinka' . . . was an incredible shock for me. Suddenly, it all became true."[48] He found a Polish locomotive engineer who ran the train carrying Jews to that fatefully designated station and had him run that ride over again, the camera riding with him along those tracks as if it were a Jew being transported to Treblinka again and again. *Shoah* is the ultimate documentary of repetition.

Beyond the claim that "*Shoah* is not a documentary," Lanzmann makes another claim: "The film is not at all representational."[49] He seems to equate representation with the photographic reproduction of appearances, whether the archival images he would not use in his film or the feigned images of reality in a dramatization such as Steven Spielberg's *Schindler's List* (1993). "No one can recreate what happened here. Impossible!" Does this mean that it is impossible to represent the Holocaust? Alain Resnais and Jean Cayrol's *Night and Fog* (1955), largely composed of archival images and before *Shoah* the most notable documentary to deal with the Nazi camps, likewise acknowledges that no one can adequately depict what happened there. According to Phillip Lopate, "*Night and Fog* is, in effect, an anti-documentary: we cannot 'document' this particular reality, it is too heinous, we would be defeated in advance."[50] That is to say, the Holocaust is unrepresentable. It is true that no representation can be equal to the heinous reality of the death camps, but then any particular reality, any concrete experience in all its aspects, always exceeds its representation. Photography, the image taken directly from actual things, seems to have furnished our culture with its paradigmatic idea of representation, but there are other kinds. Michelangelo's *Creation of Adam* in the Sistine Chapel doesn't pretend to represent the actual event.

It is an old rhetorical commonplace to declare that words fail you, that you lack the capacity to describe what you are alluding to. The biblical commandment against graven images has a similar rhetorical effect of inspiring awe at a higher power beyond our human capacity to represent. Something like that comes into play in the notion that the Holocaust is unrepresentable or unimaginable. It is part of the rhetoric of *Shoah* that it rules out archival images, just as it is part of the rhetoric of *Night and Fog* to use them eloquently while admitting that they are inadequate to the reality they evoke. To call something rhetorical is not to deny its validity, only to recognize how it works on us. We must recognize that both *Night and Fog* and *Shoah* are documentary representations of the unimaginable that, in their different ways, gain rhetorical force by declaring their limitations. The problem with *Schindler's List* is not that it gives us feigned images of the Holocaust but that it never lets us know, never makes us feel, how far they come short of the reality.

It is sometimes said that *Shoah* forswears visual representation in favor of spoken testimony. But words as much as images are a means of representation, and images in *Shoah* are an indispensable means of testimony. The camera bears witness visually to the act of bearing witness verbally; the barber's tears are as testimonial as his words. The documentary images in *Shoah* give their own testimony. Even when they only show us an emptiness where once there was a death camp, they attest to the vestiges of atrocity, the marks of the appalling past discernible in a place or on a face. It is sometimes supposed that images, being more physical, more directly present to the audience, convey the illusion of fully represented reality, while words, being less explicit, leave more to the imagination. But images can be as suggestive as words, as subtle and mysterious and as engaging of the imagination. If images have the capacity to show, then words have the capacity to tell, to explain, and if *Shoah* declines to show, it equally declines to explain. "Here there is no why": the words Primo Levi heard at Auschwitz, Lanzmann has made his own.[51] Graven images are not to be worshipped because they are not acceptable substitutes for God. But the images and words we see and hear in *Shoah*, like those in *Night and Fog*, give us a representation without ever soliciting our acceptance as a substitute for a reality that neither the eye nor the mind can adequately comprehend.

The Village Church

At the start of *Shoah*, Srebnik sings a Polish folk song he sang on that river when he was a boy. Later Lanzmann has him sing a Prussian military song, again on the river, in a flat-bottomed boat, but now with the steeple of the village church visible in the background, which prompts a cut to the organist in the church as he plays during Mass and sings. Drawing a parallel between the sung church music and the military song the Nazis taught the captive Jewish boy—musical metonymies for the church and the Nazis brought into metaphoric connection—this cut is the first step in Lanzmann's indictment of the church for its part in the Holocaust.

Next we see Srebnik in front of the church with a group of villagers around him. The frontal, symmetrical arrangement of this shot—he stands squarely in the middle facing the camera, the villagers evenly on both sides, the church door straight behind him so that it seems to make an arched frame for him—ironically mimics the sort of snapshot in which old friends welcoming back a returnee pose with him at a local landmark. No doubt the villagers saw it that way; the irony is at their expense. Srebnik remains silent in their midst, while Lanzmann, from behind the camera, asks them questions about the past. He asks them if they remember—and indeed they remember—that the Nazis used that church as a place for rounding up Jews before their extermination. In that church, Jews were imprisoned until the gas vans that administered death came to pick them up at that arched door.

A religious procession now comes out of that door, interrupting Lanzmann's conversation with the villagers, yet serving to extend his line of argument. His camera dwells on the procession not as a bit of local color but as a way of pointing his finger at a church whose rituals he leads us to see as tainted by its culpability. The village church where Jews were locked up is a synecdoche for the church's complicity in the Holocaust. But how far did that complicity go? How large is the whole this part stands for? When, after showing us the procession, the camera tilts up the church steeple and zooms into a close-up of the Christian cross at the top, this much smaller part—a synecdoche within a synecdoche—implicates a much larger whole. It indicts not just the Catholics of Chelmno, not just the Polish church, but the whole of Christianity as bearing responsibility for the Holocaust. While it is true that the Nazis weren't particularly Christian, it is also true that they drew on a long history of Christian anti-Semitism. Resuming his conversation with the villagers—again gathered around Srebnik in front of the church, and now joined by the church organist—Lanzmann asks them why they think all this happened to the Jews. Because they were the richest, some reply, but the organist steps forward and brings up the traditional commonplace of Christian anti-Semitism, that the Jews are to be blamed for the death of Christ.

Were the villagers willing accomplices, or were they forced to surrender their church to the Nazis? Lanzmann doesn't ask them. For him, it is enough to expose their anti-Semitism, which isn't theirs alone but has been fostered by Christianity over the centuries. It happened that their house of worship was once turned into a prison house for Jews, and Lanzmann's rhetoric takes advantage of that historical fact—that metonymic connection—in an accusatory synecdoche.

Shoah does not altogether refrain from explanation. Only one person interviewed in the film was not an eyewitness: Holocaust historian Raul Hilberg, whom Lanzmann brings in as an authority with his evident endorsement. Hilberg posits a "logical progression" from the early Christians who would convert the Jews ("You may not live

among us as Jews") to the late medieval rulers who expelled the Jews
("You may not live among us") and finally to the Nazi extermination
("You may not live"). Christian anti-Semitism was a necessary condition for the Holocaust, but surely not a sufficient one. Anti-Semitism
can be understood historically, but its singular virulence under the
Nazis cannot be accounted for simply as the logical consequence of
that deplorable history.

Another intellectual in the film, shown at home against a background of books, was a key participant and gives riveting testimony.
A courier for the Polish underground state during the war, Jan Karski
was approached in the fall of 1942 by Jewish leaders who wanted him
to alert the Western nations fighting Nazi Germany to the desperate
situation of the Jews. He was taken to the Warsaw ghetto so that he
could see for himself, and in an unforgettable interview toward the
end of *Shoah*, he describes the horror he saw. Yet Lanzmann omitted
what Karski, as he says in an admiring though not uncritical article
on the film, thought was the most important part of his interview:
the account no one else could have given of his report to "the Allied
governments, which alone were capable of providing assistance to
the Jews [but] left the Jews to their own fate." *Shoah* "creates an
impression that the Jews were abandoned by all mankind," Karski
argues. "This is, however, untrue and disheartening. . . . The Jews
were abandoned by governments, by those who had the physical or
spiritual power."[52]

Karski died in 2000. A novel about him by Yannick Haenel was
published in France in 2009 and aroused controversy. For one thing, it
depicts the Polish courier delivering his report on the urgent plight of
the Jews to an uncaring and distracted Franklin Roosevelt. Lanzmann
wrote an outraged review attacking the novel as a falsification of history and a defamation of Roosevelt. To set the record straight, he
brought forward the omitted part of his interview with Karski, out of
which he made a new film, *The Karski Report* (2010). It is an extraordinary film, both for the story it tells and for its portrait of the man telling the story, a talking head holding the screen all the way through.
It does not, however, lay to rest the contention that Roosevelt was
insensitive to the Jewish plight. Karski says he gave the American
president a succinct report because he expected questions on which
he was ready to expand, but Roosevelt asked none about the Jews.
Nor does he seem to have taken any special action in response to their
cry for help. So the question remains: Why was the story of Karski's
report left out of *Shoah* in the first place? Why did it have to wait for
Haenel's novel and the new film it prompted Lanzmann to release?

In one of the few unfavorable reviews of *Shoah*, Pauline Kael raised
the issue of representativeness, especially with regard to the coarsely

anti-Semitic Polish peasants Lanzmann presents as representative: "In some passages he seems to be conducting his interviews at Woody Allen's convention of village idiots."[53] When a part is to stand for a whole, we can always ask how well the chosen part represents the intended whole. Some Polish peasants helped the Jews, and if those were exceptions—the penalty for helping a Jew in Nazi-occupied Poland was death—they were exceptions representing the whole best hopes of humanity. What about genteel ruling-class anti-Semitism? The village church that confined Jews before their murder is an eloquent synecdoche for Christian complicity in the Holocaust, but it is a synecdoche that should have included the powerful who did nothing as well as the peasants in the vicinity.

The Revolutionary Battleship

In one of his essays, Sergei Eisenstein discusses his use of synecdoche—"that most popular of artistic methods, the so-called *pars pro toto*"—in the close-up of the ship doctor's pince-nez dangling from a rope in *The Battleship Potemkin* (1925).[54] Here, Eisenstein says, the pince-nez plays the role of the doctor, who has been thrown overboard by the mutinous sailors. But we have already seen that whole action—no fewer than eight successive shots in overlapping montage show us the doctor being thrown into the water—when we come to the dangling pince-nez left behind. Rather than taking the place of the action, this part comments on it, sums up its meaning, widens its significance. Here as elsewhere in Eisenstein, the close-up serves, as he puts it himself, "not only and not so much to *show* or to *present*, as to *signify*, to *give meaning*, to *designate*."[55]

This synecdoche refers us back to an earlier episode that occurred at the start of the sailors' revolt and involved the doctor and his pince-nez. Called upon to examine a rotten piece of meat intended as food for the sailors ("A dog wouldn't eat this"), the doctor holds his pince-nez up to the meat swarming with maggots and declares that there are no maggots in it. The rotten meat is itself a synecdoche, not just for the bad food the sailors get on the ship but for all the mistreatment the Russian people suffer under the czar—a synecdoche and also a metaphor for the rottenness of the czarist regime. The doctor, himself a synecdoche, represents the intellectual explaining away that rottenness, the ideologist denying the reality under his nose.[56] In another synecdoche, the mutinous sailors represent revolution, the people rising to overthrow their oppressors. After they throw the doctor overboard, Eisenstein inserts a flashback shot of the maggoty meat followed by a title, "Down to feed the maggots," before cutting to the close-up of the dangling pince-nez. We don't need the pince-nez to tell us that its possessor has been flung into the sea. This part stands for a whole much larger than that. It represents, in a kind of microcosm, oppression and liberation, ideological falsification and revolutionary justice.

Potemkin in its entirety is a synecdoche. On the anniversary of the 1905 revolution—suppressed by the czar but a prelude to the successful one to come—Eisenstein had planned to make a film, *The Year 1905*, which would have depicted several revolutionary episodes that took place during that year, including the sailors' mutiny aboard the armored cruiser *Prince Potemkin* of the Black Sea fleet. But when, looking for locations in the Black Sea port of Odessa, he saw the massive steps descending to the waterfront, he was inspired to stage a scene there as the centerpiece of a film solely devoted to the *Potemkin* episode, which thus came to be the part that stands for the whole.

In the famous Odessa steps sequence, Eisenstein characteristically brings together the figurative and the physical. When we speak of troops *descending* on people, we use a spatial metaphor for the exercise of power, which we think of as coming down from above, as something *over* the people *under* it. This metaphor finds eloquent embodiment in the actual space of the Odessa steps. The figurative is made vividly, brutally physical as the Cossacks, their descending movement given emphasis by the repeated synecdochic image of their treading boots, come down those steps, take command of that space, and massacre the people of Odessa who have gathered there in solidarity with the sailors of the *Potemkin*.

In his experimental theater work, Eisenstein once staged a dramatically tense scene with an actor on a tightrope. "The tension of such an 'act on wire,'" he writes, "extends the *conventional* tension of acting and transfers it into a new level of *real* physical tension"[57]—a new level rather of *metaphorical* physical tension: the tension embodied in the tightrope is not the dramatic tension in the scene but a physical equivalent, a parallel set up to elicit analogous emotions in the audience (though it might have been a distraction—we don't know how well that act on wire worked). Like the Odessa steps on which power descends, the tightrope is a physical metaphor. The difference, however, is that the tightrope is merely a metaphorical prop, extrinsic to the action it serves to stage, whereas the Odessa steps are part of a real situation, an intrinsic part of the action staged on them and shaped by their massive descent. They are a metaphor made not only physical but real because they are not only a metaphor but also a synecdoche. As a synecdoche, the Odessa steps sequence represents, beyond a particular incident of bloody suppression, the general brutality of power exercised against the people.

The montage of three stone lions as the sailors retaliate with gun-fire from the battleship—the first lion asleep, the second awakening, the third rising to its feet, shown in quick succession so that they strike us as one statue come to life—is a metaphor and not a synecdoche. A synecdoche partakes of what it represents, and these three statues, impossibly quickened, are removed into a symbolic space apart.[58] But what exactly do they symbolize? The rising of the people? This is presumably the meaning Eisenstein intended, but lions are often a symbol of power, and these lions, which seem aroused not by the massacre on the steps but by the sailors' retaliation, may with equal plausibility be taken to symbolize the ruling power reacting to the popular uprising. It's not clear whether the stone lions are rising in anger or recoiling in alarm. While noting the ambiguity in meaning, David Bordwell emphasizes the visceral impact of the lion montage, especially its stirring visual evocation of a sound, on which he quotes Eisenstein: "The jumping lions entered one's perception as a turn of speech—'The stones roared.'"[59] Yes, but is this the roar of revolution or the roar of reaction? At the time of the *Potemkin* mutiny, there were workers' strikes and uprisings in Odessa, but revolutionary coordination was lacking, and in reality the sailors, when called upon to help their fellow rebels, didn't fire on the town with live ammunition but only with blanks.[60] Not wanting to go into that, Eisenstein fell back on the abstraction of a pure metaphor, a self-contained symbol. However, his roaring stone lions, intentionally or not, make an ambiguous symbol allowing the implication that czarist reaction actually prevailed.

It would be wrong to suppose that a metaphor always works better or becomes more real when it is also a synecdoche. Less well known but no less impressive than the Odessa steps sequence is the massacre of the workers at the end of *Strike* (1925), which Eisenstein metaphorically juxtaposes with documentary images of a bull being killed in a slaughterhouse. Although extrinsic to the slaughter of the workers, the slaughter of the bull carries the impact of the real thing, the stomach-turning impact of actual blood being spilled, and makes the staged massacre more real to the audience. With its rhetorical use of actual butchery, the slaughterhouse metaphor affects us so strongly that it can only bring the film to its conclusion.

Potemkin ends not in tragic defeat but in revolutionary triumph. The revolution defeated in 1905 triumphed in 1917; the massacre on the Odessa steps represents the defeat, and the film's ending looks forward to the triumph. The closing sequence depicts the encounter between the rebel battleship and the czarist squadron deployed to subdue it. In real life, the *Potemkin* mutineers had some trouble running the ship, but in Eisenstein's film, as they prepare to meet the squadron, the sailors run their own ship with unfaltering collective competence. A vigorous rhythmic montage renders their concerted activity, with the men at their various tasks and the various pieces of the ship's machinery all working together, all orchestrated in dynamic ensemble. Synecdoche and metaphor are here again compounded. The sailors taking charge of their own ship and running it themselves represent the people taking charge of their own government, running their own lives, in control of their own destiny. A ship is a microcosm. As a part—the sailors as part of the people, the running of the ship as part of the running of the country—it represents the whole. And it also resembles it: the "ship of state" is an old metaphor comparing the state to a ship in its internal order and its course toward a destination.[61] Eisenstein could have shown us the sailors learning to run their ship, which would have elicited our sympathy; but his rhetoric lays stress on their capacity to act and calls for a more active identification. We are asked to identify with them as the people they are identified with, the people seizing power rightly theirs and leading the ship of state toward the socialist future.

In *Potemkin*, the ship of state is a battleship, and the sailors who take it over in the name of the people are members of the armed forces. Beginning with a quotation from Lenin on revolution as war, Eisenstein's film portrays military action as central to revolutionary action.[62] Among the civilian crowd on the Odessa steps we don't see many workers, which may seem odd for a film of proletarian allegiance. But the citizens on the steps are merely supportive bystanders: revolution is identified with the sailors, and the sailors are identified with the proletariat. Since the workers of Odessa play little part in the film, and because within the microcosmic ship the sailors are the workers to the officers' ruling class, in *Potemkin* the sailors are the proletariat, the people. They represent revolution both as armed conflict and as mass movement, and their triumph at the end is not so much military as popular.

Historically, the mutinous battleship was allowed to pass through the czarist squadron without a shot being fired. That remarkable turn of events concludes the film. Their fellow sailors on the squadron meet the rebel sailors with a fraternal cheer, and in the final image, the advancing prow of the *Potemkin*, seen from below, seems to break forth from the screen and to sweep over us in the audience with that cry of revolutionary solidarity. "But where does the *Potemkin* go?"[63] Eisenstein puts the question at the start of an essay whose title gives the historical answer his film withholds: Constanţa, a Romanian port on the Black Sea, was where the ship ended up and the mutineers took refuge. The omission of Constanţa from the film cuts the historical episode short, but as Eisenstein explains, at a point of "revolutionary consciousness, the maximum conceivable in the circumstances." An account of what followed would have been a comedown from "the great public significance of the fact that the admiral's squadron did not open fire."[64] To have shown us the sailors of the *Potemkin* escaping into Romania would have diminished their stature as heroes, not just of a mutiny they got away with but of the revolution they represent, not just as participants in 1905 but as precursors of 1917, and not just in Russia but wherever the people rise up against tyranny. To have told us more about the sailors would have reduced the meaning of their story. The choice of a rhetorically appropriate part is key to the art of synecdoche.

Allegory and Extended Synecdoche

Allegory is traditionally defined as extended metaphor. Quintilian cites a passage from Horace in which the metaphor being extended is the ship of state: "O ship, new waves will take you back to sea: / what are you doing? Be resolute, make harbour." Here the poet allegorically "represents the state as a ship, the civil wars as waves and storms, and peace and concord as the harbour."[65] Constanța was the harbor the *Potemkin* mutineers actually reached, but allegorically the sailors in Eisenstein's film are the people steering the ship of state toward the new socialist order that will be their true harbor. The ending of *Potemkin* may be called an allegory of revolution advancing. The entire film is an extended synecdoche taking the *Potemkin* episode as representative of revolution. Should such an extended synecdoche come under the heading of allegory?

Potemkin is not an allegory in the way that, for example, *The Cabinet of Dr. Caligari* (1920) has been understood to be. Made in Germany right after World War I, *Caligari* does not represent the war directly but rather through a parallel horror fantasy, a bizarre tale of insane authority compelling youth to murder. Hans Janowitz, a war veteran who wrote the screenplay together with Carl Mayer, says that their horror story was meant to allegorize the war. This interpretation of the movie was taken up and elaborated by Siegfried Kracauer and has gained wide acceptance.[66]

"Caligari is both the eminent doctor and the fairground huckster," Lotte Eisner observes; the director of a mental institution doubles as a mountebank and turns a patient into a fairground somnambulist who kills at Caligari's bidding.[67] The film may be construed as an indictment of callous military psychiatrists who would send shell-shocked soldiers back into combat.[68] For Janowitz, however, the mad doctor didn't just represent psychiatry gone mad but a "State

Authority that called upon us and forced us to participate in an insane war led at absurdum."[69] If Caligari is taken as a war psychiatrist, he comes closer to a synecdoche, a part of military authority standing for the whole; and if this were a war movie, and if instead of a doctor it portrayed a deranged general ordering his soldiers into indiscriminate slaughter, it would likewise have enacted an extended synecdoche for the insanity of war rather than the scriptwriters' extended metaphor. As Caligari is doubled into upstanding authority and sinister charlatan, so the young somnambulist under his spell, Conrad Veidt's unforgettable Cesare, who sleeps in a coffin like a corpse and whom Caligari summons back to life and hypnotically commands to go out and murder, is doubled into killed and killer. Slowly awakening from his entombed slumber, his face in tight close-up, his eyes opening to confront the viewer with a fearful stare, Cesare can be seen to symbolize both the dead and the agents of death that so many young men became under the authority sending them to war.

Janowitz tells us that he and Mayer felt betrayed by a change made in their screenplay as *Caligari* went into production. Following a suggestion by Fritz Lang, who was unable to direct the film because of another commitment, Robert Wiene, who took over as director, added a prologue and epilogue framing the narrative and gave it a narrator, a young man who tells the story of Caligari's insanity and who turns out to be insane himself. Kracauer comments:

> The original story was an account of real horrors; Wiene's version transforms that account into a chimera concocted and narrated by the mentally deranged Francis . . . Janowitz and Mayer knew why they raged against the framing story: it perverted, if not reversed, their intrinsic intentions. While the original story exposed the madness inherent in authority, Wiene's *Caligari* glorified authority and convicted its antagonist of madness. A revolutionary film was thus turned into a conformist one.[70]

The original story was not, however, an account of real horrors, as the synecdochic story of a deranged general would have been. It was a shadowy allegorical fantasy, inspired by the war but a thoroughly subjective rendition of it. Already as conceived by its writers, who envisioned something like the nightmarish painted sets for which the film is famous, *Caligari* takes place in a world of the mind, a mind in the grip of anxiety and horror. The disturbed subjectivity informing the writers' narrative is ascribed by the director's framing to a dramatized narrator. (Horror stories often make the narrator unreliable, so that we're not being asked to accept fantasy as reality but as something that could either be real or imaginary.) In his study of the *Trauerspiel*, the German "sorrow play" of the seventeenth century, Walter Benjamin stresses the subjectivity of allegory: "The absolute vices, as exemplified by tyrants and intriguers, are allegories. They are not real, and that which they represent, they possess only in the subjective view of melancholy. . . . By its allegorical form evil as such reveals itself to be a subjective phenomenon."[71] What Benjamin says about subjectivity in the *Trauerspiel* may not apply to allegory in general—*Pilgrim's Progress*, for example, allegorizes Christian doctrine, beliefs shared by a culture, not a subjective view—but it applies to expressionist allegory. Even without the added unreliable narrator, the evil of insane authority in *Caligari* reveals itself to be a subjective phenomenon by its allegorical form.

Allegory (from *allos*, "other," and *agoreuein*, "to speak publicly") says one thing and means another in a sustained way. It consistently refers the meaning of things to a figurative level apart from the literal and parallel to it. According to its etymology, allegory speaks other than publicly—that is, covertly (it often comes into play when one can't speak openly, as under censorship) or subjectively (as in expressionism or surrealism). But allegory can be clear as well as obscure; it can be didactic (the hare and the tortoise) or simplified (political cartoons) as well as secretive or enigmatic. Even an obscure metaphor, Angus Fletcher argues, will tend to gain clarity through its extension into allegory.[72]

In the romantic era, Goethe and Coleridge set allegory in opposition to the symbol, which they identified with synecdoche:

> The Symbolical cannot perhaps be better defined in distinction from the Allegorical, than that it is always itself a part of that, of the whole of which it is representative.—"Here comes a sail,"—(that is a ship) is a symbolical expression. "Behold our lion!" when we speak of some gallant soldier, is allegorical. Of most importance to our present subject is this point, that the latter (allegory) cannot be other than spoken consciously;—whereas in the former (the symbol) it is very possible that the general truth may be unconsciously in the writer's mind during the construction of the symbol. . . . The advantage of symbolic writing over allegory is, that it presumes no disjunction of faculties.[73]

Coleridge saw allegory as mechanical, an arbitrary assignment of meaning without organic relation to things; the allegorical disjunction of literal and figurative senses amounted in his view to a "disjunction of faculties," reason and imagination split apart. Synecdoche (from *syn*, "with," and *ekdochē*, "sense") joins the figurative sense with the literal, the general with the particular, the meaning with the thing. Coleridge's synecdochic symbol, "the general truth [that] may be unconsciously in the writer's mind," could perhaps be related to the psychoanalytic unconscious, but Freud's interpretation of dreams treats them as allegories, of the secretive, subjective kind. And in common usage, allegories and synecdoches (simple or extended) are alike called symbolic, which indicates that the line between the two is not so clear cut.

Imagine *Caligari* done as the story of a deranged general. That general could be portrayed realistically or made demonic like the doctor in the film or some shade in between. The more rounded and realistic the portrayal, the more the story would become an extended synecdoche; the more demonic the general, the more sheerly a figure of insane authority, the more the story would tend to allegory. A character personifying an idea, a quality, an abstraction, is allegory; a character representing a kind of person, a social type, a larger situation such as that of militaristic Germany or revolutionary Russia, is synecdoche. In allegory, the idea comes first and the character embodies it. In synecdoche, the character comes first, and larger truth emerges out of the characterization. But it may be hard to tell which comes first. Do the sailors in *Potemkin* personify the idea of revolution, or do they represent the situation of the people rising against their oppressors? No sharp distinction can be drawn between allegorical personification and synecdochic representativeness. Just as synecdoche often shades into metaphor, so does extended synecdoche into allegory.

Although the rhetorical tradition gives us no special term for it, extended synecdoche is a figure widely employed (whether consciously or not) in a medium like the movies, which make meaning out of details arranged in sequence. If every shot on the screen is a part synecdochically implying a whole sequence, then a film from beginning to end, the film as a whole, may likewise function as a part signifying a larger whole. Realism, as Jakobson says, heavily relies on metonymy, which in his sense includes synecdoche, and realistic films are usually extended synecdoches. Take a celebrated work of Italian neorealism, *Bicycle Thieves* (1948, written by Cesare Zavattini, directed by Vittorio de Sica): the man whose bicycle is stolen when he needs it for his job represents the poor faced with unemployment in postwar Rome. And many other movies besides the realistic signify by extended synecdoche: in a romantic comedy like *It Happened One Night*, for example, Peter is the workingman and Ellie the rich, and their romance and final marriage symbolize the happy hope of transcending class conflict in Depression America.

Even when vividly realistic, extended synecdoche can shade into allegory, as in Erich von Stroheim's *Greed* (1924), whose characters may be seen as synecdochic social types or as products of an environment, or as driven by essential impulses (the greed of Trina and Marcus, the violence of McTeague) they allegorically personify. In his treatise on allegory, Fletcher describes its characters as "daemonic," meaning not just demonic like Dr. Caligari but in a broader sense possessed, or acting as if possessed, by a spirit good or evil, by some dominant trait or driving force. "If we were to meet an allegorical character in real life," Fletcher writes,

> we would say of him that he was obsessed with only one idea, or that he had an absolutely one-track mind, or that his life was patterned according to absolutely rigid habits from which he never allowed himself to vary. It would seem that he was driven by some hidden, private force; or, viewing him from another angle, it would appear that he did not control his own destiny, but appeared to be controlled by some foreign force, something outside the sphere of his own ego.[74]

Greed was adapted from a naturalistic novel, Frank Norris's *McTeague*, and this is a genre Fletcher considers allegorical. And comedy? Aren't its characters frequently prisoners of a ruling idea, a quality that defines them all too well, a one-track mind or rigid pattern of behavior? Like the characters in *Greed*, comic types can work both ways: as synecdochic social types or as allegorical personifications of abiding traits and tendencies of human nature—sometimes more the former, sometimes more the latter, most often some combination of the two.

The Monster and the City

The monster in a horror tale is an allegorical personification of fear. What the fear is of we may not exactly know, but we know the monster is a fantasy, so it can't be literally fear of the monster that affects us. It must be fear of something else, something that the monster stands for. Dr. Caligari and the somnambulist Cesare together make up the monster in *The Cabinet of Dr. Caligari*, with the one standing for the fear of authority and the other for the fear of death. The vampire in *Dracula*—the Bram Stoker novel and the many stage and screen versions—has often been construed as a figure of wicked sexuality. A different vampire, though, looms in the first, and best, film rendering of *Dracula*, F. W. Murnau's *Nosferatu*, made in Germany in 1922, shortly after *Caligari*. With no suggestion of the sexual predator about him, nothing of the seductive Dracula whose bite doesn't kill but transmits vampirism, Nosferatu is, like Cesare, a figure of impending death.[75]

Expressionism portrays fear from the point of view of the frightened, confusion from the point of view of the confused. Whether ascribed to a character or not, that is what expressionism expresses—the outlook of an anxious subjectivity, the perspective of the injured self on an inhospitable world. The epitome of that fear and confusion is the city—not any real city, but an idea of the city, a dark and disturbing city of the mind that is the scene for the expressionist allegory of modernity. Another successor to *Caligari*, Fritz Lang's *Dr. Mabuse the Gambler* (1922), paints a memorable picture of the expressionist city and its shadows, its paranoia, its alienation, its unsettlement—the sort of locale later typical of film noir. In Martin Scorsese's *Taxi Driver* (1976), the city is seen as a loathsome, threatening phantasmagoria through the eyes of a protagonist who is himself the monster, himself the personification of what he loathes and fears.

In Murnau's *Sunrise* (1927), the city comes to the country in the person of a seductress, a femme fatale. She is the monster, and the country husband she seduces turns into a monster under her spell. During a moonlit rendezvous in the marshes, she persuades him to kill his wife. "Come to the city!" she bids him, and as the illicit lovers embrace in the country night, the expressionist city is conjured up explicitly as a figment of the mind. But the next morning, he can't go through with her dark plan in the clear light of day. (Like Nosferatu, the woman from the city is undone by daylight, though in her case it takes two sunrises to dispel the monster.) It's with the wife he almost killed but truly loves that the repentant husband now goes into the city, where he's forgiven and the couple reconciled and symbolically remarried in a church they come upon during a wedding. Just as a frenzied city of the mind was evoked in the adulterous country night, so when the reunited husband and wife come out of the church, an idyllic country of the mind is evoked in the midst of the city blessing their regained happiness. Though not yet near the happy ending—further trouble lies ahead, trouble associated with the night and not resolved until the sun rises again—the film now switches into comedy, a scherzo of the country couple in the city where they celebrate their reconciliation.

The husband, the wife, and the woman from the city are simple, generalized figures in an allegorical scheme of binary oppositions: country and city, day and night, the good and the bad woman. But the allegory built on this scheme isn't so simple. It's not an agrarian allegory upholding the good ways of the country against the bad ways of the city. If it were, the husband and wife would have been reconciled in the country rather than in the city. To the expressionist city, the city of darkness and disorder, *Sunrise* counterposes another idea of the city, the city of order and light, the site of civilization. This is the city the country couple go into, the city that civilizes love in the institution of marriage—call it the classical city. In *Sunrise*, the enlightening powers of the classical city prevail over the dark impulses unleashed by the woman from the expressionist city.

The monster in Lang's *M* (1931) is a serial killer of little girls. Based on the actual case of such a killer in Düsseldorf, this is a lifelike monster, socially as well as psychologically, and he inhabits a lifelike expressionist city. He throws the city into fear not because he is outlandish but because he is ordinary, anonymous, because he could be anybody and casts a shadow on everybody, a synecdoche for a violence implicating the whole city. "Peter Lorre portrays him incomparably," Kracauer writes, "as a somewhat infantile petty bourgeois who eats apples on the street and could not possibly be suspected of killing a fly."[76] We don't know exactly why, but the psychopathic serial killer seems to be a creature of modernity—Jack the Ripper in late nineteenth-century London was perhaps the first one—and this somewhat infantile petty bourgeois is seen as a child of the city driven to kill its children.

The child-murderer in *M* may be compared to figures out of expressionist allegory, as Kracauer proposes: "He resembles Baldwin in *The Student of Prague*, who also succumbs to the spell of his devilish other self; and he is a direct offspring of the somnambulist Cesare. Like Cesare, he lives under the compulsion to kill. But while the somnambulist unconsciously surrenders to Dr. Caligari's superior will power, the child-murderer submits to his own pathological impulses."[77] This Cesare who is his own Caligari is a much more realistic character, though, and just as the more realistic story of a deranged general would turn the *Caligari* allegory into an extended synecdoche, so *M* is an extended synecdoche for the sickness and the violence of modern life. Yet Fletcher's description of the allegorical character as "driven by some hidden, private force," or as "controlled by some foreign force, something outside the sphere of his own ego"—in this case his alter ego, the Caligari inside him—fits the child-murderer perfectly. Taken realistically, he is of course insane, but he isn't just a clinical case: his insanity, like Caligari's, is an epitomizing metaphor. *M* combines realism and expressionism, synecdoche and allegory.

Both frightened and frightful, both effect and cause of disorder in the city, the child-murderer personifies that fear and that disorder. As Eric Rhode observes, "The murders stir up a murderous element in most of the inhabitants of the city. We enter a time of panic, almost insanity, in which good and bad are hopelessly intertwined. Everyone suspects everybody else. A timid elderly man needs merely talk to a girl by a tram-stop and a threatening mob arises round him. Witnesses quarrel. . . . Perceptions are doubted. . . . Irrationality reigns, and the Lord of Misrule is the murderer."[78] One might expect *M* to be about the child-murderer and the efforts of the police to track him down. But there is a third party: a gang of criminals who, regarding the police as inefficient, decide to take the law into their own hands and themselves track down this madman disrupting their business as usual. Order must be restored, but how? If the child-murderer is disorder personified, the parallel pursuits of him by the police and the criminal gang represent two different approaches to the restoration of order, two different ways, which the film compares, of dealing with a problem that urgently calls for a solution. Thus *M* becomes a political allegory.

Ahead of the police, the criminals catch the child-murderer and put him on trial in an abandoned brewery. At this kangaroo court, complete with defense attorney, the apprehended man movingly confesses to the criminals that crime for him is an uncontrollable impulse, an unshakable specter that haunts him in the streets. But the gang leader, who assumes the role of prosecutor, holds that someone who can't help killing must for that very reason be put to death. We sympathize with the child-murderer, the monster now brought forward as a human being, and are put off by the harsh, dictatorial gang leader, himself a murderer. The message of *M* is often taken to be a repudiation of capital punishment. Yet the gang leader has a point: send the child-murderer to an institution for the insane, and he may escape or be released as harmless—which in fact he was the last time, as the police have found out—and once again he'll be out in the streets killing little girls. Rather than siding either with the defense or with the prosecution, the rhetoric of *M* forcefully presents both sides of the issue and leaves the verdict to us in the audience as an implied jury. The issue of capital punishment is only part of the film's political allegory, which encompasses the large crisis of democracy at the end of Weimar Germany.

If *Caligari* allegorized the beginning, *M* does the same for the end of that troubled republic shattered when Hitler came to power. The child-murderer stands for the problem, the police for the democratic solution, and the gang of criminals and their Führer-like leader for the Nazis and their lawless authoritarian solution. The inefficiency of the police expresses the difficulties faced by democracy. In keeping with his thesis in *From Caligari to Hitler*, Kracauer sees *M* as offering no alternative to the Nazis looming on the horizon. The police in the film are not to be discounted, however. Pointing to Chief Inspector Löhmann as a figure of lawful democratic authority and a redoubtable counter to fascism, Rhode argues with Kracauer and maintains that both *M* and Lang's subsequent film featuring Löhmann, *The Testament of Dr. Mabuse* (1932), "explicitly reject the Nazi solution."[79] Löhmann

.

is indeed a good cop, solid and smart; his lack of glamour, in contrast to the charismatic gang leader, only befits a hero of democracy. Working within the constrictions of the law, the inspector and his men are just a little slower than the criminals in tracking down the child-murderer. But the criminals, by being quicker, save the life of one little girl. The threat of disorder can seem to justify any measures taken to restore order. The enduring value of *M* as a political film lies not in its outright rejection of the Nazilike criminals but in its ability to dramatize both the case against them and the case they make, both the virtues and resources of democracy and the appeal of fascism, what it was the Nazis had to offer to so many Germans who voted for them in the confusion and disarray of the Weimar republic's last days.

Steamboat Willie[80]

Steven Spielberg's *Saving Private Ryan* (1998) focuses on a group of American soldiers taking part in the invasion of Normandy during World War II. One of them is a Jew who cries with rage against the Nazis when he learns that a German killed at Omaha Beach had been a member of the Hitler Youth. (It's not clear why the Hitler Youth should particularly upset him, since there were more vicious, more virulently anti-Semitic manifestations of Nazism.) Another in the group is an intellectual who speaks French and German but lacks experience in combat; awkward with a rifle, he has brought along a typewriter, but the captain (Tom Hanks) suggests that he use a pencil instead. (Metonymically, the typewriter may be mightier than the rifle, but metaphorically, as a penis substitute, the rifle is bigger than the pencil.) These American soldiers are assigned to find Private Ryan, who parachuted somewhere in the region and, his three brothers having all been killed in action, is by order of the high command to be sent back home to Iowa as the only son that his mother has left.

The fighting at Omaha Beach is brutal, and so graphically, gut-wrenchingly depicted that some have taken this film as an indictment of war. But it was a warrior, not a pacifist, who said that war is hell. Surrendering German soldiers are more than once briskly gunned down, the sort of thing that happens in the heat of battle and might have been presented as a regrettable fact, but the film expresses assent, even approval, and conveys the feeling that this enemy does not deserve humane treatment. Later on, the soldiers looking for Private Ryan capture a German who killed one of them and whom most of them would put to death. But the intellectual, who alone among them can talk to the German—called Steamboat Willie in the credits because he tries to ingratiate himself with his American captors by mimicking the Disney cartoon—argues that this prisoner of war should be treated according to the rules of warfare agreed on by civilized nations. The captain is persuaded, and the prisoner, who can't be taken along on this mission, is set free. Steamboat Willie returns with a vengeance. He is a synecdoche for the unworthy enemy, the enemy deemed beyond the pale, and his story is an extended synecdoche for the proposition that civilized rules must be suspended, the niceties of humane treatment set aside in the face of the enemy's perceived inhumanity. Looking back to the so-called last good war, *Saving Private Ryan* anticipated the ideology and policies of the Bush–Cheney administration in waging a war on terror that wasn't so good.

When finally found, Private Ryan (Matt Damon) doesn't want to go home but to remain and play his part in the effort to hold a strategically important bridge. Tom Hanks as Captain John Miller and his group decide to stay too, and they join forces with the other Americans in the upcoming battle. The Germans mounting an attack on the bridge notably include Steamboat Willie. In the line of fire, the intellectual breaks down and behaves like an utter coward. He tremblingly stands by, too afraid to intervene, as his Jewish fellow soldier struggles hand to hand with Steamboat Willie and succumbs. The German kills the Jew while the cowardly intellectual does nothing. Synecdoche is here pushed into allegory, with the three characters personifying different sides of a tragic historical situation. Spielberg pushes too hard, though, and the allegory feels imposed on the synecdoche. What the Nazis did to the Jews while others failed to intervene was not done in battle. And his anti-intellectualism (though tempered by his making the Tom Hanks character a schoolteacher) comes to the fore. Surely the intellectual is unfairly singled out for blame in this historical allegory: if there were intellectuals who stood by and did nothing while Nazis killed Jews, there were also politicians and officials, industrialists and financiers, military and religious leaders, newspaper publishers and movie producers, others who did nothing and had more power to do something. But the intellectual was the one who argued for adherence to the civilized rules of warfare, and Spielberg's rhetoric seeks to discredit that argument by portraying its exponent as a pusillanimous accomplice to the Nazis.

At liberty thanks to the principles voiced by the intellectual, Steamboat Willie returns to kill not only the Jew but also the Tom Hanks captain. A personification of Nazi villainy, he stabs the Jew with sadistic relish, and he picks out the captain, the man who set him free, from afar with his rifle. But the Germans lose the battle, and Steamboat Willie surrenders. Now, however, the intellectual summons up courage, disregards civilized rules, and with his rifle, symbol of his found manhood, shoots the surrendering German. That, we are to conclude, is what should have been done in the first place; too bad it took so long for the intellectual to give up his foolish scruples.

Figura Futurorum

In his essay on the word *figura* and its various senses and uses in late antiquity and the Middle Ages, Erich Auerbach distinguishes between allegory and figural interpretation, or typology, the Christian construction of persons and events in the Old Testament as prophetically foreshadowing, *prefiguring*, persons and events in the New Testament. He quotes a passage from Tertullian in which Joshua leading the people of Israel out of the wilderness and into the promised land is construed as a *figura futurorum*, a figure of things to come, a prefiguration of Jesus leading us out of the wilderness of this world and into the promised land of eternal life. Joshua and Jesus remain actual persons doing actual things even as Joshua is interpreted as a figure whose fulfillment is Jesus. Whereas allegory deals in concepts or abstractions, Auerbach argues, "*figura* is something real and historical which announces something else that is also real and historical."[81]

Figural meaning in the *Divine Comedy* extends beyond the Bible to pagans such as Cato of Utica, the Roman politician whose righteous opposition to Caesar ended in suicide: "Cato's voluntary choice of death rather than political servitude is here introduced as a *figura* for the eternal freedom of the children of God . . . for the liberation of the soul from the servitude of sin."[82] Auerbach reads the whole poem as a figural composition. Dante's portrayal of Virgil, "taken by almost all commentators as an allegory for reason," he sees as figural instead of allegorical: "The older commentators had no objection to a purely allegorical interpretation, for they did not, as we do today, feel that allegory was incompatible with authentic poetry. Many modern critics have argued against this idea, stressing the poetic, human, personal quality of Dante's Virgil; still, they have been unable either to deny that he 'means something' or to find a satisfactory relation between this meaning and the human reality."[83] The answer is the figural relation, in which the human reality is what it is at the same time that it is something else:

> Thus Virgil in the *Divine Comedy* is the historical Virgil himself, but then again he is not; for the historical Virgil is only a *figura* of the fulfilled truth that the poem reveals, and this fulfillment is more real, more significant than the *figura*. With Dante, unlike modern poets, the more fully the figure is interpreted and the more closely it is integrated with the eternal plan of salvation, the more real it becomes.[84]

To the poet and his contemporaries and many others afterward, the *Divine Comedy* was allegorical, but Auerbach subscribes to the view, inherited from the romantics, that allegory is abstract and lifeless, "incompatible with authentic poetry." Allegory has made something of a comeback in critical thinking since Auerbach's day, but mostly on account of the notion that all representation is illusory, arbitrary, unreal—just what allegory is supposed to be. For Auerbach, Dante's poetry is too real to be allegorical, and he learnedly theorizes and perceptively analyzes a mode he calls figural through which Dante achieves the realism that sets the *Divine Comedy* apart from such allegories as the *Roman de la Rose*. If I am prepared to insist that the figural mode is nonetheless a kind of allegory, it is not to relegate it to unreality but to defend the diverse capacities of allegory for the representation of reality.

The figural connection between the promised land into which Joshua led the people of Israel and the eternal life that Jesus promises us, or between Cato the free man who preferred death to life in servitude and the freedom from bondage to sin enjoyed by souls in heaven, is analogical, in Jakobson's sense metaphorical. The connection, though it may retain the historicity of Joshua in the Old Testament and Jesus in the New, of virtuous Cato in republican Rome, is not itself historical, not a matter of cause and effect but of similarity, not a path from here to there but a leap to a parallel elsewhere. Figural meaning, for all the importance it may attach to human reality down on this earth, yet views it, as Auerbach says, "primarily in immediate vertical connection with a divine order which encompasses it."[85] Such a vertical connection, such an encompassing metaphor, is allegory. What Auerbach's figural mode demonstrates is that allegory need not retreat into thin abstractions but can marshal a living concreteness to its purposes.

For the representation of reality in Third World countries in the era of global capitalism, Fredric Jameson has posited the necessity of allegory, and specifically of national allegory. He argues that in the Third World, where the split between the personal and the public does not obtain as it has in the West, all stories necessarily move from the personal to the public: "The telling of the individual story and the individual experience cannot but ultimately involve the whole laborious telling of the experience of the collectivity itself."[86] But why is the collectivity necessarily a nation? There are different groups an individual can belong to. And why is allegory the necessary form? There are different ways of relating the individual to the group. The novel has characteristically taken the way of synecdoche, the individual as a part standing for a whole group, the individual story (in extended synecdoche) as a part representing the larger social story.

Balzac's novels tell social, even national, stories, but they are not allegories. Presumably nothing like *Lost Illusions* could be written in the West today, but why summarily rule out a Third World equivalent? Some critics of Jameson, thinking that art in the West has progressed beyond allegory, accuse him of consigning the Third World to an outmoded form. Allegory is not outmoded in the West—look at Kafka or Brecht or Buñuel, to mention artists on the cutting edge of Western modernism—but Jameson himself seems to think it is, since he assumes that the Third World does allegory while the West does not.

You could argue that allegory is necessary when you can't get there from here, when no part of experience, no laborious recounting of many parts of experience, can adequately stand for the whole and comprehend its meaning. Then you have to leap to another level. Maybe that's what Third World countries must do in order to come to terms with their situation in the world of global capitalism. Jameson considers the work of the Senegalese writer and filmmaker Ousmane Sembène, whose 1973 novel and 1975 film *Xala* (Curse) he interprets as a national allegory. As Senegal wins independence from France, a politician and businessman with two wives marries a virginal third, but is cursed with impotence. Allegorically the independence is cursed with impotence. Allegorically the curse on this man signifies the revolt of indigenous traditions against the rule of the likes of him. At one level this is a sexual (did one of his older wives put the curse on him?) and at another level a political satire (it turns out that the curse came from the dispossessed, the paupers he has wronged in his dealings and wants out of the city). The protagonist stands for the native comprador bourgeoisie selling out the country to foreign capital and in effect keeping it under colonial dominance. In various unavailing ways, he tries to have the curse dispelled, but that can only be done by the paupers spitting on him, which is where, grossly and gleefully, the story ends.

Another story Sembène tells goes as follows. The princess is kidnapped by a commoner; the king's son, and after him the knight betrothed to the princess, come to the rescue, but the commoner, armed with a bow and arrow, kills them both. The king dies, in all likelihood assassinated, and the usurper now sitting on the throne sends two men against the kidnapper—two against one, and the two are armed with rifles while the one fights the age-old way—and this time the commoner is killed and the princess brought back. However, on her return, she seizes a rifle and kills the usurper. Such is the plot of Sembène's film *Ceddo* (1977), the plot of a folk tale, a fable, an allegory.

In real life, such a political kidnapping wouldn't have been carried out by one man alone; nor would a rescue have been attempted by one man at a time, or even two. Actions in *Ceddo* are performed in the manner of a pageant, a ritual rather than a reality, with characters not meant to be credible as actual persons but to be taken as allegorical personifications. The kidnapper personifies the Ceddo, the common people attached to their traditions. He kidnaps the princess in an act of resistance against a foreign religion being imposed on the village, Islam, personified by the imam gaining power behind the throne and finally usurping it. A white trader—another personification, a lone man standing in for a large nasty business—supplies the rifles, the new instrument of violence, in exchange for shackled villagers to be shipped abroad as slaves. The slave trade, the conversion of the Wolof people to Islam—*Ceddo* was banned in Senegal, which is today a predominantly Muslim country, for its portrayal of Islam as a usurper—such momentous historical events are woven into the fabric of this national allegory.

When in the African past *Ceddo* is supposed to take place is purposely left imprecise; things that happened over a long stretch are run together. "I can't give a date," Sembène says. "These events occurred in the 18th and 19th century and are still occurring." After quoting the director James Leahy elaborates: "Just as the village in the film is an exemplary microcosm of African (or at least West African) society in the throes of a crucial transition brought about by external pressures, and internal greed, ambition and dissension, so the time-span of the film (approximately a day and a half) offers an exemplary survey of two or more centuries of West African history."[87] This telescoping of history destabilizes the illusion of the past and makes us aware of its reconstruction in the present. There are deliberate anachronisms, like a modern beach umbrella as a canopy for the king or the imam, and one sequence (paradoxically a fantasy) is set in contemporary Senegal, with figures from the past— the kidnapper, the princess, the imam, the matrilineal claimant to the throne—in surprising present-day garb. As Philip Rosen stresses, the film "invite[s] spectators toward a consciously present-oriented consideration of options and consequences, even as they observe this enactment of the past."[88]

To put it another way, *Ceddo* adopts the form of a tale rather than a novel.[89] A novel, though usually narrated in the past tense, involves us in a kind of present. It creates the illusion of ongoing events, puts us in the place of characters taking part in them, and generates suspense as to what will happen next. A tale relates something clearly past and removed from ordinary experience, something that happened once upon a time if it happened at all, not something we are to enter into as if it were happening to us. Yet the novel lives by the written word and the printed page; the tale is an oral form—a novel brings us into a present of the story, but in a tale it is the storyteller that is present, the act of telling. Like a tale, *Ceddo* is unmistakably a telling, a relation of things, done in a hieratic manner that keeps them at the remove of once upon a time, yet these things have an equally unmistakable historicity and a direct bearing on African life.

Besides the narrative, the language of the characters—except for the whites, who never speak, and the imam and his circle, who invoke the Koran—also takes an ancestral oral form, abundant in proverbs and received metaphors and involving a *gewel*, a village storyteller who comments, embroiders, and mediates all exchanges with the court. The imam promptly bans the *gewel* after assuming power, as Serge Daney notes in his review of *Ceddo*, which construes the film as the story of indigenous oral discourse suppressed in favor of the written word, the holy book.[90] This interesting reading attenuates into an abstract opposition between oral and written language an allegory grounded in concrete reality, bodying forth the historical experience of a people.

The form of a folk tale suggests the perspective of traditional Wolof society, the way the villagers would relate their own history, not the perspective of any individual—the characters in *Ceddo* who stand out individually stand for groups—but the collective sense of things. Yet the film breaks with that traditional collective perspective in a significant way. From the start, we see villagers being sold to the white trader as slaves, and we see them being branded—with a fleur-de-lis, which alludes to the fact that France was a leading slave trader in the region long before Senegal became a French colony—and on the soundtrack we hear an African American gospel song, "I'll Make It Home Some Day." In this talky film, full of ceremonious discussion about Islam versus the old fetish religion and about the old matrilineal versus the Islamic patrilineal succession, no one, noble or commoner, raises the issue of the slave trade, which goes on undisputed, like any other business as usual—no one, that is, except the author, who not only raises the issue but also the question why no one raises it in the village.

The princess is quick to remind her kidnapper that he is a slave: the common people in *Ceddo*, the peasants who resist in the name of tradition, are slaves of the throne. They do not resist a slavery and social hierarchy well established in local life, part of the traditions of the village. They are slaves with certain rights and privileges, including ownership of their crops and a voice in public assembly, but they are still slaves liable to be sold to the white trader—liable to a more terrible slavery than they know. Brave enough to protest and eventually to fight the Muslim infringement on their customary ways and rights, they tacitly accept the practice and export of slavery; they even sell their own children to the white trader to acquire rifles for the fight over religion. "I'll Make It Home Some Day," which of course they can't hear, is not only outside the world of the film, like all background music, but inconceivable inside it, part of another order of experience. It is a kind of *figura futurorum*, a prefiguration of the future that awaits these local slaves far away from home.[91]

In his article on Sembène, "An African Brecht," David Murphy supposes that the Ceddo take a stand against Islam and slavery both. He sums up in this way the speech of a Ceddo elder at the assembly convened after the kidnapping: "No to slavery. No to Islam."[92] This, in the film's English subtitles, is what the elder says, addressing the king through the intermediation of the *gewel*: "We want this iniquity to cease. Our crops belong to us. You must put an end to plundering. . . . As King, you must decree that no one will be persecuted, no one will be enslaved. The obligation to be Moslem is abolished. No faith is worth a man's life. . . . May oppression cease today." Plundering, religious persecution, escalation of the slave trade—Islam has aggravated the subjugation of the common people, and the Ceddo call for an end to this growing oppression, this iniquity. We would call for an end to the iniquity of slavery, but the whole emphasis of the Ceddo revolt falls on Islam. The elder does say, "no one will be enslaved," "no faith is worth a man's life," but the Ceddo acquiesce to traditional slavery and are willing to give their lives for their traditional faith. Murphy would see them as revolutionaries, but they are traditionalists, and Sembène brings out the contradictions, the tragedy, in their position. At the other extreme from Murphy, Rosen pronounces the film "a condemnation of a massive failure of traditional Africa to take care of its own."[93] But Sembène does not condemn the Ceddo; he portrays them with sympathy, questioning sympathy. He wants Africans to identify with their history. The task of the Third World filmmaker, he asserts, lies in "allowing the people to summon up their own history, to identify themselves with it,"[94] even while holding it to critical scrutiny.

Formalized gestures punctuate this historical fable. Only from the princess will he accept a drink of water, the knight betrothed to her declares at the village assembly. He has just, in a rhetorical gesture, struck down a young peasant woman who offered him water, and she lies on the ground, where she remains, motionless, until the king's nephew, told that Islam disallows his matrilineal claim to the throne, orders her sold to the white slaver for a jug of wine, which the claimant nephew, in another rhetorical gesture, drinks in defiance of Muslim law. Before he gets to drink much, the imam has the jug broken to pieces, the wine exacting so dear a price from the woman spills into the sand like the water she brought. A mere pawn in this political game played by noblemen who don't care in the least what happens to her, this peasant woman is Sembène's own eloquent gesture of unspoken accusation against a selfish and insensible local aristocracy. Yet the haughty princess has a change of heart. This is signaled by an offering of water, which identifies her with the peasant woman, though the princess makes an imagined rather than an actual offering. In a reverential gesture no less decisive for being performed in her mind, she offers water not to her knightly betrothed but to his killer, her kidnapper, himself now killed before her eyes in an unequal duel with the Muslim intruders who, as she has just learned, have assassinated her father and taken over his throne. The princess makes common cause with the commoner by the drink of water that at his death she imagines herself giving him, a fantasy on which she acts in reality when she makes common cause with the common people on her return to the village.

The sequence, set in the present day, is another fantasy, entertained by a priest who personifies missionary Christianity and imagines a Catholic Senegal in which even the imam takes communion—a wishful prefiguration of things that were not to come, a future that never happened. *Ceddo* not only makes manifest its construction in the present and its address to the present, but also asks us in the audience to view the past, and by extension the present where we sit, in terms of the future, the actual sorrowful future of the slaves shipped across the Atlantic and the possible futures that might have or may yet come true. This film about traditionalists looking to the past looks to the future.

Over the burnt dwellings of the vanquished Ceddo, who now have their heads shaved and their names changed in their forcible conversion to Islam, we again hear "I'll Make It Home Some Day." But we switch to the jaunty, jazzy score played off and on through the film—also the music of the future, of that future further along which is the present day—when the princess goes swimming in the ocean. Her beautiful nude body emerging from the water, watched by her kidnapper on the shore, feels like an assertion of her power, a rebirth of the energies of Africa. She seems to be taking a step toward joining forces with the Ceddo, and though she first offers a drink of water to her kidnapper in an attempt at seductive manipulation, this prepares the way for the transcendent offering she makes to him in fantasy yet in earnest, as if ready to marry the man being buried standing up, killed but not bowed, like a monument to the common people. When she, back in the village, grabs a rifle from a Muslim warrior, the Ceddo swiftly move and put all the other rifles in their mouths, so that these one-shot rifles can't be fired against her. The princess kills the imam in a collective action. And yet even if undertaken in solidarity with the common people and carried out with their indispensable support, this is an action she alone could have performed. Hers is the revolutionary act that the Ceddo fail to accomplish or even to envision. What exactly does she personify? For the Ceddo who kidnapped her, she was the aristocracy allied with Islam in oppressing them, but in the end she allies with them against Islam, and they all rally behind her. What does her action, as hieratic and removed from reality as anything in the film, signify? Nothing that actually happened in the past. Class divisions were never overcome; aristocrats never joined forces with commoners, nor was Islam ever shot down in a country where it is still going strong. The princess shoots the imam in the crotch; the woman does away with the man who personifies masculinist Islam by emasculating him. Does this mean she has put an end to male rule? Traditional Africa, though matrilineal, is nonetheless patriarchal, and even without Muslim law, even in the absence of surviving male successors, a woman on the throne would have been impermissible. The meaning of her revolutionary act cannot be found in the past but only in the future. Having confronted the imam, she turns to confront us. After she kills him, we cut to her and zoom in to a close-up of her face. She raises her eyes and looks straight toward us in an emphatic gesture of address to the audience. Her act is meant to have an effect not on the mythical past but on the actual present where we, and especially the African audience, are watching— watching in amazement at what she has just done, and in wonder at what it means. Then, in her African colors, she walks toward us past two Muslims in white, and the image freezes to close the film as she again faces the audience. Her gaze, directed at a present where subjugation and injustice, class divisions and patriarchy, remain and endure, tells us that the meaning resides not in what happens next in a story coming to an end (Is she taking power? Is she going to do away with slavery along with Islam?) but in what will happen next in the future of Africa.

What, then, does she personify? "I think the princess is the incarnation of modern Africa," Sembène says. Why a woman? "Often in Africa it's only the men who speak. . . . There can be no development in Africa if women are left out of the account."[95] Why an aristocrat rather than a commoner? Because she is formidable, self-possessed, invincible; she is an aristocrat who comes into her own only through her identification with the people. She embodies both tradition and the break with tradition, both the indigenous and the new. She is, or gets to be after she comes out of the sea and returns to the village and fires a rifle into the seat of power, a *figura futurorum*, a prefiguration of an African fulfillment that the film calls on its audience to strive for.

Earlier I asked whether *The Battleship Potemkin* is best understood as an extended synecdoche or an allegory. It becomes more of an allegory in its final section, when the sailors take over and run the ship, an extended metaphor for the people taking over and running the country. Their encounter with the czarist squadron sent against them dissolves into a cheer of solidarity among sailors who are the workers of the world uniting, their cheer resounding beyond the *Potemkin* mutiny, beyond the suppressed revolution of 1905, in triumphant anticipation of 1917. The rebel ship sailing ahead is a *figura futurorum* announcing the revolution that was to come, an equivalent, in Marxist terms, of the Christian figure and fulfillment—a closer equivalent than the princess in *Ceddo*, a figure whose fulfillment is yet to come.

The Marriage of East and West

If emergent Third World nations have produced national allegories, so has the nation that emerged after World War II as the most powerful on earth and had its founding story related over and over again, with variations and different implications, in a popular genre that by no coincidence was then in its heyday. The national allegory of the United States was furnished by the Western. The Western is a genre of beginnings, the civilizing of the wilderness, the building of a town, the establishing of values and beliefs by which a community comes together—simple beginnings generically rendered as an embryonic epitome of social and political matters that have shaped the life of the nation. The Western hero is often supposed to be a rugged individualist, and sometimes he is, but even then, he's not so much an individual as a figure of individuality, of the communal value of individuality.

At the start of John Ford's *My Darling Clementine* (1946) Wyatt Earp (Henry Fonda) and his brothers are on their way to California with their cattle when they stop near Tombstone for the night. Wyatt attempts to get a shave in town but is interrupted by gunfire, which he subdues single-handed like a good Western hero, though still an unshaven one who returns to find his cattle rustled and his youngest brother killed. He stays on as marshal to settle this personal matter, which turns into a social matter as the marshal brings law and order to the unruly town. On a peaceful Sunday morning, he gets not only a shave but a haircut and even a touch of perfume at the local barbershop. He looks at himself in the mirror that the barber holds and sees a changed man. The sign "Tonsorial Parlor" on the barbershop window, reversed when seen from inside, is reversed again in the mirror and reads right as if seen from outside: the change in the man, the change inside, reflects the change in the town, the change outside. The personal has become the social and the social the personal.

In a parallel yet opposite moment, not in a public place now safe for civilized amenities but in the privacy of despair, Doc Holliday (Victor Mature) looks at his image in the mirror and finds a changed man too. He is by himself in his dark hotel room. His mirror is his framed medical diploma hanging on the wall. He pours himself a stiff drink, and throws his whiskey glass at his diploma, breaking the glass reflecting back to him the image of the Western outlaw that the Eastern doctor has become. He is responding to the arrival in town of his old girlfriend, Clementine (Cathy Downs), who has come from the East looking for him. If Wyatt Earp is the Western hero, Doc Holliday is his complement, not the usual outlaw villain but a parallel protagonist, a tragic hero who aptly takes up Hamlet's soliloquy on suicide when a drunken actor in a tavern can't remember the lines. Wyatt Earp and Doc Holliday are doubles, reverse mirror images of each other, the Westerner drawn to the civilizing East and the Easterner seeking the wildness of the West. They are allegorical personifications of the encounter between East and West on the frontier.

While the marshal pays a visit to the barber, others are going to church on Sunday morning, to the first service at the church under construction. Rebuffed by Doc Holliday and preparing to take the next stagecoach back East, Clementine hears the church bells and asks Wyatt Earp if she may accompany him to the service. As the two start walking side by side toward the church, we cut to a long shot down the covered walkway and watch the steady advance of this newly formed couple toward the camera. As they turn the corner, we start moving with them, the thin posts of the walkway going by in the foreground, as if the couple's forward movement were impelling the camera movement. In a low angle looking up at them against the sky, the two leave frame toward the front, and in a reverse angle they reenter frame and proceed toward the back, where the bare wooden frame of the church steeple appears in the distance. Their joint onward course has a certain solemn deliberateness pointed up by Ford's camera and cutting. Although they have only just met, they bear an arresting resemblance to a couple being married and facing the future together. Two American flags flown at the church gathering lend it a national implication and call to mind the American "civil religion."[96] The sense of ceremonial solemnity is adroitly combined with comedy—the comedy of a perfumed frontier marshal, the comedy of a church service that turns out to be a dance, of Wyatt Earp bashfully hesitating to ask Clementine to dance and then taking to the dance floor in his best backwoods manner, almost as awkward on his feet as Fonda's young Mr. Lincoln at the party in Ford's film of 1939. Yet in his awkward dancing, Fonda's Wyatt Earp achieves a grace, a bliss, of his own. And comedy, remember, often ends in marriage.

No marriage actually takes place—nothing more than a dance. It's a dance that stays in the mind, though, and Clementine decides to stay in town and teach school. At the end, Wyatt Earp goes away with his surviving brother and says good-bye to her, promising to return and stop by the schoolhouse.[97] The marriage so eloquently suggested is left hanging on a promise. Alongside the personal story runs the national allegory: allegorically it is the East and the West that are to be married. That marriage, too, hangs on a promise, yet it's a promise that stays in the mind, the promise of the dance, the promise of the frontier.

All Westerns are about the frontier as the formative scene of the American nation. But the frontier has meant different things socially and politically, from a Jeffersonian natural democracy to a Darwinian rule of the fittest as a natural aristocracy. Ford's Westerns are in keeping with Frederick Jackson Turner's historical account of the frontier not as a natural affair but as an encounter between culture and nature, a transaction between civilized order and the loosening, leveling wilderness, a continual new beginning for American society with a continually renewed tendency toward liberty and equality. The dance in the unfinished church enacts the promise of that new beginning as East and West meet on the frontier road to democracy. If Wyatt Earp is the cowboy becoming civilized and Doc Holliday is the civilized man drunk on wildness, Clementine, the woman who goes West after the renegade Easterner and who shifts her affections to the reciprocating Westerner, personifies civilization seeing its best hope in the frontier marriage of East and West. But neither the actual nor the allegorical marriage has occurred yet—a happy promise that may or may not be kept, an aspiration that may or may not be realized. Ford looks back to a frontier past that looks forward to a future. Turner worries about the future of American democracy after the closing of the frontier. Hopeful rather than worried, *My Darling Clementine* gives us the image of the refined woman and the rough-hewn man dancing together as a *figura futurorum*, a figure for a dream of liberty and equality yet to find fulfillment, a striving as unfinished as the church open to the sky that houses their glorious dance.

Seen from afar against the background of Monument Valley, the landscape that Ford made into an icon of the frontier, Wyatt Earp takes leave of Clementine and rides off on his horse. Her hat in her hands, the desert sun shining on her, she closes the film watching him vanish into the distance. As she slowly walks ahead toward the receding frontiersman, a cut on her movement brings us around in front of her, and as she comes to a stop, we cut back behind her. These reverse angles keep her in long shot, somewhat closer and lower when facing her but still pretty far, so that she remains a small figure in a vast landscape. Yet each cut pivots on her as the center of attention and keeps her in the same place on the screen, so that she seems to abide like the landscape, a figure of civilization with its future at stake on the frontier.

Like the princess and her kidnapper, like the elder and the imam and the *gewel* in *Ceddo*, Clementine and Wyatt Earp and Doc Holliday in *My Darling Clementine* are allegorical personifications vividly, bodily brought to life. They may not be realistic characters, but they are far from lifeless abstractions. They have their reality in a realm where concrete actuality intersects with the imagination—which in a national allegory is the imagination of a people. Allegory of the kind that Auerbach calls figural enables the story of the national past to be also the story of the future.

The Walls of Jericho

"The walls of Jericho" is Peter's name for the dividing blanket he puts up between his bed and Ellie's in *It Happened One Night*. When, having recognized her as the runaway heiress in the news, he first arranges for the two of them to share a room for the night, she's displeased with the arrangement and casts a disbelieving eye on the blanket: "That, I suppose, makes everything quite all right." They don't have enough money for separate accommodations, he explains, offering to help her get to New York and assuring her that he has no amorous intent but only wants, as a newspaperman, the exclusive story of her "mad flight to happiness." These "walls of Jericho" hanging from a clothesline strung between their beds are, he tells her, safer than the ones Joshua blew down with his trumpet: "You see, I have no trumpet." Like the train whistles and the piece of sky in *Man's Castle*, the blanket in *It Happened One Night* is the characters' own trope. "The walls of Jericho" is Peter's metaphor, and Ellie's joining in it makes it their metaphor, bringing them together even as it keeps them apart. It is a metaphor extended into a story and thus an allegory, as Cavell says: from the moment the blanket is set up as a barrier between the two lovers, also set up is the narrative expectation that these "walls of Jericho" will end up toppling just like the biblical ones, though exactly what has to happen for them to topple—who or what blows the allegorical trumpet—is the narrative question.[98]

When Ellie consents to Peter's arrangement and undresses and gets into bed on her side of the blanket, a chaste but sexy scene unfolds. Cavell construes the blanket as a metaphor for the movie screen and especially for what it conceals from our view:

The thing that was to "make everything all right" by veiling something from sight turns out to inspire as significant an erotic reaction as the unveiled event would have done . . . The barrier works, in short, as sexual censorship typically works, whether imposed from outside or from inside. It works—blocking a literal view of the figure, but receiving physical impressions from it, and activating our imagination of that real figure as we watch in the dark—as a movie screen works. I cannot doubt that the most celebrated Hollywood film of 1934 knows that it is, among other things, parodying the most notorious event of the Hollywood film's political environment in 1934, the acceptance of the motion picture Production Code.[99]

To construe the blanket as the movie screen, to take what it conceals as alluding to the Code, the systematic self-censorship that began to be enforced in Hollywood the year of the film's release, is to construe it allegorically. Any work that calls attention to itself, to its means and its medium, to the conditions of its own making, is thereby being allegorical. Such a work might be thought literal in its emphasis on its materials and its procedures, but what was involved in the making of a work is not what is literally there in the work before us. A work of art referring to itself refers us to another level of meaning beyond what it says or shows, a meaning we are to find in what we infer or imagine, went into its making.

The blanket as "the walls of Jericho" is the characters' own trope; the blanket as the movie screen is not. Two different allegories hang on that blanket—"the walls of Jericho" and the self-referential allegory—and Cavell joins them in his reading of Peter as a figure of the film's author or director. It is Peter who, in putting up the blanket, metaphorically sets up the screen, and though this isn't his metaphor, it is his prop and his staging, as if he were directing the scene. He in effect writes a script for Ellie and himself to follow on the road to New York, and he often acts as director, as her director. A character standing in for the author is always an allegorical figure, a metaphor leading us outside the work to its maker.

Peter may be compared to another author figure: Will Rogers's Judge Priest. Judge Priest is much more in control; he presides over the film in a way that Peter does not. But it isn't his own story—it is, rather, the story of Rome and Ellie May and Bob Gillis—that Judge Priest presides over. Peter tries to write and direct the story of his own relationship with Ellie. When she crosses over to his side of the blanket and declares her love for him, she departs from his script, and he can only send her back to her assigned place, where he expects she will remain while he, rewriting the script and trying to arrange a happy ending for their romance, goes off without her to sell their story to a newspaper. He tells the editor that this will "tear down the walls of Jericho," but he's wrong. His own metaphor gets away from him, along with the woman he loves—an "allegorical confusion," Cavell calls it, with Peter "behaving as though announcing the event in the newspaper will not only make it public but make it happen. And maybe this could work, for some story other than his own."[100]

Cavell gives the allegorical blanket a philosophical turn by taking it to symbolize something like the barrier between ourselves and others, the problem of other minds, the limitation in our individual capacity for human community. To surmount that barrier, Peter has to let go of his assumed role as scriptwriter, director, and public storyteller—the authorial posture keeping him outside a true reciprocity with Ellie. In this interpretation, *It Happened One Night* is an allegory of human finitude, of human reciprocity achieved in the recognition of finitude. "You have to act," Cavell writes, "from within the world, within your connection with others, forgoing the wish for a place outside from which to view and to direct your fate."[101]

Peter's authorial posture, which Cavell sees as an attempt to stand outside the ground of our common humanity, may also be characterized as patriarchal, an assertion of male authority over the woman. Gender relations are complicated by class relations, though, and Peter's posture is also an assertion of his workingman's dignity, a refusal to defer to the rich heiress, a resistance to class hierarchy. Peter must relinquish his authorial attempt in order to win Ellie, but what he forgoes is more than the wish to transcend human finitude. That we must all forgo, however socially situated we may be, if we want a genuine connection with others. But Peter has to give up something else besides—not his male authority in a patriarchal society, but his resistance to the upper class, to the authority, if not of Ellie, of her tycoon father. It is he, rather than Peter or Ellie, who in effect blows the allegorical trumpet and brings down "the walls of Jericho." Class reconciliation amounts to surrender to the class that rules, surrender made sweet because Ellie's father turns out to be a wise and kind ruler, which implies, synecdochically, that on the whole, things are well with the society. Although at first he seemed a blocking figure, a domineering *senex iratus*, in the end, father knows best, a self-made man portrayed as having earned his privilege and the right to pass it on to his dear daughter and deserving son-in-law. It's with the blessing of the ruling class, not in defiance of it, that class boundaries are crossed and the workingman marries the heiress. As is usual in New Comedy, the young lovers come together not for the sake of love alone but of the social good their union represents.

If Cavell's philosophical allegory universalizes the story of Ellie and Peter, a synecdochic interpretation in terms of social relations merely generalizes it from the protagonist couple to the society in which they live.

Technique as Metaphor

Self-referential metaphors like the blanket for the movie screen—or like mirrors or windows as screens within the screen—are not uncommon in Hollywood movies. Such self-consciousness, such acknowledgment of the artifice of art, can be found in both popular and elite art, in works obeying tradition as well as in the avant-garde. But avant-garde or modernist films often go further and make metaphors or allegories of film technique itself.

Bruce Baillie's *All My Life* (1966) lasts exactly as long, almost three minutes, as it takes to play on the soundtrack a 78 rpm recording of the title song. As we hear the voice of Ella Fitzgerald, with the backing of Teddy Wilson and his orchestra, singing "All my life / I've been waiting for you / My wonderful one / I've begun / Living all my life," the camera moves along a country fence, old and run down just like the scratchy 78 recording, yet adorned with flowering grasses in the sun and clusters of red roses, beautiful just like the recorded voice and music. We may take the camera movement along the fence as a metaphor for the course of one's life, the blooming roses as the good times, the sparser sections and the missing or broken pickets as the tougher times. As the song ends, the camera tilts up to the blue sky, which we may take as the upward movement of the soul departing for the hereafter. But aren't the roses red and alive in the ground? They are roses recorded on 16 millimeter film, their red not quite the color of life, the film a bit scratched like the 78 recording. Is this then a remembrance of things past while sitting in a garden and listening to an old song? But surely the camera is not sitting; it seems to be traveling close to the fence along a path parallel to it, metaphorically reliving the ups and downs of one's life rather than recollecting it in tranquility. The thing is, however, that Baillie makes it difficult to tell whether the camera is traveling or panning, actually moving along a path or just turning its head from a stationary position and taking an inspective look around, a metaphorical backward glance. The metaphor, the allegory, hinges on a point of technique.

In *Seven Types of Ambiguity*, William Empson considers two lines from Arthur Waley's translation of a Chinese poem: "Swiftly the years, beyond recall. / Solemn the stillness of this spring morning."

The human mind has two main scales on which to measure time. The large one takes the length of a human life as its unit, so that there is nothing to be done about life; it is of an animal dignity and simplicity, and it must be regarded from a peaceable and fatalistic point of view. The small one takes as its unit the conscious moment, and it is from this that you consider the neighboring space, an activity of the will, delicacies of social tone, or your personality. The repose and self-command given by the use of the first are contrasted with the speed at which it shows the years to be passing from you, and therefore with the fear of death; the fever and multiplicity of life, as known by the use of the second, are contrasted with the calm of the external space of which it gives consciousness, with the absolute or extratemporal value attached to the brief moments of self-consciousness with which it is concerned, and with a sense of security in that it makes death so far off.

Both these timescales and their contrasts are included by these two lines in a single act of apprehension, because of the words *swift* and *still*. Being contradictory as they stand, they demand to be conceived in different ways; we are enabled, therefore, to meet the open skies with an answering stability of self-knowledge; to meet the brevity of human life with an ironical sense that it is morning and springtime, that there is a whole summer before winter, a whole day before night.[102]

The large scale lets us see recurrent, circular time, the small scale only current, linear time. Panning is circular, a movement of contemplation; traveling is linear, a movement of action. *All My Life* creates an ambiguity between panning and traveling similar to that between *still* and *swift* in the Chinese poem. Panning stands back and here suggests a looking back at the passage of life, the cycle of life and death, on the large timescale; traveling conveys a sense of the present, experienced moment by conscious moment on the small timescale. Baillie's camera is actually panning, but panning in a way that feigns traveling. A telephoto lens brings the fence close and gives the impression of motion alongside it, so that the roses surprise us as if we were encountering them in the midst of life; and rose bushes disguise a corner of the fence so that the circular movement seems to proceed in a straight line. Toward the end the fence somewhat recedes and angles away—the circularity becomes more noticeable—which prepares for the final tilt up to the sky, the metaphor for death.

Either way we look at the fence and the garden and the sky allegorically—the song ensures that—but in each case with a different sense of time and our movement through it. The ambiguity brings both timescales into play together, as befits a film that has a moment stand for a lifetime. We may look at the pretty flowers and the sunny day literally depicted and ironically cherish the compensation they offer for the brevity of human life, for which the film's own brevity is of course a metaphor.

The Road of Life

Like *It Happened One Night*, Hiroshi Shimizu's *Mr. Thank You* (*Arigato-san*, 1936) is the story of a bus ride at the time of the Depression, which was worse in the United States but also afflicted Japan. Among the passengers on the bus in *Mr. Thank You*, traveling with her mother, is a young woman being sold by her impoverished family into prostitution, headed for Tokyo and an unhappy future.

In the 1930s, David Bordwell tells us, Japanese studios produced as many movies as Hollywood, with a popular audience as much in mind, but they "differed from their American counterparts in encouraging directors to cultivate individual styles."[103] Like Ozu, Mizoguchi, and Naruse, his better-known contemporaries, Shimizu has a distinctive style. Like Ozu, he favors frontal shots with a background wall parallel to the picture plane, thereby bringing the plane to our notice along with the camera's perpendicular line of gaze, an axis he sets up as an organizing principle rather than, in the manner of classic Hollywood, keeping it subservient to the actors and their lines of gaze. Unlike Ozu, Shimizu frequently moves the camera, especially when out on location, where his "beloved camera axis finds tangible expression in the highway," with "tracking shots up and down the road translat[ing] . . . axial depth into forward and backward movement."[104]

As an example of such axial camera movement, Bordwell describes the prologue of *Mr. Thank You*. We see two road workers as the bus moves toward them, the driver thanking them for getting out of the way, the workers receding behind the bus; then the same thing with a man and horse-drawn cart we see straight ahead and after the driver's thanks see straight behind; then the bus advances on two men toting piles of wood, and we hear but now do not see the driver thanking them as we diametrically dissolve to the receding men; then we see four women carrying bundles and again axially dissolve from the road ahead to the road behind without an interpolated view of the driver saying thank you. "That's why people call him 'Mr. Thank You,'" an intertitle explains: the young bus driver always smilingly thanks those who step aside on the road to let him pass.

With cuts or dissolves or fades, Shimizu skips their stepping aside and shifts from our approaching them to our watching them retreat into the distance, so that the bus overtaking them seems to be moving steadily, unperturbedly ahead. The swift transition from an advancing to a receding view, from a shot traveling forward—toward the various persons, groups, vehicles sharing the road—to a shot looking back at the slower travelers left behind, as if the bus had passed right through them in its course along the road, is a visual theme repeated with variations throughout the film, a theme that freshly enacts a familiar trope: life as a road, the road of life.

From the early days of cinema, the camera traveling in a vehicle—a train or a trolley, a boat or a bus or a car—has metaphorically evoked the passage of life. The camera is identified with the vehicle whose movement it shares, and we identify with the camera and feel as if we were traveling in the vehicle ourselves. We look back at the past behind us; we look ahead at the future before us. Moving in space signifies moving in time. This metaphor, this translation of space into time, arises almost automatically, which only makes it more affecting because life by and large passes automatically, impersonally. We may think we are in control, but in the main, life carries us along, like a train, like a bus. Certainly the young woman being sold as a prostitute is being carried along toward a future not of her choosing.

The bus in *Mr. Thank You* starts its journey in a coastal village and drives up into the mountains, a journey rendered on the screen with documentary vividness and a lively rhythm of shots inside the bus and shots looking out at the environment going by. Sometimes we look out the front from the driver's perspective or out the rear from the perspective of the young woman sitting beside her mother in the backseat, but more often the point of view is not attributed to any individual. It is in effect the collective point of view of the people riding in the bus, traveling on the road of life. Passengers get on and off, and people encountered along the road come in and out of view. The paths of many people's lives intersect the bus's path, and the way the bus seems to pass through other travelers on the road, all merging into its route like water flowing into a stream, suggests that the movement of life encompasses a larger collectivity than any particular group of passengers.

The driver is drawn to the unhappy young woman at the back of his bus. The camera takes his perspective as he sees her crying in the rearview mirror, then turns around to look directly at her and almost drives the bus off a cliff. Like *It Happened One Night*, *Mr. Thank You* depicts a romance burgeoning on the road, but Capra's film concentrates on the individual love story. According to romantic convention, Capra's film treats it as the right boy meeting the right girl, a couple made in heaven. Shimizu's embeds it among other stories, even other possible couplings between the handsome driver and girls he meets along the road. At one point in *It Happened One Night*, however, the passengers "start to sing a song—'The Man on the Flying Trapeze'—and the bus becomes a scene of community," as James Harvey writes. "It's only for a moment, but the transformation is still amazing: one of those scenes that everyone who sees the film remembers."[105] The audience at the movies is said to consist of discrete individuals sitting in the dark, but everyone remembers this moment when we feel addressed collectively and invited to join in the singing. Such is the feeling we get throughout *Mr. Thank You*, where the bus and the road it travels are always a scene of community, a locus of interweaving stories.

Shimizu's traveling camera looks out the side windows as well as the front and back. Time and again, the camera watches the passing scenery from various successive angles, the sea or a valley or houses from the climbing road, trees or grasses or a truss bridge laterally speeding by. If axial movement, forward or backward, predominates, it does not proceed in a straight line but along a curving, winding road. At one point, we look straight back at a sunlit hill withdrawing from view. The image darkens as the road turns, and we find ourselves inside a tunnel whose receding entrance suddenly gives way, in an exact match of horseshoe shapes across a cut, to the approaching opening at the other end. Like forward and backward in the advance toward slower travelers and retreat from them, backward and forward are here smoothly reversed. Later the bus stops for a rest at the entrance to another mountain pass. A young woman from Korea, a construction worker who, this stretch of road now finished, is moving on with her fellow immigrants to work elsewhere, says good-bye to the driver and asks him a favor: would he from time to time bring water and flowers to the grave of the father she's leaving behind? The driver promises he will, and, seen through the entrance to the tunnel she helped build, she recedes far into the distance—whereupon, in another match of horseshoe openings, lights at each end of the tunnel, the film cuts diametrically from retreat to advance, from the Korean woman standing on the road to the young woman on the bus looking back at her vanishing counterpart.

"Just crossing this pass," says the young woman on the bus, "I feel like I'm in a different country." "So far this fall, I've seen eight girls cross this pass," the driver responds, "headed for paper factories and cotton mills . . . and who knows what else. Sometimes I think I'd be better off driving a hearse." The road of life may be sad, yet the bus he's driving briskly keeps going, with bouncy music on the soundtrack, the sadness complicated and qualified by a light and airy tone. A pretty, somewhat older woman traveling alone brings humor and wit to the journey. Evidently a prostitute, as the young woman seems destined to become, she calls herself a migratory bird. "Birds always return to their nests," the driver says. "The girls who cross these passes rarely make it back." But a little later, the migratory woman catches him gazing again at the young woman in the rearview mirror and softly tells him that with the money he has saved to buy a bus of his own, he could rescue from prostitution this girl who has crossed these passes of no return. As he silently drives on, the scene dissolves to the receding road at sundown, and the migratory woman now takes the part of voice-over narrator: "This road's only twenty miles long, but so much has happened along it. Just think what's possible in this big wide world." Then the image fades out as the day draws to a close, and an intertitle reads: "Next day, clear skies on the road back." We are to infer, seeing the young woman heading back with the driver, that out of our view he has asked her to marry him. Their romance isn't so much dramatized as translated into movement along the road.

We skip the story's turning point, which coincides with the bus's turning point, as we skip the slowing down for travelers passed on the road. Driving up a hill on the way back, the bus overtakes a hay cart, and as usual approach and retreat fluidly blend; but other travelers not seen approaching are now seen retreating in swift succession as the driver gives them his thanks. Earlier the young woman looked back in sorrow at the receding road, at the life she thought irretrievably behind her; now the overtaken travelers are like a happy road chorus cheering the fact that she leaves behind a future she never wanted. As the smooth axial shifts from forward to backward or backward to forward have all along been suggesting, you can reverse direction on the road of life. This sense of life as possibility rather than inevitability makes *Mr. Thank You* a comedy rather than the fallen-woman melodrama it seemed headed for.

The Striped Box

Allegory is for Coleridge a rational scheme split from the imagination, but Walter Benjamin sees it as the rule of the subjective. Benjamin was writing at the time of the expressionists and the surrealists, heirs to the romantic delving into the inner and fascination with the mysterious, and exponents of allegory in a subjective rather than schematic mode. There may be a disjunction of faculties in expressionist and surrealist allegories, but not in the way Coleridge thinks, not because reason dictates meaning but because meaning eludes reason. And surrealist allegories purposely challenge reason and meaning. Perhaps the main difference between surrealism and expressionism is that surrealism has a sense of humor, and it is a humor that laughs at meaning and reason.

Just as you can define expressionism simply by pointing to *Caligari*, so for a definition of surrealism you need only point to *Un Chien andalou* (*An Andalusian Dog*, 1929, written by Luis Buñuel and Salvador Dalí, directed by Buñuel). Buñuel said that he and Dalí based their screenplay on their dreams and left out anything that they thought might make sense. *Un Chien andalou* means to defy meaning, to frustrate interpretation. But many have attempted to interpret it nonetheless. Have they all been misguided? Have they been merely trying to explain away a film that disturbs them precisely because it can't be explained? Phillip Drummond goes through various interpretations of the film with a certain exasperation, finding that they often give inaccurate accounts of it, and feeling that they are just ways of dodging the challenge it poses to our constructions of meaning, our social and aesthetic conventions.[106] Yet at the same time that it defies, this is a film that invites interpretation. As in a dream, everything in it seems to mean something, to stand for something, to be telling us something that eludes our grasp. Like an allegory, *Un Chien andalou* keeps us from taking things on a literal level and gestures toward a figurative level, where we seek a meaning we're not allowed to find: an allegory frustrated. "Nothing in the film symbolizes anything," Buñuel states,[107] but everything feels like a symbol, a symbol whose meaning may be unfathomable but still a symbol.

Take the striped box, for example. It first appears hanging from the neck of a young man riding a bicycle, and after the cyclist collapses in the street, the striped box is seen to contain a striped tie. Later it contains a severed hand, and a young woman who looks like the cyclist stands in the middle of the street clutching it to her chest as she's about to be run over by a car. Although it's impossible to ascertain what that striped box is a symbol of—it would seem to have some association with death because the cyclist drops dead while wearing it, the woman is killed while clutching it, and at the end it turns up as a wreck by the sea—it's equally impossible not to regard it as a symbol of something, calling for interpretation. At the Buñuel centenary conference held in London in the year 2000, Spanish film scholar Román Gubern rose to settle an argument about the meaning of that box. Its stripes, he said, reiterate the slanted lines of falling rain in a scene that was to have come before but was cut out. Gubern contributed an interesting piece of information, but, though he seemed to think he had established that the box has no meaning to worry about, the "purely formal connection" between the stripes and the rain on the cutting-room floor only augments the mystery that attaches to the box, the impression of secretive symbolism. *Un Chien andalou* as a whole creates that impression. This is not a film we can just sit back and let happen to us; it is not a film we can just watch without trying

to make sense of its disconcerting imagery. It is a film that dares the
viewer to decipher it, that calls for the connections of meaning even
as it thwarts them, that demands interpretation even as it blocks it—a
radically enigmatic allegory.

Surprise

Alfred Hitchcock often talked about the difference between suspense and surprise. Rather than surprising the audience with
something they didn't know, the master of suspense prefers to let
the audience know the situation and build up excitement and anxiety as to the outcome. He demonstrates how effective a rhetorical
strategy suspense can be. Surprise, however, can be no less effective.
"Astonish me," directs the impresario (Sergei Diaghilev) of the poet
(Jean Cocteau), and the surrealists aimed to astonish. This may seem
modern, avant-garde, but there is an old tradition behind it. Aristotle
appreciates the poetic and rhetorical uses of surprise. Reversal and
recognition, the two parts of the plot that he considers "the most
powerful elements of emotional interest in tragedy," both "turn upon
surprises."[108] He points out how metaphor gains impact through surprise, with the surprise arising from similarity perceived in the dissimilar:

> Metaphors must be drawn . . . from things that are related to the orig-
> inal thing, and yet not obviously so related—just as in philosophy also
> an acute mind will perceive resemblances even in things far apart. . . .
> Liveliness is specially conveyed by metaphor, and by the further power
> of surprising the hearer; because the hearer expected something dif-
> ferent, his acquisition of the new idea impresses him all the more.
> His mind seems to say, "Yes, to be sure; I never thought of that."[109]

Aristotle characteristically recommends the mean between two
extremes: "Metaphors must not be far-fetched, or they will be difficult to grasp, nor obvious, or they will have no effect."[110] Doubtless
he would have disapproved of the surrealists, who take surprise to the
point of shock and like their metaphors difficult to grasp. But what
could be more obvious than the resemblance, in the famously shocking metaphor at the start of Un Chien andalou, between a thin cloud
slicing across a full moon and a razor slicing an eye?

That eye slashed before our eyes, which recoil at the sight as if
themselves under attack, epitomizes the surrealist rhetoric of shock,
of aggression on the audience. Expecting that the audience would

throw things at him, Buñuel once came to a screening of *Un Chien andalou* armed with stones in his pockets to throw back at the audience. His aim was not to please but to displease, not to persuade but to provoke; aggression is as rhetorical as ingratiation, as much a way of engaging the audience. Noël Burch talks about "structures of aggression" and about the slashed eye as an initial shock coloring everything that follows.[111] What follows is a succession of shocks (an ant hole swarming in the palm of a man's hand, dead donkeys with their eyes bloodily plucked out lying on grand pianos being dragged along the floor in arduous striving toward the object of desire) or at least surprises (a fatally wounded man beginning to fall in a room and ending up in a field, a woman shutting a door behind her and finding herself no longer in an apartment house but on a breezy beach). The images of *Un Chien andalou* combine a blunt, charged physicality with a dreamlike dislocation of time and space. It further compounds the power of these images to startle and unsettle us that we keep feeling they must mean something but don't know what.

The Slashed Eye and the Primal Scene

After the opening words "Once upon a time," *Un Chien andalou* begins with a man (played by Buñuel himself) sharpening a razor. He goes out onto a balcony and looks up at the moon. A woman who wasn't there before suddenly appears, in frontal close-up, looking straight out toward us. A gaze meeting ours invites our identification. The slicing of her eye, presumably by the man wielding the razor and contemplating the moon as a cloud slices it, feels like violence done to our own eyes. It hits the viewer in the very organ of viewing. It may be taken as sheer rhetoric, a shock tactic with no other aim than making an impact on the audience, an inaugural act of aggression setting the stage for the images to come, which hit us again and again. But the strongest hit comes first. Rather than building up to a climax in the usual way, leading us from one thing to another toward a conclusion, *Un Chien andalou* starts at its peak moment, giving us the sense that what counts the most, the crucial thing, occurs in the beginning, "Once upon a time."

The slashed eye has been construed as signaling a break with customary seeing at the start of a film we are to watch with a new eye. That the filmmaker himself plays the role of eye slasher fits in with this line of interpretation, which proposes a self-referential allegory—or an allegory of rhetoric, of the film's effect on us. The woman's eye is identified with the viewer's eye, which flinches not merely at the sight of violence but of violence inflicted right where sight resides, so that the image can be taken to represent the experience of watching it, the slashed eye to symbolize its impact on our eyes.

Like the striped box and the rain, the eyeball slit by a razor and the moon slit by a cloud make a formal connection, a geometric metaphor. But we can't rest content with a parallel of lines and shapes alone; we want to know what it means. Besides the self-referential or rhetorical, various other interpretations of this eye-slashing prologue have been offered. For some, the slit eyeball with the jelly bleeding out symbolizes the birth of a child whose story the film goes on to relate in similarly symbolic fashion. Other interpreters stress the romantic aura of this prologue—it is evening, the moon is full, the man seems to be getting ready for some amorous rendezvous and dreamily looks up at the moon—and construe the razor cutting into the eye as a metaphor for sexual intercourse. In this sexual line of interpretation, the scene would be about the brutal, revolting violence lurking behind the moonlit trappings of romanticism.

Both the self-referential and the sexual enter into Linda Williams's reading of this prologue. She counts four strokes sharpening the razor on a strop and four shots alternating between the man's hands and his face, four strokes of film cutting; she takes Buñuel the actor to personify Buñuel the filmmaker, the seer and the cutter, the eye and hands putting the film together.[112] She agrees with those who construe the slashed eye as "a symbol of sexual penetration of the female body," though penetration by the cutting edge of a razor implies to her that "the latent meaning of the metaphor can only be castration."[113] In psychoanalytic theory, Jeff Smith remarks, "the latent meaning of *anything* can only be castration."[114] But you needn't accept the assumptions of psychoanalysis to recognize its influence on the surrealists. Buñuel himself, looking back on *Un Chien andalou* two decades later, notes that "the only method of investigation of the symbols would be, perhaps, psychoanalysis."[115] Williams is clever to combine the eye-cutting razor as a penetrating penis with the threat that its cutting edge poses to a penis. This is what Freud (for whom the fear of castration was so fundamental that he used it to explain the fear of death) called condensation.

Rhetorically, as Williams points out, the slit eye/slit moon metaphor does something special. Whereas a metaphor is normally a comment on the action, a parallel to it serving as embellishment or intensification, here the metaphor seems to make the action happen. It feels as if the slicing of the moon were bringing on the slicing of the eye, one slit round shape leading to the other as cause to effect.[116] Let me take her insight further. In *Un Chien andalou*, as in surrealism more generally, metaphor is action and action is metaphor. Metaphor is in the mind, but the mind and the body, dream and reality, are surreally as one. If the slit moon is metaphor as action, metaphor resulting in action, then the slit eye is action as metaphor, action demanding to be read as metaphor.

The slit moon is for Williams the vehicle of the metaphor and the slit eye the tenor. But the reverse has equal claim: as much as the eye to the moon, the moon is being compared to the eye. (The moon is there in the scene, but it isn't clear where the woman comes from or where the slashing of her eye takes place—perhaps in the man's imagination as he looks at the slit moon and thinks of the slit eye.) Like Vertov's comparison between the woman washing and the washing of the city, this is the kind of reversible cinematic metaphor in which cutting between two things places them side by side so that the comparison goes both ways. Where the figure acquires an irreversible direction is not in the comparison, the metaphor, but in our sense that the slit moon brings about the slit eye, the metonymic connection of cause and effect.

We may grant that the man looks at the full moon in romantic anticipation, and that seeing a cloud swiftly approaching the moon and cutting across it puts him in mind of the sexual act and prompts him to carry it out as an act of aggression on the woman, mind turning to body forthwith. But if this prologue allegorizes male desire and its aggressive consummation, surely a common occurrence, why is it presented as something that happened in some fairy-tale beginning, "Once upon a time"? And why is it such a shock? It would be a shock to the woman, but it is the man's desire that is presumably being enacted, the man's mind that, as Williams interprets the scene, condenses sexual penetration and fear of castration into the image of the slashed eye. Or is another desire in play, another mind? If the razor is both a penetrating penis and a threat of castration, which penis is being aggressive, and which feels threatened? In the Oedipal triangle, the father's penis penetrates, possesses the mother, and the son's penis, which desires the mother, is afraid of castration. We may further ask, why should that penetration and that fear be represented as violence done to the eye, the eye of the woman and the eye of the spectator?

Let me propose another condensation at work here. In what Freud calls the primal scene, the boy observes his parents having sex, and he perceives their sexual intercourse as violent, just as the slicing of the eye represents sexual penetration as violent. The child is traumatized by the sight; violence is done to his eye just as violence is done to the woman's eye by the penetrating razor and to the spectator's eye by the image. No matter how the image of the slashed eye may be construed, its effect on the spectator amounts to something traumatic, a trauma of the eye like the trauma of the primal scene, and moreover an initial trauma that colors the rest of the film just as the primal scene colors the rest of the child's life. And so the slit eye that follows from the slit moon, the shock of violence in romance, can be taken as a condensation of the primal scene and what it does to its spectator, the impact it makes on the child whose eye perceives a physical assault and thereby receives a psychological one. "Once upon a time" would then refer to the primal scene as a Freudian fairy tale.

Interpretation of *Un Chien andalou* must be tentative. The slashed eye as a metaphor for both the sexual act seen as violent and the violence the seeing does to the mind is a condensation that clicks with me. (The one proposed by Williams is its Oedipal corollary: fear of castration supposedly originates in the son's fear of the father's violence.) I'm not a Freudian, though. I hold no brief for the Oedipus complex—certainly not as a universal condition—and in any case I wouldn't presume to settle the meaning of this prologue by reference to the primal scene. But even if not in its meaning, this prologue is in its rhetoric, its effect on the spectator, a kind of primal scene. Freud offers us a myth, or fairy tale, of primal spectatorship, traumatic and formative, original sin as original seeing. The startling scene at the start of *Un Chien andalou* does something uncannily similar to our spectatorship, our way of seeing the images on the screen.

Once upon a time a little boy had a sled called Rosebud. *Citizen Kane*, which like *Un Chien andalou* is its director's first film, is likewise a film in which first things, the earliest wounds, matter most. Kane may remain a mystery in the end, but he is a mystery we at least know to be rooted in the beginning. *Un Chien andalou* can be understood as telling the same kind of story. The difference is that *Citizen Kane* digs into the past for that decisive beginning, whereas *Un Chien andalou* enacts it in its own beginning, has it happen before our eyes, to our eyes.

The Priest and the Pineapple

One of the last films Buñuel made in Mexico, within a commercial movie industry where he found freedom enough for his surrealist art, was *Nazarín* (1959), based on the 1895 novel by his fellow Spaniard, Benito Pérez Galdós. A character with something distant and exotic about him, something foreign to his environment (Francisco Rabal, a Spanish actor, plays him in the movie, set in the period of the book but transposed to Mexico), Nazarín is a saintly priest who not only preaches but in every way seeks to practice the teachings of Christ, renouncing all earthly possessions and even breaking away from the church in uncompromising pursuit of the true Christian life his conscience dictates. There were Catholics at the time who hailed *Nazarín* as a religious film and thought that Buñuel the unbeliever had come around to the faith. He soon laid that notion to rest with his well-known remark: "Thank God I am still an atheist."

Nazarín's way of life, in the film as in the novel, is an imitation of Christ. His story, insofar as its meaning resides in that parallel, is an allegory. As Fletcher says of the allegorical character, Nazarín has an absolutely one-track mind and does not allow himself the slightest divergence from a set pattern of behavior. He personifies an idea of life conducted according to strict Christian principles by which he defines himself and everything he encounters in the world. But both Galdós's book and Buñuel's movie hinge on an ambiguity as to whether the protagonist is inspired or misguided, a saint or a fool. The Christian allegory is called into question through a realistic irony; a tension arises between the meaning of life found in following Christ and the facts of actual existence.

This irony, this tension, is more marked in the film. When Nazarín goes into a plague-stricken town and offers help, a scene that is not in the novel (it was derived instead from a dialogue by the Marquis de Sade), the priest tries to console a dying woman with talk of Heaven, but she tells him she doesn't want Heaven, she wants Juan, the man she loves. Juan arrives, sends away the priest preoccupied with the salvation of her soul, and tenderly kisses her pestilential lips. Two women accompany Nazarín in his pilgrimage, two Magdalenes to his Christ: Andara, a feisty common prostitute, and Beatriz, a hysteric consumed with love for Pinto, a brutish man who mistreats her.[117] In the novel, Andara and Beatriz are both seen to benefit from their faith in Nazarín and what he represents; thanks to his influence, Beatriz is able to let go of her obsession with Pinto. But in the film, when her mother points out to her that her attraction to the priest is physical, not just spiritual, Beatriz relapses into hysteria and Pinto carries her off in his arms. Like the novel, the film portrays Nazarín sympathetically as a good man with the best intentions to do good, but it conveys a stronger sense that the good man doesn't actually do much good in the world.

Along with the two Magdalenes, a bad thief and a good thief figure in the story. When Nazarín is put in prison among common criminals, one of them beats him up and another defends him. The priest thanks his defender and asks him if he doesn't want to be good, if he wouldn't like to change his life. Here Buñuel departs decisively from Galdós. In the novel the good thief, in keeping with his biblical counterpart, embraces the righteous change of life set out for him. In the movie he asks the priest in turn: "Wouldn't you like to change yours?

. . . Your life, what's it good for? You on the good side and I on the bad side, neither one of us is good for anything." Nazarín is dumbstruck. Never before at a loss for words, his flowing pious phrases always at the ready, now he says nothing at all, on his face a look of consternation rather than his usual high-minded serenity, and from here on he scarcely speaks. It's Nazarín's life that has been changed. If Christ on the cross felt that God had forsaken him, Nazarín seems to feel forsaken by the ideas that have ruled his life and the words on which he has relied to express them, by the imitation of Christ that until now has defined him. Buñuel brings to the breaking point the irony his film shares with Galdós's novel, the tension between allegory and reality. The unchanging allegorical character changes after all, and changes momentously: if Christ died on the cross and rose to Heaven, Nazarín comes down to earth and finds his lofty notions unavailing, his sense of life thrown into crisis.

The priest is separated from the other prisoners and assigned his own guard, who leads him back to the city on foot. Beatriz rides off with Pinto on the same road, but as their carriage passes by, her head resting on her lover's shoulder, she takes no notice of Nazarín, and the downcast, brooding priest is equally unmindful of her. The guard stops with his prisoner at a roadside stand, bites into an apple he doesn't pay for, and shrugs when the vendor, a peasant woman, asks him if she may give the prisoner something. She offers Nazarín a pineapple. Nazarín has never had any qualms about accepting charity; as well as giving to others, receiving what others give him has been for him a matter of Christian principle, in no way diminishing his priestly dignity. Yet now, faced with the pineapple, he looks perplexed, perturbed, and recoils from the woman's gift. Drums start to be heard on the soundtrack. (The drums he heard as a child during Holy Week in Calanda left an enduring impression on Buñuel, whose first sound film, the oneiric, satirical *L'Age d'or* [1930], also has a final sequence accompanied by a sustained drumroll.) After a moment of hesitation, Nazarín changes his mind, takes the pineapple from the peasant woman, thanks her with an uneasy smile ("May God repay you"), and walks forward carrying her sweet, spiny gift as the drums play on and the film comes to an end.

This ending is Buñuel's own; nothing of the sort occurs in the novel. What does it mean? What does the initially refused, finally accepted gift signify? And why a pineapple? It is a fruit of rough texture and substantial body, a palpable representative of the material reality the priest is coming to grips with. It is good to eat, but you can't just bite into it as the guard bites into an apple, taking it for granted as his due. The pineapple is a prickly, rather unwieldy fruit, a gift you have to do some work to appreciate. It may be construed, then, as a symbol of the gifts we are given on this earth, the sweetness together with the thorniness of physical existence. (If you think of the pineapple as a kind of apple and associate it with the biblical forbidden fruit, you could read this ending as allegorizing Nazarín's fall from grace. But *piña*, the Spanish word for pineapple, has no "apple" in it.) The pineapple is also a fruit native to the New World, a gift of the Mexican earth, and the film's Nazarín is a European transplanted to Mexico—born of Spanish parents, educated in Spain, played by a Spanish actor with a Castilian accent—so that the pineapple he is given may be taken to stand for the Mexican reality he has been given to live in.

Beginnings and endings, the boundaries of a work, have special importance to its construction and its rhetoric. Like the beginning of *Un Chien andalou*, the ending of *Nazarín* is the film's boldest and most resounding stroke. As William S. Pechter writes, "Though the specific effect on Nazarín of the woman's gift of the pineapple following his disillusionment with saintliness may not be knowable, the affective impact that the woman's mundane charity has on him is unmistakable in every detail of the scene's realization, from his stunned bewilderment to the final, shattering roll of drums; indeed, it is a case of the final moment of the film (like the last line of Waugh's *The Ordeal of Gilbert Pinfold*) retrospectively transforming everything that we have experienced before."[118] That Nazarín at first refuses the pineapple implies that he has renounced, or is at least seriously questioning, his lifelong belief in Christian charity; it must be on new or at least renewed terms that he finally comes to accept the woman's mundane charity. Christian charity calls for humility in giver and receiver alike, but humility as a lofty principle has about it a certain pride, a detachment from common humanity, that Nazarín's saintliness hasn't been free of. Now, however, it is with something like true humility, as one human being receiving the kindness of another on the ground where they both stand, that the priest takes the pineapple offered to him. Perhaps he has fallen from heavenly grace, but he may be on the road toward such grace as can be reached down here on this earth—the kind of grace the peasant woman demonstrates with her spontaneous gift to a stranger in trouble, the grace under pressure of living in the world.

Critics of idealism and debunkers of spirituality themselves often idealize the practical and material and celebrate the blessings of the physical world. Not Buñuel. He doesn't see much to celebrate in the physical world he depicts: the plague killing the woman who wants Juan, the sexuality driving Beatriz to hysteria and binding her to Pinto, the stunted body of a dwarf who incongruously falls in love with Andara. And yet the dying woman has a moment of bliss when

Juan comes and kisses her, and the dwarf too has his bliss, touchingly, by virtue of his capacity for love, which he bestows without hope on a woman twice his size, unattractive, disreputable, but by him, as he puts it, esteemed. Born of the body, the dwarf's love, like the dying woman's, comes up against the limits of the body. Their bliss is attained in humility, the recognition of limitation. Even Pinto shows some humility in his wanting Beatriz back despite her attachment to the priest, and though there's little more hope for her future with Pinto than for the dwarf's with Andara, her submission to the lover taking her away at least gives Beatriz her moment of bodily bliss. All around the forlorn Nazarín is this humility before the physical, this acceptance of our material human nature—not because it is good but because it is. The good priest takes the pineapple and joins the rest of humanity.

Tragedy is about isolation, comedy about incorporation into human society, as Northrop Frye says; and he notes that in tragedy, "hubris is the normal precipitating agent of catastrophe, just as in comedy the cause of the happy ending is usually some act of humility."[119] Buñuel's Nazarín may be seen as a tragic character who at the transformative end takes the first step toward comedy.

Irony and Realism

Nazarín is a descendant of Don Quixote, the idealist who, armed with his ideals, meets up with the actual world. Broadly speaking, the realistic novel descends from *Don Quixote* in the way it undertakes to construct meaning, which has to do with ideas, out of the observation of reality, its concrete detail and circumstance, the stuff of facts. The irony informing Galdós's novel and Buñuel's film, the irony arising from the discrepancy between meaning and reality, ideas and facts, has been since Cervantes a kind of irony characteristic of realism.

Jean Renoir's *The Rules of the Game* (1939) is a work of realism that, ironically, takes the form of a comedy. It has been called a social satire, with some justice, but its sympathy for its characters runs warmer than that, and its irony goes deeper. Satire mocks the beliefs and conventions, the hypocrisies and absurdities, of society; comedy may make fun of society, may throw it into disorder, but in the end is happily reconciled to a restored social order. Along with the form, *The Rules of the Game* assumes the charm of a comedy, the lightheartedness that would seem to promise a happy ending. It does not mock the conventions of comedy or even of society; it genuinely cherishes the communal aspirations in the comedic portrayal of society. But in the end, those aspirations are dashed, through the very mechanisms—the confusion of roles, the intricate geometry of amorous couplings and jealous third parties—by which comedy would realize them. In the climactic irony, a redoubled comedic device, a mistaken identity leads to the killing of the film's one true romantic lover. The order that is restored is not living but deathly, an order of walking shadows like those that loom in the haunting final shot. Society as theater is a familiar trope, but here the theater of society is adverse to nature and human nature to the point of doing violence to life, as in the semidocumentary sequence of the hunt, where what we might have expected to be an excursion into a comedic "green world" turns into a shocking spectacle of ritualized slaughter. The meaning that comedy proposes is seen to be tragically inadequate to the actual situation.

Unfolding much like a bedroom farce, but a farce played by real characters in a real world, this film does not portray a comedic integration of individuals into society but the disparateness of individuals and the disintegration of a society. If tragedy is the form of singularity and comedy the form of community, then *The Rules of the Game* is a comedy gone wrong, a tragedy of community. Such a thing defies Frye's assertion that "to make a sombre action end happily is easy enough, and to reverse the procedure almost impossible. . . . Even Shakespeare, who can do anything, never does quite this. . . . None of Shakespeare's tragedies impresses us as a comedy gone wrong."[120] But Renoir manages it in his great ironic, realistic tragicomedy.

"King Lear attempts to achieve heroic dignity through his position as a king and father, and finds it instead in his suffering humanity." Such irony, Frye holds—the kind of irony that "looks at tragedy from below," that "stresses the humanity of its heroes" and "supplies social and psychological explanations for catastrophe"—marks the "sincere, explicit realism" of novelists like Tolstoy, Hardy, and Conrad.[121] In irony, Quintilian writes, "we are asked to understand the opposite of what is said."[122] "For *irony*," Burke suggests, "we could substitute *dialectic*."[123] Irony is the figure of opposition, discrepancy, contrast, contradiction. Contrast may be thought of as a form of similarity, and Jakobson perhaps means to subsume irony under the umbrella of metaphor (as Quintilian subsumes it under allegory, understanding the opposite being a special case of understanding something other than what is said). Yet the negative of similarity, the play of contradiction, takes us to a quite different place rhetorically. Art, even at its most lifelike, works through the imagination; irony is central to the rhetoric of realism because the endeavor to portray life as it is calls for a contrast, a contraposition, a dialectic, with what it is imagined to be. Realism favors metonymy over metaphor, as Jakobson teaches us, but he neglects another favored realist trope: irony.

The Bridge and the Ballad

R enoir derived *Toni* (1935) from "a news item, a love-story that really happened in Les Martigues and was told to me by my friend Jacques Mortier, who at the time was Chief of Police in that small town."[124] He went to that small town in Provence and shot the movie entirely on location right where the story took place, with actors mostly recruited locally, stripped of theatricality and speaking in regional or foreign accents bearing the mark of a place. "*Toni* has often been described as the forerunner of the Italian neo-realist films," Renoir writes, but he points out that the usual Italian practice of shooting the picture on location and afterward dubbing the sound in the studio was not his way: "I am a passionate believer in authentic sound. I prefer sound that is technically bad, but has been recorded at the same time as the picture to sound that is perfect but has been dubbed. . . . In *Toni* the sound of the train arriving at Les Martigues station is not merely the real sound of a train but that of the one which one sees on the screen."[125] *Toni* begins on that train, where migrant workers are coming to work in the south of France and singing songs of the homeland they left behind. They pause to have a drink from a bottle of wine they pass among them, and we suddenly hear the loud sound of the train whistle and cut to a long shot of the train crossing the bridge leading to the station at Les Martigues. The sweet human sound of the folk songs contrasts with the harsh industrial sound of the train whistle, a contrast made more vivid by the actual sound recorded on the spot and a representation of the experience of peasants arriving in an alien land where they are to do alien industrial work.[126]

The migrant workers get off at the station. Toni (Charles Blavette) is among them, and the camera singles him out long enough to indicate he is the protagonist, but more than once it lets him leave view and focuses on other arriving workers, which suggests that any one of them could have been the protagonist. The three workers shown singing on the train now reappear, walking down a hill on their way into town, and one of them plays his guitar and sings: "Tonight I sing below your window / Tomorrow I will leave for France / And I shall never see you again." His voice continues to be heard after he and his friends are gone from view; the camera pans and tilts up to the trestle bridge over which the train carried him and all the other immigrants to their destination in France. Song and bridge, peasant tradition and industrial modernity, are again strikingly juxtaposed.

The panning and tilting to frame a view of the bridge is a gesture identifying the camera with the bridge, as William Rothman argues:

Gradually, the camera slows, so that it no longer keeps up with the immigrants, who file through the frame. When all the human figures have left the frame, the camera—still haunted by the singing of the workers now unseen—continues its slow movement until it composes a perfect picture of the bridge.

This bridge functions as one of the film's main settings, but only the ending of the film declares its significance as a symbol. Toni dies just past the end of the bridge. As the camera tilts up, we see a new train arrive, a whole new potential cast of characters filled with hope. The film ends on a final camera movement that exactly repeats the first, and again it concludes by framing the bridge, as if it is in this bridge, not in any of its human subjects, that the camera finds its own likeness.[127]

Why would Renoir identify his camera with a bridge? For Rothman, the answer is the "apparent indifference" of Renoir's camera. Yet this is a camera that sympathetically moves with Toni as he flees from the police across the bridge where at the other end death awaits; and the microphone, too, is right there with him, poignantly recording the sound of his hurried footsteps on the bridge, an eloquent human detail resounding against the big alien machinery about to crush him. When Toni dies and the train passes by with its load of new immigrants, this is a camera that, by cutting to the other side of the train so that he seems to be run over by the iron wheels through which we see him, tells us that it is the bridge, the train, industrial modernity killing him.

The camera, anyone's camera, is of course a machine, and the identification between the camera and the bridge acknowledges the fact that film is itself a product of industrial modernity—and not only the camera; realism too is a modern invention. It was not by happenstance that the photographic camera emerged at around the same time as the realistic novel. Both responded to an increased appetite for details and particulars in the representation of reality. *Toni* is Renoir's most naturalistic film, the one most steeped in the actual sights and sounds of a particular place and time. And so the camera identified with the bridge can be taken as declaring its alliance not only with the machine age but also with the methods of realism. The migrant workers in *Toni* surely wouldn't tell their own story in this naturalistic way, which belongs to a modernity alien to them. But the camera is also, in Rothman's word, haunted by the song that is the immigrants' own means of expression.

In keeping with Renoir's preference for direct sound, there is no background music in *Toni*. The music is provided by the immigrants themselves singing their folk songs, which recur throughout the movie like the refrain of a ballad. One scene with sung accompaniment was cut out of the picture because the producers objected. Let me briefly fill in the plot. Toni loves Josefa (Celia Montalván), an immigrant from Spain, his love for her bound up with his wish to return to his peasant roots. He asks her uncle for her hand, but Albert (Max Dalban), the foreman at the quarry where Toni works, seduces her, and Josefa is forced to marry the abusive Albert and eventually is driven to kill him. Toni comes to her aid and proposes that they make Albert's death look like suicide. In the omitted scene, they carry his body into the woods hidden in the laundry cart—recalling their early love scene, in which Toni hauled the laundry cart for Josefa—and are joined along their path by an unwitting, lighthearted funeral cortege of migrant workers singing. The producers deemed this music inappropriate at this dramatic moment in the story. But the incongruity, the ironic counterpoint between music and drama—rather than their consonance in melodrama—was just what Renoir had in mind.

The film's closing sequence repeats the opening not merely in the final gesture of panning and tilting up to the bridge but also in the shots of the arriving train and the immigrants getting off at the station and walking downhill toward the town, and even in the song we hear one of them singing, this time without a guitar: "Tonight I sing below your window / Tomorrow I will leave for France / And I shall never see you again." Visually as well as aurally, this is like the refrain of a ballad. *Toni* brings together and bounces off each other the modern form of realism and the traditional form of a ballad—which is the way the immigrants would tell the story themselves.

By extending realism into the life of the lower classes—and "with this film," as Christopher Faulkner notes, Renoir "moved outside his own class for the first time to encompass a different social life"[128]— naturalism faces the problem of a class difference between the author and the characters. The author's higher social position often results in an attitude of superiority and condescension toward the characters. Renoir solves the problem in *Toni* by inflecting a realistic mode belonging to the author with the strains and structure of a ballad belonging to the characters. Realism grounds the narrative in concrete detail and social circumstance; the ballad sings a sad love story. In a prose speech, Cicero says, one feels an "obscure song,"[129] but here the prose of realism meets a song voiced and heard. If in *The Rules of the Game* the irony of realism arises in interplay with comedy, then the irony in *Toni* comes out of the transaction with another traditional form: the juxtaposition between the bridge and the ballad.

Dramatic Irony

Out the window we see the candy man in the distance. His coming is always an occasion for the children, but not this time in *Pather Panchali*. The camera tilts down to Durga, sick in bed, and she doesn't even notice; she is beyond candy, and so, we fear, not long for this world. It is a very affecting moment. When this dear girl who got sick in the rain dies in a house too run down to protect her from another storm, we are heartbroken. Yet the point of highest pathos, the moment that brings us to tears, comes when her unknowing father returns. Why is it so moving to see him arrive in the aftermath of the tragedy, only to find out what we know already? The answer is dramatic irony.

It was partly his fault that she died, partly the result of his not being a good provider and letting the house fall into disrepair; but he comes back having earned some money and thinking the family's fortunes have turned for the better. He steps up to the porch and, while his wife says nothing, cheerfully pulls out things he has brought—a board and rolling pin for the kitchen, a picture of a goddess, a new sari for Durga—at which point his wife starts crying, and the music of wailing strings takes over on the soundtrack, the film's way of crying with her. She clutches her daughter's sari and sobbingly drops to the ground. Her husband leans over her, the camera moving closer to him but letting him leave the frame as he stands up; he drops back down into view after a moment, having finally realized that his daughter is dead, and the camera moves down with him toward his prostrate wife and pulls back as, over the wailing strings, he cries out Durga's name. Cut to little Apu on the road with the umbrella he now carries in case it rains again.

When the audience knows more than the characters about their situation—as we know more than the returning father about what has happened in his absence, or as when, in a horror movie, we are made aware that the monster threatens an oblivious character—we have dramatic irony. Our superior knowledge may at times induce detachment, but it heightens our involvement with the father who doesn't know what awaits him on his return or with the character in a horror movie who doesn't know what lurks around the corner. We may think of identification as sharing a character's consciousness, knowing no more than the character knows, but surely in a horror movie we identify with the oblivious character threatened by the monster. For we are frightened, and that can only be because we put ourselves in the character's place, imagine ourselves in his or her situation, which we know to be reason for fear even if he or she doesn't know. Our sentiments can be more keenly aroused, our emotional (rather than epistemological) identification made stronger, when we feel for a character what we know he or she should be feeling or will feel in due course. This is the case with the returning father in *Pather Panchali*. We feel more because we know more and know he'll soon come to know.

The Hurdanos and Us

In his early period—many years passed before his career resumed in Mexico—Buñuel made three films, the surrealist *Un Chien andalou* and *L'Age d'or* and the documentary *Land without Bread* (1932). (All three films were financed privately, *Un Chien andalou* with family money, *L'Age d'or* by an aristocratic patron of the arts, and *Land without Bread* by an anarchist teacher, Ramón Acín, who promised to pay for the film if he won the lottery—and who kept his promise when he won.[130]) After the dreamlike stream of imagery "uncorrupted by plausibility" (as the surrealists put it at the time), Buñuel took his camera up into the mountains of northwestern Spain for a look at an external reality no less astounding than the most far-fetched surrealism. Here, according to Octavio Paz, "the poet Buñuel withdraws, keeps silent, so that reality may speak for itself."[131] But the reality depicted in this documentary is unspeakable: it's hard to imagine, even though we see it, that human beings can live under the wretched conditions prevailing in the isolated region of Las Hurdes, literally a land without bread. Reality in any case never speaks for itself; realism must resort to the irony of speaking for it, giving it a meaning not its own but always a construction, a matter of interpretation and supposition, ideas necessarily at a distance from the facts. *Land without Bread* is of a piece with *Un Chien andalou* and *L'Age d'or* in the way it enacts a defiance of meaning. It is one of the most incisive and provocative works of ironic realism in the movies.[132]

Buñuel keeps silent, yes, but he sets up a voice-over narrator who speaks throughout in the tones of a travelogue, in the manner of a visitor to some exotic land who takes a casual interest in its picturesque sights and in the quaint customs of its inhabitants. A pocket of stagnant misery, a land not only without bread but without adequate agriculture and even without windows in cramped houses perennially full of smoke, it is treated as just another tourist spot. Assuming that Buñuel couldn't have been responsible for this narration, a film professor I've heard about would turn off the sound when screening *Land without Bread* for his students. But such off-putting, out-of-keeping narration was indeed what Buñuel intended.

Voice-over narration is common in documentaries. It is less common in fiction films, where it is of course fictional and is often in the voice of a character, a dramatized narrator telling us the story from his or her point of view. The documentary voice-over is factual and usually impersonal, authoritative, an account we are to accept as the truth. Buñuel radically breaks with that convention. He gives us a voice-over narration purposely not to be trusted. The untrustworthy or unreliable narrator is a device that, in fiction, merely augments the subjectivity of a character's first-person account. But with his unreliable travelogue narrator, Buñuel undermines the documentary claim to objectivity. He challenges the authority of documentary.

The narrator tells us that the Hurdanos eat goat meat only when this happens, and we see a goat falling off a cliff. But we watch the goat fall in two successive views, first facing the cliff from a distance, then looking down from above. If this was an unforeseen, accidental occurrence, how, we may wonder, could it have been captured from two such different angles? We may notice a puff of smoke at the edge of the screen, evidently smoke from a gun used to shoot down the goat, whose fall we can see was no accident.[133] A scene arranged for the camera, staged in some manner, is nothing unusual in documentary, which always has some admixture of fiction. The unusual thing here is that the admixture is acknowledged, brought to our attention in the audience. The fictionality that most documentaries would dissemble Land without Bread declares. Lately it has been much admired as a deconstruction of documentary by postmodern-minded commentators who take documentary to be as fictional as fiction—or even more so, they would argue, because it puts up the fiction that it is not fictional. If the professor who shut off the sound saw the film's realism but missed its irony, then these admirers see the irony but miss the realism. Land without Bread has been aptly characterized as a parody travelogue, but it is a parody set against a troubling reality being documented all the same—a reality made more rather than less troubling by the ironically inappropriate style of representation.

There is, deliberately, something wrong with the narration in Land without Bread. This doesn't mean, however, as a scholar of documentary like Bill Nichols thinks, that the Hurdanos are doing all right and the film merely caricatures our tendency to misunderstand and misrepresent people who are different from us. Nichols talks about the "outrageously judgmental, if not ethnocentric, voice-over commentary" ("How profoundly disrespectful; how contemptuous! How little regard for the hardships and difficulties of those who confront an inhospitable environment") and takes Buñuel "to be hinting to us that this is not a factual representation . . . but a criticism or exposé of the forms of representation common to the depiction of traditional peoples."[134] Ethnocentric? The Hurdanos are Spaniards, just like Buñuel, and he would have laughed at the notion that we should respect them as a "traditional people." For him, that would have been as much a conventional piety as the usual profession of pity for the unfortunate. Not factual? Unreliable though it may be, this representation of the Hurdanos is factual enough to make palpable the notion that something is wrong with the way they live, not just the way they're represented—and what, the film tacitly asks, could be the right way to represent their astonishing misery? If Nichols finds nothing wrong with the Hurdanos in their difference from us, Buñuel leads us to recognize that they are not so different as we may think, that what's wrong with them may be wrong with us too—terribly wrong.

The narrator is lying about the goat that didn't fall accidentally, but such accidents happen, and the gist of what he's saying may well be the truth: that only when they do happen are the Hurdanos able to eat goat meat. We have no way of ascertaining. Buñuel wants neither our ingenuous belief in documentary veracity nor our contented disbelief. He is not simply out to expose the lies of documentary; his irony is not the cynical postmodern sort that would foster in us the attitude of knowing better. Rather, he throws on us the task of inspecting the evidence we have and making of it what we can. Perhaps the narrator exaggerates the misery of the Hurdanos, but he doesn't seem much perturbed by it or much concerned with its amelioration; far from a caring observer appealing to our humanitarian sentiments, he strikes us as callous in his travelogue superficiality. If this narrator we distrust and dislike does not speak for the author, then what is the author hidden behind him silently saying? Whenever we can't be sure where the author stands, whenever we find ourselves in uncertainty as to how we should respond, we are in a situation of irony.[135] That, to an uncomfortable, unsettling extreme, is our situation in this film.

Sometimes we feel like laughing at the Hurdanos, and feel that Buñuel may be laughing too at a group of people whose efforts to cope with adverse circumstances often only make things worse; but our laughter is held in check by the fact that these people are real, that this is after all a documentary. Laughter is a barbarous response to the spectacle of human want; the civilized response would be pity. It's not clear, though, that Buñuel the surrealist doesn't prefer barbarity to civilization. In a rhetorical move as shocking to our sensibilities as the living conditions in Las Hurdes, he withholds pity, the compassion we would extend to the people who live there. His parody travelogue suggests that no matter how compassionate we may be, there is always something touristy about our watching the misfortune of others. For this, the film criticizes itself along with its audience. Pity is too easy an outlet for our emotions. Laughter may be preferable because we find it more difficult, because we feel bad about mocking the Hurdanos but feel good about feeling sorry for them. What comes easier has the tendency to confirm our assumptions; what makes us uneasy has the capacity to incite questioning. Buñuel's withholding of pity is a provocation to thought.

The rhetoric of *Land without Bread* puts the audience on the spot. Not that audiences are ever passive—it's a mistake to think otherwise—but here we are called upon to play an unusually active role. Irony is a figure whose inexplicitness asks for our participation. It may invite us into complicity with an author who lets us in on a meaning that others might not get; or, as here, it may leave us on our own to find a meaning that the author declines to assign. "Irony is naturally a sophisticated mode," Frye remarks, "and the chief difference between sophisticated and naive irony is that the naive ironist calls attention to the fact that he is being ironic, whereas sophisticated irony merely states, and lets the reader add the ironic tone himself."[136] Once we have added the ironic tone, Buñuel presses us further—presses us by the combination of disturbing content, unsuitable form, and authorial elusiveness—to raise questions and search for answers he leaves up to us.

At one point in the film, we see a bunch of Hurdanos going off to look for work elsewhere, and then we see them coming back, not having found it. The brisk juxtaposition of hopeful departure and dispirited return is one of the things we can take as making fun of the Hurdanos. It is the closest the film comes to putting the question, why don't they get out? Though isolated, the region is not inaccessible. Obviously they can get out, but then they come right back. Why don't they just go? What keeps them there, and has kept them for generations? And if they must remain in that inhospitable region, why do they persist in their ways, their inhibiting habits of existence, their counterproductive practices? Some of them are cretins born of inbreeding, but most of them are as normal as we are. Yet stuck in that pocket of wretchedness, they stay.

Why don't they get out? If the narrator had asked this question, if it had been spelled out for us, it wouldn't have had the import it has when we ask it ourselves. We can give an answer to this question, and as we pose the question and ponder the answer, we are bound to see how we are implicated. It's not the physical world that entraps the Hurdanos, not the mountainous geography that keeps them stuck in Las Hurdes. The reason they don't get out is that this is their culture, their way of life. They don't get out because they are social animals just as we are, conditioned just as we are by shared values and beliefs, established patterns of behavior, entrenched customs and conventions that seem to allow no alternative. The question we ask about them we may well ask about ourselves: why don't *we* get out, why don't *we* break free of the entrapments in our own lives? We may be better off than they are, but we too are stuck inside the horizon of a culture, we too are prisoners of a society determining the shape of life as we know it, we too have learned to live with the habitual thwarting of the best human possibilities. The Hurdanos are but an aggravated case of the constrictions and frustrations of human culture and society. Las Hurdes is a grotesque microcosm of the human condition. The Hurdanos are us. They are not an example of barbarity but of the pathology of civilization. There lies the film's deepest irony.

In his theory of literary modes, classified according to the hero's standing relative to us, Frye has this to say about the ironic mode: "If inferior in power or intelligence to ourselves, so that we have the sense of looking down on a scene of bondage, frustration, or absurdity, the hero belongs to the *ironic* mode. This is still true when the reader feels that he is or might be in the same situation, as the situation is being judged by the norms of a greater freedom."[137] This may seem like an odd conception of irony, but it fits *Land without Bread* perfectly. Irony in this film yields allegory (or its close cousin, extended synecdoche): an allegory identifying the poor Hurdanos with all of us, a documentary allegory of the way we human beings dig our own traps.

Ironic Self-Effacement

Documenters should be self-effacing, or so it is commonly assumed; their job is to let the facts speak for themselves. This may be called the convention of objectivity—the convention governing the pretense of objectivity, the posture of impartiality, in most documentaries and television news shows. The more biased you are, the more fair and balanced you claim to be. Michael Moore, who has brought documentary to unprecedented popularity, often comes under criticism for putting too much of himself into his films and supposedly breaking the rules of documentary. But the notion of an unadorned report of the facts, a straight documentary unadulterated by fiction or rhetoric, is itself a fiction, a rhetorical ploy for gaining the audience's trust. Behind the pretense of objectivity, the self-effacing documenter disguises the work of representation, the choices and emphases it involves, the slant it brings to the things represented. *Land without Bread* parodies that pretense and that notion. Buñuel is ironically self-effacing—self-effacing with a vengeance.

In the writing of history, there is a similar convention of objectivity, which for Roland Barthes rests on the suppression of the first person:

> This occurs when the historian intends to "absent himself" from his discourse and where there is, consequently, a systematic absence of any sign referring to the sender of the historical message: history seems to *tell itself*. . . . On the level of discourse, objectivity—or lack of signs of the "speaker"—thus appears as . . . the product of what we might call the *referential illusion*, since here the historian claims to let the referent speak for itself. This illusion is not peculiar to historical discourse: how many novelists—in the realistic period—imagine they are being "objective" because they suppress signs of the *I* in the discourse![138]

In a work of fiction, however, the presence or absence of the *I* is part of the fiction, part of its conventions, different from those of a factual or historical account. Fiction films conventionally ignore the presence of the camera, and some would see the "referential illusion" in that, but fiction films are dramatic enactments and can't be said to suppress an author's *I* normally absent from drama. It should be added that the eyewitness account, which highlights the *I*, also develops a convention not of objectivity but of firsthand veracity. As Barthes well knows, rhetoric, the attempt to persuade the audience in one way or another, always enters into discourse.

Another ironically self-effacing documenter is Errol Morris. Quite unlike Moore and Lanzmann—who in their different ways are both aggressive interviewers, documenters who feel free to intrude into the document—Morris keeps himself as much as possible out of the picture and lets the people he interviews tell their own stories with minimal interference from him. They don't even talk to him face-to-face. Instead he has them speak into an interviewing machine he devised, where they see his reflection in a mirror and past the mirror they face the camera head on, so that when we watch them on the screen they appear to be bypassing the interviewer and addressing the audience. More than interviewees, they become, in effect, narrators.

A self-made death-house engineer from Massachusetts who went to Auschwitz on his honeymoon and denies that the Holocaust ever took place is the subject of one of Morris's documentaries, *Mr. Death: The Rise and Fall of Fred A. Leuchter Jr.* (1999). Fred Leuchter is here the principal storyteller, not just the subject. This doesn't mean, however, that his own account of his curious, sad story is allowed to stand unchallenged. Morris asks few questions yet is felt all the while as questioning. The ultimate self-effacing interviewer, he nonetheless seems to be pressing us, by his very silence behind the camera, to ask the questions not being asked. It is the irony of the hidden author sensed in the unstated.

Such irony can be found in much prose fiction. Frye links the hidden author to the *eiron*, the self-deprecating person, a prime example being Socrates, who pretends to know nothing in the famous brand of irony that bears his name. "The term irony," Frye writes, "indicates a technique of appearing to be less than one is, which in literature becomes most commonly a technique of saying as little as possible and meaning as much as possible."[139] He's talking about telling, recounting stories verbally rather than performing them dramatically. How does this apply to the movies? In a fiction film, as in a stage play, actors moving and speaking before the eyes and ears of the audience enact a story without the intermediation of a storyteller. The author is out of the picture not as a matter of irony but as a matter of course. Although an author may be implied, may be sensed by the audience, it is an author that can only be hidden, that can only be sensed as an absent cause.

Showing rather than telling, action rather than account, drama rather than narrative, predominate in fiction films. Documentaries are more about telling, more like a recounting than an enactment. Their frequent use of voice-over narration and talking heads attests to this. What a documentary shows is often merely an illustration of what it tells. But who is telling the story? The talking heads seldom tell more than bits and pieces of it. The authoritative, impersonal voice that usually narrates documentaries may be considered authorial but sounds like no human storyteller. If in fiction films the author gives way to the actors, in documentaries the author yields to the facts—or rather to the fiction, the referential illusion, of facts related without embellishment, without manipulation, without bias. This is the exact opposite of *eiron* irony, a pretense not to be less but to be more than one is, an attempt to give the impression of irreproachable objectivity. As in most fiction films, the author in most documentaries is conventionally rather than ironically self-effacing.

Morris is an unconventionally self-effacing interviewer. Like Lanzmann and Moore, he departs from the convention of objectivity, not by coming forward as they do but by going in the opposite direction, by assuming the posture of the *eiron* and intruding so little into what his interviewees have to say that we are led to question them ourselves. The conventional interviewer will neither intrude too much nor let the interviewee, the talking head, talk too long; other interviewees should also have their say, and the voice-over narration should put it all in proper perspective. Morris lets the talking heads in his films talk for longer, often much longer, than usual. He almost never interrupts them with questions, and even though he may insert assorted images, highlighted details, imagined reconstructions of events, bits of old movies or television, the talking voice will often continue unbrokenly as first-person voice-over narration. While the usual interviewee looks off to the side, visibly addressing an interviewer whose presence off screen we are to keep in mind, Morris's interviewees look straight into the camera, straight at us, as if they weren't talking to an interviewer but directly to the viewer. They are given center stage and free rein to tell their stories, and they are, we feel, telling *us* their stories. They take over as storytellers.

Morris did a television series in 2000 and 2001 with the title *First Person*. It's not his own first person but that of his subjects, the talking heads facing his camera and talking to us, addressing us like the first-person narrator of a story. And it isn't just that they speak in the first person—which of course every interviewee does—but that their eyes are fixed in our direction as they speak, that the viewer rather than the interviewer is their second person. The *I* isn't just in their words but in their eyes, in the meeting of their eyes and ours. Before he developed his interviewing machine, Morris would position himself right by the camera when conducting his interviews, so that the subjects looking at him would give as much as possible the impression of looking at us—which approximated but did not fully achieve the first-person effect.

One of his subjects in *First Person* is a man convinced we can defeat death by having our bodies frozen before we die and kept that way until medical science advances enough to cure the illness killing us, at which time we'll be thawed and brought back to life. The man has tried this on his own dying mother. He had her body frozen and her head cut off and stored away in a freezer—whether or not she was decapitated while still alive is an issue that got him into trouble with the law—and he believes she'll be resurrected many years hence in another body. Crazy and incredible though this story may sound, Morris passes no judgment on the sanity or credibility of the storyteller. The man has the floor, and on his proposal for immortality, on his mother's frozen head, Morris takes no position, for or against. By inserting footage from *Frankenstein* (the man says Dr. Frankenstein has always been a hero for him), or from Leni Riefenstahl's *Olympia* (the man talks about the beautiful bodies we'll all have when we rise from the frozen), Morris makes a kind of ironic comment. But mostly he withholds comment, and his irony resides mostly in his withholding of comment. It's the irony of the *eiron*, the man who pretends he knows nothing, who has nothing to say.

Morris's storytelling interviewees may be considered unreliable narrators—not because they're liars, not because they're crazy, but because we can't be sure how far to trust them, because the ground on which to credit them or discredit them has been pulled out from under us. Morris does not endorse them, but neither does he disparage them. His irony is not so much at their expense as it is directed at us in the audience, and it leaves us unsettled, in suspension. Like Buñuel's in *Land without Bread*, it's what Wayne Booth has called *unstable* irony.[140] What are we to make of this wacky, self-assured man who would deal with our mortality through some amalgam of religious faith in everlasting life and faith in science and progress such as has been prevalent in our culture? Or of an autistic woman who has a singular empathy with cattle, is able to put herself in their place and, as she says, not just imagine but really feel what that's like, and so is able to design the best, most humane slaughterhouses?

On television we are to trust news announcers who may be lying or dissembling; in Morris's films we are to distrust interviewees who may be telling the truth. To distrust but not to discount: we are called upon to pay them sustained even if skeptical attention. They are allowed to speak at length but left on their own, and we are left on our own to assess the truth of what they say. Morris gives them a hearing, a forum for telling their stories they wouldn't usually have. His unstable irony asks us to question them without presuming we have the answers, to question not only them but ourselves too. It doesn't simply undercut them; it also undercuts the complacency of simply disbelieving them. These narrators may be unreliable, but Morris credits them enough to lend them in his films the authority of storytellers, which normally they wouldn't enjoy.

His method requires subjects who open up before the camera and microphone and rise to the narrator role he gives them. As a rule he has more than one first-person storyteller in his feature-length films. An exception is *The Fog of War* (2003), where he interviews Robert McNamara and stays with him all the way through. This may have been a mistake, and not just because McNamara never lacked a forum for his stories. On the issue of the Vietnam War, which he admits was wrong and for which he takes a share of the blame, McNamara is still self-justifying and evasive—not a reliable narrator, but not a very interesting unreliable narrator either.

The film's subtitle, *The Rise and Fall of Fred A. Leuchter Jr.* suggests something like a tragedy but with a certain irony, for Leuchter is a little man with nothing like the stature of a tragic hero. Nevertheless, his is a story of rise and fall, and what led to the rise also led to the fall. The self-taught son of a prison guard, Leuchter achieved success as the designer of electric chairs and other execution equipment. Prisons around the country sought his services. He presents himself as a humane man whose technical skill has ameliorated the suffering of those undergoing capital punishment. That was the rise. The fall began when a German in Canada who wrote a pamphlet denying the Holocaust and was being brought to trial for knowingly spreading lies approached Leuchter with the idea that the expert in methods of execution would find evidence in his support and testify in his behalf. This, Leuchter tells us, was an issue of freedom of speech. It was also a project that the self-made engineer took on with the homespun American know-how that had always served him well. He went to Auschwitz and, having just been married, brought his bride along on the trip. Armed with a chisel, he dug into the walls of chambers where Jews were killed with cyanide gas and collected some sample powder for chemical analysis. No cyanide was found in that powder. He testified at the trial (the German was convicted anyway) and published a report saying that Auschwitz couldn't have been an extermination camp. He didn't know what he was doing in his rash excursion into the camp, as a chemist explains to us: cyanide doesn't penetrate past the sheerest layer on the surface of a wall, and any remnant in that powder would have been diluted beyond detection.

This chemist is one of the alternative storytellers enlisted by Morris in this film. Originally, I gather, the plan was to let Leuchter tell the whole story, and to have his version of it called into question by authorial irony alone. But irony, and especially unstable irony, is not something people can be counted on getting, and Morris felt it necessary to discredit Leuchter's Holocaust denial unequivocally, unironically. Apart from that, Leuchter is an unreliable narrator of the same sort as the various others in Morris's films, neither exactly trustworthy nor readily dismissible, somewhat odd and off-putting but with a story to tell that we want to hear. And the fall of Fred Leuchter—the way his business, his marriage, his life fell apart after he collected that powder and testified at that trial and published that report—is another story. Though in Auschwitz he was out of his depth (or his surface), he was nationally recognized for his expertise in capital-punishment engineering—maybe not the most commendable line of work, but one in regular demand—yet nobody would hire him anymore. A little man who didn't know what he was doing may not be a tragic hero, but Leuchter is still a tragic little man who ruined his life by blundering into the politics of the Holocaust. He was persecuted, it seems fair to say, for denying that the Jews were persecuted. And that is another irony.

Open Synecdoche and the Reality Effect

The Deer Hunter (1978), Michael Cimino's Oscar-winning movie about the Vietnam War, has many admirers who have praised it for its "realism." Though a great admirer of the film—and of Cimino's subsequent, spectacularly unsuccessful *Heaven's Gate* (1980)— Robin Wood objects to that way of praising it. The term "realistic" is for him "merely obfuscatory: if not exactly without meaning, its meaning is so vague and diffuse, so prone to slipping from one sense into another . . . as to invalidate it for critical use."[141] It's true that the term often serves just to express approval; anything people find convincing they tend to associate with realism, which since the nineteenth century has been a prevalent idea of what carries conviction. It's also true that in some respects *The Deer Hunter* departs far from realism. But in other respects it may be accurately described as a realistic movie, and precisely because we are dealing with a work that both is and is not realistic, the term is useful and even indispensable. A term having various senses (another such term is "romantic," which can be opposed to "realistic" or allied with it and opposed to "classical") isn't necessarily a disadvantage to critical thinking.

Wood lists several factors he sees as entering into the notion of realism in the movies:

> (1) Identification with sympathetic characters, but also, and more important, with commonly experienced emotions such as delight, excitement, pain, fear, rage. . . . (2) "Suturing": the binding of the spectator, through camera position and editing, into the dramatic situation, either with point-of-view or shot/ reverse-shot figures, or simply by bringing us in so close that we are denied the possibility of contemplative distance. (3) Physicality: suggestions of physical sensation that automatically evoke an empathic response. . . . (4) Spontaneous, naturalistic acting derived from the Method school/Actors' Studio. (5) Superfluity: the use of redundant or irrelevant detail that draws on our sense that life is not a coherent narrative and that lots of things happen simultaneously, giving a sense that this is indeed "life," not an organized fiction. The entire wedding party scene is an unusually sustained and elaborate example of this strategy.[142]

The first three items on this list have to do with identification, sympathy, empathy, involvement—things that may contribute to realism but hardly distinguish it from thrillers or melodramas or horror movies. Take the work of a director dear to Wood, Alfred Hitchcock, a master of identification and "suture," but not a filmmaker anyone would call realistic—least of all himself: "For me, the cinema is not a slice of life," he once said, "but a slice of cake."[143] Though "bringing us in so close that we are denied the possibility of contemplative distance" may be a feature of certain forms of realism, it seems to me that a more distinctively realistic strategy is to pull us back from a closer to a more distant view showing us the characters in relation to their social and material environment. This is a favored strategy of Italian neorealism, and Cimino, who learned much from the neorealists, often uses it in *The Deer Hunter*. I might also add that Brecht, who famously advocates distance, considered himself a realist.

Few will quarrel with Wood's fourth item, "naturalistic acting," though there are different styles of naturalism, and such acting need not be "derived from the Method school," as it mainly is in *The Deer Hunter*. A realistic factor that should have been on the list is shooting on location—the use of actual places rather than studio sets. The documentary quality of the photographic image, the camera's direct rendering of things in the world—even if those things are made part of the world of a fiction—is surely central to most cinematic realism. The long opening section of *The Deer Hunter*, which takes place in Clairton, Pennsylvania, the hometown of three friends being sent to fight in Vietnam—Michael (Robert De Niro), Nick (Christopher Walken), and Steve (John Savage)—"conveys a very distinctive love of rootedness and of the values of people whose town is their world," Pauline Kael writes in her review. "This town of Clairton is actually a composite of a number of locations, most of them in Ohio, but it becomes a clear geographical entity for us, and even the double mobile home that Michael and Nick share feels so accurate that it, too, seems rooted. Nothing was shot in a studio."[144]

The most interesting item on Wood's list is the fifth: "Superfluity . . . redundant or irrelevant detail." This brings to mind the "reality effect" discussed by Roland Barthes.[145] Thinking of realism as a kind of effect rather than a kind of content puts the emphasis on its rhetoric, its relation not to reality but to the audience. Barthes argues that realistic description tends to exceed the compass of meaning, to give us more information than seems relevant; the described aspects and details often go beyond the function of setting the scene, fleshing out the characters, motivating and grounding the story. That excess, according to Barthes, that superfluity of concrete detail we encounter in realism, that attention to particulars signifying nothing in particular, serves to signify the real, the real perceived as "a resistance to meaning."[146] Shooting on location, amid the incalculable detail of actuality, is conducive to such superfluity, such excess. Realism looks for meaning in reality, and its meeting with resistance makes palpable its endeavor to find the significant in the larger field of the real.

The reality effect should be distinguished from the apprehension of reality as a limitless whole, the immensity of mountains or the ocean, the life that goes on beyond measure. Rather than an excess of the whole, what produces the reality effect is an excess of the parts, a sense that the parts exceed their place in the whole. Such is the effect Dickens characteristically achieves through his use of detail, as George Orwell notes: "The outstanding, unmistakable mark of Dickens's writing is the unnecessary detail. . . . Dickens is obviously a writer whose parts are greater than his wholes."[147] Synecdoche, which fits parts into wholes, is a chief means to meaning in realistic representation, and Barthes's point, put another way, is that we get a keener impression of reality just when the part doesn't fit into the whole that would subsume it—open synecdoche, you might call it, the detail that signifies the real by resisting signification, the part that stands for no specifiable whole but for the weight of reality arresting the movement of meaning from part to whole.

Ellipsis goes with synecdoche, and with open synecdoche goes open ellipsis. When a part stands for a whole, the omitted rest of that whole is an ellipsis we can account for; but when the whole is left open, indeterminate, the omission is a gap in our knowledge. Parts in excess of the whole overflow the container, making fluid the boundaries of what fits in, raising our awareness of what is left out, giving us the feeling that any number of aspects and details omitted and unaccounted for could as well have been included. Paradoxical as it may sound, superfluity consorts with its opposite, insufficiency. The inclusion of too much implies the omission of still more. If the sense of a reality resistant to meaning is a mark of realism, then it is a resistance arising from both too much and too little, excess and ellipsis, more than seems necessary and less than seems sufficient. Renoir's realism combines a use of deep focus bringing extra detail into view with an activation of the space off screen calling attention to all that is left out of view. The best episode in Rossellini's neorealist *Paisan* (1946), and the most realistic, is the concluding Po River episode, which is the most elliptical.[148] The lengthy Clairton opening of *The Deer Hunter* achieves its realistic effect both by its profusion of lifelike detail and by the gaps it leaves open—the pieces we feel are missing from the picture. We see, for example, that Linda (Meryl Streep) has an alcoholic father who beats her, but we only get a glimpse of her troubled family life, a brief glimpse suggestive of much more than we ever go into.

Hometown and War

The rhetorical reality effect is not the same thing as the truthful representation of reality. Realism in the sense of truthfulness may be opposed to idealization, which is what Kael sees in Cimino's picture of the Pennsylvania hometown: "an enraptured view of common life" with "a detailed clarity: we feel that we're storing up memories. There's something nostalgic about this ceremonial view of ordinary American community life even as it's going on."[149] It's not all charm and ceremony, however; look at Linda and her abusive alcoholic father, or at Steve and his pregnant bride, whom he marries just before going off to Vietnam but who, as he confides to Nick after the wedding, carries another man's baby. Wood (following Andrew Britton) compares the wedding party, which seems to involve the whole town and is also a farewell party for Steve, Nick, and Michael, to the church dance in Ford's *My Darling Clementine*, though he perceives a difference: Cimino's film "cannot be read simply as endorsing a nostalgia for the organic community."[150] But then neither can Ford's, which portrays an unfinished church and an unfinished community, a frontier past looking forward to a future, a nascent town idealized as an aspiration rather than an attainment. Cimino's Clairton is less idealized, more realistically depicted; but Kael accurately detects something nostalgic about the picture—nostalgic for a traditional, endangered way of life. The Russian Orthodox church where the wedding takes place and the ethnic community to which the Russian American main characters belong are an enclave of the old under threat from the ambient modernity. Here the future is nothing to look forward to.

The Deer Hunter begins with a big truck rushing through the streets of Clairton in the early morning, an image both realistic (trucks going too fast are common in this country, where truckers are paid by the job rather than the hour) and symbolic of an unstoppable outsize modernity imposing itself on the everyday life of Clairton. Then we cut to the blast furnace in the town's steel mill, where Michael, Nick, and Steve are working the night shift for the last time before reporting for duty. The film draws a parallel—Wood calls it "the inferno motif"[151]—between the fires blazing in the Clairton steel mill and the fires of war in Vietnam, and this metaphoric connection intimates an actual connection between the industrial capitalism ruling over the workers' hometown and the war they're being sent to fight overseas. The workers themselves don't seem to make this connection, however, and there is a certain irony in the discrepancy between the characters' consciousness and the author's.

"Cimino is not much interested in the men's working-class status," Wood maintains (agreeing with Britton and with Mike Westlake).[152] I would have thought unmistakable the working-class allegiance of this movie. True, it gives no analysis of class relations—it doesn't show factory bosses or anyone in Clairton from a higher class—but its whole picture of the town is a portrayal of life among the working class, the class from which, in disproportionate numbers, the American soldiers who went to Vietnam were recruited. And in its picture of the war, the film stays with its main characters, within the ambit of the enlisted working class. None of the other Vietnam movies—*Coming Home, Apocalypse Now, Platoon, Full Metal Jacket*—makes so clear to the audience the fact that, like every war waged by the United States since, it was a war fought by the unprivileged. But again, the characters don't seem to be aware of that fact, of that unfair burden falling on them; nor would they think of protesting even if they were.

The ironic sense that the author knows more than the characters is salient at two moments during the wedding party. When the three Vietnam-bound friends encounter at the bar a returned Green Beret, they ask him, "What's it like over there?" The only reply they get is a repeated, "Fuck it." They don't register as we do what this portends for their upcoming tour of duty. The second moment occurs when Steve and his bride drink wine together from a double-cupped wedding goblet, a traditional ritual in which they are to drink the wine down without spilling a drop, which means good luck for the rest of their lives. But we are enabled to see, in tight close-up, what neither bride nor groom notices: two red drops of wine spill on her white dress, a presage of bad luck and also, metaphorically, of spilled blood. Here Cimino's camera is not merely an observer but a knowing narrator letting us know that something bad is in store for this couple and for the groom going away to war.

This is dramatic irony of a kind having to do not so much with the occurring action as with authorial comment and foreshadowing. It is, however, rather unstable irony. Although we sense a discrepancy between the author and the characters, where the author stands isn't entirely clear. "Unlike such makers of epics as Coppola and Bertolucci," Kael remarks, "Cimino doesn't seem to want his themes to rise to our full consciousness (or perhaps even to his own)."[153] Despite the Green Beret's "Fuck it"—and despite Vietnam scenes in which, as Kael describes them, the "American helicopters are like Walpurgisnacht locusts coming down on your head, and no one who believed that the Americans behaved honorably in Vietnam would have staged the evacuation of Saigon as Cimino has done, with thousands of Vietnamese abandoned and despairing"[154]—*The Deer Hunter* can't be said to be against the Vietnam War, though it can't be said to be for it either.

With Steve off with his bride on their brief honeymoon, Michael takes Nick and three of their friends in his white Cadillac up into the mountains to hunt deer. When, in this "last, ritual hunt before Vietnam," as Kael writes, "Michael climbs to the top of a virgin mountain and, with a snowcapped peak behind him and a male choir in the sky singing a Russian Orthodox liturgical chant and rain clouds swirling about him, stalks a buck and fells it with one clean shot,"[155] realism is left behind and something like myth or allegory comes into play. Michael is being identified with the mythical frontier hero, the cowboy whose white horse has become a white Cadillac with tail fins. This deer hunter traces his ancestry back to the deerslayer of Fenimore Cooper's Leatherstocking Tales. This scene "cannot be taken ironically," Wood says, but at the same time he recognizes that neither is it "simply to be read straight, the 'standard emblems of romantic uplift' (Britton) being clearly placed, as it were, within quotation marks."[156] What are such quotation marks if not a form of irony? The deer hunt up in the mountains outside the town, the Russian Orthodox chant, the heady communion with nature, the ritual of felling the deer with one shot, even the frontier mythology—these are all part of the characters' world, but their compound effect of romantic grandiosity belongs to the author. It's an ironic effect, though nothing undercuts it, because of the author's distance from characters who would never see themselves and their experience in quite that way, and because of his earnest yet less than confident striving—hence the quotation marks—to call forth a mythical past in opposition to a menacing future. The full-blown heroic portrayal of Michael the deer hunter ironically marks itself off as a departure from the reality that until now the film has been depicting. And that departure serves as a transition from hometown to war.

When *The Deer Hunter* moves on to Vietnam, it moves away from the realism of the Clairton preamble to an allegory of brutal, indiscriminate, engulfing violence. This corresponds to the experience of characters whose reality is their hometown and who now find themselves in a strange land fighting a strange war. The shift in style of representation reflects the characters' subjectivity—Walter Benjamin's point about the subjectivity of allegory certainly applies here—but it is the characters' subjectivity embroidered by the author and writ large on the canvas of Vietnam. The war's dirty violence and the clean violence of the hunt, however different they may be, are both violence all the same, and they are both presented in terms of feeling rather than fact, a feeling of exaltation in the ritual hunt, a feeling of degradation in the bloody mess of Vietnam, but in neither case an objective, realistic picture.

Those who find the Vietnam sequences "realistic" are responding to the graphic violence, which has a strong visceral impact (the third item on Wood's list, "physical sensation"); but by this measure the oozing sliced eye in *Un Chien andalou* would be the most realistic image of all. Kael points out both the skill and the slant of Cimino's action scenes, as well as his metaphoric rather than realistic use of physical sensation:

> It's in the contrast . . . between the Clairton sequences, with all those people joined together in slowly rhythmed takes, and the war in Vietnam, where everything is spasmodic, fast, in short takes, with cuts from one anguished face to another, that Cimino shows his filmmaking instinct and craft. But also his xenophobic yellow-peril imagination. . . . [Michael, Nick and Steve] are taken prisoner and are tortured strictly for their captors' pleasure. The prisoners are forced to play Russian roulette in teams while the Vietcong gamble on which one will blow his head off.
>
> The Vietnam War—and, more particularly, Russian roulette—serves Cimino metaphorically as the Heart of Darkness. . . . These prison-camp torture sequences are among the finest-edited action scenes that I know of. . . . They are the very center of the film. . . . The sheer force of these pulp atrocity scenes takes over one's consciousness. I say "pulp" because the Vietcong are treated in the standard inscrutable-evil-Oriental style of the Japanese in Second World War movies and because Russian roulette takes over as the ruling metaphor for all the action scenes in the rest of the movie.[157]

Some have upheld the "realism" of this ruling metaphor by claiming that the Vietcong actually played Russian roulette with their prisoners. This seems unlikely. The Vietcong may have tortured prisoners, but the systematic, sadistic game of chance they play in the film bears the stamp of fabrication. In any case, factual accuracy is not the issue. Fiction can take liberties with the facts it draws on—as Cimino does by constructing a Pennsylvania town out of several locations in Ohio—but realism requires lifelikeness, verisimilitude. The Clairton sequences are convincingly lifelike; the Vietnam sequences are a nightmare whose central, recurring image is Russian roulette. After Michael, Nick, and Steve escape from the Vietcong, the nightmare continues, and so does the Russian roulette, to which Nick becomes addicted—addicted to the risk of blowing his head off—and which he plays compulsively in Saigon gambling dens. Verisimilitude, by this point, is nil—try to figure the odds against your survival if you repeatedly put to your head a gun with one bullet in the barrel and pull the trigger—yet the film holds its audiences by force of metaphor. The utter contingency of such violence potently allegorizes what the soldiers in Vietnam felt they were up against.

This viscerally gripping allegory allows no ironic distance. Instead it manifests a close identification between Cimino and his characters, between what he expresses and what they experience. His "xenophobic yellow-peril imagination" reflects what many ordinary Americans felt in Vietnam—or what he takes them to have felt and feels with them, which hardly clears him of blame. But he "is not merely trying to move people by pandering to their prejudices," as Kael says. "This movie may offend conventional liberal thinking more by its commitment to parochial, 'local' values than by any defense of the Vietnam War—for it makes none."[158] Though *The Deer Hunter* is, I daresay, one of the best pictures to win the Academy Award for best picture, I can think of no other so widely attacked after it won. But look at other war movies; look at such Vietnam movies as *Apocalypse Now* and *Platoon*, which take a position against the war, and you will find few that even for a short stretch sympathetically adopt the enemy's point of view. War movies, as Diane Stevenson has argued, are nearly always about our side, not the enemy. *The Deer Hunter* portrays the Vietnam War from the local, parochial point of view of small-town working-class Americans sent to fight over there, which may not be a way to understand the war but puts us in touch with their sentiments in its midst. Soldiers at war tend to see the enemy as brutal and vicious— and modern nations enlisting soldiers from the common people tend to demonize the enemy in order to promote the willingness to fight it. The nightmarish subjectivity of the Russian roulette allegory represents the subjective experience of soldiers thrown into the maelstrom of Vietnam. This is not to excuse the xenophobia or racism of ordinary Americans, but to question the self-righteousness of those who complacently feel superior to them.

A famous Vietnam photograph, Eddie Adams's *Saigon Execution*, shows a South Vietnamese officer killing a Vietcong in the street by putting a gun to his head. Cimino acknowledged that horrifying picture, which many in the audience would have seen, as the inspiration for the game of Russian roulette in *The Deer Hunter*. But the gun to the head is transposed from the photograph's summarily executed Vietcong onto American soldiers compelled to play Russian roulette, first by their Vietcong captors and finally by the internalized demons of war. Sylvia Shin Huey Chong has aptly construed this transposition as making an identification between Americans and the Vietnamese with a gun to his head whose place they assume in the picture.[159] Chong seems to think, though, that all the violence in Vietnam was

American violence inflicted on the Vietnamese, and she deems it unwarranted, narcissistic, for Americans to assume the victim's place, which in her view belongs to the Vietnamese alone. Like other critics, she takes no account of class in *The Deer Hunter* and sees its characters as privileged Americans, privileged because Americans. But the workers from Clairton sent overseas as combatants represent the unprivileged Americans who, because unprivileged, bore the brunt of war in Vietnam. They are indeed war victims and can rightly step into the picture with a gun to their heads.

Leaving Nick behind, Michael returns from Vietnam, and finds that Steve has returned already as a cripple. On another hunt with his friends, Michael now spares the deer. He seems to have renounced violence, but the way his friends play with guns makes him violent, and he could have killed one of them whose gun he angrily turns on him in a round of Russian roulette. Violence has failed Michael. It can no longer be exalted but only degraded. Though close enough to a war hero, he can no longer be identified with the frontier hero but only with the Vietnamese with a gun to his head. The shock of this recognition comes when he goes back to Vietnam in search of Nick, his childhood friend and in effect his double, who shared with him not only a double mobile home but also, in a way never spelled out, a love for Linda, who stays in their mobile home while they are away. In the gambling den where he finds him, Michael tries to rescue Nick from the insanity of continually staking his life with a gun to his head. The two friends play Russian roulette against each other, and Nick, just before he shoots himself, smilingly recalls the "one shot" with which, in the mystique of the hunt, the hunter is to fell his prey. The frontiersman allegory and the Russian roulette allegory, the clean, skillful violence of the deer hunter's one shot and the dirty random violence of the war in Vietnam, are here brought together in a conclusive repudiation of violence.

God Bless America

Nothing is more important to the rhetoric of a work, to the way it affects its audience, than our sense of the author's attitude toward the characters. In Clairton the author knows more than the characters—not about the town where they have lived all their lives but about what awaits them in Vietnam. Over there he identifies with their disconcerted subjectivity, which informs his whole picture of the war. In the realistic rendering of the hometown community we sense an unhurried sympathy shaded with concern, a nostalgia for the present apprehensive about the future; in the deer hunt before Vietnam we sense an effort to dispel that apprehension by invoking a mythical heroic past; in the allegory of the war's arbitrary brutality we sense a heightened, quickened, alarmed empathy verging on expressionism. Cimino assumes toward his characters and their situation a variable attitude not always easy to gauge, and thus conducive to authorial irony. Take the memorable final scene, which some regard as simple flag-waving patriotism. Yet this is an ending colored and deepened with irony of a special, poignant kind.

Michael returns again from Vietnam, this time with Nick's body, which is buried in Clairton. After the funeral, Michael, Linda, Steve in his wheelchair, Steve's wife, and several other friends gather for breakfast. While making scrambled eggs for the group, one of the friends tearfully starts humming and singing "God Bless America." Linda at the table starts singing too, and then the whole group of friends sings "God Bless America." After what America has done to them, after burying a dear friend killed where America sent him, and with another friend at the table crippled in the name of America, how can they sing its blessings? The film leads us to ask this question, which puts us in the position of irony. But the scene is heartbreaking, and the irony that enters into our response is complex, unstable, certainly not the derisive or dismissive kind.

Aren't the characters singing "God Bless America" aware of how America has betrayed them? By now they must be aware, maybe not fully but at least dimly, and to the extent they are aware they are themselves being ironic. But we can't doubt the sincerity of their patriotism, and in their tragedy they seem to cling to the feeling that America is their home sweet home. Who are we to tell them they're wrong to cling to that feeling? What makes the scene so moving is that we may think they're wrong, but we still feel with them—feel with them all the more because we think they're wrong. The author, and we with him, may have an awareness they lack, but he neither feels nor allows us to feel superior to them. Irony often undercuts sentiment, but this is irony that increases sentiment.

The High of War

The Hurt Locker (2008) is the lowest-grossing Oscar winner for best picture and the first movie to win for a woman, Kathryn Bigelow, the Oscar for best director. It's a war movie about the war on terror, though Bigelow maintains, and many have agreed, that it's not a political film but a character study. The central character is Sergeant William James (Jeremy Renner), leader of a squad of American soldiers in Iraq assigned to the task of disarming terrorist bombs.

Aristotle, who believes in nothing in excess, defines courage as a mean between fear and confidence; the coward has excessive fear, the rash man excessive confidence, and the brave man strikes the right balance between the two.[160] A "redneck piece of trailer trash," as a riled member of his squad calls him in the washroom, Sergeant James is bold and deft at his hazardous job but also cocky, imprudent, prone to recklessness rather than what Aristotle considered true courage. The film opens with a quotation from Chris Hedges: "The rush of battle is often a potent and lethal addiction, for war is a drug." At the end James has returned home from his tour of duty, but he feels restless there and tells his little boy that "the older you get, the fewer things you really love, and by the time you get to my age maybe it's only one or two things. . . . With me I think it's one," whereupon we see him back in Iraq for another tour of duty disarming bombs. Just as Nick in *The Deer Hunter* is addicted to Russian roulette, so, it becomes clear, James is addicted to the high of war.

You don't know who your enemy is, who among the Iraqis around you may be a terrorist, when a bomb may blow up that will tear you to pieces: "Every time we go out," says a distraught squad member sitting in an army truck beside James, "it's life or death, you roll a dice." Like the game of Russian roulette in *The Deer Hunter*, *The Hurt Locker* gives us an excruciating sense of the contingency of violence, of life or death as a matter of chance, though it conveys that sense through a more realistic picture of war. Grippingly photographed on location not in Iraq but right across the border in Jordan, *The Hurt Locker* uses roving multiple cameras that plunge us into the midst of the ongoing action with the immediacy of a newsreel. James and his fellow soldiers are well trained in the skills of war; they are better equipped for the deathly game of chance than their counterparts in *The Deer Hunter*, and better suited to be war heroes. At a screening of Bigelow's film at the Museum of Modern Art followed by a panel with the director, the scriptwriter (Mark Boal), and the three main actors, the moderator of the occasion called James a "superhero"—not the word for a man with an unappeasable craving for war's adrenaline. Still, despite his flaws, James is a likable, in some ways admirable, character. He can be placed in a long line of American heroes, like Cagney, Bogart, Mitchum, James Dean, Clint Eastwood—the bad boys who break rules and take chances and go too far. *The Hurt Locker* is a sympathetic character study, and at the same time, like *The Deer Hunter*, it incisively questions American heroism.

Unlike Cimino, however, Bigelow invokes no myth, no legendary frontier heroism against which to measure the protagonist as we measure Michael in *The Deer Hunter*. James the adrenaline addict is a particular case realistically observed but not clearly invested with

a general significance. We can't take him as a typical American soldier in Iraq; we can't take his addiction, as we take Nick's in *The Deer
Hunter*, to represent the trauma so often suffered by soldiers in war.
He's Nick and Michael combined into one: his addiction is indistinguishable from his heroism. If he's too singular to typify the common
soldier, then he's too ordinary, too low in social class and military
rank, to symbolize the aberrations of ruling power. We can't aggran-
dize his craziness into the insane authority responsible for the war—
he's no Dr. Caligari.

After a devastating explosion, probably the work of a suicide
bomber, James thinks that the perpetrators may be alive and somewhere around, hiding in the night, and he stubbornly leads his squad
into the dark streets on a futile search resulting in serious injury for
one of the soldiers and retreat for the group. Searching in the dark for
an enemy nowhere to be found could be construed as an image of the
whole American invasion and occupation of Iraq. And such an allegorical reading can be carried further. It can be argued that, at least
since the time of the Cold War, at whose end there was no peace but a
continuation of bellicosity through to the war on terror with no end in
sight, the people of the United States have been living in a climate of
continual war, have been nationally addicted to war as James is individually, so that he personifies a disorder afflicting the whole country.
Yet *The Hurt Locker* is not an allegory, and it is not quite an extended
synecdoche either. It stays acutely close to the actuality of agonizing
peril, which exerts a strong gravitational pull down from the level of
ideas, and it doesn't readily move from the particular to the general.
Call it an extended open synecdoche, open to possible paths of meaning between the particular and the general. *The Hurt Locker* is a political film in the way of irony—the irony of the author who keeps mum
and lets us see, as if things spoke for themselves. But they don't, and
it's up to us to draw inferences and make connections in our quest for
a meaning that the author declines to assign to things.

Reflexivity and Comedy

The Merriam-Webster dictionary defines *reflexive* as "directed or
turned back on itself," and also, with regard to works of art, as
"overtly and usu. ironically reflecting conventions of genre or form."[161]
A movie is reflexive when it calls attention to itself as a movie, when
it makes manifest to the viewer its conventions and its artifice.

Acknowledging the artifice of art is characteristic of modernism
and the avant-garde. But reflexivity is no modern invention or avant-
garde innovation. Art can be reflexive in different ways, for different

motives, with different aims. Look at a child's playacting, the pretend people and pretend objects not soliciting belief but offered in a
spirit of make-believe: there you have a spontaneous reflexivity at the
earliest stage of artistic activity. Modernist or avant-garde reflexivity
comes at a late stage when artists grow self-conscious and alienated
from society, strangers in the big city who find their own community
in their art itself, their shared medium and practice of expression.[162]
Consider the filmmakers of the American avant-garde, from Maya
Deren and Stan Brakhage to Ernie Gehr and Su Friedrich, and the way
they have seen themselves as an artistic underground at odds with
the commercial illusionism of Hollywood.

In Ernie Gehr's *Serene Velocity* (1970), the camera stands in an
empty corridor for twenty-three minutes. Nobody comes or goes;
neither the camera nor anything else in the corridor moves. Only the
lens itself changes, the eye of the beholder. It is a zoom lens rapidly
alternating between two different focal lengths growing farther and
farther apart, so that the corridor seems to shake faster and faster. We
are made aware that a film is composed of still frames mechanically
animated into the illusion of motion, aware that a movie's movement
is a deception of the eye—and also aware of the lines of perspective converging at the center of the picture and acting like well-oiled
tracks along which the walls and floor and ceiling appear to slide
back and forth with mounting speed. *Serene Velocity* lays bare the joint
workings of the camera and the projector, the machine that sees and
the machine that sets in motion.

Not long afterward, a theory of the cinematographic apparatus
became fashionable in the academy: a theory about the "bourgeois
ideology" supposedly built into the apparatus, whose imitation of the
perspective of an individual eye was taken as ready-made bourgeois
individualism.[163] *Serene Velocity* depersonalizes the individual eye and
in that way could be said to subvert individualism; but it is never
made clear exactly what the ideology is that the bourgeois conform
to. It is assumed, though, that illusion is a bad thing—Plato's cave is
invoked—and it follows that a film reflecting on itself and dispelling
illusion does a good thing. But the illusion of movement in *Serene
Velocity* is so potent that no reflexivity can dispel it. We know very well
that a corridor doesn't move, yet we can't help seeing it move on the
screen and gain velocity. This reflection on the means of film serves
to exhibit the inescapability, the indispensability, of illusion. Lauded
in some quarters as the right thing to do, the answer to the lies of
illusion and ideology, reflexivity is not morally or politically superior
to illusionism but an artistic and rhetorical strategy like any other.[164]

Reflexivity in art goes back to antiquity. Ever since Aristophanes made fun of Socrates in *The Clouds* by having him brought down from his lofty thoughts onto the stage in a basket, comedy has been disposed to show its hand, to let its audience see the contrivance of its representations and invite our knowing, smiling assent to its fancies and fabrications. It differs from tragedy not in being less serious but in taking itself less seriously, not in dealing with things that are less real but in making us more aware of its remove from reality. It thus enables us to laugh at things that in real life wouldn't be so funny, like Chaplin snowbound in *The Gold Rush* (1925) with a burly companion driven by hunger to imagine him as an appetizing outsize chicken. Comedy has a long tradition of manifest artifice.

The reflexivity of comedy is perhaps most evident in parody. Parody is inherently reflexive; it calls for awareness of the work, the genre, the conventions being parodied. W. C. Fields's mordant short comedy *The Fatal Glass of Beer* (1933, directed by Clyde Bruckman) is a parody of wilderness melodramas, and its point of departure is a parody of country ballads. "There was once a poor young man who left his country home," a mock-sad song by the vaudeville comedian Charlie Case, is sung to a weeping Mountie in the opening scene by Fields as a Yukon prospector intoning the tale of his wastrel son, Chester, whose first drink in the wicked city led straight to perdition ("And he staggered through the door with delirium tremens"). *The Fatal Glass of Beer* was originally a theater piece, and it flaunts its theatricality, its hammy performances and stagy props, its cabin in the frozen north that is obviously a set. Just as, in a running joke, Fields gets a handful of patently fake snow thrown in his face on cue each time he looks out the cabin door and says, "And it ain't a fit night out for man nor beast," so the film keeps throwing its fakery in the viewer's face. Its theatricality is all the more flagrant because it is a film and because, being a film, it could have gone out on location and shown us the real frozen north. Instead it uses stock footage and back projection in a manner as purposely, pointedly phony as the snow in Fields's face, a parody of the convention that would have us accept as a real setting for the action inserted or back-projected footage of a locale where the actors never set foot.

After drinking the city's fatal glass of beer and going to jail for stealing some bonds and money, Chester returns to his country home and repentantly confesses that he was indeed guilty of the theft, first to his Ma, who says she knew and asks him not to tell his Pa because it would break his poor old heart, and then to his Pa, who says he knew and asks him not to tell his Ma because it would break her poor old heart. Pa Fields segues to the question, "Chester, have you any of them bonds on you, or any of that money?" No, Chester replies, no bonds and none of that tainted money. Whereupon Pa and Ma crossly break a pitcher and two bowls on Chester's head and throw the prodigal son in his pajamas out into the frozen wilderness.

Reflexivity, the dictionary tells us, is usually ironic. Irony gainsays figuratively what it says literally, the trope of contradiction. *Serene Velocity* could be called ironic because it has the projector contradict the camera: the camera depicts a corridor while the projector sets it in motion, quite unlike a corridor. Parody is ironic in the way it adopts a form or style only to subvert it, to negate the meanings and sentiments normally expressed through it. *The Fatal Glass of Beer* ironically gives the lie to the common view that the country is clean and wholesome and the city dirty and corrupt. The unctuous overacting brings out the falsity of the rustic characters; the bogus country setting shows up as bogus the notion of the country's moral superiority to the city. Much in the manner of Brechtian alienation, reflexivity in *The Fatal Glass of Beer* serves to perform a critique of ideology—not of some vague "bourgeois ideology" but of a precise and still prevalent way of thinking about the country and the city.

As well as critical detachment, however, reflexivity can bring on involvement. Comedians from Charlie Chaplin to Woody Allen often directly address us in the audience. When Stan Laurel does something particularly foolish, Oliver Hardy will cast a glance in our direction, asking us to share his exasperation with his partner. While reflexively reminding us that we are watching a movie, pulling us back from the illusion, the comedian's aside to the audience establishes a rapport with us that at the same time draws us in. It may break the conventional fourth wall between actor and spectator, but it brings us closer to the comedian through the breach. Chaplin's tramp is a character oriented toward the audience, a social outsider who turns to us for human sympathy and understanding. Even if nobody loves him in the uncaring world he inhabits, we do; it's to us watching him on the screen that he primarily relates. What he can't get in life, he gets in art.

"Fields's alienation effect is absolute, surpassing Brechtian imitations," writes Harold Bloom in his essay on *The Fatal Glass of Beer*, his favorite movie.[165] He claims absolute alienation yet shows ardent appreciation. The fact is that to be effective, the alienation effect cannot be absolute: it must always be relative to some degree of illusion, some sort of involvement it works to restrain. Brecht never aimed to do away with illusion and emotion, only to hold them in check. He knew that theater without them wouldn't be theater. If he sought to pull us back, he would also draw us in, would enact a give-and-take between drawing us in and pulling us back. Sour, irascible Fields seems to have detested sweet, endearing Chaplin, but Brecht greatly admired him; he even lifted from him for one play half the plot of *City Lights*, the half about the millionaire who befriends the tramp when drunk but repudiates him when sober.

In *Monsieur Verdoux* (1947), his most Brechtian movie, Chaplin gives up his lovable tramp and plays a businessman whose business is marrying and murdering women. Yet this unlovable character still turns to us in the audience. Pressed to raise a large sum of money by the next morning, Verdoux rushes to one of his wives, whom he plans to kill, but first he must talk her into taking all her money out of the bank before it closes. She sits grim-faced on a couch, and he steals glances at the clock as he mellifluously endeavors to persuade her. Standing behind the couch, he says: "Life can so easily degenerate into something sordid and vulgar. Let us try to keep it beautiful and dignified." He's speaking to her but looking toward the camera, facing us (who know what he's up to), and addressing us with his eyes. Is Verdoux seeking our complicity, or is he defying our judgment? Is he shameless or ashamed? Is he admitting to us that he's doing something sordid and vulgar? Is he pleading with us that he's trying to keep life beautiful and dignified—not for this wife, of course, but for his real wife in their placid suburban home, for the real family he would keep secure by means of all these killings? In *Monsieur Verdoux*, Robert Warshow observes, "there is no solid point of reference; everything is open to question. The meanings shift and turn and spread until the whole movie, and ultimately the whole world, is enveloped in ambiguity and irony, and it is no longer certain whom the joke is on. Not only is Verdoux caught in his own irony; sometimes it is we in the audience who are caught, and sometimes Chaplin himself."[166] Verdoux has something of the tramp in him, and looking right at the camera helps him achieve a rapport with the audience not so different from the tramp's—albeit an unstable and complicated rapport. At moments unmistakably reverting to the tramp, Chaplin reflexively plays on our awareness of him as the actor long famous as that character and now before us as Verdoux. Verdoux is the tramp corrupted, the lovable individual who turns his lovability, the personal humanity that had earlier set him apart from an impersonal society, into a business asset in the business of murder.

Fields's alienation effect cuts through the ideology of rustic morality and unmasks his Yukon prospector as greedy and nasty. Isn't that what, under a mask of refinement rather than rusticity, Verdoux basically is? Aren't both these films unambiguous in their critique of capitalism as greedy and nasty, whether in the country or the city? Yes, but the critique in *The Fatal Glass of Beer* is the author's critique, not the character's, whereas Verdoux is himself a critic of his ruthless business practices, which he sees as something he has been forced to do in order to provide for his family, and moreover something that is done all the time, and on a much larger scale, in a ruthless world. Verdoux's critique is a self-justification, a self-deception, as Warshow argues:

> Despite the clarity of his original perceptions, Verdoux becomes corrupt, and with the corruption not so much of a murderer as of a businessman. It is a hard struggle, he tells us; I go into the jungle only because I must fight for my wife and my child, all that I love in the world. When he says this he is not to be trusted. The jungle is everything to him and his home is only his convenient excuse—characterless blond child and colorless dull wife (how useful that she is crippled!), existing only so that he may have a symbol to justify his ambition.[167]

The critic is part of what he criticizes, and his critique is itself part of the ideology that rationalizes his participation. Chaplin's alienation effect thus performs a double critique: it criticizes the critic's illusion of a firm ground on which he can stand back and criticize, which is why in *Monsieur Verdoux* irony endlessly reverberates.

Modernist Parody

Parody is always reflexive and ironical but not always comical. It has been put to serious use in the art of modernism.[168] Modernist painting can be said to begin with Manet, whose *Déjeuner sur l'herbe* and *Olympia* are both parodies of Renaissance paintings, the *Déjeuner* of the *Pastoral Concert* attributed to Giorgione or Titian and *Olympia* of Titian's *Venus of Urbino*. According to Aristotle, the inventor of parody was Hegemon of Thasos, who, one gathers, would make epic poetry ridiculous by altering the words, twisting them into the coarse and common, while keeping to the stately meter, the noble style of epic. Giving low content an elevated form is just what Manet does in *Olympia* by portraying a recognizable prostitute, a *demimondaine*, in a composition deliberately evoking the *Venus of Urbino*. Neither Titian's painting nor his own is thereby made ridiculous, however. We may smile at the Venus turned into a courtesan, but *Olympia*, even if no longer shocking the way it was in its day, still has an unsettling effect and demands a serious response. Manet did parodies but not mockeries.

Whether the low in the form of the high or vice versa, incongruity between form and content has been an enduring method of parody. It is a breach of decorum, the rhetorical principle that calls for the fitting, the appropriate. Decorum prescribes a style appropriate to the subject matter: the high for the high, the low for the low. Comical parody plays against decorum yet in that way keeps it in place. We know what would be fitting when we laugh at the unfitting, know what the rules are that are being broken, and know how we are to respond. Modernist parody pulls the rules out from under us. It holds decorum in negotiable suspension, opens to question what the fit between style and subject should be, and what on our part would be a suitable response. Modernism gives us unstable parody.

A prime example in film is Buñuel's parody travelogue about Las Hurdes, which arouses a laughter acutely uncomfortable. Andy Warhol's movies—such as *Sleep* (1963), whose six hours of a man sleeping, fixedly depicted, can be seen as a parodic inversion of the avant-garde dream film[169]—are another example. For another, look at the irony verging on parody—ambiguous enough to have gone undetected by audiences at the time—of Douglas Sirk's Hollywood melodramas of the 1950s, or at the outright parody melodramas made in the 1970s by his admirer, R. W. Fassbinder. And a dedicated practitioner of unstable parody over a long career, and for many an epitome of cinematic modernism, is Jean-Luc Godard.[170]

Incongruity is central to Godard's way with parody: incongruity between form and content, between fiction and documentary, between the story and the image and between the image and the word, between action and reflection, spontaneity and calculation, sad truth and splendid beauty. The very beauty of his images rests on an incongruity. Godard always films with available light: he takes the camera out into the world and uses only the world's light, the light of day, the city lights of night, the actual light of an actual place, without recourse to the concealed lamps and reflectors normally used to light a scene for the camera. Available light incongruously combines naturalness and artificiality. It is a documentary light, a light that visibly comes from reality, yet at the same time it yields an image prone to being overexposed (when the daylight is too bright) or underexposed (when the light indoors or in the streets at night is too dim) and so draws attention to the camera's difference from the human eye, the contrivance of the photographic image. Whatever it is—it's obviously not just a matter of leaving the camera open to the light of things in the world—no one else does with available light what Godard does, which brings about a singular beauty. "Everything beautiful," Novalis says, is "self-illuminated."[171] Lit by a light seen to shine from the depicted things themselves, Godard's images have that quality. Yet in their mixture of palpable actuality and undisguised artifice, they also have a paradoxical quality characteristic of a body of films everywhere marked by the play of incongruity and the concomitant tendency to parody.

In his second film, *Le Petit Soldat* (1960), his first with Anna Karina, she is the splendid beauty and the sad truth is the Algerian war. (The film was banned by the French government for its political content and was not released until after the war was over.) Godard's love affair with Karina, who became his wife, began during the filming—not an unusual thing to happen, but no other film makes a director's falling in love with an actress so luminous on the screen. "Photography is truth, and the cinema is truth twenty-four times a second," muses the wordy, opinionated hero (Michel Subor) while taking photos of Karina, a woman who captivates him the moment he lays eyes on her. An objectionable character and an unreliable narrator, this protagonist is nonetheless a surrogate for the author, with whose camera he is identified as he focuses on Karina, photographing beauty and talking about truth. The photographer and his subject come together romantically but are on opposite sides politically, he with the militant right-wing French and she with the fighters for Algerian independence. She dies at the hands of his thuggish comrades, yet her beauty and her truth abide in this film he retrospectively narrates and lead him to reflect on the error of his political ways. He quotes a phrase he attributes to Lenin, "Ethics are the aesthetics of the future," which he finds "very beautiful and very moving too. It reconciles the right and the left." But actually the phrase is Maxim Gorky's and goes the other way: aesthetics as the ethics of the future. Neither the character nor the author can be trusted. We are to think for ourselves about the relation between ethics and aesthetics, which Karina personifies. *Le Petit Soldat* ironically assumes the form of a spy thriller, a genre that touches on political issues but usually treats them as a pretext for melodramatic action. Godard turns that around. Here melodramatic action serves to deal with political and philosophical issues. He parodies the spy thriller not to make fun of it but to take it more seriously.

If in *Le Petit Soldat* Karina is beauty awakening the hero to truth, in *Alphaville* (1965), a parody of two genres together, science fiction and the secret agent movie, she is beauty awakened by the hero to truth. Godard's films of that time—his New Wave period—freely made use of popular film genres, the crime movie in *Breathless* (1960) and *Bande à part* (1964), the musical in *A Woman Is a Woman* (1961), the fallen-woman melodrama in *Vivre sa vie* (1962), the fugitive couple melodrama intermittently crossed with the musical in the finally suicidal *Pierrot le fou* (1965). All these films draw on generic conventions but never settle into them. *Bande à part*, for example, though based on a crime novel, idiosyncratically transforms it into something "like a reverie of a gangster movie as students in an espresso bar might remember it or plan it," as Pauline Kael writes in her review, which describes the film well:

> The two heroes . . . begin by playacting crime and violence movies, then really act them out in their lives. Their girl, wanting to be accepted, tells them there is money in the villa where she lives. And we watch, apprehensive and puzzled, as the three of them act out the robbery they're committing as if it were something going on in a movie—or a fairy tale. The crime does not fit the daydreamers nor their milieu: we half expect to be told it's all a joke.[172]

It's not a joke, however—it's a parody but not a mockery. Nor is it a simple case of Brechtian distance and disbelief. "The distancing of Godard's imagination," Kael observes, "induces feelings of tenderness and despair which bring us closer to the movie-inspired heroes and to the wide-eyed ingénue"—played by Karina and named after Godard's mother, Odile Monod—"than to the more naturalistic characters of ordinary movies."[173] If Godard is to be called Brechtian, it must be understood that, like Brecht, he seeks not merely to alienate us but concurrently to involve us, so that we enter into a transaction between distance and closeness, belief and disbelief.

The crime does not fit the milieu. The crime is a movie-inspired fantasy; the milieu, a rather bleak terrain on the outskirts of Paris, is evoked with documentary veracity. Movies regularly go out on location to enact fantasies against a backdrop of reality, but Godard brings the reality forward and sets it in conflict with the fantasy. The crime fantasy expresses the wish for another existence on the part of restless, dissatisfied characters, which is what such fantasy usually expresses—the movie gangster represents the drive for success, the ambition to rise in life at any cost—but *Bande à part* is less an enactment of crime fiction than a playful meditation on the genre and its hold on the imagination. Realism gives a documentary portrayal of the characters' milieu and tells stories accordingly, but Godard tells stories discordantly, so that they seem out of place in reality, fictions declaring their artifice. It could be said—he has said as much himself—that he just isn't very good at telling stories and borrows them from here and there without really believing in them. But out of that deficiency he has made a method of modernist art calling into question the adequacy of fiction to reality.

Detective (1985) is *Bande à part* two decades later. It is also a crime story that Godard treats insouciantly and doesn't bother to make believable. This fractured generic story provides him with the occasion for moments of beauty and moments of truth. Its central situation, punctuated by a lovely metaphor of three balls on a billiard table, is again a triangle of a woman (Nathalie Baye, described by a Mafia don in the movie as looking like a faux Botticelli) and two men, one of whom is played by Claude Brasseur, who was one of the two young heroes in *Bande à part*. The barren yet open suburban horizon of *Bande à part* gives way to the enclosed space of a Parisian grand hotel. Though still inspired by crime movies, what were dreams of escape are now dreams of holding on: *Detective* is a movie about getting old. As well as Brasseur, it has Jean-Pierre Léaud, aging icon of the French New Wave, the boy in Truffaut's *Les Quatre cents coups* (1959) and the young hero of Godard's *Masculine Feminine* (1966), in a comic part as the ineffectual hotel detective. The sight of Léaud grown paunchy and unhandsome bears witness to the passage of time.

Brecht advocates the separation of elements, and in the different medium of film, Godard is of the same mind. Brecht separates the actor from the character, and so does Godard; Brecht separates the performance from the drama, and with Godard this translates into a separation of the image from the story, the image, which in most movies is a vehicle for the story, set at odds with it. Parody (from the Greek *para*, "beside," and *oide*, "song") originally signified, according to Giorgio Agamben, "the rupture of the 'natural' bond between music and language, the separation of song from speech. Or, conversely, of speech from song. It is, in fact, precisely this parodic loosening of the traditional link between music and *logos* that made possible the birth of the art of prose with Gorgias. Breaking this link liberates a *para*, a space beside, in which prose takes its place."[174] If for Agamben the separation of speech from song led to prose, speech that does not sing, with Godard the parodic loosening of image from story enables the image to speak, and sing, in its own language. The contradiction between story and image—the story that robs the image of autonomy, the image that brings the story to a halt—has never ceased to preoccupy him. In *Detective*, as in several of his New Wave films, the story is a purposely implausible, skippingly rendered generic fabrication, and the image is a slowing down, an arresting pause, at once interruptive and crystallizing. The image separated from the story, no longer a container for the action, becomes a place for astonishment and reflection. Godard's parodies of genre rupture the story, break the "natural" bond between story and image, and liberate a space where the image can sing its song of light.

Beyond the genres of popular film, Godard did parodies of *Carmen* (1983) and *King Lear* (1987), of the Gospel story of the virgin birth (*Hail Mary*, 1985) and the myth of Amphitryon (*Hélas pour moi*, 1993). And it isn't just stories that he parodies. When Karina in *Vivre sa vie* goes to see a famous Joan of Arc movie, he parodies Falconetti's performance and Dreyer's close-ups by cutting to her teary face in the audience. In *Masculine Feminine, Two or Three Things I Know About Her* (1967) and *La Chinoise* (1967), he portrays his characters, or his actors, in the form of interviews—not real interviews, for he would feed the actors their lines, but not mock interviews either, for he would feed them their lines at the last minute while they face the camera, so that, caught between the scripted and the impromptu, they reveal more of themselves than people usually do in interviews. If every film is a documentary of its actors, as Godard notes, nowhere does this hold truer than in this unstable parody of documentary. From the beginning critics would describe Godard as more of an essayist than a storyteller, but it was near the end of his New Wave period that he really began to make cinematic essays, inquiries into a situation, explorations of a scene: French youth mixing politics and pop culture in *Masculine Feminine* and embracing activism in *La Chinoise*, which saw the revolt of May 1968 coming; a Parisian neighborhood undergoing in *Two or Three Things* massive modernization in line with consumer society, the titular *Her* referring to the place as well as the protagonist (Marina Vlady), a housewife who, to acquire commodities, turns herself into one as a part-time prostitute. Documentaries, even when they tell stories, are formally more like essays or reports, so rather than parodies of stories, these more essayistic films are documentary parodies.

At the start of *Passion* (1982), we look up at the purplish-blue sky with some dark and some white clouds and an indiscernible airplane tracing in its wake a straight white line. In that steady mark of human making across the face of nature, the rather unsteady camera seems to recognize its likeness. Cut to a woman working in a factory; cut back to the sky, the white line gone from view, the camera panning and tilting in search of it. Cut to the factory worker on her bicycle, holding on with her hand to a slow-moving car and talking to the man driving it; cut back to the sky, the white line reappearing from behind a cloud and rising. Cut to a woman getting dressed and a man leaving the room, evidently after lovemaking; cut back to the sky, the white line beginning to spread and disperse.

Let there be light—light shining from the sky and painting on the screen an image as natural and as artificial as the thin, elongated wake of an airplane taking its place among the clouds. The sky is the image separated from the story, set parallel to it; the characters intercut with the sky are the story. In this prologue, we glimpse the story to come and its main characters, Isabelle the factory worker (Isabelle Huppert), Jerzy the filmmaker (Jerzy Radziwilowicz), Hanna the worker turned bourgeois (Hanna Schygulla), and her husband Michel the factory owner (Michel Piccoli). Yet the sky tells its own story in a parodic space beside, the story of the celestial white line on its onward path, lost and sought after the cut to Isabelle in the factory, then found and seen to be rising with regained potency after the cut to her riding at the side of Jerzy's car, and then seen to be dissipating after the cut to Hanna and Michel having had sex. *Passion* is a film about work and love, art as work and art as love, passion lost and regained, sought and dissipated, the image as metaphoric parody.

A filmmaker obsessed with light and with the image at the expense of the story ("Why must there always be a story?" he asks), Jerzy is Godard's parodic surrogate. The film he strives to make and abandons at length consists of elaborately mounted, inevitably unsatisfactory reconstructions of great paintings—Rembrandt's *Night Watch*, Goya's *Third of May*, Delacroix's *Constantinople*, El Greco's *Assumption of the Virgin*—as *tableaux vivant* in a movie studio. Though unachieved as wholes—which paintings are, whereas film images are details usually conceived as pieces of a story—these tableaux achieve a beauty of their own as the camera enters their space and captures the play of light on details. They tell their own kind of story, the inchoate story of images in the making. As well as parodies of the paintings, these staged replicas are a parody of Jerzy's, and Godard's, aspiration, or pretension, to paint with light. The light in them, which never pleases Jerzy, who keeps finding fault with the lighting and seldom gets around to filming, may count as available light because we can see the studio lamps that are its source; but it's not the same as the light of actuality, and by cutting between the studio and the world outside—the sun shining through trees as the camera travels by, or a room illuminated by bluish daylight from a window and a brighter, yellower bedside lamp shining behind Isabelle, tenderly silhouetting her as she sits naked in bed—Godard brings out the difference. *Passion* reflects on the difference between painting and film. With mischievous seriousness, it parodies not only painted images but the film image itself.

Folk Tale and Revolution

Like Eisenstein's *Strike*, Alexander Dovzhenko's *Zvenigora* (1928) is an amazing early work that dropped out of sight for many years. It was *Potemkin* and *October* (1928), *Arsenal* (1929) and *Earth* (1930), that won Eisenstein and Dovzhenko their international renown in the heroic period of Soviet cinema; and it was not until the Khrushchev Thaw, after they were both dead, that *Strike* and *Zvenigora* began to be shown again. Eisenstein seems to have disowned *Strike*—in a 1934 essay he writes that it "floundered about in the flotsam of a rank theatricality"[175]—but Dovzhenko says in his 1939 autobiography that *Zvenigora* "has remained my most interesting picture for me. I made it in one breath—a hundred days. Unusually complicated in structure, eclectic in form, the film gave me, a self-taught production worker, the fortuitous opportunity of trying myself out in every genre. It was a catalogue of all my creative abilities."[176]

While Eisenstein theorized the "montage of attractions," Dovzhenko was arguably the better practitioner. Eisenstein started in the theater. Montage, though central to his theory of film and usually taken as a theory of film editing, started as a theory of theater, the "montage of attractions" he expounded in a 1923 essay—attractions as in a circus or variety show, different sorts of performance assembled together, different ways of engaging and affecting the audience arranged in succession to produce a composite effect.[177] In its mix of documentary realism and caricatural stylization, *Strike* exemplifies the "montage of film attractions," but Eisenstein apparently thought that the stylization was too theatrical and went on to make the more consistently realistic *Potemkin*. In the theater, Eisenstein saw himself less as a director of actors than of spectators he endeavored to sway, and he was no different as a film director; he remained chiefly concerned with making an impact, eliciting a response. All his films are highly rhetorical, all theatrical in the way they play to the audience. But none after *Strike* combines dissimilar modes of representation so markedly. If *Potemkin* adopts a more consistent semidocumentary mode, *Ivan the Terrible* (1944) adopts a more consistent semioperatic mode. Except for *Strike*, montage in Eisenstein's films is not so much montage of attractions as the quick, assertive editing of shots.

Dovzhenko was born in a Ukrainian village, the son of illiterate peasants, their seventh child but, by the time he was eleven, the oldest surviving one. He went to school and became a teacher, which exempted him from fighting in World War I. In the complicated strife following the Soviet revolution, he was with the Borotbists, a faction of Ukrainian nationalists espousing a homegrown, peasant-based communism. He served as a Soviet diplomat in Warsaw and Berlin, but his mediating position between Bolsheviks and nationalists was made untenable when the Red Army slaughtered nationalist prisoners who refused to join its ranks, and his diplomatic stint came to an end. He turned to the arts—he studied with George Grosz in Berlin— and found a congenial atmosphere among artists and writers in the flourishing Ukrainian culture of the 1920s. He published caricatures and had aspirations as a painter before he started on his career as a filmmaker.

Zvenigora was his breakthrough film. It boldly mixes the legendary and the contemporary, the traditional and the experimental, the manner of Ukrainian folk poetry and the methods of avant-garde theater and cinema. The administrators at VUFKU, the Kiev studio that produced it, didn't know what to make of it and sought the opinion of Eisenstein and Pudovkin, who were invited to a screening in Moscow. *"Zvenigora* leaps!" Eisenstein writes in his account of the occasion. "As the film goes on it pleases me more and more. I'm delighted by the personal manner of its thought, by its astonishing mixture of reality with a profoundly national poetic imagination. Quite modern and mythological at the same time. Humorous and heroic."[178] The film opens with mounted Ukrainian Cossacks from the seventeenth century riding into view in magical slow motion; an old grandfather joins them as they shoot Poles down from trees and search for a treasure reputedly buried in the Zvenigora hills. But the grandfather also lives in the present, the time of world war, revolution, and civil war, and he has two grandsons, one a revolutionary who extends his hand to German soldiers in the trenches as fellow workers and the other a reactionary who puts on a suicide act before a paying bourgeois audience in the West, all eager to watch him shoot himself onstage, so that he can raise funds for an expedition back to his native land in quest of its buried ancestral treasure. More than any Eisenstein film besides *Strike*, Dovzhenko's *Zvenigora* has the stylistic diversity, the bent for disparity, of the montage of attractions.

The Cossacks on horseback, one of them carrying a *bandura*, invoke right at the start, as Ray Uzwyshyn observes, the Ukrainian tradition of bardic song. Laying stress on the Dada connection, Uzwyshyn sees the slow motion as a mockery in the vein of René Clair's *Entr'acte* (1924) and takes the whole sequence as a burlesque of the Cossacks and their bardic tradition similar to Duchamp's mustache on the Mona Lisa.[179] But Dovzhenko's slow motion lends the opening a strange sort of majesty—more akin to Jean Vigo than René Clair—and the jokes about such things as shooting down Poles perched on trees blend laughter with a fairy-tale wonderment. "Humorous and heroic," as Eisenstein says, the humorous accompanying the heroic as often in epic poetry, the humorous qualifying but not repudiating the heroic. Dovzhenko brings to the bardic tradition a modernist sensibility—he was certainly aware of the international avant-garde, Dada, and surrealism as well as cubism, constructivism, and the rest—and he does a kind of parody of Ukrainian folk poetry, but in a fashion essentially serious. And he doesn't so much parody the legendary as level it with the contemporary, put it incongruously together with the actual. Like Manet in *Olympia*, he gives an old form a new content.

When it shifts from the legendary past to the present time, the film goes into its most lyrical passage of Ukrainian folklore. We may think we are still in the realm of legend when maidens in festive peasant garb, one named Oksana singled out among them, perform the midsummer ritual of Ivan Kupala and send wreaths of flowers with lit candles floating down the river. "Destiny flows by," the intertitles read. "Oksana watches it." Time-honored belief has it that a maiden's wreath caught by a young man signifies marriage, while an overturned wreath or a candle blown out by the wind foretells misfortune. Oksana is alarmed to see that the old grandfather catches her wreath and throws it back into the water after blowing out the candle. Between these two figures of traditional Ukraine there seems to be a split, and in the next scene we are introduced to the two grandsons personifying a split, Pavlo the reactionary and Tymishko the revolutionary. Then comes another lyrical passage, a bucolic celebration of the land, its fruits and its beasts and its people, the growing of wheat and of children, a poem of fertility expressing in material terms much the same sentiments that the midsummer ritual expressed in mystical terms. Thus *Zvenigora* proceeds as a montage of scenes, of whole sequences more than of shots within a sequence, scenes linked together in their diversity by a play of correspondences and cross-references.

The idyll of the land is interrupted by a bell calling the men to the world war. Pavlo stays home with the grandfather and the two go digging for the Zvenigora treasure, but a fat general stands above them and tells them digging is forbidden. Tymishko becomes a soldier, though he shakes hands with the enemy in the midst of battle and challenges the authority of a frail old general who orders his execution to no avail, then just topples over. The actor who plays the old grandfather also plays the frail old general, and even if we don't recognize him in this other role, at some subliminal level we register the parallel. The digging for a national treasure, the gesture of solidarity with the enemy, the fat and the frail generals, the collapse of old authority: like much else in the film, these are symbolic, theatrical, frankly unrealistic representations of reality—reality in the mode of legend, of bardic song, but still reality rendered with the physical directness, the documentary immediacy peculiar to the film image.

On a horse painted white, Pavlo leads nationalist troops in the civil war, and Tymishko and the Communists retreat from the village. The revolution fights back, as the film represents it, armed with the pick digging in the mines, the hammer at work in the factories, and the sickle in the fields—the industry and agriculture that are the real treasure of Zvenigora, as Tymishko learns. Pavlo goes abroad, and after his profitable suicide act, he returns and persuades the grandfather to sabotage the advancing train symbolic of revolution. But Tymishko is on that train and Oksana is with him—the old man caught her wreath, it seems, for the benefit of his good grandson—and the grandfather joins them on board. Pavlo faces us as if we were the audience for his suicide performance and now actually puts a bullet through his head. *Zvenigora* is a complex national allegory. If the grandfather personifies old Ukraine, so does young Oksana, who is doubled in the legendary Roksana, heroine of a story related by the grandfather and visualized in misty, layered images like pictographs excavated from the distant past. The grandfather is the old fixated on tradition, Oksana the old with its eyes on the future; he is the old set in its ways, she the old that is continually renewed. In the original Zvenigora folk tale (as outlined by Uzwyshyn), a poor peasant discovers a treasure in a cave and, warned that it is cursed, takes only two gold coins from it, which are enough for him to prosper. Tempted to go back for more, he finds snakes and vipers in the cave, and the wind howls, "Take only what you need."[180] The grandfather's digging may be construed as the desire to hoard, to accumulate riches selfishly, but the treasure he dreams of is real and can be made to yield riches for all. He belongs on the train with Oksana and Tymishko in a final alliance of old and new.

"There was a mother who had three sons," *Arsenal* begins. A peasant woman is alone at home in a held posture of distress. "There was a war." Soldiers on a train travel to the front. In the village streets, women stand still and a one-legged veteran walks on crutches with a child following. "And the mother had no sons." A woman trying to sow a large field all by herself totters and falls to the ground. The intertitles assume the manner of folk poetry and the images are stylized in kind—theatrical, hieratic, with a distinctive use of immobility as a way to counterpoint and crystallize movement, and at the same time real. A soldier in the trenches under the influence of laughing gas confronts the audience like an actor on a stage. A woman beating her hungry children in frustration is intercut with a disabled veteran beating his horse in a field lying fallow, and the horse tells him he's hitting the wrong target. Horses speak in *Arsenal* as in any folk tale.

The bardic mode, as Uzwyshyn notes, tends in *Zvenigora* toward "comedy and Menippean satire" and in *Arsenal* toward "lament and tragedy."[181] *Zvenigora* ends happily with the hero and heroine together and the old man reconciled to the new order; *Arsenal* ends with the hero, also named Tymishko and played by the same actor, indomitably baring his chest before gunfire in the rebel arsenal's last stand, symbolically defying yet actually meeting his death. To a greater extent than any other Soviet portrayal of revolution, *Arsenal* is tragic, terrible, sorrowful. Its most dynamic depiction of revolutionary action is a rush to the grave. A dying Red soldier asks to be buried at home, and his comrades, together with speaking horses "flying with all the speed of our twenty-four legs," hurry him across a wintry embattled landscape to his final rest. Dovzhenko's mastery of the rhythms of motion and stillness is manifest in this dazzling fast-cut sequence in which militant excitement joins hands with mournful sadness. If *Zvenigora* mixes genres and styles more diversely than *Arsenal*, is more of a montage of attractions, then *Arsenal* cuts more disjunctively than *Zvenigora*, is more of a montage of shots. In *Arsenal* more than in *Zvenigora*, and in *Earth* more than in *Arsenal*, Dovzhenko treats shots as self-contained units, each holding the screen on its own and carrying equal weight, the ensemble forming an aggregate space like a medieval altarpiece or a Cubist painting.[182]

Cinema is both theatrical, a medium of actors performing for an audience, and documentary, a medium of images recording actual appearances. Like Godard, like Sembène, like Andy Warhol, like Jean-Marie Straub and Danièle Huillet, Dovzhenko pushes in both directions at once, and his films, like few others of his time, combine overt theatricality with vivid documentary imagery. Take the great love scene in *Earth*, the sole scene in the movies that portrays not just love's intimacy but also its commonality, not just its personal but also its sacramental quality: a sequence of lovers standing immobile in the country moonlight after a day's work, one peasant couple after another posing theatrically for the camera yet exhibiting, in a steadfast gesture of solemn bliss, the subjective as well as shared reality of love. Or consider the way that, in *Ivan* (1932) or *Aerograd* (1935), the documentary rendering of a massive hydroelectric dam being built on the river Dnieper, or of the Siberian frontier with its vast ancient forests and its airplanes in the sky heralding the future, is punctuated by the theatricality of characters looking at the camera and addressing us in the audience, implicating us in their struggle, facing our judgment, acknowledging their shame, asking us to witness their grief, reciting poetry to us in summation of their experience.

Earth was Dovzhenko's last silent film and is generally—and justly—regarded as his masterpiece. It is a marvel, a poem of change and of permanence, of death and of life, epic and lyric, tribal and revolutionary, passionate and imperturbable. But it was not a lone masterpiece. Worthy to stand beside it are *Zvenigora* and *Arsenal*, which compose with it a kind of trilogy, *Ivan*, which augments that into a tetralogy, and *Aerograd*, for once made outside his native Ukraine.

Each Scene for Itself

Brecht's separation of elements is a form of montage, the juxtaposition rather than the blending of different things. His alienation effect meant the estrangement not only of the audience from the play

but also of the performance from the drama. As well as the spectator's, the actor's identification with the character he or she plays is to
be curtailed. And, perhaps most important, it meant the autonomy of
the scene from the overarching story, the treatment of "each scene for
itself." Brecht contrasts traditional "dramatic" theater, which sets its
"eyes on the finish" and arranges its scenes in "linear development,"
each leading to the next, with his own "epic" theater, which keeps its
"eyes on the course," moves in "curves" and "jumps," and puts the
focus on "each scene for itself."[183] "As we cannot invite the audience
to fling itself into the story as if it were a river and let itself be carried
vaguely hither and thither," he writes two decades later, "the individual episodes have to be knotted together in such a way that the knots
are easily noticed. The episodes must not succeed one another indistinguishably but must give us a chance to interpose our judgment. . . .
The parts of the story have to be carefully set off one against another
by giving each its own structure as a play within the play."[184] "Dramatic" plot construction proceeds by causality: one scene the cause,
the next the effect. But how are scenes to be linked together when
each stands on its own? Scenes in linear development are connected
metonymically—cause for effect or effect for cause is metonymy—
while "epic" theater connects its self-sufficient scenes largely by
means of comparison (metaphor in Jakobson's sense). Holding back
causality and contiguity, Brecht brings forward relations of similarity
and difference, parallels, correspondences, cross-references, repetitions, oppositions, variations on a theme. If metonymy leads from
one thing to another, metaphor leaps, and with each scene for itself,
we have to leap across the gaps between scenes in order to make the
connections required for coherence.

In the same year as Brecht's "A Short Organum for the Theatre,"
1948, André Bazin published his essay on Rossellini's *Paisan* and the
aesthetic of Italian neorealism. Bazin and Brecht might be thought
antithetical, one championing realism and the other calling attention
to theatrical artifice. But look at Bazin's characterization of neorealist narrative technique and compare it with Brecht's "each scene for
itself":

A child cries beside his dead parents: there it is, this is a fact. How did
the Germans find out that these peasants were culpable? Why is the
child still alive? That's not the film's business. Yet a whole concate-
nation of events has led to this result. To be sure, a filmmaker never
shows everything—that would be impossible—but even so, his or her
choices and omissions will usually reconstruct a logical process in
which the mind goes without difficulty from causes to effects. Rossellini's technique undoubtedly maintains a certain intelligibility in

the succession of facts, but these do not mesh with one another like a chain on a sprocket wheel. The mind must make a leap from one fact to another in just the way one jumps from rock to rock when crossing a river. It may happen that one's foot hesitates between two rocks, or misses a rock, or slips on one. The mind does the same. For rocks are not there for the purpose of allowing travelers to cross rivers without getting their feet wet, any more than the lines on a melon are there to facilitate its division into equal slices. Facts are facts, our imagination makes use of them, but it is not their *a priori* function to serve it. In the usual arrangement of shots in a film (according to a process similar to that of classic narrative technique in the novel) a fact is seized by the camera, taken apart, analyzed, reconstituted; it may not totally lose its factual nature, but it is enveloped in abstraction as the clay of a brick is enveloped in the wall as yet absent that will multiply its parallelepiped. Facts, with Rossellini, take on a meaning, but not in the manner of a tool whose function has, in advance, determined its form. Facts follow one another, and the mind is compelled to perceive that they resemble one another and that, resembling one another, they end up meaning something that was in each one of them and that, if you like, is the moral of the story.[185]

Bazin's simile of the rocks that serve us to cross a river calls to mind Brecht's "each scene for itself": each rock, each fact in Rossellini's film, is there for itself, and it is by making leaps from rock to rock, fact to fact, that we are able to get across, to put together a story with a meaning. Brecht and Bazin alike use the image of a river, which for Brecht signifies our immersion in a story sweeping us along (just what he didn't want in his theater), while with Bazin we make the story precisely by avoiding immersion, crossing the river without getting wet, the kind of storytelling that would have pleased Brecht. As in Brecht's "epic" theater, in Bazin's simile we keep our "eyes on the course" and move not in a straight line but in "curves" and "jumps." Bazin's image of the foot hesitating between two rocks before making a leap, or missing a rock, or slipping, concurs with Brecht's "episodes [that] must not succeed one another indistinguishably but must give us a chance to interpose our judgment."[186]

Open synecdoche—or open causality, or open metonymy—is the term I propose for the way realism conveys the sense of picking out the significant from the larger space of the real. In realism, as Jakobson says, metonymy rather than metaphor predominates, but with metonymy left open, causality in abeyance, metaphor comes into play. A part pried loose from a particular chain of events, the crying child in *Paisan* is a metaphor as a microcosm is a metaphor, a part that resembles a whole, a sorrow that stands for all the sorrows of war.

Let me quote again the last sentence from Bazin: "Facts follow one another, and the mind is compelled to perceive that they resemble one another and that, resembling one another, they end up meaning something that was in each one of them and that, if you like, is the moral of the story." Facts follow one another, and we perceive that they *resemble* one another—did Bazin really mean that? It may seem odd to shift from succession to resemblance, one thing after another to one thing *like* another. When I read this passage in Hugh Gray's translation, which says *resemblance*, I thought that might be wrong, and I turned to the Spanish translation, which sounded right: "Facts follow one another, and the mind is forced to notice that they come together." But then I went to the French original and found that Bazin did say *resemble*, and said it twice, so there can be no doubt that he shifted from succession to resemblance, or—in the terms later formulated by Jakobson—from the axis of metonymy to the axis of metaphor. It was an apt shift. Bazin sees that when the links of causality and contiguity wane, things can come together only by virtue of resemblance and comparison.

Insofar as realism aims for a slice of life, a transparency to reality, it can be seen as antithetical to the modernist acknowledgment of artifice. But realism and modernism share in common an opposition to classicism, which for Brecht is represented by Aristotelian drama, with its linear development and its beginning, middle, and end. He quarreled with Georg Lukács, a fellow Marxist but a champion of nineteenth-century realism, because he saw his own methods as a newer form of realism better equipped to deal with twentieth-century reality. Bazin likewise saw Italian neorealism as a new realism he sought to distinguish from earlier forms.

Classicism is art secure in its conventions, settled within the rules of decorum, of what is fitting. The parts are designed to fit perfectly into their assigned place in the whole, like bricks into a wall, as Bazin says: treating shots as bricks in the edifice of a story serves to put a film together in classical fashion. But film has other possibilities. It may, as a modernist art, defy conventions or break rules of decorum. It may, instead of subordinating the parts to the whole, allow them autonomy. It has, as a realist art, a special capacity for conveying, through the animated photographic reproduction of actual appearances, the sense that "there it is, this is a fact."

The history of cinema has sometimes been divided between the descendants of two pioneers, Lumière and Méliès, the realist and the magician. Jean Vigo has found favor with both camps, a filmmaker alike admired for his earthy naturalism and for his imaginative experimentation. Neither slices of life nor flights of fancy, his films inseparably combine realism and modernism and demonstrate how well that mixture takes to the expressive capabilities of the medium. In *Zero for Conduct* he recruited the schoolboys from real life and made the teachers into monsters of the imagination. For one scene he set the boys loose in the school dormitory and let them have fun in a freewheeling pillow fight until a sudden, lyrical swell of slow motion turns naturalistic spontaneity into an eerie and exalted ritual of rebellion.

You could say that *Zero for Conduct* assumes the point of view of the boys, who see themselves realistically and their teachers exaggeratedly, and whose pillow fight escalates in their minds from fun and games into transformative ecstasy. But the film gives us the boys' subjectivity in a curiously objective way. We get no point-of-view shots through their eyes. More than their perspective, we share their whole sense of reality. Though an autobiographical work—Vigo spent his childhood in schools like this—*Zero* has no individual protagonist: the boys as a group are our hero, and we're brought into their collective subjectivity. Together they construct the world they know, just as any other human group constructs the world of their experience and calls it objective reality. If surrealism (a visible influence on Vigo) would merge dream and waking life, *Zero* makes it impossible to draw a line between subjective and objective. That's part of its modernism, a challenge to the convention that draws such a line, as between the designated point-of-view shots and the rest, and also part of its realism—no "magic of childhood" here but a vividly actual world as children perceive it.

Zero for Conduct was made on a very low budget. Despite his bad health—scarcely two years later he died of tuberculosis at the age of twenty-nine—Vigo had to work in haste. For the most part, as we learn from the biography by Salles Gomes, "there was no question of more than one take of any scene."[187] The producer, Jacques-Louis Nounez, wanted a film longer than a short but shorter than a feature—he thought there was a market for movies of that length—and even after the scenes that didn't turn out right on the first try were discarded, *Zero* had to be further cut down. Salles Gomes describes Vigo as faced with the decision

> whether to concentrate on the clarity of the whole, and choose those scenes and shots which, irrespective of their inherent quality, could help one to understand the action better, or whether to choose the most authentic and appropriate sequences without worrying too much about overall rhythm and so forth. In short, given the practical impossibility in which he found himself of attaining an ideal unity, he had

to choose between unity of action or unity of style. He opted for the second solution.[188]

Neither unity of action nor unity of style—let alone an ideal blend of the two—did Vigo seek. Like the surrealists, though with a lighter touch, he pursued incongruous juxtaposition, the clash of one thing with another, the unsettling disparity, the fraught disharmony. He shortened *Zero* by concentrating on each scene for itself. He may have done this under pressure from the circumstances of production, but each scene for itself wouldn't have been an option unless the scenes as they stood were already capable of standing on their own. There could be no string of pearls without pearls to string. Lindsay Anderson, who happily acknowledged *Zero*'s influence on his own *If . . .* (1968), calls this "Vigo's poetic method, episodic, fragmentary, charged."[189]

Yet Salles Gomes was right to raise the question of unity: even if not unity of style, *Zero* does achieve unity of some kind. With a larger budget, a longer running time, it might have been more cohesive, but all the same, it hangs together. Its stylistic incongruities, its very disparities—the different acting styles for the boys and their teachers, the realistic pillow fight shifting into dreamlike slow motion—help it gain coherence. Incongruity and disparity promote richness and complexity, and the richer and more complex each scene is, the more paths of association it makes possible, the more ways of connecting it with other freestanding scenes without recourse to the causal links of a story line. Disparity and incongruity may interfere with metonymic linear development, but they lend themselves to the kind of unity *Zero* manages, the metaphoric coherence attainable by discrete, disjunct, juxtapositional construction.

Consider the scene depicting one of the schoolboys, Caussat, at his guardian's house on a Sunday afternoon. It is a cherished moment away from school. Caussat and a little girl in knee socks, his guardian's daughter, are in the parlor by a window, playing a mysterious game. The scene is brief and simply done in one static shot. On the left sits the guardian, reading a newspaper that mostly hides him from view, while on the right, toward the back, the children play. A handkerchief covers the boy's eyes as the girl climbs onto the piano and hangs a goldfish bowl from a wire strung in front of the window. Then she sits next to the boy and takes off his blindfold, and the two of them gaze with hushed delight at the goldfish bowl hanging before them. That is all. What are we to make of it?

When he introduced the film to a Belgian audience at the time, Vigo addressed "the little girl of those rare Sunday outings" and made it clear that the scene is a memory of his childhood:

Do you remember how I loved to watch you climb up on the piano and hang the goldfish bowl from a wire which we had strung up, the two of us, our hands touching?

You used to cover my eyes with your handkerchief, smelling so nicely of your mother's lavender, because I looked at your plump, babyish thighs. And then gently, as one does with the sick, you would remove the festive bandage, and in silence we would both watch the goldfish bowl.[190]

Good to know that the scene is a personal reminiscence. But is it just a charming, dangling nostalgic vignette? Good to know too that the film as initially released had a follow-up scene in which Caussat mimed and embellished the game he played on his Sunday outing for the benefit of his friends at school. But *Zero* was soon banned, and nothing of that miming scene survives. In the film as we have it, the scene with the little girl and the goldfish bowl stands all on its own, very much a scene for itself. How does it fit in with the rest?

The first person of Vigo's introduction seems to have no equivalent in the scene on the screen. If Vigo identified himself with Caussat, his camera does not identify with the boy's perspective. It observes the boy and girl from a distance. We see the two of them in a stuffy bourgeois room cluttered with furniture, an ornate lamp, potted flowers, a china cabinet, the piano, and a goldfish bowl they borrow from the adult world for their childish game—a room the guardian behind his newspaper presides over. Yet the dominant adult is indifferent and immobile, and as the blindfolded boy sits still in a chair by the window, only the girl moves. It is she most of all who draws our attention, she who silently, entrancingly disrupts the adult order. The effect is of something like Vigo's second person, his address to "the little girl of those rare Sunday outings," as if the camera were saying to her, "I loved to watch you climb up on the piano and hang the goldfish bowl from a wire." The subjectivity of the boy and girl quietly playing in a corner holds us in thrall and somehow colors the whole scene—which thus partakes of the interpenetration of subjective and objective that characterizes the whole film. What may be called the objective subjectivity—or subjective objectivity—of *Zero for Conduct* is its central conjoining of contraries, and in different ways we find it in every scene.

The hanging goldfish bowl, bright with the light from the window, and the little girl whose thighs and bloomers we see even though the blindfolded boy cannot may be taken to represent the dawning of sexuality in preadolescent children. Vigo matchlessly evokes physical sensations, whether the grossness of a fat, filthy teacher petting a student, a gesture repulsive enough to trigger the boys' revolt against the school, or the sweet, delicate rapport between Caussat and his guardian's daughter, the whiff of lavender in the air. But more important than their fledgling romance is the children's construction of the world—not their retreat into a fantasy world of their own but their way of seeing and construing the material world we all inhabit.

What happens in the scene with the boy and girl and the goldfish bowl is the same thing that happens again and again in *Zero for Conduct*: children transform through play an adult-governed environment, a constituted objective reality they reconstitute according to their sense of things, subjective yet shared in common and thereby gaining objectivity, an alternative social construction of reality no less valid than the governing one and more stirring of the imagination. Like Caussat and his friend Bruel returning to school in the opening scene and astonishing each other in the dim railway carriage with a vivid array of games, like the pillow fight uncannily culminating in a slow-motion transfiguration, this scene connects with the rest by way of similarity, analogy, metaphor. It fits in as a variation on a theme, the boy and girl appropriating their corner of space and reconfiguring it for their purposes, having it suit their sentiments and dreams. If *Zero* as a whole is a microcosm of society and its subversion—which is why the censors banned it—each scene is a part that resembles the whole, a microcosm in itself.

Black Sheep

Chaplin's comedy of the machine age, *Modern Times* (1936), begins with a metaphor: we see a flock of sheep from above then dissolve to a view, also from above, of people coming out of the subway on their way to work.[191] People as sheep is an old metaphor that in days of faith meant something good: "The Lord is my shepherd; I shall not want . . . Yea, though I walk through the valley of the shadow of death, I will fear no evil: for thou art with me; thy rod and thy staff they comfort me" (Psalm 23). Chaplin's overhead angle may suggest a godlike perspective, but no benevolent god shepherds these subway riders toward their dehumanizing assembly-lined employment.

Charles Burnett made *Killer of Sheep* (1977) as his thesis film at UCLA. Born in Mississippi to an African American family that emigrated to Los Angeles when he was a child, Burnett grew up in Watts, and his film attentively depicts daily life among the black poor in that neighborhood. The protagonist, the killer of sheep, works at a local meatpacking plant. Stan (Henry G. Sanders) says he's not poor. He sometimes donates to the Salvation Army—a claim both funny and poignant, like much else in the film—and no doubt he could be doing worse; he has a steady job and lives in a house with his loving wife (Kaycee Moore) and their two children (one played by Burnett's own little daughter). But he is an unhappy man, at work, at home, everywhere he turns, and nothing that happens to him or anyone around him seems to offer much hope that things will get better. The sheep regularly killed at his place of work are a central, heartbreaking metaphor for him and his fellow blacks trapped in poverty.

The film ends with Stan at work guiding sheep to their slaughter. Here is a critic's take on the sheep metaphor reiterated one last time: "For all the vaunted warmth and sympathy of Burnett's images, it's pointless to deny that his vision is a profoundly fatalistic one."[192] Over this ending, we hear Dinah Washington singing a sad song: "This bitter earth / What fruit it bears / What good is love / That no one shares." Not wholly sad, though: "But while a voice / Within me cries / I'm sure someone / May answer my call / And this bitter earth / May not be so bitter after all." The film's theatrical release was delayed for three decades because Burnett hadn't cleared the rights to the music (from Paul Robeson to Faye Adams, Scott Joplin to Little Walter) he uses as more than background to the images. Another Dinah Washington song, to which the rights couldn't be obtained, was originally heard at the end: "Unforgettable," which in a way was meant ironically but could also be taken straight as a parting love song sung by the film to its unforgettable characters. Without gainsaying, either song qualifies the final sadness. *Killer of Sheep* is not hopeful, but that doesn't necessarily make it fatalistic, let alone resigned.

In both the original and the theatrical-release version, "This Bitter Earth" accompanies an earlier scene. "What good is love / That no one shares," sings Dinah Washington over the image of Stan and his wife dancing at home to a record of the song. Lit by a bright window, an overexposed screen within the screen behind the underexposed couple, the scene is done in one held shot. As husband and wife dance together, she caresses his naked back and puts her head on his shoulder, while he remains impassive, physically close yet emotionally distant. After the music stops, she clings to him but he backs away, and she forlornly goes to the window, whose bars now suggest a prison she wants to break out of. Cut to the sheep in the slaughterhouse, the first time the film presents them in a manner unmistakably metaphorical.

Burnett says that he aimed to make something different from "social-realist pictures where the issues are very clear: for example, there's exploitation in a shop, the manager is exploiting the workers,

so you have to have the people come together and form a strike. . . .
And then boom, you get your worker's rights, and everyone is
happy."[193] *Killer of Sheep* has no such dramatic arc. It could have told
the story of a black husband feeling depressed and becoming impotent with his pretty wife, with sexual impotence as a symptom and a
symbol of social impotence. That story is there in the dancing scene
but is not developed dramatically. Then you would have to have a
resolution—either a happy ending when the husband regains his sexual drive or an unhappy ending when he doesn't. And since in such a
story his sexual drive would stand for everything else, his regaining
it or not regaining it would either way mean an answer for the future
of the blacks in Watts: yes, things will turn out all right, or no, they
won't. Stan dancing with his wife is a scene for itself. It leads to no
scenes to come, serves as no link in a chain of events. And cutting
from Stan's distraught wife to the sheep answers nothing about her
future with her husband. It only makes a troubling comparison, raises
a fraught question.

The focus on the impoverished, the grounding in a particular
place, the use of actual locations and nonprofessional actors, the
episodic construction reflecting the haphazardness of real life—in
many ways *Killer of Sheep* shows the influence of Italian neorealism,
and Vittorio de Sica may especially come to mind. Yet *Bicycle Thieves*
and *Umberto D.*, though episodic, even digressive, have much more
of a dramatic structure—a man searches for a stolen bicycle he needs
for his job, an old pensioner faces eviction from his rented room—a
story with a beginning, a middle, and an end. There is no such thing
in *Killer of Sheep*, which takes to an extreme the treatment of each
scene for itself, and which moreover uses a calculated disorientation
and estrangement, a strategy of giving us pause, so that each scene
demands that we ponder it for itself, more in the way of Jean Vigo
than Vittorio de Sica.

Stan is helping a friend fix up a ramshackle car for which they buy
a motor. With great exertion, the two of them carry the heavy motor
down a steep flight of steps and put it in the back of Stan's pickup
truck—not all the way in, though. The friend hurts his finger, and
they leave the motor a bit too close to the edge. The truck is parked
at an upward incline, and the moment it gets going, the motor falls
from the back and rolls down the street, irreparably broken. Stan's
daughter has her head pressed to the back window, and as the truck
moves on, we take with her a backward look at the dropped motor,
the effort gone for naught, receding down the sloping street into the
distance: "an image of futility," as J. Hoberman describes the motor,
"rolling through the movie."[194] Dispiriting yet also humorous, a scene
for itself with large implications beyond itself, the motor episode is

physically affecting and at the same time symbolically resonant in the way that it embodies in a concrete object the whole weight of circumstance.

Piano ragtime playfully accompanies the image of rolling futility, and then a startling image of play springs before our eyes. From the dropped motor, we fade to a shot looking up at the sky between two buildings and watch one boy after another jumping across the gap. From the unconquerable gravity of the motor, we turn to leaps conquering gravity, from dejection to daring, fall to rise. Armond White sees the leaps as frightening, even suicidal: "The camera fixes on the feat, looking up like a circus spectator, an incredulous citywalker focused on a potential suicide, like an appalled parent or social worker. This sight of vaulting youthful (both carefree and careless) becomes, well, dreadful. So goes one of the film's key ambivalent moments. An essential poetic image of trepidation and potential tragedy."[195] Parents and social workers might be appalled, but these leaping kids are adept at it and are having fun. Like the schoolboys in *Zero for Conduct*, the kids at play in *Killer of Sheep* carve out of an adverse world a free space of their own. Still, it seems accurate to call the jumps from roof to roof "both carefree and careless" and reckon this "one of the film's key ambivalent moments." The soaring in the sky qualifies but does not cancel the dropping to the ground that just took place. Soon after the show of audacity, one of the boys is brought to tears: the play that liberates can also hurt, and we see how vulnerable these kids are, how liable in their youthful reaching to come to grief. These children represent the future, but the future is stacked against them.

A girl about ten years old takes the laundry out to dry, and a group of boys runs past and throws dirt on it. If the leaping boys defied gravity, these defy plain decency. The girl doesn't scream at them; she just looks without uttering a word. Rather than anger at the boys, she seems to feel something like perplexity at the world's meanness, as if this were her first brush with evil. Her face in close-up is an image of innocence despoiled like the fresh laundry. What kind of world is this, she seems to be asking herself, what violence does it harbor? From her face, as if in answer to her unspoken question, the film dissolves to sheep in the slaughterhouse. It is an answer we want to resist. Though we know that in her life this sweet girl will surely meet with worse violence than the boys' mischief, we draw back from seeing her as a sheep destined for slaughter. No, that can't be, we want to say; such misfortune can't be inevitable. That's just the response Burnett is after; that's how this governing trope works in *Killer of Sheep*. What can't be too often is; not fatalism but realism motivates the sheep metaphor. It is a metaphor we are meant to resist. Were we simply to accept it, we would tacitly be acquiescing to the terrible condition it signifies—a metaphor gaining much of its power from the way we resist it but are unable to shake it off.

Flowers

Abbas Kiarostami crouches over a frying pan that has two eggs in it, and beside him is the original movie camera, the *cinématographe* invented by the Lumière brothers, focused like him on the eggs being fried. I am describing a photograph taken during the shooting of *Lumière and Company* (1995), a film that, on the hundredth anniversary of the Lumière camera, enlisted filmmakers from all over the world to make one-minute shorts using it. I think Kiarostami made the best one. On the screen, against the dark background of the frying pan, we see the butter melting and bubbling and the eggs being dropped in one at a time, one of the yolks breaking and spreading—fried eggs, sunny-side up, taking shape in close-up before our eyes. Isolated and enlarged, the two eggs cooking over an unseen fire appear strange and wondrous, something mysteriously primal, some microcosm of organic matter evolving in the dark. The eggs done, the frying pan is swiftly removed from the heat, and the unmoving close-up camera lingers for an extra moment on the clean, cold, metallic geometry of the burner now extinguished. The organic has suddenly given way to the mechanical.

The burner, with its central circle of reflective metal, may be taken as a metaphor for the camera with its central lens; the burner's final unveiling may then be seen as the unmasking of the mechanical behind the illusion of the organic created on the screen. Like the burner it ends up facing, the camera is an inanimate machine yet an instrument of animation, a lifeless thing yet implicated in the stuff of life.

On the soundtrack, besides the fizzing and crackling of butter and eggs, we hear a telephone answering machine on which a woman is leaving a message. "Hello. It's me. Are you there?" The woman sounds rather anxious as the butter fizzes. "Hello. Not back yet?" The first egg is cracked and dropped into the pan. "Hello. Well . . ." The second egg is dropped in. "Listen . . . I'm here. I won't move. Good-bye. Call me back." The eggs are frying. The pan is whisked away. The blank burner stares out at us. "Well, bye then." As the woman hangs up, the film ends.

This disjunction between sound and image calls for our taking an active part in putting them together. We can make a metonymic or a metaphoric connection between them. We can assume spatial contiguity, imagine the answering machine we're hearing to be located somewhere off screen near the frying pan, and surmise that whoever is cooking the eggs—all we see of that person are brief glimpses of a hand over the pan—is choosing not to answer the woman's call. Out of this little documentary of fried eggs and this voice leaving a message, we can thus make a story. Alternatively, or additionally, we can draw a comparison between image and sound as separate elements. If we construe the image as a meditation on the organic and the mechanical, the soundtrack—the voice of a woman trying to reach someone and talking to a machine instead—offers a parallel. And if we take the image as an acknowledgment of the inanimateness of film even as it beguilingly simulates animation, the sound of the anxious voice, mechanically registered, reminds us that the machines in our lives are not themselves alive, and that even those designed to put us in touch with one another are liable to come between us.

This short exhibits, on a small scale, several qualities typical of Kiarostami's work. It stays close to documentary, to the observed fact, and at the same time it makes us aware that even as simple a fact as eggs in a frying pan is complicated by a context, a larger frame of reference on which its meaning depends. The visible, the detail tangibly before our eyes, is seen to acquire meaning in relation to the invisible and the intangible. Kiarostami has a gift for embodying thought, having abstract ideas resonate in concrete things, investing mind with the weight of matter and matter with the import of mind. He successfully combines the documentary nature of film with its symbolic, evocative, ruminative capabilities. Characteristic of his approach, too, is the way he calls on us to complete the film. He wants the audience to "put the pieces together on their own," he has said. "When you see a film, you should come away with your own personal interpretation, based on who you are. The film should allow that to happen, make room for that interaction."[196] I'm not sure that my interpretation of his little Lumière film is exactly what he was after, but I am certain that he intended to give me room for it. No film, no work of art, is so complete in itself as not to admit different responses, as not to require the work of interpretation. But some art allows more room for our response, is more open to our interpretation. Kiarostami is that kind of artist. He draws our attention to the means of his art and invites our participation in the construction of its meaning.

Kiarostami's most frequent metaphor for the camera is the car. Many of his scenes take place in cars, and many of his shots look out of a car window identified with the movie screen as a frame within the frame. *Ten* (2002) consists of a series of conversations between a Tehran woman driving a car and the passengers beside her. In a car we are both inside and outside, in a private as well as a public space. The director drives a car in his documentary *10 on Ten* (2004) and

gives us lessons in the way he makes films. Kiarostami got his start
making films for children, and the best of his early shorts, *Orderly or
Disorderly* (1981, also known as *Regular or Irregular*), takes the form
of a lesson—a double lesson. The film sets out to teach us that order
is preferable to disorder in the conduct of life, and at the same time
it gives us a lesson in the techniques it uses and the process of its
making, where to put the camera, how long to hold a shot on the
screen, what effect this is to have on the audience. But the teacher
filmmaker runs into trouble arranging in his film the order he would
uphold in life, and the filmmaking lesson ends up ironically calling
into question the order lesson. *10 on Ten* has some of the same questioning irony. Kiarostami mostly talks about *Ten*, which he shot on
digital video with two little cameras affixed to the car dashboard, one
pointed at the driver and the other at the passenger. He thinks digital video offers great possibilities to the art of film, first because he
believes in film as an art, and the video camera gets rid of complicated
technology and enables the filmmaker to work alone as an auteur, as a
writer or a painter works alone and second because the video camera
minimizes artifice and enables the filmmaker to capture life just as it
is. Which is it, then, the video camera serving the personal artistry of
the auteur or effacing artistry and auteur in favor of real life? Kiarostami must be ironically aware of the contradiction. His entire career,
from well before he started using digital video, has been built on it.

The influence of Italian neorealism on Iranian cinema has often
been noted. In the endeavor to render life as it is, Kiarostami adopts
the neorealist practice of taking the camera out into the actual world,
grounding the story and its characters in a concrete setting integral
to the film, and recruiting nonprofessionals as performers—ordinary
people who bring their reality to the roles they play. And Kiarostami
does neorealism one better. He almost never uses professional actors,
and for dialogue he relies as much as possible on his nonactors' own
words. The Iranian censors, he tells us in *10 on Ten*, have learned that
they can't expect him to follow a prepared script. When he writes one,
he says, he loses interest in filming it and usually hands it over to
someone else. He prefers to discover the story during the filming, to
let it grow out of the reality of the place and the people. Sometimes,
as in *Close-up* (1990) and *Through the Olive Trees* (1994), he relates a
true story reenacted where it happened and performed by its actual
protagonist and other participants as themselves.

Yet the realism of *Close-up* and *Through the Olive Trees* is not the
transparency to reality sought by Italian neorealism, the illusion of
actually being there. Rather, it is a realism declaring its artifice, vividly depicting a reality without letting us forget we're watching a
film. Kiarostami blends realism and modernism, a representation of

life and a reflection on how life is represented on the screen. The protagonist of *Close-up* is an unemployed printer who gained entry into
a prosperous family's home by impersonating a famous Iranian film
director, Mohsen Makhmalbaf. The impostor reenacting his impos-
ture is giving a performance of a performance, an impersonation of
an impersonation. We're in a hall of mirrors. This poor man has our
sympathy from the first close-up scrutiny of his earnest, gaunt face,
but even so we remain aware that he's performing for us, playing a
role in a movie, albeit his own role. At the end Makhmalbaf himself
appears, the real person joining the impersonator, both of them real
and both of them impersonating themselves.[197]

Through the Olive Trees begins with an actor (Mohamad Ali Kesha-
varz, one of the few professional actors in Kiarostami's films) looking
straight into the camera and addressing us in the audience. Standing in a field, with a tree behind him and a group of women in dark
clothing behind the tree, he tells us that he is "the actor who plays
the director. The other actors were hired on location. We're in Koker,
about 400 kilometers . . . no, 350 kilometers north of Tehran, where
an earthquake destroyed everything last year." So far we can take him
as an actor speaking in his own voice before the fiction starts. But
now a woman hurriedly emerges from the background and interrupts
him: "The girls are hungry, they've still got a long way to go. Can we
speed it up a bit?" With this interruption, the film deftly shift gears
and takes us into the fictional situation in which the actor plays the
director. It's no longer in his own voice but in the role of director
that the actor wraps up his preamble: "We have come to this rebuilt
school to choose a young actress." Cut to the other side of the tree
(of what is now revealed to be a line of trees; Kiarostami has a way
of surprising us with a cut that revises our sense of what we've been
seeing), where many local young women have gathered hoping to get
a part in the movie being made in their home territory. We're shown
how a director like Kiarostami goes about recruiting performers on
location, and we register the fact that for all their reality, these are
performers nonetheless.

As the actor playing the director walks among the would-be
actresses, we cut to reverse angles showing us their reactions to him,
the camera moving and pausing among them as if from his point of
view. He's a fictional director, but they're real young women from
the region who want to be in his movie—who, as we see, *are* in his
movie. "You're filming us," one of them says, and asks him if they'll
be able to see the movie on their televisions. We seem to be watching
a documentary of these aspiring movie actresses reacting not to the
fictional but to the real director making this movie. Having shifted
gears from documentary into fiction, the film as deftly shifts back. Its

poise on the edge between fiction and documentary is characteristic of Kiarostami.

The address to the audience, the director figure, the movie within the movie, the ambiguity between fiction and reality—*Through the Olive Trees* exemplifies the artistic self-consciousness, the modernism of Kiarostami's films, the way they call attention to their artifice and to the artificer behind it. In both *Close-up* and *Through the Olive Trees*, the story taken from real life and reenacted in its midst is a story involving film. The closer Kiarostami brings us to real life, it seems, the more he wants to acknowledge the intervention of film, not only how the camera and the screen shape our viewing experience but how the act of filming reality affects the reality being filmed.

Through the Olive Trees was the third of three films Kiarostami made, each taking up from the previous one and referring back to it, in and around the village of Koker in northern Iran. The start of this Koker trilogy—and, together with his great documentary *Homework* (1990), the culmination of his films about children—was *Where Is the Friend's House?* (1987), less self-conscious than the films that followed, more like neorealism, but at once simpler than neorealism and richer and stranger, distinctively the work of Kiarostami and one of the best things he has done.

Where Is the Friend's House? takes its title from a poem by Sohrab Sepehri. (Modernist Persian poetry has been an inspiration for Kiarostami and other Iranian filmmakers, as Hamid Dabashi has shown.)[198] In Sepehri's poem a traveler in a strange land is instructed to ask a child where the House of the Friend is. In Kiarostami's film the world is depicted through the eyes of a child, a schoolboy determined to find the house of a friend whose notebook he accidentally brought home with him at the end of the school day. That day the teacher threatened to expel the friend from school, not for failing to do his homework but for not doing it in his notebook as the teacher requires. And so the boy, though his mother has other ideas about how he should be occupied, embarks on a search for the friend's house to return the notebook that means so much. For most of the film we follow the boy in his quest. He makes his way up a hill to the next village, where he's heard the friend lives, and back down to his own village, where he's led to suppose the friend and his father have gone; then he dashes up the hill again, chasing after a man who pays him little attention, who heedlessly tore out of the friend's notebook a page to write on for his own business use, but who could be the friend's father riding off on a mule. The boy is a traveler in the strange land that is the world around him.

We share the path and the perspective of this boy facing the odd requirements of the adult world, not challenging them—he endeavors with sweet earnestness to help his friend comply—but throwing them into question nevertheless as he explores the world for himself and we explore it with him. His search for the friend's house turns into a journey of discovery of the world, what it offers and what it withholds, its mysteries and its possibilities. He often retraces his steps, returns to places he has seen before, but as the philosopher said, you can't step in the same river twice, and the same places are each time seen in a different light, revealed in a different aspect. This is a film about wonder, the wonder of seeing things with fresh eyes, the wonder from which philosophy is born. It's a wonderful film.

Usually we're invited to identify with children from a position of superiority—we find them endearing and feel for them without ceasing to feel that as adults we know better. Our identification with the boy in this film is not like that. It's more like the way we share the schoolboys' construction of the world in *Zero for Conduct*. Unlike *Zero*, which brings us into the group consciousness of the boys, *Where Is the Friend's House?* has an individual protagonist and center of consciousness, a boy alone in his quest for the most part; but his affinity with other children at school and along his journey suggests that they share a way of looking at things with one another and not with the adults making the rules. *Zero* has no point-of-view shots; the group subjectivity of the boys objectively colors everything. *Where Is the Friend's House?* has few, and some of these are given to the boy's grandfather, a traditional, petty disciplinarian who distantly and disapprovingly observes his grandson going up and coming down the hill on a zigzag path and going up again in pursuit of the mule rider; but taking the unsympathetic grandfather's point of view only increases our sympathy for the boy we watch from afar. A point-of-view shot from the boy's perspective—as when he spots a child's pants hanging on a clothesline and guesses they belong to the friend—is all the more striking for being rare.

In contrast to the sleek and fast editing style prevalent in movies today, with shots like soft clay being molded at will, Kiarostami cuts sparingly, like a carver respecting the character of the stone. It's not cutting to what the boy sees that establishes his perspective in *Where Is the Friend's House?* It's putting the camera oftentimes at his eye level, as when the man rips a page from the friend's notebook or a washed white sheet suddenly drops into view from above, surprising us as much as it surprises the boy. It's almost always staying with him, coming upon what he comes upon, and almost never letting us know anything he doesn't know. It's a kind of steady empathy with his way of seeing.

Twice the film departs from the boy's perspective for a bit, and each time we shift to an old man. The first time, before the boy repeats his run up the hill, we tarry with the unfriendly grandfather as he sits and talks. The second time, near the end, after the boy at last gives up on finding the friend's house, we turn to an old craftsman in whom he has found a friend. The sole adult willing to help him in his search, this old man used to make carved doors and windows for local houses, and as the day darkens into sundown, he points them out to the boy at the slow pace of old age. They look beautiful at dusk as the light inside shines through the carving. (The mule rider makes doors and windows too, but in a newer, businesslike fashion lacking pride of craft.) An artist working in the modern medium of film—whose light it is that shines on the screen—Kiarostami identifies himself with this old-fashioned village craftsman, an artist whose work resides not apart from ordinary life but right in its midst. While attempting to lead the boy to the friend's house—and instead leading him to the mule rider's house, where he has already been—the old man offers him, and us, a haunting experience of beauty in the twilight. And he gives him a flower to press inside the friend's notebook. The shift in perspective to the old craftsman, whom we follow inside his house as night falls and the wind blows, enables the film to skip the boy's return journey and the parental scolding that surely awaits him—an ellipsis calculated to lend a mysterious suddenness to the images of the boy back home, in a familiar environment where everything seems somehow to have changed for him.

Ellipsis is a figure central to both realism (because reality always exceeds its representation, so any representation necessarily leaves out much of reality) and modernism (because art that would acknowledge its means and its choices must own to what it leaves out), and on both fronts it is central to Kiarostami's art. *Where Is the Friend's House?* abides with the boy and gives an unhurried rendering of his tireless comings and goings, yet there are things it noticeably omits, and what it leaves out it brings into play.

Back home, the boy gazes at his mother—and here we do get a point-of-view shot through his eyes—as she takes down in the dark night the windblown white sheets hanging out to dry. From this eerie image, we slowly dissolve to the classroom the next morning. This is the film's only dissolve—Kiarostami's technical austerity enhances the impact of a device when he sees fit to use it—and it marks another ellipsis. The boy hasn't as yet turned up in class, though the friend is there and the teacher is going around checking each student's homework. Not until the boy arrives and returns the notebook to the friend do we learn that, after failing to find his house, the boy did his homework for him. The teacher looks over the notebook with approval. And as he flips through the pages, suddenly the flower pressed inside comes into view. We had forgotten about it, and now we remember it with astonishment as the old craftsman's gift. Kiarostami, who knows when to cut a shot short, swiftly concludes the film at the point of our surprised recognition. This is a rhetorical figure that to my knowledge has no name but can be put to startling effect; call it the return of the forgotten, or the surprise of rediscovery, not of the newly encountered but of the once again brought to mind.

The flower represents beauty. This gift from the old craftsman, this reminder of his beautiful carved doors and windows, is a metaphor for the boy's beautiful act of friendship—as if its successful conclusion were somehow the old man's gift, as if the craftsman who took care and pride in making things the right way stood behind the boy who has gone to such lengths to do the right thing for his friend. Ethics and aesthetics come together here, the beauty of an action, a bit of human doing, and the beauty of a work of art, a piece of human making, both moving us to admiration and both calling for the best in us. Philosophers have pondered what an action and an object of contemplation have in common that we should find them both beautiful, and Kiarostami's pondering takes concrete form in a film that is itself beautiful.

A taxi driver waits outside a gated suburban house in the opening scene of *Close-up*, and we wait with him. A reporter covering the story and two policemen who have come to arrest the Makhmalbaf impostor are inside that house, which belongs to the deceived family. Our remaining outside with the taxi driver makes us aware of the limitation in our access to the story, aware that reality doesn't allow us the kind of entry into stories we can get in fiction. From a pile of autumn leaves the driver picks out some pretty flowers to adorn his taxicab. An empty aerosol can is set loose, and he gently kicks it and watches it roll down the sloping street until at length it comes to rest against the curb, an inconsequential yet peculiarly absorbing detail. Does it mean anything? If nothing else, it's an observed fact, and it emerges as the driver gathers flowers—which may be taken to suggest that the pursuit of beauty is called upon to deal with actual facts. Later the reporter kicks the aerosol can hard, sending it up in the air and denting it so that it hits the ground with a noisy, crooked spin—which is how reporters have been known to treat facts. This time, without much lingering, we cut from the rolling can to a printing press.

The encounter at the end between the impostor and the real Makhmalbaf was arranged to take the impostor by surprise, to capture his spontaneous response, on his release from jail, when he finally gets to meet the director he has all along insisted he impersonated out of great admiration. The camera was hidden in a van, and Makhmalbaf carried the microphone, but much of what he said to the impostor Kiarostami was considered unsuitable for the film.[199]

Because the scene couldn't be redone, the sound was, under pretense of defective equipment—we hear voices in the van talking about a problem with the mike or the jack or a loose wire—intermittently erased on purpose. Kiarostami feigned the faulty sound recording. It was an inspired move. The inadequate sound fits in well with the barely adequate shots taken from the distant van, the two men often lost from sight or not seen clearly, glimpsed in the side-view mirror or through the cracked windshield. Sound and image together conspire to heighten the documentary sense of something real caught as it happens. It was a rhetorical move, the way these actual or simulated shortcomings in the pursuit of truth induce a feeling of truth.

The van follows the two men riding on Makhmalbaf's motorcycle. They are on their way to visit the family that sued the impostor for fraud but agreed to let him off—and to take part in the film. They stop to buy flowers for their visit. The impostor chooses a pot of yellow flowers, but Makhmalbaf instructs him that red ones are better. As they get back on the road, the camera hidden in the van brings the red flowers into the closest views it manages in this whole sequence, the faulty on-the-spot sound ceases, and we start to hear music. It seems we are headed for a happy ending.

The manipulation of the directly recorded sound may be dissembled, but in the striking shift to the music that takes over, Kiarostami shows his hand. He invites us to compare the two different accompanying sounds, one rough and the other smooth, documentary and fiction, and so to recognize that if the meeting of impostor and director is a matter of fact, then the happy ending promised by the music and the pretty flowers is a flight of the imagination. It's an ending we, and he, wish would come about, an ending he could have contrived for us, but it is not what reality likely has in store for the penniless delinquent and lover of art. We close on a freeze-frame as the shamefaced impostor, holding the pot of red flowers, stands at the walled gate of the prosperous house he may now enter in Makhmalbaf's company, but probably not in the future, probably not on his own.

Truth and beauty are goals of art as well as life, ends to be sought. But they are also means of persuasion. The best way to tell a lie is to envelop it in truth, with truth used as a means to make the lie more persuasive. That's just what a movie does when it enacts a fiction in actual locations; the ambient reality makes the fiction more convincing. Beauty, too, serves to win us over. Usually the hero or heroine we are to side with is beautiful. Tropes gain much of their effect through the persuasion of beauty; a metaphor expresses something more forcefully because more beautifully. Often truth and beauty are looked up to as ultimate things and rhetoric is looked down on as mere deceit, but as Kiarostami knows, truth and beauty are regular instruments of rhetoric. At the end of *Close-up* he uses them rhetorically and sets them in conflict, rough documentary versus smooth music and flowers.

If they can be at odds, truth and beauty can also be in congruence. When the impostor comes out of prison and sees Makhmalbaf, he hugs him and weeps. We watch from a parking lot across the way, through slightly blurred green leaves whose intervening beauty is appropriate to the emotional truth of this moment. Whether by accident or design, the aerosol can is green and red, the same colors as the leaves and flowers, and the driver's soft kick sets it rolling down the street gracefully, with the beauty a thing can have when in accord with its own nature. Anything done right is beautiful. "With him, a shot is beautiful because it is right," Godard said in praise of Rossellini.[200] The boy's search for the friend's house is beautiful because it is right, and it fittingly culminates in a flower. The unsettling, otherworldly beauty the boy encounters at twilight in the old craftsman's work, and back home as his mother gathers the flapping sheets in the windy night, means that his own endeavor, his transaction with the world, is not yet settled, beauty and truth not yet in harmony together.

II

MELODRAMA AND FILM TECHNIQUE

Between Tragedy and Comedy

Everybody speaks of melodrama, often disparagingly, but it's not easy to define it. The definition I heard as a kid was that melodrama makes the characters subordinate to the plot, but when I read the *Poetics* I saw that Aristotle prescribes the same thing for tragedy. Some would define melodrama by its play on our feelings, by the intensity of emotion it elicits; but that again scarcely distinguishes it from tragedy. Looking to the audience, others would distinguish melodrama as popular art from tragedy as elite art, but then few tragedies would make the grade besides the courtly French ones, and Shakespeare's would be melodramas. Once I asked an older colleague at the school where I teach what the difference was between tragedy and melodrama, and he answered, "If you don't like it, it's melodrama."[1] Still others would say that the crux of melodrama is a simplified moral scheme, an unqualified conflict between good and evil, virtue and villainy; but look, for example, at *Stella Dallas*, a melodrama if there ever was one, and you will find no villains.

If, like tragedy, melodrama tells a sad story, it often comes to a happy ending like comedy. It must be considered not only in relation to tragedy but to comedy as well. Stanley Cavell has noted a kinship between the Hollywood genres he calls the "melodrama of the unknown woman" (*Stella Dallas, Now, Voyager, Letter from an Unknown Woman*) and the "comedy of remarriage" (*It Happened One Night, The*

199

Awful Truth, His Girl Friday).[2] To see how close to comedy melodrama can be, look at the way Chaplin blends the two in *The Kid* or *City Lights* or Lubitsch in *To Be or Not to Be* or Capra in *It's a Wonderful Life* or Hawks in *To Have and Have Not* or *Rio Bravo*.

Comedy and tragedy are ancient, whereas melodrama, Peter Brooks maintains, "appears to be a peculiarly modern form" whose origins "can be accurately located within the context of the French Revolution and its aftermath."[3] But a form arising out of a break with tradition may still have links to traditional forms. The connection between social and political history and the history of artistic representation is never simple. Those who say that melodrama derived its violence from the bloody French Revolution forget all the blood spilled in human history before that time and depicted in art as far back as the *Iliad*. What was new about melodrama and related to the French Revolution was not violence but an egalitarian spirit. Tragedy deals with the high and mighty, the death of kings. In melodrama the sorrows traditionally represented in tragedy befall on ordinary people traditionally represented in comedy.

This is how John G. Cawelti describes the melodrama of the late eighteenth century:

> The central figure . . . was usually a virtuous young lady of some lower or ambiguous status—village maiden, orphan, daughter of parents in reduced circumstances—who was pursued by a male character of higher status and dubious intentions, a figure of aristocratic, erotic, financial, and social power; in other words, some form of the stereotypical squire with curling mustaches. The sorely beset heroine commonly loved a more worthy and innocent young man, who was himself enmeshed in status difficulties, often because his true parentage was concealed for one reason or another. This primary triangle was the essence of melodrama and was capable of two major permutations, corresponding loosely to comic and tragic modes of action. In the first case, the heroine resisted the entreaties and threats of the villain and was ultimately united in marriage with the noble young man. . . . In the tragic melodrama, the heroine succumbed to the villain's plots. . . . The single most important outcome of any melodrama was the marriage of the virtuous heroine to the right man—or, in the tragic version of melodrama, the degradation and death of the fallen heroine.[4]

This pretty much remains, well over a century later, the plot of D. W. Griffith's *Way Down East* (1920), except that the Lillian Gish heroine, even though she succumbs to the villain, nonetheless abides in her virtue, narrowly escapes death, and marries the noble hero. The tragic and comic modes of melodrama that Cawelti differentiates come together here. They are not so far apart after all. The desired outcome, marriage to the right partner, is in both cases the same. And that's also the desired outcome of comedy, what Aristotle might call the final cause of the plot. Whether comic or tragic, melodrama can be said to be in that way essentially comic.

The melodramatic plot outlined by Cawelti recalls the plot of New Comedy, in which young lovers contend with older characters blocking their union and, through developments as improbable as those in melodrama, eventually prevail. There are differences, of course. In comedy neither virtue nor villainy, neither pity nor fear, is played up the way it is in melodrama. The heroine's virtue is not so crucial, the young woman herself not always so central, the blocking figures not so sinister as the villain of melodrama. Marriage in comedy is not the matter of life and death that it is in melodrama. But it's a matter of life: comedy seems to have originated in rituals of fertility, and the concluding union of the young lovers celebrates procreation. More than a personal affair, their marriage is a matter of life in society. Like the melodramatic villain, the comedic blocking figures enjoy social prominence and power, and the young lovers' triumph represents a renewal of the social order. Tearful like tragedy, melodrama, even when it ends unhappily, shares with comedy a reaching toward a happy marriage implying a larger social happiness. *Way Down East* ends not just with a marriage but with three at once. After the awful winter storm that almost kills the heroine unjustly expelled from home and hearth, in this communal happy ending, spring triumphs over winter as in the ancient ritual at the root of comedy.

Comedy, as Northrop Frye says, is about incorporation into society, and tragedy about isolation from it. Melodrama unstably combines isolation and incorporation. Much of it takes place in privacy, within closed doors, yet no form has been more social: family secrets, illicit loves, personal crises—all that would be kept inside reflect the world outside. A bourgeois form, whose original villain in the days of bourgeois struggle with aristocratic rule was a figure of the aristocracy, melodrama expresses the contradictions of bourgeois thinking, the individualist emphasis on privacy coming into continual tension with the public business, the capacity to determine social existence, of a once rising and now ruling class.

From Theater to Film

Melodrama (from the Greek *melos*, "song") originally meant drama with music. It has come to mean drama heightened, embellished, whether with music—most opera is melodrama, and much

film music is melodramatic—or with emotive acting, sensational staging, intense close-ups, or other affecting ornament. Words, which
Aristotle considers the medium and the substance of drama, are not
enough for melodrama. If rhetoric is embellishment, then melodrama
is rhetorical beyond words. Its home is the theater, then the show put
on for an audience, and even in literature, where it often enters, it can
muster an almost bodily theatricality.

Film, inasmuch as it tells stories dramatically, brings them to life
with actors in performance, is a variant of theater, a different yet
similar medium. A. Nicholas Vardac traces the ways in which the
nineteenth-century theater led to the movies.[5] The theater director,
precursor of the film director, was a job that came into being in the
nineteenth century as methods of staging grew more elaborate and
the visual dimension of theater got to be more prominent. Griffith,
one of the first to take up the job of film director with pride of craft,
had sought a career in the theater before he turned to the movies. In
the popular theater of his time, melodrama reigned. Although realism or naturalism offered an alternative to its improbabilities, melodrama would be staged with all the props and trappings of realism,[6]
which, as Vardac argues, anticipated the camera's more direct and
convincing reproduction of reality. A great founding innovator of film
technique—even if not the single-handed pioneer described in old
histories of cinema—Griffith does not so much break with the theater as continue it by other means. The techniques he developed, the
closer view that enhances emotion, the crosscutting that builds up
suspense, chiefly serve the purposes of melodrama. His use of camera
and cutting provide visual ornament for melodrama in the movies.

His debt to the melodramatic theater of the nineteenth century is
perhaps most evident in *Way Down East*, which he adapted from a play
that had been around since his youth. He paid a lot of money for the
screen rights to this theatrical warhorse; he was thought foolish but
was proved right. *Way Down East* turned out to be, after *The Birth of a
Nation* (1915), his biggest popular success. Even today, when a silent
movie based on an old-fashioned play—a play already old-fashioned
at the time—would seem certain to strike audiences as hopelessly
archaic, it holds up remarkably well. One may credit Griffith and Lillian Gish and say that directorial genius and an extraordinary performance made a superior film out of an inferior play. Melodrama has
a bad name acquired from plays like this. But it is a play with roots
in a century of melodrama, so typical as to be almost archetypal, a
repository of generic power that Griffith and Gish were able to draw
on and bring to eloquent fruition on the screen. Because melodrama
has a bad name, Griffith's admirers would rather see him as a realist

than as a melodramatist. The winter storm that climaxes the film was a real storm, Gish's frozen eyelashes were really frozen, and the breaking ice was really breaking on a real river. According to Richard Schickel, Griffith's biographer, the wind of reality blows away all the melodramatic contrivance of the story.[7] But such sensational realism only bolsters the contrivance. Like the realistic staging of theatrical melodrama, it lends to the dramatically far-fetched the impact of the visually lifelike. Film can do this much better, though; Griffith wouldn't have been nearly as good a melodramatist had he stayed in the theater. "*Way Down East* was not the first, or last, theater melodrama to be filmed," Stanley Kauffmann notes, "but, through it, one can almost hear Griffith saying to the audiences of twenty-five years before, 'Here! This is what you *really* wanted.'"[8]

Thinking and Feeling

Melodrama notoriously deals in exaggeration. While making a case for its artistic validity, Brooks calls it "the mode of excess."[9] Excess of what, and relative to what? Relative, we may suppose, to the norms of realism, which presumably shows us things as they really are. But Roland Barthes sees realism as a mode of excess too. In its description of things, realism characteristically goes beyond the requirements of the story; it gives us an excess of detail that produces what Barthes calls "the reality effect."[10] Realism is often opposed to melodrama, but both realism and melodrama are modern forms that emerged in opposition to classicism. Classicism is art that exhibits just what is necessary, the right measure of information and emotion, the perfect fit of form and meaning. Realism feels real because it exhibits more than seems necessary in the way of concrete observation, because it imparts the sense that the world exceeds our assumptions of meaning, that there are more things out there than we can account for. Both realism and melodrama are excessive relative to the norms of classicism. Realism is excessive objectively, in its representation of fact; melodrama is excessive subjectively, in its expression of emotion. Melodrama is to the inner world as realism is to the outer world. Like the inner and the outer, the subjective and the objective, melodrama and realism may be opposed but are better looked upon as complementary. In the work of a writer like Balzac, a great realist and also, as Brooks argues, a melodramatist, the two come together to mutual enrichment.

Why shouldn't we compare apples and oranges? They alike grow on trees and please the taste. Are realism and melodrama alike enough to admit comparison? Realism is not a kind of story but a way of telling a story, not a genre like melodrama but a principle of representation like classicism. There are smaller and larger genres, however, and melodrama has shown itself to be, like tragedy and comedy, a large genre encompassing various smaller ones. If, more than genres, tragedy and comedy are outlooks on life, ways of apprehending and interpreting our experience—Chaplin once said that tragedy is life seen in close-up, comedy life seen in long shot—is melodrama, too, a genre that is more than a genre? Brooks seems to think so. He calls it a "mode of excess" and an "expressionist aesthetic"—and by "expressionist" he means not merely the familiar German variety but any mode of representation that puts pressure on appearances in order to disclose their meaning.[11] He looks to Balzac and Henry James, and he also mentions Dickens, Dostoevsky, Conrad, Lawrence, Faulkner—quite a list of writers he considers excessive, expressionist, melodramatic. He is right to regard melodrama as a major form of expression in modern art high and low, but he shouldn't characterize it all the same as an innately moralistic genre that everywhere sets up an unequivocal opposition between virtue and villainy.

"Melodrama is the fundamental mode of popular American moving pictures," Linda Williams declares at the start of an article expounding the proposition that melodrama is no mere genre but "a peculiarly democratic and American form" that has governed the Hollywood movie from the silents until now.[12] Democratic, yes, tragedy brought down to the common people, but neither peculiarly American—melodrama originated in Europe and has spread far and wide—nor confined to the popular. In academic film studies melodrama used to be thought of as the genre of women's pictures or weepies, and Williams rightly claims for it a more extensive domain. But the whole field? Even if most serious movies are melodramas of one sort or another, what about all the comedies? You could argue that comedies are often pretty close to melodrama. What seems to me more of a problem is that, even while striving to widen our notion of melodrama, Williams, like Brooks, still wants to define it in ways that are too narrow. If melodrama is nostalgic for lost innocence and dedicated to the recognition of virtue through victimhood and driven by Manichean conflicts between good and evil, then how can we possibly expect it to be the fundamental mode of all movies?

Melodrama has often been construed as inherently conservative. Kauffmann thinks that "its one essential ingredient is earthly justice," which "is always seen to be done," so that "melodrama is an artistic strategy designed, *and desired*, to reconcile its audience to the way things are."[13] Williams says that melodrama retrieves from the past "an absolute innocence and good" and thereby shows "profound con-servatism."[14] But earthly justice and heavenly innocence are neither necessarily conservative nor necessarily to be found in melodrama. What justice is done when Stella Dallas gives up the daughter she loves? What innocence is retrieved in *Casablanca* or *Gaslight* or *Letter from an Unknown Woman*? In *Way Down East*, however, justice is done and innocence is retrieved. Does that make it a conservative film?

Lillian Gish's character, Anna Moore, is a country girl who goes to visit wealthy relatives in the big city and meets the seductive vil-lain, Lennox Sanderson, who tricks her into a sham marriage and abandons her when she tells him she's pregnant. Alone in the world after the deaths of her mother and her baby, she finds employment at Squire Bartlett's farm, a surrogate mother in the squire's kindly wife, and true love in the squire's son, David (Richard Barthelmess); but her past, which she keeps secret, makes her feel unworthy of David's love and returns in the person of Sanderson, whose country estate is nearby and who is now after the squire's niece. When the squire finds out about the unwed mother and points his patriarchal finger out the door, banishing her into the cold and the wind, Anna in turn, before she goes, raises her finger and points to Sanderson, telling everyone about *his* past and the way he deceived her. Rescued in the nick of time from inclement nature, she receives an apology from the squire and an offer of marriage from the shamed seducer, but it is David she marries in the final joint ceremony. Yet, as Williams observes, it is the squire's wife, the mother rather than the son, whom we see Anna kissing at the end, which signifies that, quite cleansed of sin, she has regained the innocence she had with her mother in their country home at the beginning.

Way Down East turns the original aristocratic villain of melodrama into a callous and spoiled high-bourgeois heir. With the rise of the bourgeoisie, melodrama may have lost its subversive edge, but bour-geois society retains divisions of class, and *Way Down East* retains something of that edge in the conflict between its impoverished middle-class heroine and its upper-class villain. Like many other melodramas (*Stella Dallas, The Strange Love of Martha Ivers, Written on the Wind, Titanic*), it brings forward class differences in an ostensibly egalitarian society. This is a pastoral melodrama, though, the story of a country girl who, led astray in the city, regains her roots in the household of a rich farmer and finally marries his heir. As often hap-pens in America, the conflict between the poor and the rich gets mixed up with the opposition between the country and the city. Tak-ing the good squire to represent the ruling class no less than the vil-lain does, it seems fair to say that the movie reconciles its audience to the powers that be. But the stern squire virtually sends Anna to her

death, and though she forgives him, Griffith has him, in tandem with
Sanderson, offer her what amounts to a class apology.

As Williams sees it, rescuing "Anna's personal innocence" avoids
"the more deep-seated problem that causes her suffering . . . the per-
sisting double standard"—which condones the seducing man but
condemns the seduced woman—and "its source in a flawed patriarchal law."[15] But the whole movie is about the injustice of that patriarchal double standard, which Griffith's florid intertitles couldn't make
clearer and which Anna's personal innocence serves to make more
dramatic. That's what melodrama does. The culminant moment is
not the squire's condemnation and casting out of Anna but Anna's
answering accusation of Sanderson. Why, then, don't we end there,
with everyone's recognition of her virtue and his villainy? Why must
she go out and face the storm? It isn't just the squire, it's the movie,
with our full consent in the audience, that sends her out into this trial
by fire, or rather by ice. If it feels right dramatically that she should be
put through this purifying ordeal, doesn't it feel right morally? Don't
we see her as tainted after all? Yes and no. Intellectually we can have
no doubt of her innocence, but emotionally we seem to need this ultimate proof; otherwise the storm sequence wouldn't work so well on
us. You can say that at some level the movie holds on to the double
standard it opposes. Or you can say that we all live in a patriarchal
society, that the double standard has a tenacious hold on many of us,
and *we* must be put through this purifying ordeal—that the storm is
in that way cathartic for us.

The prejudice against melodrama is a prejudice against emotion. It
seems to be assumed that the more we feel, the less we think. A rejection of feeling in the name of thinking (and in the name of Brecht)
dominated academic film theory for years. Williams takes the contrary view: "We go to the movies not to think but to be moved."[16] The
mistake she still makes, however, is to separate feeling and thinking,
to suppose they are incompatible. Likewise she separates the personal
and the social. She holds that while realism deals with social issues,
melodrama cannot because it centers on personal emotion. But the
viewer who loves the heroine and hates the villain in *Way Down East*
is responding to socially representative figures. The film certainly
raises social issues and addresses them no less seriously because it
does so emotionally. What audiences moved by it may conclude from
the experience we shouldn't presume to know; it gives reason both to
accept things as they are and to call for their change. Rhetoric must
find common ground with its audience, and the rhetoric of melodrama often looks to the past for views and values on which people
can agree, but that doesn't rule out questioning the present or looking to the future.

The Close-up as Aria

When we say close-up, without a modifier, it goes without saying that we mean a close-up of the human face. Yet Griffith, for all the technical strides he made during his pioneer years (1908–13) at the Biograph Company, was slow to come to the face. Objects like the wrench that passed for a gun and foiled the robbers in *The Lonedale Operator* (1911) he would show in close-up, but almost never the face. He got to that only later, and then he became famous for his close-ups, especially his close-ups of women. Here is Jean Renoir, reminiscing about the movies of his youth and their impact on him: "I followed the work of Griffith with intense interest. The marvel of marvels was the close-up. I have never changed my opinion about this. Certain close-ups of Lillian Gish, of Mary Pickford and of Greta Garbo are imprinted on my memory for life. The enlargement enables us to delight in the texture of the skin, and a slight quivering of the lip tells us something about the inward life of the idealized woman."[17] Theorists of the male gaze have seldom discussed the close-up,[18] perhaps because they theorize the camera as a Peeping Tom, and peeping is not what we do when looking at a face displayed in close-up for us to look at, or perhaps because the male gaze is supposed to objectify the woman, and the close-up magnifies the most subjective part of her body. Still, there is an erotic dimension to the close-up, and Renoir describes a male gaze enamored of the female face. In real life it is a lover's privilege to come this close to a woman. And that must have been why at first Griffith held back from the face; it is a privilege he was reluctant to assume.[19]

In his Biograph films he boldly took the liberty of switching scenes, cutting from one place to another and back again, and bequeathed to the movies thereafter the convention empowering the camera to be in two places at once like no observer in real life. But moving around in the physical world is not the same thing as moving into the personal, sentimental territory of the human countenance. Even after he began taking the liberty of personal proximity, one senses that Griffith didn't take it for granted—which is, I think, why his close-ups of the female face are unforgettable: he treated those moments of intimacy as a singular privilege, above and beyond the camera's other empowerments.

The close-ups of Lillian Gish in *Way Down East* stand out from the action like arias in an opera, and like arias in an opera they amplify and embroider moments of emotion. At times they are visually mismatched with the rest of the scene, most noticeably in their lighting. By the rules of smooth continuity, already conventional in 1920, this

208 Melodrama and Film Technique

is a technical error, but Griffith surely intended, if not for us to notice the visual discontinuity, then for us to register the shift in emotional intensity. One of Gish's finest moments occurs when Anna discloses she is with child to the man she thinks is her husband, and he lets her know they were never actually married. She pulls out her wedding ring to show that can't be true, and we stay on her face as her disbelief turns into pleading and then into tears. The close-up has a light of its own, coming from behind and encircling her face with a sweet radiance. In the casting-out scene there is also a changed light in her close-ups, the light of righteousness rather than sweetness illuminating her face as she spiritedly responds to the punishing squire who has found out about her past. And there is a jump cut—a pointed break with smooth continuity—between a fiery Anna in backlit close-up and a meek Anna in flat-lit medium shot who seems ready to pack up and go without uttering a word. We want Anna to stand up for herself, and Griffith shows us in abrupt succession two different aspects of her character and keeps us in suspense as to which one we are going to see, the submissive or the spirited Anna. Her forceful exposure of her villainous seducer feels as if she were breaking out into an aria of accusation.

An aria is a sung soliloquy. A close-up, as Béla Balázs describes it, is a "silent soliloquy, in which a face can speak with the subtlest shades of meaning" and "find a tongue more candid and uninhibited than in any spoken soliloquy."[20] In a spoken soliloquy or in an aria, however, a character speaks or sings to the audience, whereas in the usual close-up it is not the character but the camera bringing the face to our attention that silently speaks to us. Griffith's close-ups are unusual. The pregnant Anna, looking at the false husband who is abandoning her, looks almost straight in our direction; the accusatory Anna, looking at the squire who has expelled her and fingering a welcome guest in his house as a scoundrel, looks right at us. We are on her side, where Griffith puts us, but he also puts us, and himself behind the camera, in the place of those who have wronged her, those who must set things right. Like the voice singing an aria, the face in these close-ups addresses us in the audience.

Way Down East is critical of society but not subversive. If the villain, Sanderson, represents what is bad about the ruling class, then Squire Bartlett represents what is good, and he is the presiding authority, the patriarch. The film condemns the patriarchal double standard but not the patriarchy; otherwise the patriarch would be a villain rather than the stern yet benevolent arbiter before whom the heroine speaks out against the villain. Anna's look toward the squire as she denounces Sanderson is at the same time a look into the camera, toward the audience, so that we are identified with the figure of social authority.

She is speaking to the patriarchy inside and outside the film. She is asking the patriarch, and asking us in a patriarchal society, to recognize her wronged innocence and the injustice of a social order that would find her guilty. *Way Down East* may not be subversive, but it is critical of society.

Melodramatic Argumentation

A *Corner in Wheat* (1909) is one of the most innovative of Griffith's Biograph films and one of the most interesting rhetorically. A reviewer at the time called it "a daring step . . . out of the domain of the picture drama" and a "demonstration of the force and power of motion pictures as a means of conveying ideas": "This picture is not a picture drama, although it is presented with dramatic force. It is an argument, an editorial, an essay on a vital subject of deep interest to all. . . . No orator, no editorial writer, no essayist could so strongly and effectively present the thoughts that are conveyed in this picture."[21] *A Corner in Wheat* tells the story of the Wheat King, a ruthless financier who corners the market in wheat and greatly enriches himself while impoverishing the farmers who grow the wheat and driving up the price of bread so that the poor go hungry in the city. The reviewer did not consider it a picture drama because the farmers, the urban poor and the Wheat King, though interrelated economically, never interact dramatically, never even come together face-to-face. They are shown in separate places, parallel sites of action—a farm, an urban bakery, the stock market, or a dining room where the rich celebrate their getting richer. In shifting from one place to another and back again, Griffith's crosscutting usually builds up a suspense of separation that leads to conjunction, as in his last-minute rescues, when he quickly cuts back and forth between increasing peril and approaching rescue until in the nick of time the parallel lines meet. But in *A Corner in Wheat* the parallel lines never meet. Here the crosscutting is comparative rather than conjunctive; it makes thematic rather than dramatic connections. At one point we see the rich at their lavish banquet, then the poor in a breadline—a contrast laying bare an injustice.[22] This is editing as editorial comment; it develops an argument rather than a plot.

As George Pratt notes, *A Corner in Wheat* draws on two works by Frank Norris, the short story "A Deal in Wheat" and the novel *The Octopus*.[23] "A Deal in Wheat" begins with a farmer in southwestern Kansas, a wheat grower ruined and forced to abandon his farm because the price of wheat in the Chicago market has sunk too low; then we turn to the speculation in wheat, the "battle between Bear and Bull," and the resulting price upswing; we then return to the farmer, now an unemployed worker in Chicago who stands in a breadline at night and waits for hours in the rain, only to find that bread has ceased being distributed because the price of wheat has risen too high. In "A Deal in Wheat" the story of the farmer gone to the city frames the story of the wheat market; there is no alternation between the two, nothing like crosscutting. But in a passage from *The Octopus* (1901) we go back and forth at an accelerating rate between a sumptuous banquet of the rich and the starving poor—a clear literary precedent for cinematic crosscutting, and specifically for the similar alternation in *A Corner in Wheat* between the Wheat King's banquet and the urban bakery where the price of bread has doubled and at the end of the day most of the poor standing in a breadline are turned away empty-handed. In Griffith as in Norris, the contrast between wealth and poverty is authorial rhetoric, editorial argument; but if it's not in the usual sense drama, the pointed juxtaposition of the extravagance of the rich and the plight of the poor is surely melodramatic.

On a visit to the grain elevators, right after he receives a message from his accountant telling him he has made millions and controls the entire world market, the Wheat King accidentally falls and drowns in a torrent of wheat. This concluding divine retribution was derived from *The Octopus*. There the villain is the railroad, the Southern Pacific expropriating the farmers of the San Joaquin Valley, "the snake in the garden," as Alfred Kazin describes it in his reading of the novel as "unconsciously conceived in terms of the Biblical legend of evil"; and "the rascally railroad agent," just like the Wheat King, "falls to his death amid circumstances reminiscent of the cheapest Victorian melodrama."[24] The melodramatic drowning of the rapacious schemer in his own wheat is even more contrived in the film than in the novel, for the Wheat King, as opposed to the railroad agent, is a financier dealing solely in money and is not likely to come near the actual grain whose price he manipulates. "There is no vengeance possible here but the hand of God," says the *Biograph Bulletin*, the hand of God often to be sensed in melodrama behind such improbabilities as the Wheat King falling into the grain elevator: "One of the sins that cries to heaven for vengeance is denying food to the hungry."[25] Tom Gunning takes issue with this "homily" and points out that Griffith intercuts the tycoon's death with a bread riot suppressed by the police, thus "comparing the violent death of the Wheat King to the violence he has unleashed in society."[26] Gunning is right to observe that the ending of *A Corner in Wheat* is melancholy rather than happy, but the *Biograph Bulletin* was not wrong to invoke divine intervention. Only, as often in melodrama, this is divine intervention presented not as what believably would happen but as what ought to happen.

Novelistic Characterization

"**H**e is the best novelist of the films," Erwin Piscator notes of Erich von Stroheim, whose *Wedding March* (1928) he likens to a novel by Balzac.[27] That was the last film Stroheim completed as a director. He may be better known as an actor ("the man you love to hate," as in *La Grande Illusion* and *Sunset Boulevard*), but in the history of film, he made more of a mark as a director. It was his painstaking attention to detail, his untiring accumulation of it, that earned Stroheim his place in old film histories as the exemplar of realism. His descriptive excess achieved a reality effect. It also added to the cost and length of his pictures. Again and again he ran into trouble with his producers and had his films taken away from him and cut against his wishes, *Greed* (1924) being the most famous case. After a while nobody would employ him behind the camera; his career as a director lasted barely a decade. This was the second reason for Stroheim's place in old film histories. He represented the artist at odds with the commercialism of Hollywood. The tendency of some recent film historians has been to regard the artist with suspicion and bow to the "genius of the system," and Stroheim's reputation has suffered as a result.

The Wedding March tells the story of a Viennese prince, Nicki (Stroheim), who seduces a beautiful commoner, Mitzi (Fay Wray), and abandons her even though he loves her. Their tender, ardent encounter in a setting of apple blossoms is intercut with a brothel where his father arranges his marriage to Cecelia (ZaSu Pitts), the limping daughter of a rich manufacturer of corn plasters. At the end money sets the tune for the wedding march, and the Grim Reaper's hands are symbolically at the keyboard. If that's not enough melodrama for you, what was to have followed (and was made into a sequel now lost, *The Honeymoon*) included Cecelia taking a bullet meant for Nicki and choosing to die rather than remain paralyzed for life and a burden to a husband in love with another woman. But the melodramatist does not negate the realist. Like Balzac, Stroheim shows how the two can be complementary. Nicki is a melodramatic character portrayed with realistic complexity, a character in whom the brothel and the apple blossoms intermingle, at once heedless seducer and romantic lover, aristocratic villain and sentimental hero.

In the terms put forward by E. M. Forster, you could say that Stroheim was able to portray "round" characters, whereas those in melodrama tend to be "flat," simple and unchanging, types lacking in nuance.[28] But this familiar dichotomy is itself flat. "The test of a round character," according to Forster, "is whether it is capable of surprising in a convincing way."[29] Yet Lillian Gish's Anna—the very type of beset innocence, a simple character who reaffirms in the end what she was from the beginning—surely passes the test when she faces the squire and denounces the villain both surprisingly and convincingly. Despite the common critical notion that characters should change in the course of a story, Anna doesn't change, but she still surprises us, still discloses an unexpected side of her character. What she surprisingly exhibits, her righteous anger, is typical rather than individual, something that any woman in her situation would likely harbor. It's not a matter of flat typicality versus round individuality but of our coming to recognize that there is more to typicality than we had thought. Anna surprises us at a climactic moment, a turning point in the plot—call it dramatic surprise. Stroheim can be called novelistic for the way he gives us the sense, moment by moment, through his multiple details and perspectives carrying multiple implications, that there is more to know about his characters, that they may have the power to surprise us.

At the start of *The Wedding March*, Nicki's aristocratic parents grumpily wake up in the morning of a feast day. Annoyed by his wife's lapdog, which intrudes on his side of the bed, the father throws the furry little animal brusquely back to the mother. "You—ugly old fool!" she exclaims, and he retorts that she should take a look at herself: "It's pitiful!" Their son rises, dresses for the day, and, pinched for money thanks to his gambling and womanizing, goes to see his father, who tells him to blow out his brains or else marry money, and then goes to see his mother, who also tells him to marry money but indulges him and gives him some. Mother and son visibly carry on a flirtation. Nicki kisses his mother as he kisses all the housemaids; she seems to be displacing onto her son the amorousness missing from her marital bed. And when the father in the brothel avidly arranges for his son a loveless marriage like his own, it can be viewed as jealous paternal revenge or, as Freud might put it, the father's castration of the son. While the chief motivating force here is money, the Oedipal subtext adds another layer to the characterization. Stroheim's characters thus acquire a novelistic density and depth. Imagine *Way Down East* if Griffith had so much as hinted at an amorous dimension complicating the relationship between the squire and Anna.

Stroheim made more frequent use of the close-up than Griffith— the close-up not a lyrical soliloquy but an instrument of scrutiny, proximate and at the same time detached. If with Griffith the face sings, then with Stroheim it speaks mundane or unprepossessing yet revealing prose. As a storytelling medium, film lies somewhere between theater and the novel; Griffith tended to theatrical display, Stroheim to novelistic observation. If Griffith's close-ups enlarge emotion operatically, then Stroheim's close-ups probe into the face as a novelist probes into the mind of a character.

The Reverse Angle

"What does acting add to a play?" Eric Bentley asks, and by way of an answer, he first points out

> that the actors' eyes meet. This is probably not true of some of the older theatres, and some of the Oriental ones, but in our modern Western theatre it is a well-established, if not essential, feature. . . . Watch the acting of any intimate scene between a man and a woman— say, the last scene of *Pygmalion*. One can imagine an ancient Greek or a more recent devotee of classical Chinese theatre or Kabuki finding in our acting of *Pygmalion* a lack of formality and pattern, no special significance in where the feet are going, no special beauty in the way the body moves or stands. "Why, they're not doing anything," any of these visitors might say, "but alternately looking at each other and looking away." And this is essentially true. Acting, in such an instance, has come to concentrate itself in the eyes. . . . The meeting of eyes constitutes a kind of center of human communication. The contact established is more personal than touch. . . . On stage this is an aliveness of the actors, which they add to the much less directly physical life of the script. Spectators who might have difficulty with the written script have none responding physically, by empathy, to the actors' looking at each other. . . . Conversely, the overliterary spectator who has seized Bernard Shaw's ideas all too readily, may not have lived through the drama of a Shavian scene until he, too, receives it from the actors' lips, through the actors' bodies, and especially through the actors' eyes. Usually, when we speak of seeing something through another's eyes, we are speaking only of the mind's eye. In the theatre, the actors' feyes guide us through the labyrinthine ways of the scenes; and all that joins us to the actors' eyes is the magnetics of looking. In the theatre, we may not be led by the nose: we *are* led by the eyes.[30]

What Bentley says about the theater applies even more to the movies. The movies are primarily a medium of the eye, and our eyes in the audience respond to the actors' eyes on the screen, which often look off screen and prompt the camera to look where they are looking, thus guiding us through a space more closely observed and indefinitely larger than a theater stage. The exchange of looks, the meeting of the eyes, can be more forcefully enacted in the movies by the exchange of shot and reverse shot. In a point-of-view shot, which assumes the perspective of an actor looking off screen and brings before our eyes the object of that look, we see through another's eyes not in the mind's eye but with the camera's physical immediacy, by a more direct perceptual empathy than can be managed on the stage. In the eyes, the inside encounters the outside. And in the movies, the actors' eyes can more pointedly draw attention to what goes on both inside the characters and in the world outside.

After watching Griffith, students in my film classes find it striking how much more modern Stroheim looks. Why? The answer is the reverse angle. A shot lets us see a piece of space; the reverse angle turns to the facing area, shows us the space in which we were situated a moment earlier and situates us in the space we were just viewing. Such reversal does away with the theatrical demarcation between the space of performance, which belongs to the actors, and the space from which we view the performance. The reverse angle usually pivots on an actor's glance. It identifies the actor's eyes with our own by cutting to what is in front of them, so that we see what they are seeing, not necessarily from their exact point of view—the point-of-view shot is a special case of the reverse angle—but from their side of things. Our eyes are aligned with the actor's to greater or lesser degree, and to greater or lesser degree we are brought inside the space of the film. (Lacanians say we are "sutured" into the film, but our involvement is more variable than they allow.) Griffith uses the reverse angle sparingly; he prefers to keep the camera outside the action like a spectator at the theater, one armed with opera glasses for taking a closer look without trespassing into the actors' space. Stroheim uses the reverse angle intensively, leading us by the actors' eyes into the characters' world and situating us right in the midst of the action vividly and assiduously. At the outset of the first film he directed, *Blind Husbands* (1919), we are introduced to the husband, the wife, and the seducer, played by himself, not in theatrical and then conventional tableaux but in angled and reverse-angled close views that bring us inside the horse-drawn carriage in which the characters are riding and show us their perspectives on one another.

An interlocked pair of reverse angles is the figure known as the shot/reverse shot (or shot/countershot). Two characters face each other, and the camera cuts back and forth between the two, each in turn seen from the other's side. The exchange of glances between a man and a woman has nowhere been more expressively rendered than in the shots and reverse shots alternating between Stroheim as Nicki and Fay Wray as Mitzi in *The Wedding March*. Their first meeting is an eloquent meeting of the eyes. At the parade on the feast of Corpus Christi, which she has come to watch with her family and friends, Mitzi stands beside the young butcher who wants to marry her when

Nicki, up on a horse in military regalia, takes a position by her other side and catches her eye. She looks up at the mounted nobleman, and we look up with her; he looks down at the pretty plebeian, and we look down with him. Unable to speak to each other under the circumstances, they carve out a silent intimacy between them by exchanging glances and gestures, and the language of Stroheim's silent cinema rises beautifully to the occasion in a sustained mutuality of shots and reverse shots. In his next film, the unfinished *Queen Kelly* (1928–29), Stroheim enacted another great angled and reverse-angled scene of unspoken flirtation between a prince on horseback and a commoner on foot.

Frightened by the ceremonial gunfire at the parade, Nicki's horse kicks Mitzi, and the flirtation thus interrupted resumes in her hospital room, where the apologetic nobleman visits the injured plebeian. Then he goes to her neighborhood and sees her at the outdoor tavern by the river, where she plays the harp with her broken leg in a cast. In his shots and reverse shots, Stroheim often puts the camera on or almost on the eye line, the line of eye contact between the characters, so that a character looking at the other looks right in our direction and we look right into the character's eyes. In Nicki's eyes, we see the seducer ready to take advantage of Mitzi's vulnerability, yet we also sense his own vulnerability, sexual attraction touching him more deeply and turning into something like genuine love. Although Stroheim was never what you would call a romantic lead, his scenes with Fay Wray in *The Wedding March* have a singular poignancy and authenticity of erotic feeling conveyed above all in the eyes.

"Tonight I crave apple blossoms," Nicki says as he takes leave of the brothel where his father remains and, swapping drinks from a bottle with the corn-plaster magnate, negotiates the marriage that dooms the romance at that very moment being consummated in the flowery night. After a passionate kiss, Mitzi draws back from Nicki, draws back from the sexual act toward which he pulls her, and they gravely look at each other as the virgin hesitantly gives in to the seducer. In an extraordinary shot/reverse shot, the camera repeatedly crosses the line of gaze and movement joining the characters to each other, so that at this fraught amorous juncture they seem to be at cross-purposes as he, facing her, slowly backs up toward the left of the screen, while she, yielding to him, slowly advances in tight close-up across the screen from left to right. It feels as if at this decisive moment the two were at once being united and divided, bound together and split apart.

Stroheim was an early master of the reverse angle. In his hands the device has a freshness we can still sense. He used it with a freedom that was later curtailed by the rules of conventional filmmaking. One such rule is that, in a shot/reverse shot, the camera should not cross the line along which the actors' eyes meet, for staying on the same side of the line keeps one actor looking toward the left and the other toward the right of the screen, and the audience may be disoriented if the apparent direction of an actor's glance changes from one shot to the next. Another rule is that an actor should not look directly at the camera, which presumably breaks the fourth wall, the dramatic illusion, by addressing the audience. When Lillian Gish's Anna looks at the camera as she accuses the villain in *Way Down East*, she's addressing the squire, but no reverse shot of him alternates with the sustained shot of her, and we feel she's addressing us too, which may break the fourth wall yet has the effect of heightening the drama like an operatic aria. With Griffith we are for the most part outside the world of the film, essentially in the position of spectators at a theatrical performance. Stroheim's actors look at the camera much more often than Griffith's, but we never feel they're addressing us in the audience, for we're brought into the space of the film, situated inside the characters' world, in such a way that the fourth wall disappears.

The Wedding March ends with a polyphony of faces and eyes meeting and gazing toward us as we take the place of one character after another. On their way out of the church after their wedding, Nicki and Cecelia encounter Mitzi and her rebuffed suitor, the young butcher, Schani, who has a gun in his pocket and threatens to kill the aristocrat who stole and then broke the heart of the plebeian beauty whom Schani still hankers for. Mitzi looks at the camera as she looks at the truculent Schani and promises to marry him if he desists from his murderous intent; Nicki looks at the camera as he and Cecelia pass by and he looks at Mitzi and at Schani; Schani looks at the camera as he looks at Mitzi and at Nicki; Mitzi looks at the camera as she looks at Nicki; Cecelia looks at the camera as she looks at Nicki and asks him about that sweet girl in tears and that awful man they just saw, and tells him she'll always remember these beautiful apple blossoms in her bridal bouquet. An actor's glance toward the audience is supposed to break the illusion. In Stroheim it increases the illusion; the way we meet their eyes as their eyes meet enhances our identification with the characters.

McTeague and *Greed*

"Norris crammed into it the darkness of that world of the poor which always beckoned to him like Nemesis, a world frozen in necessity, merciless to those who lost their foothold, savagely inexorable even in death. It was a melodrama, as all Norris's books were melodramas," yet it "was arranged, for once, on a scale of genuine determinism; blindness became the arena and accident the avenging angel; the universe was a wasteland in which men grappled for bread, and life was emptied into the sewers of the city." Thus Alfred Kazin on Frank Norris's novel *McTeague*, which, "despite all its extravagance and crudity," the extravagance of its melodrama and the crudity of its naturalism, "glows in a light that makes it the first great tragic portrait in America of an acquisitive society."[31]

Benjamin Franklin Norris Jr., an admirer of Émile Zola and a champion of American literary naturalism, was born in Chicago in 1870 to a wealthy family that moved to San Francisco when he was fifteen. He went to Paris to study painting but developed an interest in writing, and he returned home and attended the University of California at Berkeley. He started publishing during his college years, but like the eponymous dentist in *McTeague*, he never earned a diploma. Norris got the idea for his novel from a story in the San Francisco newspapers. In 1893 a murder took place in a kindergarten: when one Sarah Collins, who worked there as a janitor, refused to give her estranged alcoholic husband any of her money, he stabbed her to death. Norris began his novel in a writing course he took at Harvard as a special student.

A well-off young man looking down from the heights of Harvard at the likes of that janitor woman and her brutish husband will for some exemplify the trouble with naturalism, the social distance separating the author, and the reader, from lower-class characters, and the condescension likely to result. But for Norris, the trouble with realism—as he wrote in an article on Zola, whom he considered a romantic writer, as opposed to a realist like William Dean Howells—was that the "characters live across the street from us, they are 'on our block.' We know all about them. . . . We ourselves are Mr. Howells's characters, so long as we are well behaved and ordinary and *bourgeois*." By contrast, he continues,

> The naturalist takes no note of common people, common in so far as their interests, their lives, and the things that occur in them are common, are ordinary. Terrible things must happen to the characters of the naturalistic tale. They must be twisted from the ordinary, wrenched out from the quiet, uneventful round of every-day life, and flung into the throes of a vast and terrible drama that works itself out in unleashed passions, in blood, and in sudden death.[32]

What, according to Norris, realism lacked and naturalism supplied was the inordinate eventfulness and emotion of melodrama.

Stroheim's *Greed* is a silent version of *McTeague* that survives only

Melodrama and Film Technique

as drastically truncated by MGM but nonetheless remains the director's most celebrated work. If Norris did something new in the literature of his country, then Stroheim was breaking ground in the new art of film. This is a singular case of adaptation. Neither the novel nor the film suffers by comparison with the other, with the film faithful to the novel yet an original work in its own right.

Erich Oswald Stroheim was born in 1885 in Vienna; he added the "von" to his name upon his arrival in the United States in 1909. He fabricated an aristocratic background for himself, a persona as someone like the character he plays in *The Wedding March*, and not until after his death in 1957 did it come to light that he was actually the son of a Jewish hatter and never an officer in the imperial army. He may have also made up the story that in his early years of immigrant poverty he found a copy of *McTeague* in a seedy hotel room, read the book straight through in one night, and became determined to film it one day. But if Stroheim was a liar, an impostor, he told the truth as well. The aristocratic officers he plays in *Blind Husbands* and *Foolish Wives* (1922) are shown up as liars and impostors, and in *Greed* he tells a story that carries to an extreme something he lived himself when, in anger and despair over lack of money, he beat his first wife, Margaret Knox. Perhaps it was then that he read Norris's novel.

McTeague is full of doublings, interlocked lives: McTeague and Marcus, best friends turned mortal enemies who die handcuffed together in Death Valley; Trina McTeague and the Jewish junk dealer, Zerkow, hoarders alike, living in poverty and dreaming of riches; Trina and Zerkow's wife, Maria Macapa, two women abused by husbands who eventually kill them for an unreal or useless pot of gold; McTeague and Trina themselves in their entrapping mutual dependence—what would today be called their codependency—symbolized in *Greed* by a pair of canaries in a gilded cage, a husband and wife bound together in health and forever in sickness. Stepping outside the fiction, we might also take Norris and Stroheim, the privileged boy and the immigrant, the Anglo-Saxon supremacist and the Jew passing for an imperial nobleman, as doubles of each other:

> "Nothing is more remarkable in the book," Kazin maintained, than the detachment with which Norris saw it—a tragedy almost literally classic in the Greek sense of the debasement of a powerful man—and nothing gives it so much power. For McTeague himself, it is safe to say, Norris cared very little; but out of his own instinct for brute force he invested McTeague's own brutality with an imperishable significance.[33]

How, it may be asked, can a character for whom the author cares so little have the stature of a tragic hero? Tragedy is traditionally about the death of kings, and we must care for kings, whatever we may think of them as individuals, because what happens to them happens to a whole society. Naturalism, as Diane Stevenson has observed, transposes tragedy from the high reaches of society to the low, making the low representative not of the ordinary course of life but of its terrible possibilities, cards that society may deal to any of its members. McTeague is a tragic hero not because he's personally exceptional but because, whatever we may think of him as an individual, something exceptional happens to him—and to Trina, as much a tragic figure as he—that could happen to anybody.

McTeague, a dentist on Polk Street in San Francisco, falls in love with Trina while treating her as a patient. She is his friend Marcus's cousin and sweetheart, but when McTeague confesses his passion for her, Marcus tearfully gives her up: "It was a great moment; even McTeague felt the drama of it. What a fine thing was this friendship between men! The dentist treats his friend for an ulcerated tooth and refuses payment; the friend reciprocates by giving up his girl. This was nobility. Their mutual affection and esteem suddenly increased enormously. It was Damon and Pythias; it was David and Jonathan; nothing could ever estrange them. Now it was for life or death."[34] Here Norris assumes an ironic, slighting superiority toward his characters, who are not Damon and Pythias or David and Jonathan—who haven't even heard of them. In the corresponding scene in *Greed*, as McTeague and Marcus pour out their emotions, Stroheim cuts to a player piano in their vicinity. This is also an ironic authorial comment, detached from the characters but, unlike Norris's, staying within their experience. The player piano is a mechanistic metaphor for the emotions in the scene, for the inflation of Marcus's sentiments—yet the earnest McTeague is involved too. The metaphor widens and grows unsettling, chillier. It suggests that human feelings, sincere, intense though they may be, have something mechanical about them, something programmed.

When Trina, now betrothed to McTeague, wins $5,000 in a lottery, Marcus feels cheated and resentful, and these feelings keep running in his head like an unceasing tune on a player piano. It's the same with the other characters; they are not in command of their feelings, their feelings are in command of them. Trina doesn't surrender to McTeague because she loves him; she loves him because she surrenders to him. Such a deterministic view of human character as effect rather than cause is typical of naturalism. Determinism is a matter of degree, however. Few would dispute that to some degree we are free, to some degree determined, but we like to think we are free, and naturalism reminds us that we are determined.

They would seem an ideal couple, or at least a perfectly normal

petty-bourgeois husband and wife, McTeague big and strong, Trina
pretty and tidy and thrifty. Under her civilizing tutelage his manners
and his mind improve. He's happy to submit to her socially; she's
happy to submit to him sexually. If not on our block, these characters
live close enough to it. If a tragic flaw is inseparable from a virtue,
then McTeague and Trina surely qualify: what their society normally
upholds as virtues end up becoming their vices. McTeague's manly
strength turns into brutality, Trina's wifely thriftiness turns into utter
parsimony ("'I didn't use to be so stingy,' she told herself. 'Since I
won in the lottery I've become a regular little miser. It's growing on
me, but never mind, it's a good fault, and, anyhow, I can't help it'"),[35]
and her sexual pleasure in submission to a man, just what a patriarchal society would expect of a good woman, turns into outright mas-
ochism. Talk about the psychopathology of everyday life.

Trina's winning the lottery is the turning point in the plot of
McTeague, the chance event that triggers inexorable necessity. Having
money leads Trina to save it compulsively; like everyone at all levels
of her society, no matter how much money she has, she doesn't feel
she has enough. Her $5,000 also brings out the worst in Marcus, who
out of vengeful envy informs the authorities that the dentist is practicing without a license. With a miserly wife and now the loss of his
livelihood, McTeague is doubly a victim of the lottery money (as well
as a victim of his society's professionalization, a competent enough
dentist forced, as he says, "to quit for just a piece of paper").

Victim changes into victimizer as Jekyll into Hyde, and a sequence
in *Greed* memorably dramatizes the change. Fired from a job he found
after he had to give up dentistry, McTeague (Gibson Gowland) arrives
home early, but Trina (ZaSu Pitts) commandeers all the money he
was paid and sends him right out to look for another job. In a striking
deep-focus shot taken from a low angle, we see him in the foreground,
going downstairs and pausing to ask her something, while behind
him, at the top of the stairs, she looks much smaller yet looms powerfully over him. It's going to rain, he says; could he have a nickel for
carfare? "A big fellow like you 'fraid of a little walk." So he goes out,
finds no job, and gets thoroughly soaked in the rain. A friend sees him
in the street and, to warm him up, invites him into a bar for a drink
of whiskey. "It kind of disagrees with me," he demurs—his father, we
recall, died of alcoholism—but the friend insists. As McTeague gulps
down the whiskey, Stroheim cuts to Trina at home polishing a coin,
then back to the bar as McTeague drinks another glass of whiskey,
and then, after a fade indicating a passage of time, back to Trina with
her hoard of money. Switching back and forth between husband and
wife at this significant moment links them together in the addictions

that compel each of them, her money and his whiskey. Her money, the nickel she wouldn't give him for carfare, has led to his whiskey, and his whiskey will lead to her death. He returns home full of drink and anger and almost hits her, his hand raised and clenched into a fist. "I wonder where he got the money to buy his whiskey," she asks herself after he falls asleep.

Stroheim was a favorite of André Bazin, who advocated a realism of integral space, unbroken long takes rather than short shots cutting things up into pieces, and took him to represent an approach to film-making that does not rely so much on editing: "The principle of his direction, a simple one, is to look at the world from so close and with such insistence that it ends up by revealing its cruelty and its ugliness. One can well imagine, in theory, a Stroheim film composed of a single shot, which would be as long and as close up as one liked."[36] But Stroheim in fact practiced a realism, or naturalism, of short shots rather than long takes. His films are cut faster than Griffith's and almost as fast as Eisenstein's, though they are cut more smoothly and so less noticeably. No shot transition is smoother than one cued by a glance. To cut on an actor's glance is to bring into play a character's perspective: Stroheim's editing weaves the fabric of his films out of the interplay of perspectives and details. Griffith's close-ups stand out; Stroheim's blend in. Getting close to a character was for Griffith something special, but Stroheim took it as his prerogative, the way it is a novelist's prerogative to get inside a character's thoughts and feelings. And like a novelist, Stroheim had no difficulty with going in and out of each character's point of view as he saw fit, now adopting one perspective, now switching to another, now giving us—as with the player piano inserted into the exchange between the two friends for life—the author's view of things. His intricate yet smooth editing allow him to achieve the roundedness and texture one finds in a realist novel, the intricacy making for the sense of a multiply interrelated world, the smoothness for the illusion of immersion in that world.

When the former dentist returns home drunk and advances aggressively toward his wife, we are put in her position and see him from her point of view as if he were coming right at us, up close in our face and getting closer; and when she looks up in fear at his raised hand, we see his clenched fist from her point of view as if it were about to strike us. We alternate between the two characters in a shot/reverse shot, but McTeague, unlike Trina, looks straight into the camera, which is thus more directly aligned with her perspective, more identified with her than with him at this moment when he threatens violence against her. In a shot/reverse shot we are identified with both characters as they look at each other—identified at least to the extent of being situated with each character in turn—but our identification is not necessarily equally apportioned between the two characters.

Early on in the story the dentist treats his future wife for a broken tooth. She's in pain, and he decides to use ether. In a shot/reverse shot he glances down at her and she up at him from his dentist's chair, and our identification with his point of view increases after she passes out under ether, when we see her in tight close-up from his perspective above. A white cloth covers her dark hair, which lends her a resemblance to a nun and suggests that his desire is aroused at the sight of purity vulnerable to defilement. From this close-up of her we cut to a view of him from behind the back of her head, an unusual reverse angle cued by no glance; we cut to what she would see if her eyes were open. Shot and reverse shot quickly alternate, and then, from the tight close-up of the etherized Trina, we cut to a close-up of McTeague coming in our direction and gazing straight toward us. As the dentist, driven by his baser instincts, approaches his defenseless patient, we assume her position and look from her perspective into his eyes looking at her with irrepressible desire, even though she's unable to perceive what she faces. His gaze toward the camera puts us literally though not perceptually in her point of view, in her place though not in her consciousness, and in the place of the unconscious woman our consciousness comes into play. Rather than seeing what she sees, seeing with her, we are in her position seeing what she can't see, seeing for her. After identifying with him looking at her, now we identify with her all the more because she can't look at him, because we look for her, fear for her, feel for her. And when, after several sessions, he finishes his dental work on her and thinks that this woman so close to him for a spell will never come back again, the poor fellow wins over our sympathy. We take his point of view out the windows as he watches her go away down in the street, and on the face where we previously saw feral desire and now see tearful love.

If condescension toward a lower class is the trouble with naturalism, it largely resides in the better-educated language the author shares with the reader but not with the characters. In this respect the reverse angle gives Stroheim an advantage over Norris. A point of view expressed in words inevitably carries the mark of a class, a social position, but a visual perspective we can all share. A lustful dentist advancing toward his slumbering patient, a big angry drunk getting closer, a raised fist seen from below—these look the same to everybody.

Sometimes we identify more with McTeague, sometimes more with Trina—more with the meek McTeague when the domineering Trina sends him out, more with the scared Trina when the drunken

McTeague returns. In *Greed* and in *McTeague* our identification is divided between husband and wife. If you think Norris sides with the man, look, for example, at the passage in which, after McTeague leaves one morning, the novel sympathetically stays with Trina all through the day. She thinks her husband has just gone fishing, and she worries about him and asks the neighbors when he fails to turn up, until she comes to realize as night falls that he has robbed and abandoned her. Norris's detachment, like Stroheim's, arises not so much from the withholding of sympathy as from its division, which keeps us from taking sides and allows us to stand back and observe the terrible pattern of compulsion in which both husband and wife are caught. The story of McTeague and Trina shows that melodrama can attain the depths of tragedy, the tragedy of common people who suffer as steep a descent as any of the high and mighty and evoke as much pity and fear. No one is good in this melodrama, and no one is evil. It is not sympathy but moralizing that is withheld.

The novel is a bourgeois form. In the main it portrays middle-class characters for middle-class readers. The naturalist novel, however, ventures into the life of the lower classes, foreign territory to middle-class readers. These may be more difficult for them to identify with, but they are not so far from them as they may think. *McTeague* depicts the petite bourgeoisie falling into an awful abyss in perilous vicinity to familiar reality. For all their divergence from the usual, the characters resemble us in recognizable ways, and the narrative brings us close to them and has us share the detail of their lives, yet at the same time keeps us at a distance. We observe them like insects under the clinical eye of an entomologist, these characters who are what we fear we might become.

Greed effects a similar combination of intense closeness and ento-mological detachment. Stroheim's fluid use of the reverse angle puts us perceptually in many places at once. On her wedding day Trina, afraid of the hulking husband who will now possess her, says good-bye to her departing family, and we see her mother going downstairs from Trina's perspective above, then Trina from her mother's per-spective below, then her father at the door downstairs from Trina and her mother's perspective above, then Trina and her mother from her father's perspective below, and so forth. One moment we take the blurred perspective of Trina's fearful tears, but then we go on to see, from no character's perspective, the telling detail of her small feet standing on tiptoe on his big feet as she surrenders to her husband and reaches to kiss him. We are situated with the characters but never remain with any one of them for very long, and the next moment we may be looking with the author at the funeral ominously taking place down in the street while McTeague and Trina are getting married.

We are at once right in the midst of the characters and viewing them dispassionately.

This is a detachment that observes without moralizing, without passing judgment. It has no governing moral standpoint—neither that of an omniscient author nor that of a Jamesian center of consciousness. Setting *McTeague* and *Greed* side by side lets us discern more clearly the cultural moment of naturalism. The world hasn't fallen to pieces; that will occur with the fragmentation of modernism. But if the naturalistic details and perspectives come together into a whole, it is a material, circumstantial, and not a moral or spiritual, whole.

Photographer

A cut makes a break and at the same time a connection. Like Eisenstein's abrupt cuts, Stroheim's smooth ones endeavor to make the connections of meaning, with many cuts making many connections. Bazin was wrong about Stroheim's editing but not about the way his camera bears down on reality to reveal its meaning. If Stroheim was the leading realist of the silent era, then the most influential film realism since World War II flourished in Italy. With *Rome Open City* (1945) and *Paisan* (1946), Roberto Rossellini ushered in the neorealist movement. "Things are there," he famously said. "Why manipulate them?"[37] Unlike Stroheim's, Rossellini's is not a realism of meaning but of reticence, of deference to reality, of refusal to manipulate it into sense. "The force of *Paisan* is in certain images of danger, suffering and death that remain in one's consciousness with the particularity of real experience," Robert Warshow notes. "These images have an autonomy that makes them stronger and more important than any ideas one can attach to them."[38] Meaning is an idea, a generality attached to things. If a novelist's realism moves from the particular to the general in pursuit of meaning, Rossellini's deference to things in their particularity is a photographer's realism.

With its portrayal of heroic Italian opposition to the Nazis—Catholic as well as Communist—*Open City* did much in the immediate postwar period to make Italy look better in the world's eyes. It is a political melodrama of good against evil with an emphatic meaning and little reluctance to manipulate our emotions—little in the way of reticent deference to things as they are. The scene everyone remembers, the death of Pina (Anna Magnani), shot down by the Germans in the street as she runs after her captured partisan lover, gains much of its power and pathos from the way it bursts on the screen without preparation, as if caught by a newsreel camera on the spot, after a passage of melodramatic suspense led our attention elsewhere. It may seem to interrupt the melodrama, but it actually continues it by other means, lending it what Penelope Houston calls "voracious immediacy"[39] and deepening it into tragedy, a photographer's tragedy dispensing with dramatic buildup. Like Stroheim, Rossellini combined realism and melodrama, but with him this was an uneasy and unstable combination.

Paisan carries his newsreel neorealism further. He preferred it to the more popular *Open City* and felt that it better represented what he wanted to do. Yet in its episodic construction *Paisan* still relies on melodrama, most obviously in the contrived fallen-innocence sentimentality of the Roman episode, which was the most carefully scripted and the one that took longest to shoot, while the last and best episode, the one about partisans in the Po River delta, Rossellini shot quickly, without bothering to fill in the gaps in the action, as if the camera were itself caught in the rush and confusion of things—his "most extreme experiment in off-the-cuff filmmaking," as Tag Gallagher calls it in his critical biography of the director.[40] Rossellini at his best was a cinematic equivalent of the street photography of Robert Frank or Garry Winogrand (which he surely influenced), the picture snatched from life with the rough edges of life, the uncomposed look of something that happened to be there rather than something arranged into a statement.[41] But a still photographer takes a detail out of life and lets it stand as an image, whereas a filmmaker puts together a succession of details and must not only show them but in some way link them together as an articulation of images. It's in the details themselves that Rossellini's strength lies, in the "feeling for particularity" Warshow considers "his greatest virtue as an artist."[42] His capacity for articulation is another matter.

It's not that Rossellini lets things speak for themselves—things never do—but that he lets them be silent. His attempts to make them speak—to attach an idea to them—are often unconvincing. The reaction shot is a common signifier: cutting to a character reacting to a scene tells us how we are to construe it. Rossellini tries that in *Stromboli* (1949), his first film with Ingrid Bergman, as a way to assimilate the remarkable documentary sequence of tuna fishing to the fictional story centered on her character, but the gripping, affecting spectacle of the fishes and the fishermen asserts its autonomy from the clumsy reaction shots. Never adept at film editing, Rossellini from the start of his career, "whether through laziness or genius," as Gallagher says, preferred to film scenes in long takes.[43] The long take can be a form of articulation, as it is in Mizoguchi or Renoir, Antonioni or Hou Hsiao-hsien, but in Rossellini it is nothing so organized. Rossellini didn't believe in preparing a script, rehearsing the actors, setting up the shots according to a plan. He believed in the spur of the moment. He would create a fiction but would treat it as a fact that was out of his hands, something encountered in the world. He was a careless filmmaker, but there was method in his carelessness.

"Well, who is this Ingrid Bergman?" he asked when he received a fan letter from her, offering her services. "If you need a Swedish actress who speaks English very well, who has not forgotten her German, who is not very understandable in French, and who in Italian knows only 'ti amo,' I am ready to come and make a film with you."[44] Rossellini grew up rich, and though his family lost all its money before he was out of his twenties, he never lost his taste for the sweet things in life. Having to work for a living, he drifted into cinema because that was where his pursuit of women led him. When he found out who this famous movie star who wrote him a letter was, he set about seducing her before they had even met. She abandoned her family and her Hollywood career, and married him amid an international scandal. That he fell in love with her I don't doubt, but the love doesn't come across in their movies together—*Stromboli, Europe '51* (1952), *Voyage to Italy* (1954), *Fear* (1954)—which are all melodramas peculiarly holding emotion at arm's length. At the time they pleased nobody but the French—Bazin wrote a "Defense of Rossellini," and in 1958, when the group at *Cahiers du cinéma*, which included Truffaut and Godard, Rohmer and Rivette, picked the best films ever made, *Voyage to Italy* came third, after Murnau's *Sunrise* and Renoir's *Rules of the Game*—but the French have had a large influence on subsequent movie taste.

Voyage to Italy is extraordinary in the way it focuses on characters who are ordinary to the point of banality, neither appealing nor unappealing, a bourgeois couple from Britain uneventfully traveling in Italy and having unremarkable marital problems. It is also extraordinary that the banality of these characters is presented without irony. For long stretches the film adopts the Bergman character's point of view as she wanders around Naples and takes in the tourist sites. This is Naples "filtered through the consciousness of the heroine," as Bazin notes, "and if the landscape is poor and limited, it is because the consciousness of this mediocre bourgeois woman is itself of a rare spiritual poverty."[45] Rossellini assumes no superiority toward this impoverished consciousness, which he treats as another fact out of his hands, something that was there like the streets of Naples or the ruins of Pompey. He manages a curious neutrality, neither identifying himself with his heroine nor viewing her with ironic detachment. But even the withholding of irony where we would expect it requires that one thing be presented and another implied; it requires a novelist rather than a photographer. The neutrality of *Voyage to Italy* is largely uninflected, and though that has its fascination, the effect is for the most part rather flat. But the ending is wonderful. After an hour and a half of nothing much happening, suddenly the wife and husband, who have been talking of divorce, find themselves separated by a crowd in a religious procession where what looks like a miracle has occurred. They reach for each other and are reconciled. The film is over before we know it. In a usual melodrama this would be a conclusive reconciliation, a live-happily-ever-after ending, providentially settled even if not prepared for; but here everything passes too quickly for us to determine what it means, and we may doubt (as the director himself did) that the couple will stay together for long. Who can say? This is a photographer's ending, seizing on a moment and letting it stand.

Music into Drama

Like *Way Down East*, *Aventurera* (Mexico, 1950) is a melodrama whose heroine succumbs to the villain yet marries the hero, a fallen woman who bounces back. And bounce she does. Elena is a cabaret dancer of quick beat and fast ways, tough and loud and fiery, an angry tigress ready to pounce and take revenge on those who wronged her—a far cry from the demure and dignified Lillian Gish, who has her own strength but not this indomitable energy. Elena is Ninón Sevilla, a Cuban dancer and actress who became a movie star in Mexico, where *Aventurera* was part of a cycle of melodramas called *cabareteras*, or cabaret pictures, and a very popular one. Alberto Gout directed; Alvaro Custodio, like Buñuel an exile from fascist Spain employed in the Mexican film industry at that flourishing time, wrote the story and cowrote the screenplay; and several noted musicians participated, including composer and lyricist Agustín Lara, crooner Pedro Vargas, and Ana María González, Pérez Prado, the Trio Los Panchos. So salient are the musical numbers that the movie has been called a compound of melodrama and musical, but better to call it a melodrama in the original sense of the word: a drama with music.

In the city of Chihuahua, Elena is the daughter of a respectable bourgeois family and such a good girl that when her dance class lets out early, she goes straight home, where she finds her mother kissing Ramón, the chauffeur. Elena walks away, appalled, thinking of her loving father and her betraying mother, who now runs off with Ramón. "I'll never forgive her," she says. "Ramón is a scoundrel. If some day I come across him I'm capable of killing him"—at which point the sound of a gunshot is heard. Her father has killed himself.

All this happens as quickly and disconcertingly as in a dream. Melo-drama, as Eric Bentley has characterized it, is the naturalism of the dream life.[46]

Now we move to Ciudad Juárez, where Elena is on her own. Practically an orphan, certainly in reduced circumstances, she fits Cawelti's description of the melodramatic virtuous young lady. She has a succession of jobs, which she quits because men keep accost-ing her, and then she runs into Lucio (Tito Junco), a shady character, mustachioed and good-looking, not the aristocrat of old melodrama but a lowlife. He promises her a job with a woman, Rosaura (Andrea Palma), who needs a secretary, he says, but who actually owns a caba-ret that doubles as a whorehouse, and who by deceit and force enlists Elena into her dual establishment. "You won't get out of here," she tells her. "Whoever enters this business, hear me well, never leaves it." Much later we find out—it is the biggest surprise in a film full of twists, coincidences, and improbable turns of plot—that Rosaura has another life as an aristocrat, or the latter-day equivalent, a figure of the high bourgeoisie. It is a person of higher social status who leads the virtuous young lady into perdition.

This film is crammed with incidents yet punctuated with pauses at musical numbers commenting on the action and opening it to reflec-tion. Before introducing her to Rosaura, Lucio has dinner with Ele-na—we see no eating, just drinking—in the cabaret, where there is a show on a stage. First Ana María González sings "Adiós," which alludes to Elena's impending good-bye to her life of virtue. Then Pedro Vargas sings "Amor de Medianoche" (Midnight love), Elena and Lucio get up to dance, and when Vargas intones the words "puerta de pecado" (door of sin), Rosaura, watching from her office above the dance floor, notices "Lucio the pretty boy. He brings a girl. Nobody can pick them better." Back to Elena and Lucio dancing, and from her perspective we get a blurred, intoxicated view of the singer on stage. By the time she comes to see the woman who will employ her, Elena is quite drunk: "But Lucio, I'm going to see two women instead of one." Beyond her drunken vision, this remark alludes to the two women who bring on Elena's ruin, her mother and Rosaura, as well as the two women Rosaura is: the whorehouse madam and the upper-class matron.

"It took me work to tame her," Rosaura tells Lucio after some time has passed, but now Elena "is a sensation as a dancer." Elena hasn't been tamed, though—she gets into fights so often that Rosaura fears the police may close the cabaret—and Ninón Sevilla, who choreo-graphed her own numbers, isn't an accomplished dancer. But in a way she might not have managed had she been a better dancer. She is a sensation all the same, precisely because she's untamed, appealingly unrefined. Some viewers take her numbers as camp and laugh at her expense, but the fun she has doing them is palpable on the screen, and we can have fun along with her. The musical is the genre of high spirits, and *Aventurera*, though terrible things happen to the heroine and she retaliates in kind, is a melodrama of the spirited woman.

Forcibly pulled away from one of her fights by the thug Rengo (Miguel Inclán, the nasty blind man in Buñuel's *Los Olvidados*) and dragged upstairs to Rosaura's office for a dressing down, the chastised Elena returns to the cabaret. As she steps down to the floor, Pedro Vargas steps up to the stage, and this begins a counterpoint of movements and gestures and glances, enacted between Vargas and Elena as he sings and she listens and reacts. He sings the title song, written by Agustín Lara: "Vende caro tu amor, aventurera" (Sell your love dearly, adventuress). In this remarkable sequence the song not merely comments but also impinges on the action and becomes part of it. The singer addresses the song directly to the heroine, and she assumes the position of the referent and recipient.

As Vargas intones the word "aventurera," a cut to a reverse angle shows Elena looking at him and responding with wrinkled brow to his singing about "el precio del dolor" (the price of pain). Cut back to him, returning her gaze, then back to her, who now starts moving toward him. The camera moves with her, bringing him into view just when he says "tu pecado" (your sin), and now the two are framed together. He starts moving on the stage in a direction parallel to hers on the floor and to the camera movement. At the point when she, approaching the stage, lines up with him and he halts, there is a cut to a higher, wider view, the camera continuing to move with her as she walks across the floor to the other side. He starts moving again, looking at her, but now she moves away from him and seems to be avoiding his gaze; she hides behind a pillar as if ashamed of what the song is saying about her. A cut gets closer to her as he sings about "la infamia de tu cruel destino" (the infamy of your cruel destiny), and she starts moving again, away from the stage. But she turns to look at him, prompting a cut to a close-up of him singing "marchitó tu admirable primavera" (wilted your admirable springtime), followed by a cut to a deep-focus shot with her in front and him well in back, the two of them and the camera again moving in parallel paths, now reversing direction and going from right to left instead of left to right as before. When Vargas, a distant figure on the stage, ceases moving, so does Elena, hiding behind another pillar, and the two of them again line up on the screen, so exactly that she obscures him from view. At this point, reasserting the parallel, comes a cut from her profile to his, in close-up, as he reprises "Vende caro tu amor" and turns to look at her when he sings the word "aventurera." Cut to a reverse angle, a close-up of her as, emerging from behind a curtain, she turns to look at him and faces the camera.

Judging from this film, the only one of his I have seen, Alberto Gout is a very good director. Pedro Vargas is stiff, but Gout orchestrates the singer's movements together with Ninón Sevilla's and the camera's—and with the words of the song—in a way that brings the singer and the song into arresting rapport with the action and the heroine being addressed. This is true melodrama—music not merely as accompaniment, background, interlude, but as central to the drama. First the heroine recognizes herself in the song and moves toward the singer, but then—the shift marked by a cut when she and he line up—she moves away from the singer and seems upset, shamed by the song. And when—the shift again marked by a cut at a point of alignment—Elena, in frontal close-up, looks at the singer and at the camera and for an instant appears to break out of the world of the movie and look at us in the audience, then back inside the movie looks at Lucio and at someone else in the cabaret audience, Gout does something extraordinary with her gaze and its objects.

Bringing into the action a song commenting on the action is a self-conscious move declaring the film's artifice, a kind of Brechtian alienation effect. Isn't melodrama bent on involving us emotionally, the opposite of Brecht's curb on dramatic illusion and emotion in his modernist theater? Most of his plays are in the root sense melodramas, though, dramas with music and with songs in the manner of musical comedy or comic opera. Comedy since antiquity has had no qualms about displaying its artifice, and what Brecht did, in Bentley's view, was to apply to tragic situations comedic forms and techniques[47]—not so different from melodrama. As well as making us aware of the film's contrivance, the song Vargas sings to Elena makes her aware of her own predicament. The gaze she turns toward the camera is a gaze of self-consciousness, both the film's and hers.

Though we just saw her behind a pillar, she emerges into the close-up at the song's conclusion from behind a curtain. Few will notice this continuity error, and the curtain suggests, more than the pillar would have, her emergence onto a stage, the stage that is the film, the stage that is her life. And there she is, front and center, no longer trying to hide, aware of the part she is to play, prepared to face her future without deterrents from her past, to take command of her life without inhibiting shame. *Aventurera* has been called a shameless melodrama for the way it dispenses with plausibility in its convoluted plot, and it is equally shameless in the way it dispenses with moralizing and embraces its heroine's spirited shamelessness.

When she emerges in close-up from behind the curtain, she looks first at Pedro Vargas as he finishes singing; then, momentarily, she seems to glance at the viewer. Then a reverse angle shows Lucio as the object of her gaze. Sitting at a table, he has heard the song about the life of sin he led her into, and they exchange glances, she accusingly, he with a smirk on his face. But now she looks past Lucio at something all the way across the floor, which is where she was when the song began and where she now resolutely returns. It's a return to the beginning not just of this sequence but of the whole story of her fall from grace. Now the object of her gaze is none other than her old family chauffeur, Ramón. Having spotted the scoundrel as soon as he arrives at the cabaret with a party of revelers, she briskly proceeds to break a bottle on his head, to kick him and hit him and kick him as he lies on the floor until Rengo carries her away. Spirited indeed. The gaze of her self-consciousness, directed in turn at the singer telling her story, at the audience hearing it, and at one and then another of the villains playing a part in it, lets loose her vengeful fury.

Melodrama of the Spirited Woman

Plato distinguishes three parts of the human soul: the part that reasons, the part that desires, and the part that gets angry, the spirited part. Anger is in rather low repute nowadays, an emotion often thought to call for therapy, "anger management," but Plato values it almost as highly as reason: it is the emotion that makes warriors, and the rulers of the Republic are to be warriors as well as philosophers, outstanding not only for their love of wisdom but also for their spiritedness. Elena may not be a philosopher but is certainly a warrior, and *Aventurera* celebrates her invincible spiritedness.

Doña Bárbara (Mexico, 1943, directed by Fernando de Fuentes from the novel and screenplay by Rómulo Gallegos, and photographed by Alex Phillips, who also shot *Aventurera*) is another melodrama of the spirited woman. The heroine is María Félix, perhaps the greatest star of Mexican cinema's golden age, one of the most beautiful women ever to appear on the screen, and one of the most powerful—regal rather than plebeian like Ninón Sevilla, but no less feisty and fiery. Doña Bárbara is the fallen woman of melodrama risen to the top, destroyer of men, owner and virtually absolute ruler of vast expanses of land on the plains of the Orinoco basin. As recounted in an introductory flashback, six brutal men killed her boyfriend and raped her on a boat when she was very young, after which we see her in close-up staring penetratingly into the camera, fixing us with her angry adamantine gaze. The gaze of self-consciousness, which Elena gains through the song addressed to her, Doña Bárbara has from the start. Like Elena's, this is a warrior's gaze, a gaze that doesn't just look but means action, vengeance on the wrongdoers. Doña Bárbara avenges herself for what those men did to her by assuming power over all men as far as her commanding eyes can see. The dark, intense eyes of María Félix dominate the film right to the end, when Doña Barbara the witch loses to her good daughter the man she would put under her spell, yet her spellbinding gaze, directed at the camera, seems to bring on that happy ending for her daughter, to will it into being.

Mexico, the country that gave us the notion of machismo, also gave us María Félix and these melodramas of the spirited woman and the dominant female gaze. True, melodrama often centers on women, and women in Hollywood melodramas, from Lillian Gish to Barbara Stanwyck and Bette Davis, are often stronger than people think. The theory of the male gaze may apply to some movies, but it fails with melodramas and the female perspective they frequently assume. In his study of the "melodrama of the unknown woman," Stanley Cavell argues that the women in films like *Stella Dallas*, *Now, Voyager*, and *Letter from an Unknown Woman* are not the male-deferring, self-sacrificing ninnies they are sometimes taken to be.[48] But even so, neither are they the warriors that the heroines of *Doña Bárbara* and *Aventurera* are. To find in Hollywood movies women so powerful and so assertive of their power, you would have to go to the femmes fatales of film noir, and those women are presented, unlike Doña Bárbara and Elena, from a male point of view.

Stella Dallas (I have in mind the 1937 version, with Stanwyck as Stella) and *Doña Bárbara* make an interesting comparison. Stella is the social climber who gives up her climbing and lets her daughter take over from her; Doña Bárbara, of even humbler origins than Stella, rises much higher, but rather like Stella, she withdraws in the end and passes on her power to her daughter, who inherits all her land and marries the rival landowner in the region. Like the young man Stella's daughter marries, this landowner represents not only wealth—Doña Bárbara has plenty of that already—but also the refinement of a higher class. Stella and Doña Bárbara may be perceived as the losers, which seems to have been how the authors intended us to regard them, with Stella as unworthy of the upper class and capable only of sacrificing herself for her daughter's sake, and Doña Bárbara as the embodiment of a matriarchal barbarism defeated by patriarchal civilization. But in both cases our experience of the movie is at odds with that intention. If Stella and Doña Bárbara are losers, they come across as stronger than the winners. Barbara Stanwyck's Stella and María Félix's Doña Bárbara command the screen in such a way that everyone else pales beside them, and we're drawn to take their side against the supposedly superior virtues of upper-class refinement and patriarchal civilization. That may be why Stella is an "unknown

woman"; we feel there's much more to her than the movie seems
to know. Doña Bárbara is similarly unknown, beyond the movie's
knowledge. Not Elena, however. Everything about her is loud and
clear, and the movie takes her side as much as we do.
Upbraided for making trouble at the cabaret, Elena listens to
"Aventurera" and right away makes more trouble by assaulting
Ramón. She couldn't help herself, she explains; this man brought
ruin on her family. Rosaura doesn't care and orders Rengo to teach
the unruly young woman a lesson with the slash of his knife. Lucio
bursts in and almost kills the thug, who is spared thanks to Elena,
and who from here on is devotedly grateful to her. She and Lucio
take off together with a wad of money he forces the madam to hand
over. But he lands in jail when he attempts to rob a jewelry store and
one of his gang, Pacomio, sells him out to Rosaura, who tips off the
police. Elena goes on to become a successful dancer in Mexico City,
where Mario (Rubén Rojo), a well-bred young lawyer from an old
Guadalajara family, falls in love with her (we hear the Trio Los Panchos singing a love song: "Your lips taught me to feel / What tenderness is / And I will not tire of blessing / Such sweetness"), and asks
her to marry him. To get away from Pacomio, who has caught up with
her and tries to blackmail her for her complicity in the robbery, Elena
decides to marry the upstanding Mario and accompanies him to staid
Guadalajara. There, in his family's mansion, she meets his mother, a
paragon of respectability who turns out to be Rosaura.
Elena finds herself in a perfect position for vengeance. She is the
love and the happiness of a son Rosaura loves and wishes to be happy.
Rosaura sees herself as "a mother who has sacrificed everything for
the benefit and happiness of her sons," and the last thing she wants as
a mother is for her son to discover that she has been leading another
life as a madam. Elena uses Mario to punish Rosaura—not a nice
thing to do, we recognize, but we still take her side because we also
recognize that Rosaura did much worse to her, and because we cheer-
ingly identify with her defiance of a social order whose proprieties
and hypocrisies she, and we along with her, see through. She gets
drunk at her wedding party and dances so outrageously in the eyes
of Guadalajaran society that all the guests leave. She does it on purpose, flaunting the vulgarity she knows the upper class looks down
on, and flaunting it subversively. "Wasn't I up to the level of high
society?" she asks mockingly. Melodrama here comes close to comedy
and its deflation of pose and pretense. The society matron doubling as
madam of a whorehouse can be seen as a satirical caricature, almost
a figure of comedy.
Rosaura's posture as the sacrificial mother ("If my business dealings haven't been clean, at least I have fulfilled a mother's duty") can

be taken as part of the comedy. It's like a parody of maternal pathos, and we smile when Elena shows no compassion: "You don't move me, Rosaura. I go on hating you with all my soul." Rosaura turned her into a whore, and now Elena turns that against her with poetic justice. She seeks revenge on the madam and mother by making a fool of her son and letting the world know he has married a whore. Her impudent behavior, the private brought out in public literally with a vengeance, strikes at Rosaura where she's most vulnerable. The mother withdraws from Guadalajara and goes off to Ciudad Juárez, where the madam can perhaps regain control. It just so happens that Elena's own mother is there, dying in a hospital, and Rosaura makes sure Elena gets word. She wants Elena back in the city where the young woman first fell and can fall again into her hands. She tells Rengo to take care of Elena when she comes, and take care of her he does, but not in the way Rosaura intended. Elena does return to visit her mother, who asks for her daughter's forgiveness so she can die in peace. Elena remains stonily silent, though after her mother dies she softens and weeps. As for the nefarious designs Rosaura has on her, under the protection of the grateful Rengo, neither Pacomio, who threatens her again but plummets to his death while fleeing from Rengo, nor the wicked madam can do any harm to our heroine.

Aventurera is a melodrama that not only has a woman as the protagonist but also a woman as the villain. Ramón, Pacomio, even Lucio, are minor villains in comparison to Rosaura. And if Rosaura is a doubled character, mother and madam, she is further doubled with another mother, Elena's. Rosaura represents the mother that Elena is fighting, the mother that is within her, both a figure of the upper class and of the lower depths, standing both for repressive propriety and dangerous sexuality. Mario and Lucio, who in an old melodrama would have been the noble hero who offers the heroine a good marriage and the villain who puts her virtue in peril, are here lesser figures next to the mother, the respectable mother Mario reveres and her dirty other self, the madam Lucio pimps for. Here the central conflict is between daughter and mother. *Aventurera* is a melodrama of two spirited women.

Elena would have wanted the respectable mother, not the dirty one who ran off with Ramón and whom she doesn't forgive to the end. Yet it is the dirty Elena who fights the respectable Rosaura in Guadalajara, who exposes the falseness of bourgeois respectability, who wins because she fights dirty. Such are the contradictions of melodrama. Back in Ciudad Juárez, Elena goes back to her dirty dancing, and Mario arrives from Guadalajara and rebukes her, holding up his mother as a model of respectable womanhood. In retaliation, Elena takes him to the cabaret and whorehouse and introduces him to the dirty Rosaura. Her vengeance is complete. But as she comes down to the cabaret floor, she hears again the song "Aventurera," now sung in duet by Pedro Vargas and Ana María González, who stand side by side on the stage like a father and mother posed for a family picture as they sing to the daughter gone astray. This time Elena doesn't move but is moved to tears. The spirited woman has had her revenge, but these, in tightening close-up, are the tears of the good girl.

Her earlier tears were too late to assuage her mother's sad end; these tears prepare for a happy ending. They are tears of comedy—not the comedy that mocks, the social satire lending a sharp edge to the Guadalajara scenes, but the comedy that accepts and reconciles. And Elena is ready for reconciliation with her husband, who, after the shock of seeing his mother in her guise of madam, still wants Elena back. Mario regrets what his mother did to Elena—even if Rosaura sacrificed herself for him and his brother, he says, her conduct is inexcusable—and Elena regrets what she did to Mario while settling scores with his mother. The noble hero meets the fallen yet once again virtuous heroine. But the villainous Lucio, who has escaped from prison and wants Elena for himself—all the men in the movie want Elena—has been listening in and before long breaks in on the reconciling couple. Elena is caught between two men associated with the mother's two sides, the respectable Mario and the dirty Lucio. The good girl chooses the good boy, but it takes Rengo to save the situation with his knife. The dirty mother's thug won over by a good-girl gesture on Elena's part kills Lucio in the nick of time and enables the reunited wife and husband to reach their happy ending to the strains of "Aventurera."

Isn't this finally the taming of the spirited woman? Isn't the good girl surrendering to the values of a society the spirited woman defied? Elena is, after all, a daughter of the bourgeoisie, which betrays her and which she rebels against but in the end makes her peace with. It wouldn't have been right for her to have rejected Mario and gone off with Lucio, which was what her mother did with her father and Ramón that led to all the daughter's troubles. But the good girl reconciled with her husband at the end is not the same as the good girl shocked to find her mother with the chauffeur at the beginning. The mother who was the enemy, who personified the bourgeoisie through betrayal and rebellion, is by the end vanquished and gone, and has left her place to the daughter. It is with herself that Elena makes her peace, and she surrenders but also triumphs. This is essentially the ending of New Comedy, the triumph of the young lovers that brings on a renewal of the social order—a renewal, not an overthrowing. Just like its heroine, *Aventurera* is daring but also conventional, subversive but also accepting. It reflects the divided values of the bourgeoisie.

By dirty means Rosaura keeps up respectability, by dirty means Elena combats it, and all the while both of them, villain and heroine, believe in respectability, Rosaura sacrificing herself for it, Elena getting angry when she perceives it to be false and embracing it when persuaded it will come true. Such are the contradictions of the bourgeois world finding expression in melodrama.

The Ambiguity of Stella Dallas

In the mid-1980s, on the pages of *Cinema Journal*, feminist film scholars debated over *Stella Dallas* (the 1937 movie directed by King Vidor with Barbara Stanwyck in the lead). An article by Linda Williams disputed some points in E. Ann Kaplan's account of the film; Kaplan replied to Williams, other scholars offered their views, and Kaplan replied to them.[49] This debate was never settled and, as often happens with academic as with political debates, the terms in which it was conducted were never questioned. The claim that the gaze is male—that the movie camera habitually adopts the point of view of a male protagonist—led film scholars at the time to worry the issue of the female spectator. It was noted that Stella goes to the movies on a date with Stephen Dallas and expresses the wish to be just like those glamorous people on the screen; a connection was made to the way that in the final scene she resembles a movie spectator as she stands outside in the rain and watches through a large window the marriage to a rich young man of the daughter she has given up for good. Stella was taken as a figure of the female spectator, and as such she was taken to be passive, out of the picture, rendered powerless under the patriarchy. On this the debaters all concurred. But it's not for the patriarchy that Stella gives up her beloved daughter—that's not a demand the patriarchy makes on mothers. She gives up her daughter to the upper class she is herself unable (or unwilling) to join. *Stella Dallas* is a story about class, and class hardly entered into the scholarly debate.

Who is Stella Dallas? What kind of character is she? Williams describes her as a "good hearted, ambitious, working class floozy."[50] A *floozy*? It's true that after the birth of her daughter Stella wants to have a good time, and she persuades Stephen (John Boles), against his better judgment—he feels that so soon after giving birth she should be staying home and resting—to take her to a dance at the River Club. But it's for social rather than sexual reasons that Stella wants to go to the River Club. She wants to meet people of the higher class that her marriage to Stephen gives her entry into; she has no intention of cheating on him. Before her marriage she lived in a working-class

home where her stern father enforced a strict moral code; it's a safe
bet that she came into marriage a virgin. After her separation from
Stephen, when he moves to New York where his business takes him
and she stays with her daughter in her hometown of Millhampton,
Massachusetts, it's made quite clear that, though she remains friends
with Ed Munn (Alan Hale), a man she met and danced with at the
River Club, she has no sexual interest in him. The only man Stella
has known sexually is her husband.

Stella is no floozy. But she is perceived as one by two straitlaced
older women who observe her disapprovingly on a train as she laughs
loudly with Ed Munn over a practical joke with itching powder he
played on some passengers. In this very scene, out of hearing of the
two women, Stella tells Ed unequivocally that she wants their relationship to go no further than a friendship. Stella is no floozy, and if
Williams describes her as one, it can only be because she is assuming
the perspective of those from a higher social class who disapprove
of Stella, who see vulgarity and impropriety in her working-class
demeanor.

The issue of point of view, the way a film situates its spectators,
the subject position it assigns us, is central to the dispute between
Williams and Kaplan. Kaplan is more precise in her analysis of *Stella
Dallas* and right to stress that we all cry at the end. Like everyone else
in the debate, however, she sees Stella as sacrificing herself to the
patriarchal order, and she argues that our tears keep us from being
duly critical, that the film leads us to identify with its heroine to such
an extent that, unless we step outside it, we're bound to acquiesce
with her to the ruling ideology. Williams contends that, unlike the
male spectator, allegedly always identified with the male protagonist,
the female spectator is not locked into a fixed subject position and
can identify with multiple points of view inside the film. Presumably
this enables the female spectator of *Stella Dallas* to be critical of the
heroine's sacrifice, though nobody in the film takes anything like a
feminist position. Men and women may differ in their ways of looking
at things, but not only female spectators, surely male ones too, are
capable of a divided and complex response. And not only a "woman's
film" like *Stella Dallas*, many films of various kinds (Stroheim's, as we
have seen, or *The Rules of the Game* with its much-cited line, "Everyone
has their reasons," or *Rashomon* with its famous differing narrators,
or *The Killing* or *Viridiana* or *Salvatore Giuliano* or *Andrei Rublev* or *Fast
Times at Ridgemont High* or *Cadillac Records*, and I could go on and on)
deploy, and ask us in one way or another to identify with, a multiplicity of points of view. *Stella Dallas* is not particularly notable for such
multiplicity. Unlike the original novel, Olive Higgins Prouty's *Stella
Dallas* (1923), which evenly divides its attention between Stella and

Helen, the upper-class mother who takes her place, Vidor's film for the most part situates us with Stella. She is in almost every scene, and though we may not wholly side with her, we never side with any of the other characters against her. In the train scene, when we see Stella from the unsympathetic perspective of the two snooty women, this only increases our sympathy for her and our identification with her.

Though the two women look down on her, Stella is not exactly working-class any more. She is actually in an ambiguous class position—this is key to the ambiguity of Stella Dallas—between Ed Munn and the straitlaced women. While she likes him and values his friendship, she sees his vulgarity as they see hers. Stella's ambiguous position between classes—between Ed Munn and Stephen Dallas—is dramatized most strikingly in the scene at Christmastime in which Ed, drunk and disheveled, appears at her door bringing a turkey, and Stella tries to get rid of him just as Stephen, prim and impeccable, arrives from New York to pick up their daughter, Laurel (Anne Shirley), for the holidays. A reeling oaf and a stiff patrician: with neither man does Stella belong. Usually it is assumed that she belongs with her daughter, so that her giving her up at the end is taken not only as the ultimate maternal sacrifice—the mother so loving that she renounces her motherhood—but as an act tantamount to self-eradication. But it seems to me clear that Stella and Laurel don't belong together, that, though she loves her mother, Laurel would rather be with her father—as she shows in the Christmastime scene—and fits in with him and Helen and their social circle better than with her mother. To remain with her mother would have been for Laurel a sacrifice, and it is to spare her daughter that sacrifice that Stella makes hers.

At the beginning we see Stella standing by the fence of the little front garden of her working-class home and putting on an act for Stephen, who is passing by but pays no attention to this pretty young woman reading—or pretending to read—a book of love lyrics. Stella has her eyes on the upper-class Stephen: she wants to catch him and leave the working class behind. That's why Williams calls her "ambitious." She succeeds in catching Stephen but not quite in leaving the working class behind. Why not? She seems to have no attachment to her working-class family—nor have we, for the film presents them from her perspective, and we can only be glad that she manages to get out of there. But if she is "ambitious" to rise in class, why doesn't she go with Stephen to New York? In Prouty's novel it's Stephen who doesn't want Stella with him in New York—he's in effect leaving the marriage—but in the movie it's her choice not to go. The reason she gives is that she's just getting to know the right people at the River Club. Are we to assume that Stella has no social ambition beyond

Millhampton? But she must know that without Stephen she won't have access to the "right people" even in Millhampton, and that if she goes with him she will have access to the "right people" in New York. In any case, of the people she met at the River Club, the only one she continues to see is Ed Munn, who is surely not "right." Why she wants to stay in Millhampton is a question to which the film gives no satisfactory answer. Were the filmmakers anxious to make Stephen look like the abiding rather than the abandoning husband? Or did they mean this as the first step in Stella's renunciation of the upper class?

The ambiguity of Henry James—to invoke the title of Edmund Wilson's famous essay on *The Turn of the Screw*[51]—is a function of point of view: we can't be sure exactly what's going on in *The Turn of the Screw* because we are limited to the point of view of the governess, who is an unreliable narrator. Most of the time in Stanwyck and Vidor's *Stella Dallas* we are situated with Stella, are limited to her experience and encouraged to put ourselves in her place. We share her feelings about her family; we wait with her for Stephen to walk by her house; we go with her to the local factory as she pretends to bring lunch for her brother but actually wants to make an impression on Stephen; we identify with her distress when nobody comes to the birthday party she has lovingly prepared for her daughter; we identify with her jealousy when Laurel, back from a visit to New York, gushingly likens Helen to a rare flower or a goddess; and so forth. No ambiguity arises, however—none at least of the sort that comes from limited knowledge. Nor does the inclusion of points of view in conflict with Stella's, as when the two women on the train find her vulgar and take her for a loose woman, bring on any ambiguity of that sort. We know quite well that Stella can be seen as vulgar, but she isn't a loose woman. And yet the ambiguity of *Stella Dallas* has much to do with point of view, with differences in point of view—differences not so much between individuals as between classes.

Stella internalizes those class differences; part of her looks down on the working class, part of her feels looked down on by the upper class, and hence her ambiguous social identity. To some extent Laurel too, through her identification with her mother, internalizes class differences, but she wholeheartedly embraces an upper-class identity, and the conflict inside her is between her social allegiance and her personal attachment to her mother. The points of view of mother and daughter are alike divided, ambivalent. And as class divisions form divided subjectivities, so class perceptions constitute objective social realities. Perceptions, appearances, are everything in *Stella Dallas*. None knows it better than Stella the adept pretender, the performer dressed up for a part she feels called upon to play. That's how she catches Stephen; that's how she gets Laurel to believe she wants to marry Ed Munn and will gladly let her go live with her father and Helen. If the way the snooty women on the train see Stella is a misperception, it is a misperception that becomes a nonnegotiable social fact, resulting in Stella's ostracism from "nice" society (it is the reason why Laurel's friends all stay away from her birthday party) and in the end coming to be accepted by Stella herself (as it is by Williams when she calls her a "floozy"). If all that counts is how people perceive you, the fact that different people perceive you in different ways makes for an ineradicable ambiguity.

Stella has, as Stanley Cavell says, a gift for theater.[52] As the poetry reader, as the sister who has prepared lunch for her brother, Stella puts on an act for Stephen's benefit. From the lunch he duly appreciates, we dissolve to the two of them at the movies, the projector light flickering behind them as they watch people in fancy dress dancing on the screen and the leading couple kissing at the end. "I want to be like all the people you've been around," Stella tells Stephen afterward, looking very pretty as she walks by his side in the day-for-night moonlight. "Don't be like anyone else," he replies. "I like you the way you are." "No, I don't want to be like me," she insists, but "like the people in the movie, you know, doing everything well-bred and refined." "And dull," he interjects. "Stay as you are. Don't pretend, Stella. Anyway, it isn't really well-bred to act the way you aren't." They kiss like the couple in the movie and proceed to get married without delay. If Stella is sincere in saying that she wants to be like the people in the movie, she is sincere in her willingness to feign, to play the part that others expect of you in a society she sees as a matter of theatrical performance. But Stephen tells her that you shouldn't act the way you aren't; he evidently believes that the way he acts in society is his natural way of being. The perhaps unintended irony is that Stephen seems to us artificial, thoroughly conventional, as false as the people in the movie he and Stella watched, as false as all the well-bred and refined people in this movie we are watching. While Stella knows she's performing, Stephen is performing but doesn't even know it.

Prouty's novel idealizes the upper class and regards it as "natural"—elegantly simple in its dress, composed in its demeanor, outdoorsy—in contrast to Stella's flamboyance and frills. Naturalness confers class: Helen wears little makeup; Stella lays it on like war paint. Prouty identifies with Helen and presents her as the right mother for Laurel; like Helen, Prouty condescends to Stella, descends from a superior position to sympathize with her. The novel and the earlier film version of it, the silent *Stella Dallas* also produced by Samuel Goldwyn (1925, directed by Henry King, with Belle Bennett as

Stella and Ronald Colman as Stephen), portray Stella as incapable of upward mobility, unambiguously stuck in the lower class. She lacks the gift for theater, the skill at feigning and pretense, that she exhibits in the 1937 version. The novel's and the silent movie's Stella reads no poetry book and brings no lunch to impress Stephen. She doesn't pretend she wants to marry Ed Munn; she really marries him in order to drive away the daughter who detests him. But isn't King Vidor still idealizing the upper class? How else does Stella's sacrifice make sense if not to enable the daughter to rise in class as the mother had dreamed of doing? Can't we just say that the wooden John Boles is less convincing as Stephen than Ronald Colman? It's central to the ambiguity of the 1937 *Stella Dallas* that we find it hard to decide whether the intention was to idealize or to deflate the upper class.

The scene with Stella and Stephen at the movies is neither in the novel nor in the silent adaptation of it. That Stella wants to be like the people in the movie, that she watches her daughter's wedding like a spectator at the movies, suggests that the higher class she initially aspires to and that her daughter finally attains is an illusion. But is the illusion punctured, the reality behind appearances exposed? "In King Vidor's *Stella Dallas*," Charles Affron writes,

> modes of display constitute the film's dramatic pretext. Its script explicitly calls for situations in which identity is judged and acquires moral value through outward appearances. The codes of dress and manners establish a rigid standard of suitability and fitness that is worked out according to the logical expectations of the bourgeois ethic that shapes the codes. Yet the processes of the film are not completely hospitable to such expectations. The display/concealment pattern of *Stella Dallas* undermines the fiction's ostensible values. The film finally demonstrates how feeling transcends appearance through images critical of conventional standards of appearance. . . . Stella is a mediating presence in the spectacle of the wedding, a ritual that demonstrates the affective power of appearance and decorum (people are supposed to cry at weddings). She is also a spectacle in her own right when, shorn of her habitual appearance, she *shows* her feelings. . . . As Stella smiles and jauntily walks away from the window on which was projected her daughter's wedding (a surrogate screen), she becomes a model for our emotion in watching a motion picture.[53]

In his own way Affron too sees Stella as a figure of the movie spectator. Recognizing film as an art of appearances, a producer of illusions, he maintains that Stella, finally shorn of her usual makeup and ornate dress, transcends appearance through sheer emotion. But if it is "the affective power of appearance and decorum"—upper-class appearance and decorum—that elicits her emotion, how are these "images critical of conventional standards of appearance"?

John Boles's Stephen looks like nothing so much as a tailor's dummy. That may be the way he looks to Stella, but he looks that way whether or not Stella is around, and it is a look quite consistent with the way the film generally depicts his class. While buying presents for Laurel in a store in New York, he runs into Helen (Barbara O'Neil), the sweetheart of his youth, and she seems as stiffly genteel as he, as hemmed in by upper-class decorum. Her three young sons are with her, and she introduces them to Stephen. Her oldest, though still a child, wears a jacket and tie and a felt hat; she proudly describes him as "the man of the family" since she became a widow. Her youngest has saved his money to treat the whole family to lunch and amiably includes Stephen, who smilingly leans over and says: "If you're running short, I'll lend you a couple of dollars." They're all very "nice," Stephen, Helen, and her three boys, and they all seem stilted to the point of unreality. Vidor intended the niceness, but I'm not sure about the stiltedness and unreality.

Laurel takes up with a similarly "nice" young man at a summer resort, and their blossoming romance has a similar air of unreality. She plays tennis with him and goes bicycle riding with him and other young people. She's the ingénue in paradise. When the two are alone by a stream and throw pebbles in the water and he gives her his pin, she's just tickled pink. My students laugh at this idyllic sequence. Alan Hale's Ed Munn is a comic type of the lower class, but these types of the higher class don't seem intentionally comical. You could say they are idealized as Stella idealizes them—they're an illusion like the people in the movie she saw with Stephen. But Stella doesn't witness her daughter's romance at the resort, and you might rather say that the idyllic idealization expresses Laurel's feelings—though Laurel herself is a type we may find comical. Stella has been ill in her room at the resort hotel, and when she eventually comes out, dressed more flamboyantly than ever, the "nice" young people look down on her as comical and laugh at her. But *we* don't. Stella is no type, not as Barbara Stanwyck plays her.

As she demonstrated early on in films like *The Bitter Tea of General Yen* (1933, directed by Frank Capra), Barbara Stanwyck was a great actress—and a singularly unaffected one: "downright," as James Harvey describes her, "her effects . . . plain and undecorated." While few other movie stars can match her versatility, one senses in her, as Harvey notes,

> something immovable and deeply reserved, what Douglas Sirk calls her "amazing tragic stillness." Her voice, for example, as distinctive

in its way as Arthur's or Sullavan's, is both flat and eloquent, oddly and always both nasal and husky. Though what that huskiness suggests is not whiskey or disillusion or sexual provocation—but tears. Tears which have been firmly and sensibly surmounted but somehow, somewhere, fully wept—the voice of someone who is "cried out."[54]

Stella Dallas is a tearjerker performed by an actress who contains her tears. Stanwyck plays a theatrical, ornamented character without much ornamentation or theatricality. The result is a sense of Stella's inward authenticity despite her investment in the social game of outward appearances. Stella comes across as a rounded character in a movie otherwise populated by types, a real human being out of place in a world of well-bred and refined unreality.

Rounded or flat characterization is a matter of degree—Boles's Stephen is flatter than Hale's Ed Munn, a more human type, or than Ann Shirley's Laurel, a more complex type, torn between love for her mother and the pull of her father's world—but the vivid roundedness of Stanwyck's Stella sets her apart from everyone else in the movie. One character fully rounded, the rest more or less flat: this is a recipe for identification, a way of aligning the viewer (or the reader of a novel) with one character and taking that character's perspective on all the others. Vidor's film by and large gives us Stella's perspective, her slant on things even if not directly her point of view. You could say it adopts a sort of free indirect style—which in literature is the style that without demarcation or subordination brings into a third-person narrative the words and sentiments of a character—so that Stella's way of looking at things colors their visual and dramatic portrayal on the screen. But Stella changes. The spectator on a movie date near the beginning isn't the same as the spectator outside the window framing her daughter's wedding at the end. Maybe you could say that the picture of the upper class as immaculately seemly throughout represents the young Stella's dream, which her daughter inherits, of doing everything well-bred and refined like the people in the movie.

What, then, of the ambiguity in authorial intention? Is the upper class meant to be admirable or conventionalized, false, mere appearances without reality? Did Vidor aim to idealize it, like Prouty and Henry King before him, or did he knowingly intend that apparitional hollowness? Or was he, like Henry James, ambiguous on purpose? Whatever the case may be, the ambiguity somehow works to the film's advantage. It expresses the ambivalence of a heroine who breaks away from her working-class background and comes to find herself cut off as well from the higher class of her dreams. The free indirect manner of expression implicates not just her and her daughter but the author and the audience too. Thus the film gets at something important about class in America. Ordinary Americans look up to the upper class, identify with it as an ideal, and at the same time view it as illusory, impossibly removed from common humanity.

Supposedly melodrama tolerates no ambiguity. Supposedly it requires dastardly villains and suffering innocent victims in clear-cut conflicts between wickedness and virtue. If you define melodrama that way, *Stella Dallas* doesn't qualify. Even in the novel and the silent movie, which are without the ambiguity of the 1937 version, no character qualifies as a villain, and Stella is no innocent victim. Suffer she does, though; one criterion of melodrama that her story certainly meets is pathos. But pathos also belongs to tragedy. What keeps us from calling *Stella Dallas* a tragedy? Not that the protagonist is an ordinary person—we shouldn't reserve the name of tragedy for the high and mighty alone—but that the pathos comes from such petty, superficial matters as the laughter of snobby rich kids at an overdressed woman. Stella's suffering has its source in nothing of more import or gravity than common social embarrassment.

Yet *Stella Dallas* generates enormous pathos; it's amazing how potent an emotion social embarrassment can be. Williams calls the movie "an excruciatingly pathetic maternal melodrama,"[55] and Cavell says he found it "the most harrowing" among the movies he examined while preparing his study of the melodrama of the unknown woman. The most harrowing scene in this excruciatingly pathetic movie is the one at the summer resort with the derided overdressed Stella, which Cavell describes as

> one of the most famous, or unforgettable, I dare say, in the history of American cinema—in which Stella's excessive costume at a fancy resort hotel makes her an object of ridicule to refined society and—so the accepted view goes, unchallenged as far as I know—precipitates her plan to separate from her daughter, the act all but universally understood as Stella's "self-sacrifice." This understanding is based on the assumption, as expressed . . . by Linda Williams, that Stella is "as oblivious as ever to the shocking effect of her appearance." My thought is that . . . there is massive evidence in the film that Stella knows exactly what her effect is there, that her spectacle is *part* of her strategy for separating Laurel from her, not the catastrophe of misunderstanding that causes her afterward to form her strategy.[56]

Cavell is right that Stella is not oblivious—she aims to make an impression with her attire—but what Williams means is that Stella is unaware that she's making entirely the wrong impression. In the novel and the silent movie that's quite clear: she waves at her daughter and comes toward her, but Laurel can't bear to acknowledge in front of her friends that this ridiculous person is her mother, and she runs away from her.

I don't know whether Cavell is familiar with the earlier versions of the story, but his interpretation rests on the very ways in which Stanwyck and Vidor's film is significantly different—and significantly ambiguous. How could the woman who has shown such talent for theater, such skill at social performance and mastery of dress—as Cavell points out, she makes all her daughter's clothes, which win praise from Helen herself, and in the Christmastime scene she "hurriedly and surely alter[s] a black dress in which to receive her husband Stephen," knowing perfectly well how to tone down her frills and wear something plainer that suits his upper-class taste[57]—how could this woman commit such a blunder as the gaudy attire she puts on for refined society at the summer resort? And so Cavell infers that at the resort too "Stella knows exactly what her effect is."

Her altered black dress makes the right impression on Stephen, but he recoils at the sight of Ed Munn and promptly takes off with Laurel. Stella is left alone. Her act has failed, and she "stands in that black dress, her back to the camera, watching the closed door behind which Stephen and Laurel have disappeared," as Cavell describes the moment he sees as a turning point in the story.[58] The silent version has a similar shot of the abandoned Stella, but the camera is farther away, which puts the emphasis on her empty surroundings, on the pathos of her abandonment, whereas the emphasis here is on Stella herself, what she may be thinking, her reflection on her failure. At this moment, Cavell surmises, "Stella learns the futility of appealing to the taste of those who have no taste for her."[59] In his view it is at this point, not after the embarrassment at the summer resort, that she begins planning her strategy for separating from her daughter, meaning that the spectacle she makes of herself at the fancy hotel is no blunder but a calculated effect.

After her moment of reflection Stella visits the office of Stephen's lawyer and, in marked contrast to her black dress and decorous demeanor in the previous scene, she wears a showy costume and exhibits a lower-class manner as she flatly refuses to give her husband a divorce. In the usual interpretation she refuses because she doesn't want him to take Laurel away from her, which is what she tells his lawyer. But in both scenes this theatrical character is surely performing. Neither the decorous nor the loud woman is the real Stella. If, as Cavell thinks, the real Stella has reached the decision to part from Laurel, she presumably knows that a divorce at this stage would only keep her loyal daughter with her, that it will take a drastic measure like her inviting ridicule at the resort hotel to get Laurel to part from her. Even after that Stella must play the vulgar woman again and pretend she wants to marry Ed Munn.

It's Barbara Stanwyck, her performance as a social performer wearing different masks from one scene to the next yet all the same possessing a core of substance, that chiefly conveys the sense of a real even if unknown Stella. From Laurel by the stream, ecstatically receiving her young man's pin, we dissolve to Stella before a mirror in her hotel room, preparing to go out in her excessive costume. If daughter and mother alike seem contrived, Stella at least knows she's putting on a show. But does she know it's an outrageous show? I certainly didn't think so when I first saw the film, but seeing it again in light of Cavell's interpretation, I admit the possibility that she knows, the ambiguity that she may or may not know. Unlike Prouty's Stella, or Belle Bennett's in the silent movie, Stanwyck's Stella isn't naive. At the fancy resort she's not unsure of herself and pitiful in her misguided attire; she's ostentatiously affected, manifestly playing a role and unashamedly showing off. She may be unaware of the effect of her appearance, but we could be deceived by her apparent unawareness.

The last to return from the bicycle ride, Laurel and her young man join the others at the hotel soda fountain. They're all talking about this preposterous woman who has been parading around the hotel, but the two young lovers pay little attention. Then Stella enters, and we see her reflected in the large mirror behind the counter at which the young people sit. We see her from their point of view, though Laurel takes no notice of her, and neither does Stella of her daughter. When Laurel looks up at the mirror, sees her mother, and realizes she's the woman on everyone's lips, we cut closer to Stella, but we still see her mirror image, now from the point of view of the horrified Laurel, who, "for the first time," as William Rothman says, "sees her mother through others' eyes."[60] Here, as in the earlier versions, Laurel runs away from her mother, but here Stella, perhaps pretending, remains inadvertent of her daughter's presence. Rothman construes the soda fountain mirror as another "surrogate screen"—though in this case Stella is not the spectator but the spectacle—and he maintains that "we 'identify' not with Stella but with the gazes that cruelly expose her"—the spectators of her spectacle.[61] But if we don't identify with Stella, why do we feel such acute embarrassment?

This scene is a good example of multiple identifications. We see Stella from the position of the derisive young people—who may be cruel but are still presented as "nice," and we agree with them about her ridiculous appearance—and then from Laurel's position, from the divided perspective of a daughter who identifies both with her friends and with her mother. If she didn't identify with her friends she wouldn't run away from her mother, and if she didn't identify with her mother she would laugh at her along with her friends. We are situated at the counter with Laurel and her friends, and we look at the mirror first through their eyes and then through hers. But identification isn't about visual perspective alone. Even if that's not where the camera puts us, we put ourselves in Stella's place as others laugh at her behind her back. We identify with her not because we feel what she feels but because, even if she's not embarrassed, we are tremendously embarrassed for her. Laurel is embarrassed too, for her mother and for herself, and we identify with her too, but the embarrassment centers on Stella, and we identify with her most of all. Social embarrassment may be a petty emotion, but in America it can be the clearest marker of class divisions. I have friends who like to think there's no such thing as class in this country, and when I ask them if they've ever been at a fancy restaurant, prepared to pay the exorbitant prices but still feeling embarrassed and out of place, they recognize the fact of class.

The Stella we identify with in this scene is not, however, the knowing Stella Cavell proposes. We identify with a woman unaware of being ridiculed by the very people she set out to impress. That's what generates such intense emotion, what makes the scene harrowing and unforgettable. Identification with another is an act of imagination: we put ourselves in the other person's situation as we imagine it to be, not necessarily as it is. We can identify with a Stella we think unknowing and later agree with Cavell that she knew exactly what she was doing, but then the film, as we come to understand it, must retroactively justify the suffering it put us through by encouraging a misperception. Maybe Stanwyck and Vidor were trying to have it both ways, to elicit all the pathos of the earlier versions and at the same time portray a less pathetic, more forceful Stella. They may have risked inconsistency, yet they succeeded in enriching the story by lending it ambiguity, and Cavell's interpretation, taken not as the answer but as a good question, opens up a possibility that augments and complicates the ambiguity. Even in the earlier versions Stella was never the passive, suffering spectator she's often taken to be; no other character is as much a mover of the plot. She's out of the picture at the end, but in effect she is—and Helen gives her credit for it—to a considerable extent its author.

In the novel Stella marries Ed Munn and moves to New York, where she sinks into misery with her alcoholic husband; such are the depths of her self-sacrifice. Her one joy in life is watching her daughter through the windows of Helen and Stephen's house. Helen knows this (Laurel of course doesn't) and arranges to have the shades always raised to provide a view for Stella, who at the end watches Laurel's coming-out party—not her wedding, as in the two movies, which confine the spectatorial mother to that romantic happy ending. In the silent movie Stella watches her daughter first through her bedroom window (Laurel looks out but only sees her own reflection in the windowpane) and then through the larger window displaying the wedding ceremony. Unlike Henry King, who keeps cutting from Stella's outside perspective to shots inside the house, Vidor remains outside with Stella and sustains her point of view on the nuptial spectacle. He highlights the metaphor of the movie screen down to the final kiss.

In the 1937 version Stella never intends to marry Ed Munn, and when she appears in the concluding scene she seems to materialize out of nowhere. She seems transformed: with no makeup, not the least affectation of dress or demeanor, no social mask, the performer is no longer performing, no longer putting on a show but simply watching one. She cries with a sincerity as plain as her attire, and she smiles. Bennett's Stella smiles too, but hers is the smile of a woman without any other joy in life than the sight of her daughter; and it's a brief smile, seen in long shot just before her final departure from view. Stanwyck's smile prompts Vidor's camera to move with her Stella, the kind of camera movement that doesn't merely follow a character's movement but seems to originate with the character. As this radiant Stella turns away from the window and toward the camera, as she jauntily strides toward us in the rain and the dark, we feel compelled to keep pace with her until the final fade-out. Behind her triumphant smile we sense something beyond the happy ending she contrived for her daughter and left herself out of. She seems to be headed somewhere, as if her own story were not over but beginning anew. Hers is a "secret smile," as Rothman calls it, and it suggests "the possibility that Stella is happy *not* to be inside, happy to be free from marriage and motherhood."[62] While she's happy for her daughter, she is also, we may surmise, happy to be rid of her daughter, rid of the obligation to perform in a world ruled by performance.

The ambiguity of this Stella Dallas culminates in this haunting conclusion. Stella turns her back on the past and, smiling beyond her tears, advances toward the future—but what future? "I do not feel that any future I might imagine for her is as important as the sense that she has one," Cavell writes, and at the end of this story about class he sees her as transcending class, an Emersonian figure of self-reliance and self-invention perhaps on her way to becoming a movie star—"call her Barbara Stanwyck."[63] But even if she's not going back to a life of misery with Ed Munn, she might be about to go jump in the river. Who knows? Stella is an unknown woman, unknown because all along she has been playing one part or another

in the theater of an alienated society in which appearances are everything. Now that, perhaps gladly, she's out of that theater, now that
she seems to be herself, she says nothing.

"The tragic hero has only one language that is completely proper
to him: silence." Walter Benjamin quotes this statement by Franz
Rosenzweig in the course of a comparison between tragedy and *Trauerspiel*, the German "sorrow-play." "The inarticulacy of the tragic
hero . . . distinguishes the main figure in Greek tragedy from all his
successors," Benjamin writes. "In tragedy pagan man realizes that
he is better than his gods, but this realization strikes him dumb, and
it remains unarticulated."[64] The gods represent the order of things:
the tragic hero who realizes that he is better than his gods realizes
that the order of things is not right. Doesn't Stella come to realize,
even if not quite consciously, that she is better than her gods, better
than those well-bred and refined figures she looked up to and would
emulate? Doesn't she come to realize that something is wrong with
the order of things in this society governed by outward appearances?
Invested as she has been in the ways of these gods, this is a realization
she could not express in words. She can only exclude herself from the
Olympus of the people in the movie and silently disown their order of
things, an unknown woman with a smile on her face as she goes off
by herself into the darkness. I don't mean to suggest that *Stella Dallas* is like a Greek tragedy, only that Stella has something in common
with a tragic heroine.

Moving with Characters

When the camera adopts a character's perspective, we look with
the character, we identify with the character's gaze. When the
camera follows a character's movement, we move with the character,
we identify with the character's ongoing action. And when, as at the
end of *Stella Dallas*, the camera starts moving in visible response to
the character's movement, we get the sense that the character leads
the camera, that the camera's agency in telling the story takes its cue
from the character's agency inside the story—which fits in with the
way that Stella has functioned as an author figure, a mover of the plot.

Murnau's *Sunrise* (1927) is an archetypal melodrama of adultery,
a parable of the husband, the wife, and the villainous other woman,
the femme fatale who comes from the city, seduces the country husband, and talks him into killing his sweet wife. It is also a film famous
for its camera movements. As the woman from the city sets out in
the evening on her way to a rendezvous with the unfaithful husband,
the camera pans with her from across the village street. Then, as if

under an irresistible pull, it starts traveling down the street with her and follows along behind her until she stands outside the married couple's house and signals to the husband to go meet her in the marshes. As he does so, the camera now follows along behind him in the moonlit country night, but it soon overtakes him and, swerving through the bushes, gets to the woman from the city well ahead of him—again as if the camera itself were irresistibly drawn to her. This is often considered a classic example of the autonomous camera, the camera moving on a path of its own, detached from the characters— yet here the camera leaves one character aside only to take a short- cut to another, more dominant character. After the femme fatale has persuaded the man to go along with her murderous plan, a tracking shot follows their footprints in the mud and at length catches up with her high-heeled feet making their mark on the swampy ground, she being the one governing this movement, hers and the man's as well as the camera's and ours.

In the way it moves as if under her spell, the camera identifies itself with the woman from the city. Is this just a matter of form, nar- rative design, following the character who drives the story forward? Tracking shots are a matter of morality, Godard once said,[65] and Mur- nau's camera, though not morally allied with the villainous seduc- tress, does exhibit a certain complicity with her. What about us in the audience? Don't we identify with the femme fatale? We identify with her as we do with any compelling villain. The villain in melodrama is often the prime mover of the plot, and if we enjoy melodrama we enjoy villainy and, consciously or not, we identify with it even as we also identify with virtue. Hitchcock, an inheritor of Gothic melo- drama and expressionist cinema, cunningly identifies the camera with the villain in such movies as *Shadow of a Doubt* or *Psycho*.

The husband in *Sunrise* takes his wife boating on a lake, intending to drown her but in the event shrinking from a deed that goes against his better nature. He swiftly rows to shore, where she runs away from him and gets on a passing trolley. He runs after her, asking forgive- ness, and breathlessly joins her on the trolley, where the two of them ride together into the city. It is an extraordinary sequence, this trolley ride we share with the nearly killed wife and the husband who nearly killed her. Nothing happens other than the movement through space and time as intense emotion stays in place and resonates against the flowing scenery of the country gradually turning into the city. We identify with both the distressed wife and the repentant husband we travel with. There is no more moving instance of the way moving with characters induces identification with them. It is not an uninterrupted movement; it comprises several smoothly successive traveling shots abridging the time it would take to travel from the country to the city, just as this sequence condenses the time it would take for a wife to begin to forgive a husband who came so close to murdering her. The moving camera previously in thrall to the woman from the city is now identified with the trolley's mechanical, impersonal motion, which conveys a sense of relief, of time flowing free from the villain's manipulation.

The camera can identify with a character's agency as a mover of the story; call that *efficient* identification. Or it can identify with the movement of characters whose feelings it thereby draws us into, such as the husband and wife on their trolley ride; call that *affective* identification. Efficient and affective identification are of course not mutually exclusive. When we move with Stella away from the nuptial window, we recognize her agency and we also cry and smile with her.

Kenji Mizoguchi's *Osaka Elegy* (1936) begins at a well-appointed house in the morning. The wife is still asleep, her dog beside her in bed. The husband treats the female servants peevishly and peremptorily ("The towel's damp, you half-wit" are the first words he utters) and complains about his wife ("She's always out at night. What time did she get in?") She feels a bit indisposed, and a doctor comes to examine her ("Too much rich food again?"), but soon enough she joins the two men at the breakfast table, where her husband keeps complaining about their marriage and she calmly reminds him that he married into her family. *Osaka Elegy* is a film about money, and hers is the money behind their prosperous household and the pharmaceutical company he runs. As she rises from the table and leaves the house, we follow her in a camera movement that she seems to initiate and which, after a cut, resumes as she arrives at the pharmaceutical company and walks into its offices, where we steadily follow her from a distance, with people and things, employees and desks, a tall shelf of pharmaceutical bottles and a potted palm, going by between us and this striding rich woman. She may not be exactly a prime mover of the plot, but these traveling shots give us the sense that, at home and place of business alike, she is in command of a space she traverses as its owner.

The start and the cessation of movement as well as the movement itself are deliberate, distinctive gestures of Mizoguchi's camera. When the arriving woman pauses to address a young male employee she's inviting to the theater, the camera pauses with her and then cuts to Ayako (Isuzu Yamada), the company switchboard operator, who jealously watches her boyfriend and her boss's wife. Ayako needs money to repay the sum her father embezzled, and her boss has propositioned her and will give her the money that will save her father from jail. What's she to do? Her boyfriend can't help her, and out of filial duty she agrees to become her boss's kept woman. Having left home and quit work, she sits alone in the apartment where her boss has set her up. Then the two-timing husband comes to the building, and we follow him as he walks through the lobby and up a flight of stairs, the camera movement circling back on the upper floor and concluding with a view of the apartment through a sheer window curtain as he enters and greets his young mistress. Like his wife at the company offices, he arrives at the apartment with an air of owning the space into which he leads the moving camera.

Things happen twice in this fallen-woman melodrama. The wife runs into her husband with his mistress at the Bunraku theater but is deceived into thinking that Ayako is another man's companion. It takes a second chance occurrence for the wife to realize the truth and angrily break up her husband's adultery. Ayako is glad to see him go, to have been set free of a corrupt arrangement. Perhaps her boyfriend will forgive her and they will be able to marry. Once again, however, her family lays an obligation on her. This time her brother owes money for his school tuition, and she extracts the requisite sum from another amorous businessman and curtly departs without keeping her side of the bargain. That things happen twice suggests that they are liable to happen. But it also means that paths are twice taken, choices twice made. Ayako is no mere pawn of circumstances. Neither unknowing nor exactly blameless, she twice chooses to compromise herself for the sake of her family. When Trina wins the lottery in *McTeague* and *Greed*, she has no choice in the matter; she is prey to forces beyond her control inescapably driving events on a path toward perdition. Compared with Trina, Ayako is more in control of her life, more responsible for what happens to her. This is not to minimize the terrible pressure of circumstances but to recognize that she has an active part in the way things turn out. It's the same with Omocha, the Yamada character in *Sisters of the Gion*, Mizoguchi's subsequent fallen-woman melodrama from the same year.

Thinking that she has gotten away with cheating the businessman who paid for sexual services she withheld, Ayako calls her boyfriend on the phone and asks him to come to the apartment. We see her through the curtained window as she impatiently awaits him, the camera moving with her as, whistling, she stands up and moves to the window, parts the curtain and looks out, sits down and stands up again, goes to fetch a pot of tea and brings it to the table, lights a cigarette and again moves to the window and parts the curtain— small nervous movements to which the camera attentively responds, encouraging our affective identification with her expectant anxiety. Now she sees her boyfriend arriving, and as she calls to him, the camera swiftly moves down with her gaze and proceeds to follow him as he walks through the lobby and up the stairs in the same way it earlier followed the arriving boss, circling back on the upper floor just as before and concluding with a view through the sheer curtain of Ayako and the boyfriend she hopes to marry. But if the earlier camera movement induced an efficient identification with the boss who set her up in the apartment, this reprise does something different: it follows the boyfriend following Ayako's bidding to come meet her, and it signifies her attempt to move the story in accordance with her wishes, to gain command of a space she does not own—an attempt that sadly fails. The camera moving with her boyfriend as if he were taking over that space expresses her wishful notion of his efficacy in the role she would have him play in her life. She pleadingly admits to him that she was the boss's kept woman, and before the astounded young man makes any reply, the cheated businessman arrives, and after him the police.

At the police station her boyfriend disowns her and blames her for everything ("I have no desire to marry her. She deceived me. I didn't realize she was such a terrible woman"), but the charges against her are leniently dropped, and her father takes her home. Her family offers her no welcome and shows her no gratitude, however; this woman has fallen for the sake of a family that treats her as a disgrace. For a second time Ayako leaves home. Where's she to go? She stands alone on a bridge in the city night, looking down at the water and perhaps thinking of suicide. Then, after a brief exchange with the doctor, who has no cure for her ills, she walks on, and the camera starts moving with her in a lateral traveling shot that follows her steadily and brings us gradually closer to her until we cut to a final, frontal close-up of her face. Like Stella in her final shot, she advances toward us; unlike Stella, she looks straight at us and faces us in a close-up that gets closer and closer as the film ends. More than casting a glance in our direction, she seems to be breaking out of the screen and, instead of resignedly disappearing into the darkness as we might have expected, thrusting herself into our space. Her concluding stare at the audience has been taken to express an accusation, a mute protest against an unjust society. But her countenance is composed and emotionless, a simple assertion of her ineffaceable presence before us, meeting our eyes and moving ahead. As with Stella, the final movement with Ayako conveys a sense of her agency. Unlike Stella, however, Ayako has no reason to smile as she faces an uncertain future.

Mizoguchi uses close-ups sparingly; even at moments of emotional intensity, he tends to keep the camera at a distance. Yet time and again he depicts things that call for tears, woeful, heartrending things, second to none in the annals of melodramatic (or tragic) pathos; his reflective detachment does not so much assuage the pathos as deepen and amplify it. (One of his admirers writes that

his "gentle but unwavering camera nurtures and observes his characters' often tragic lives with an emotionalism . . . as intense as any
committed to film, yet free of melodrama."[66] When melodrama gets
as good as this, the prejudice against it will lead people to deny that
it is melodrama.) What's most notable about Mizoguchi is not his
detachment but its transaction with pathos, not his serenity but its
interplay with sentiment, not his imperturbability but its entwine-
ment with turmoil. Something similar could be said of another artist famous for keeping his distance, Bertolt Brecht, who in plays like
Mother Courage or *The Caucasian Chalk Circle* stirs potent emotions and
at the same time puts a curb on them. It was a misunderstood Brecht
that the academic film theory of the 1970s and 1980s invoked, a theory opposed to all identification and illusion because it supposed that
they hold the spectator in absolute ideological thrall when in fact they
are a matter of degree and variable effect. At the time a leading film
scholar, Dudley Andrew, undertook to rescue identification in Mizoguchi from the strictures of the theory and talked about the "paradox of distance and involvement which defines the experience of his
films."[67] But distance and involvement do not preclude each other,
and their combination is not a paradox. They are combined all the
time, though rarely with Brecht's, and Mizoguchi's, dialectical force
and finesse.

Max Ophuls loves to move the camera ("A shot that does not call
for tracks / Is agony for poor dear Max," rhymes James Mason in a
poem about the director").[68] He often moves it with his characters,
but he seldom uses point-of-view shots through their eyes. His moving camera, Daniel Morgan argues, "responds to both the states of
mind of characters and the social world they inhabit," a "dual attunement" that "does not . . . create a straightforward identification with
characters."[69] All identification is partial, relative. By "straightforward" Morgan seems to mean the kind of identification created in a
point-of-view shot—a designated subjective perspective—but seeing
with a character is neither more nor less straightforward than moving with one. The "dual attunement" that Morgan thinks special to
Ophuls seems similar to the combination of distance and involvement that Andrew thought special to Mizoguchi. Surely a camera
moving with a character usually responds both to the character and
to the environment in which he or she moves.

Ophuls's *The Earrings of Madame de . . .* (1953) tells the story, set
among the French upper class around 1900, of a love triangle and
a pair of earrings. The husband is an aristocratic general, the other
man an Italian diplomat, and the wife, Louise (Danielle Darrieux),
is described in title cards at the start as a "very elegant, dazzling,
celebrated woman" who "seemed destined to a pretty life without

a story. Probably nothing would have come to pass except for this jewel." We see her hand opening a drawer and almost taking a pair of heart-shaped diamond earrings; we hear her voice saying that they were her husband's wedding present to her. So she looks among her possessions for something else she could sell to pay a debt without telling her husband. The camera is right beside her as, in a kind of secret complicity, it follows the movements of her hand, her gaze, her shadow, her body, her bending down after a dropped Bible and reaching up for a hat, her swerving back toward her dressing table and sitting before an elaborate mirror in which we get our first full look at her face. Giving herself permission after all to sell these earrings she doesn't like so much, she puts them in her handbag and stands up, and the camera draws back and unbrokenly continues moving with her as she walks toward the door.

In no other opening scene I can think of is the camera so closely, so intimately identified with a character. That for most of the scene Louise is at least partly out of view only strengthens the identification; she is with the camera, she shares with it the off-screen space extending in its direction. She hums along with a melody being played as background music—music from outside the world the characters inhabit, nondiegetic music she supposedly can't hear but seems to respond to, and music that responds to her humming like an unseen orchestra in a musical. "It's as if she were attuned to the formal logic of the film itself," Morgan comments[70]—or as if the film itself were thoroughly attuned to her. The film makes an efficient identification with Louise—she sets the story in motion, she's preparing to sell the earrings without which there would have been no story—as well as an affective one.

"Yet Ophuls is careful to keep a degree of distance and separation," Morgan adds; "he never actually creates a genuine point-of-view shot."[71] Ophuls does keep an edge of detachment—so that we may note Louise's privileged vanity and frivolity—and never exactly assumes her perspective. But point-of-view shots aren't necessary to induce identification with a character; nor are they necessarily the most binding way to induce it. They have been compared to the use of dialogue in prose fiction. Just as a writer will have a character say something, so a filmmaker will show something through a character's eyes. A line of dialogue does not take over the narration, and likewise a point-of-view shot doesn't of itself establish a narrative point of view; nothing more than a momentary identification with a character's perspective need be entailed. A novel may have a character as narrator, or it may incorporate a character's words into the narration as free indirect speech, which identifies the narration with the character to greater or lesser degree. Voice-over is the only way for a character to narrate a film, but a film can incorporate a character's perspective and movements into the arrangement of images as a sort of visual free indirect speech. That's what Ophuls does with Louise in the opening of *Madame de . . .* At any moment during the long take moving with her among her possessions he could have created a point-of-view shot by simply inserting a view of her face in reverse angle. The free indirect rendering of her viewpoint that he instead gives us mixes it in more thoroughly with his authorial narration and in that way makes for a closer identification between the two.

Near the end of *Le plaisir* (1952) Ophuls's camera moves with and at the same time sees with a character. It briskly and uninterruptedly takes the place and assumes the perspective of a suicidal woman running upstairs, opening a window, and jumping out. This might be deemed the ultimate in identification, but for me the effect is of a technical stunt. As the camera plunges forward suicidally, I draw back emotionally from the scene. A camera can imitate well enough what human eyes see, but it can't convincingly throw itself out of a window and crash into a glass roof below. This could, however, be construed as suggesting that, if the point-of-view camera movement is a theatrical gesture, so is the woman's suicide attempt, sincere yet intended to make an impression on the man who has forsaken her, and resulting not in her death but in their marriage. The camera's inordinate alignment with the suicidal woman may be taken as ironic detachment.

The protagonist of *The Reckless Moment* (1949), a suburban housewife named Lucia (Joan Bennett), seems to be constantly in motion, and Ophuls's camera seems to be constantly in motion with her. It follows her everywhere as, her husband being away on business, she attends to the incessant business of the home, the regular and the irregular demands of the family. As it follows her up the stairs and around the upper floor of the house, or down the stairs when she receives a long-distance call from her husband, the encircling balustrade suggests imprisonment, intimates that the home she assiduously rules over effectively holds her prisoner.

At the outset it follows her car as she drives into the city to confront Darby, the sleazy middle-aged man her teenage daughter, Bea, has been seeing, and it stays with Lucia as she crosses the street, goes into a hotel, and walks into the empty bar where Darby has arranged to meet her. Ophuls's camera will move with one character and freely switch to another—this is part of its dual attunement—and now it cuts to Darby and follows him into the bar, a camera movement that turns into a shot/reverse shot as he and she face each other and talk. She can handle him in the bar—he asks her for money to stop seeing Bea, and Lucia feels that telling her daughter how easily he can be bought off will suffice to get rid of him—but that night Darby comes to the house, and her upset daughter strikes him and runs away, unaware that she has accidentally killed him. Lucia can handle this too. When she finds his dead body in the morning, she manages with remarkable aplomb to dispose of it.

But the corpse surfaces, an apparent murder, and love letters that Bea wrote to Darby at the height of their affair have fallen into the hands of blackmailers. Lucia has a worried look when she arrives at the house. We follow her as she hears from the maid that a Mr. Donnelly has been waiting for her, walks through the kitchen and the dining room, and pauses when she sees a man in the parlor. Then Donnelly (James Mason) comes forward, and the camera starts moving with him as he walks past Lucia and closes a pair of slatted bifold doors, and it keeps moving with him as he proceeds to inspect other doors he decides need not be closed, turns back toward Lucia and tells her about the letters, which he prices at $5,000, and walks unperturbedly away from her, reading aloud choice passages of Bea's smitten prose. This is nothing like the shot/reverse shot face-off at the bar. There Lucia stood her ground, but here, on her own ground, in the unbroken course of a long take, Donnelly seems to be insinuating himself into the space of the family and subtly gaining control: "you'd think she was visiting *him*," James Harvey observes, "the quiet way he takes over the room, and the situation."[72] And, one might add, the movements of the camera, the cut that ends the long take with a close view of him as he turns on a lamp. Identification in this scene gravitates toward the blackmailer who comes to fall romantically in love with Lucia and to represent for her, at a more mature level, something like the freedom from suburban confinement that the lowlife Darby meant to her adolescent daughter.

In the end Donnelly dies rescuing Lucia from his partner in blackmail, who is nasty and not a bit romantic. Harvey sees *The Reckless Moment* as "noir with a twist: the *femme* here is *fatale* to the hero because she is respectable *instead* of criminal."[73] Not only in *The Reckless Moment* but in such other Ophuls movies as *Madame de . . .* , *Letter from an Unknown Woman* (1948), or *La signora di tutti* (1934), the *femme* is *fatale*—yet he portrays her sympathetically, affectionately, never as a villain. *La Tendre Ennemie* (1936, from a play by André Antoine) gives us, according to Barry Salt, "the Ophuls woman in the extreme form: vain, spoilt, selfish, and directly responsible for the death of one lover and another admirer also. She is the enemy of the film's title, and it seems likely to me that Ophuls regarded her tenderly, though the author of the original play did not, just because she is pretty and charming. We shall meet her again, particularly in *Madame de . . .* , but also elsewhere."[74] Are we to hold against Ophuls his love of beautiful women? Isn't the usual portrayal of a villainous femme fatale motivated by fear and resentment of a woman's beauty?

Helen of Troy, a femme fatale if there ever was one, is not a villain in the *Iliad*. Homer does not blame her personally for the Trojan War. Something larger than herself was involved, a power beyond her control, something the Greeks personified in a divinity. "She is a dangerous girl and she doesn't know it!" says her father about Gaby (Isa Miranda) in *La signora di tutti*, a girl who has done nothing wrong but finds herself expelled from school after her beauty drives the music teacher to suicide because he can't live without her. Her widowed father would keep her confined at home, but a boy, Roberto, passing by with other boys, notices her in the garden, gets into a fight over her, and invites her and her sister to a party at his house. Bearing on his face a scar from the fight, a wound of love, Roberto looks for Gaby at the party, and the moment he sees her, he strides down the staircase toward her. The camera moves with him as he approaches her, and it continues moving with the two of them as they dance together and, past a cut, go into another room by themselves and go on dancing and turning around and around. "I would like to dance always," she says, whirling free of her partner and swooning down to the floor, whereupon the camera itself whirls all around the room. We aren't merely following these characters; we feel immersed in the stream of their movements, their sentiments, which makes palpable the experience of falling in love and getting vertiginously caught up in something larger than ourselves, something divine and dangerous.

Roberto is leaving the next day, however, and is twice thwarted in the attempt to declare his love. First his mother, Alma, who has heard about the scandal at the school, wants to talk to Gaby, and then his father, Leonardo, a rich man away on business most of the time, happens to be returning and driving by in his car just as Gaby steals out of her house for a midnight tryst with Roberto. Alma, an invalid habitually left alone by her husband, asks Gaby to come visit her and grows very fond of this meek, sweet girl. Leonardo, for his part, decides to cancel a business trip and stay home once he lays eyes on this beautiful girl. She wears one of his wife's dresses when he takes her to the opera, which she finds enchanting, and afterward he tries to kiss her, but she puts her hand between their mouths. A scene ensues in which the camera moves now with her, now with him, as they move parallel to each other, Gaby rowing a boat in a pond, Leonardo driving his car alongside the pond, and trees, pillars, plants, flowers going by between them as we see her from his perspective and him from hers in a traveling shot/reverse shot that reverses with each cut the apparent direction of motion on the screen, so that two characters both going in the same direction seem disconcertingly opposed, she moving left to right, he right to left, as if the two were bound together on a collision course. This fraught family romance centered on Gaby is indeed headed for disaster. That night Leonardo insists that she meet him in the garden, and Alma, with the music from the opera playing on her bedside radio, anxiously rises in search of the girl who hasn't responded to her call, rushes along the corridor in her wheelchair, and crashes down the staircase to her death. Gaby is the most *fatale* of Ophuls's *femmes*, and the most innocent—innocent yet not unaware. Awareness dawns, perhaps already after the music teacher's suicide, certainly after Alma's death. A shaken smile of recognition flickers on Gaby's face as she slowly advances toward the woeful scene at the bottom of the stairs, and the camera keeps following her as she runs up the stairs toward the blaring radio, which she attacks with both fists and throws on the floor, silencing the music that for her seems to have come to represent the demonic forces unleashed by her beauty. Now it is Leonardo's turn to meet his ruin, his disgrace, and eventually his death in the street outside a theater featuring a new movie with Gaby in the lead. She has become a movie star, everybody's woman, *la signora di tutti*. After Leonardo's death she sees Roberto, who confesses he still loves her but has married her sister, and now it is Gaby's turn and she slashes her wrists. Her story, related in flashback from the operating table where doctors try to save her life, ends with her death there. Extravagantly melodramatic—as much so as *Aventurera*, whose protagonist is also a woman everybody loves—*La signora di tutti* invites an allegorical reading. Let's call it a melodrama of the beautiful woman and say that it allegorizes the irresistible power of a woman's beauty and the personal powerlessness of the woman herself.

Michelangelo Antonioni's *La signora senza camelie* (1953) is another melodrama of the beautiful woman. It also has a movie star as protagonist, or rather an aspiring one. Clara (Lucia Bosé), the "lady without camellias," is a Milanese shopgirl whose beauty catches a producer's eye and gets her a part in a film being screened as the film begins. Under the opening credits, we see her from above in a static long shot as she waits outside the screening and paces back and forth on the edge of the sidewalk, twice leaving frame and returning into view. We start moving with her, from a distance, as the credits end and she goes into the theater, and after a cut, we resume following her as she enters the screening and watches herself singing a song on the screen. Then she leaves frame and does not return into view; only her screen image abides as Gianni, the producer who discovered her, gets up from his seat together with the chief producer, and they come closer to the camera and talk about revising the script to give her the leading role in a film now to be called *Woman* (instead of *Man*) *without Destiny*. As the screening concludes and the audience applauds, the camera pans with the two producers toward the exit and cuts outside the theater, where they join a group coming out of the screening, talking about Clara and her promise as a star. The camera moves rightward with them, pauses awhile, and then moves leftward with them and a few others along the sidewalk, Gianni leaving frame ahead of the rest and reappearing in the distance as he reaches his car and notices some-one hidden from us around the corner behind a wall, whereupon we cut to Clara as he walks toward her. Characters entering and leaving frame, disappearing and reappearing, the camera moving with one character, then with another, in one direction, then in another, explor-ing, inspecting the scene, finding the lost sight of, encountering the unanticipated—such intricate arrangement of motion and attention, unhurried yet continually surprising, marks Antonioni's way with long takes.

Involvement and detachment, identification with characters and inspection of their milieu—what Morgan calls dual attunement to their states of mind and their social situation—are a matter of degree. Compared with Antonioni's, Ophuls's camera movements tend to be more identified with character movements, swifter, more rest-less, more involving. Antonioni's camera tends to be more detached from the characters, more reflective, a more acute social observer. In its portrayal of upper-middle-class suburban America in the post-war years, *The Reckless Moment* is exceptional among Ophuls's films for its precise social observation; his favorite setting is the gilded European past depicted in *Letter from an Unknown Woman* or *Madame de . . .* , a society almost as mythical as the medieval castles and for-ests, damsels and knights of fairy tales. While alike telling stories of love in society, Ophuls's films are on the whole more romantic, more immersed in the turmoil of love, and Antonioni's more realistic, more grounded in the patterns and particulars of an actual society.

Though she plays one in *Woman without Destiny*, Clara is no femme fatale, not even an innocent one like Gaby. It's not so much that men fall for her beauty as that her beauty flatters their vanity. Rather than the beautiful woman, here it's the men who are vain. Gianni does attempt suicide, but less for love than for matters of money and prestige—his misguided "art" film with Clara as Joan of Arc has utterly flopped—and in any case his isn't a serious suicide attempt. Having brought her into the movies, Gianni pushes the reluctant Clara into marriage, and once she becomes his wife, he no longer wants her to play sexy roles such as the lead in *Woman without Destiny*. They go off on their honeymoon before the picture is finished, and she's expected on set as soon as she gets back, impatiently awaited for a big scene in a posh private house hired for the shoot, the director complaining that her stand-in doesn't look enough like Clara. But when she finally shows up at the house with Gianni, he takes the chief producer aside and lets him know that he won't allow her to go on with the picture. Production is halted, preparations dismantled, cast and crew making their departure. "Are they leaving?" asks the matriarch of the house as she comes down the stairs to look over the remains of the movie set that her home was turned into. The camera follows her for a bit, lets her leave frame, and picks her up again as she notices, crying on a couch, Clara's stand-in. "Who's this girl?" she asks, and the camera moves on with her and back with her into the room, now letting her leave frame again in order to pause, as the scene fades out, on the tearful young woman who is Clara's double in more ways than one.

After the failed Joan of Arc movie and the ensuing suicidal gesture, Clara feels responsible. Before she breaks up with her husband, she goes back and finishes *Woman without Destiny* to help him recoup his losses. But Gianni has only himself to blame for his troubles. You could say the same thing about Leonardo in *La signora di tutti*—if you take him as a real person, that is, willful and domineering like Gianni, but Leonardo is a man possessed, driven by some unstoppable force in the manner of an allegorical character. Gaby's whole story is driven by the demons of her own beauty. It's a different story with Clara, a sensible, good-natured young woman from the working class who happens to be uncommonly beautiful and finds herself transplanted into another social world. Melodrama in Max Ophuls tends to the allegorical, the mythical—the Liebestod myth especially, the inescapable nexus of love and death. Antonioni's great melodramas of the 1950s—*Cronaca di un amore, La signora senza camelie, Le amiche*—are works of sobering, bracing realism, and in his famous trilogy of the early 1960s—*L'avventura, La notte, L'eclisse*—melodrama almost disappears with Anna on that desolate volcanic island but like her remains a haunting vestigial presence.

Not Reconciled

A work of mature mastery, sorrowful and self-possessed, *The Life of Oharu* (1952) introduced an international audience to the art of Kenji Mizoguchi. It is an art both attached to tradition and radically original. The son of a roofing carpenter, Mizoguchi was born in Tokyo in 1898, during the Meiji period, when Japan gave up its isolationism and opened itself to modernization from the West, including of course the movies, a line of work he took up as a young man. Of the many films he directed in the 1920s and early 1930s, little survives. His two films from 1936, *Osaka Elegy* and *Sisters of the Gion*, bitter portrayals of wronged women in contemporary Japan, were a breakthrough. By then he had developed his own unmistakable style, avoiding close-ups and reverse angles and favoring a distant, mobile camera and prolonged, choreographed takes. This style can be seen at its purest in *The Story of the Last Chrysanthemum* (1939) and *The 47 Ronin* (1941–42). A few years after the war, as if to confirm the opinion of critics who were calling him old-fashioned, he turned to classic Japanese literature for a series of films that, beginning with *The Life of Oharu* and continuing with *Ugetsu* (1953) and *Sansho Dayu* (1954), would win him a top prize at Venice three times in a row and make his reputation in the West, which was then belatedly discovering the cinema of Japan. Some Japanese critics now object to the liberties he took in adapting national classics. But that an artist can take liberties and still remain true to a tradition only attests to its vitality. As a national storyteller Mizoguchi has few peers among filmmakers anywhere.

These celebrated 1950s films don't adhere so strictly to the long-take technique he perfected in the late 1930s and early 1940s, are more amenable to cuts and closer views, but his distinctive style nevertheless abides. It is consummately at play in *The Life of Oharu*, which opens with a camera movement steadily following from behind a woman walking in the dark outskirts of old Kyoto. She is our protagonist, Oharu (Kinuyo Tanaka), and we follow her at the start as we are to follow her through the course of her life. She notices something off screen and turns her veiled face away, and Mizoguchi's camera, with characteristic tact, slows down and lets her recede in felt deference to her diffidence. A woman and a man come into view, evidently a prostitute taking a customer to an inn; he tries to break away, but she seizes him and ushers him to the inn door. This prompts a cut closer to Oharu, herself a prostitute walking the streets—a striking cut, by about ninety degrees, to a lower angle on her other side, and a cut suddenly intruding into her personal space and bringing the detached, deferential author more into alignment with her viewpoint.

Mizoguchi compared his long takes, with the camera moving and pausing and moving again—poised to move even when pausing—to the traditional picture scrolls of Japanese art. If the easel paintings of the West are windows open onto another world, picture scrolls are more like texts to be read. And if scrolls usually picture things from above, befitting the position of a reader at a table rather than a viewer at a window, in a similar way (as Noël Burch has noted),[75] Mizoguchi often photographs things from a high angle. But no less often he comes down to the ground. Movements of descent and ascent are characteristic gestures of his camera—and not only camera movements. Cuts like that first one in *Oharu* will shift perspective from lofty detachment to earthly involvement or vice versa.

Oharu was derived (by the director and his regular scriptwriter, Yoshikata Yoda) from Ihara Saikaku's *Life of an Amorous Woman*, a novel from the seventeenth century related in the first person by an unnamed woman confessing to her numerous carnal sins and thereby implicating a whole society. Though not the narrator, the film's Oharu is from the start seen to be the prime mover of the story, the principal motivator of the camera's movement. And though no saint either, she is a nobler and graver figure than the novel's narrator, and one who more palpably suffers oppression and injustice at the hands of her society. The novel is comedy, erotic and satirical and at times harsh; the film is melodrama, leavened with an incisive humor that yet does little to mitigate a mounting sadness.

Having introduced Oharu as an aging streetwalker, the film goes into an extended flashback when, at a temple housing statues of many disciples of Buddha, she sees in one of these images a resemblance to the love of her youth—a forbidden love: she was a lady at court, and the man (Toshiro Mifune) was a lowly page. In Mizoguchi, as in Kurosawa—though not in Ozu or Naruse—the actors act with their whole bodies in a gestural manner that owes much to the Japanese theatrical tradition. Look at Tanaka and Mifune when the young Oharu backs away from the impetuous page and the two enter a garden. All in one uninterrupted take, he approaches her on his knees and embraces her around hers; she further retreats, and the camera follows at a distance and pauses as, in an exquisite swooning gesture, she amorously succumbs and faints in his arms. As she drops to the ground the camera tilts down with her, and two stone ornaments rise side by side into view at the bottom of the frame. As he carries her away, the camera stays in the garden for an extra moment after they leave and, in a gesture of its own, tilts down a bit more, so that the two stone ornaments rise a bit higher into the frame, suggesting something like two erect phalluses, his and hers, for she has been as decisive as he in consummating their love.

Their breach of the feudal hierarchy entails severe punishment: Oharu and her family are banished from court, and the page is beheaded. At his execution he dictates a last letter to her in which he bids her to marry for love. The camera follows the executioner's gleaming sword as it touches the page's neck, is raised to strike the fatal blow, and, the bloody deed done out of view, is then swung back. When her dead lover's letter reaches Oharu, she reads it in held long shot, at the bottom right of the screen, by a pair of hanging kimonos that obstruct our view. We hear her crying but can't see her face. We can barely make out the knife she now intends to use on herself, though the glint of the blade recalls the executioner's sword. In the next shot, which moves out with her into a bamboo grove, the thin stems surrounding her like so many prison bars, and shows her mother wresting the suicidal knife from her and holding her back when she threatens to throw herself down a well, the camera gets no closer and takes a higher perspective—a veritable scroll shot. Why keep us at such distance at this point of heated emotion? You could say that Mizoguchi aims to cool down the emotion, to maintain composure in the face of misfortune. You could also say that he doesn't want to confine the emotion to individuals, that he wants us to feel the misfortune as spreading throughout the space the characters inhabit. The violence acutely represented by the executioner's blade is in the very air and manifests itself again in the knife that emerges from behind the handsome kimonos dissembling an oppressive social order. We are not to focus solely on the plight of individuals but to sense the pervasive strictures of a society.

Like Saikaku's novel, *The Life of Oharu* tells a picaresque story in which the protagonist wanders through various stations on the road of life. But the picaresque protagonist usually has ups and downs, and Oharu has only downs, one after another, an accumulation of sorrows adding up to melodrama. In *Sisters of the Gion* one of the two geisha sisters is a good girl, generous and compliant, the other a bad girl, rebellious and manipulative, and things turn out badly for both of them; no way can a geisha get a break in life. For Oharu, who is both generous and rebellious, things turn out badly whatever social role she assumes—court lady, concubine to a lord and mother of his heir, courtesan, wife, nun, common prostitute; no way can a woman get a break under feudal, mercantile, patriarchal rule. Women in Mizoguchi are consistently central and consistently portrayed with a sympathy that has no need for idealization. Some have questioned his feminism, which he may not have lived up to personally; some have speculated that he harbored feelings of guilt with regard to women and sought their forgiveness. However that may be, in his art he was a critic of society, whose wrongs were for him most evident in the wrongs done to women.

The flashback to Oharu's past eventually returns to the opening camera movement behind the aging streetwalker and the cut abruptly closer to her on her other side. Only after these two repeated shots does the film dissolve back to the temple where Oharu has been recalling her past. The same shots that began the author's prologue now conclude the flashback enacting the character's memories. The cut shifts from a more detached to a more involved perspective, and the two shots are initially outside and finally inside the flashback. The images of Oharu's past are thus to be seen as both the character's and the author's. Mizoguchi at once detaches us from Oharu's subjectivity—these are not her mental images but an objective reality—and identifies his enactment with her recollection.

The author's epilogue—Saikaku's novel has nothing of the sort—seems to promise a happy ending to the character's sad story. The son Oharu bore when she was chosen for her beauty as a lord's concubine has succeeded his father and, as the new lord, wants to take his old mother into his care. Once again, as she was in her youth—this is a film of repetitions—Oharu is ceremoniously carried in a palanquin to the lord's manor. But there she's peremptorily told that she has disgraced the clan by becoming a prostitute and will not be allowed to live with her son or even to see him, except briefly, from afar, as she saw him once before in the street when he was a boy and was passing by with his entourage. The scene of her last look at her son unfolds in a sunlit garden as he and his attendants stride along a veranda. On her upward glance at him we cut not to her point of view, as we might expect, but to a distant perspective on her from the veranda where no one returns her glance, the lordly group entering and leaving view in the shadowy foreground, the camera moving with her as she rises to her feet in pursuit. After another cut she reenters view, again a small bright figure seen from the veranda, and again the large dark figures come and go in front, the camera moving with her as she keeps trying to get a closer look. Mizoguchi's skill at cutting is seldom noted. Here each cut punctuates her feeling of being put back in her place, at an insuperable distance from the looming, ruling shadows.

Her story ends as it began: the hierarchy that cruelly thwarted the passionate love of her youth now thwarts the old mother's love for her son. She escapes his prohibitive domain and becomes a mendicant nun. The film's concluding shot follows her as she goes from one house to another reciting a prayer for mercy, which a chorus on the soundtrack takes up as she moves along. The camera moving with her comes to a pause as she pauses and bows to a pagoda in the distance, but when she starts moving again, it does not keep pace with her, letting her leave view and at the same time ascending, so that the final image centers on the screen the pagoda pointing toward the sky. In his later years—he died of leukemia in 1956, at the age of fifty-eight—Mizoguchi was drawn to Buddhism. But the Buddhist recognition that suffering is inevitable does not mean resignation to injustice. In every circumstance she finds herself in, Oharu stands for an alternative to the dominant order. To the world she is soon to leave she is surely not reconciled.

In the Mood for Love

When I first saw Wong Kar-wai's *In the Mood for Love* (2000) I thought, like many others, that the love affair between Li-zhen (Maggie Cheung) and Mo-wan (Tony Leung) was never consummated. On further viewings, though, that doesn't seem to me so clear. This is a film of fragments rather than long takes, of repetition rather than progression, elliptical, off-centered, oblique. I found it and still find it to be very sexy in the way it dwells on the aroused possibility, the sustained expectation, the mood rather than the fact of love. This is melodrama with the accent on melody rather than drama— particularly a recurring waltz accompanying slow-motion images in a transformation of ordinary movement into a kind of mating dance.

On the same day in Hong Kong in 1962, Li-zhen and her husband and Mo-wan and his wife move into rooms the two couples are renting in adjacent apartments. At that time housing was scarce in the city; many moved there after the merchant city of Shanghai came under Communist rule. This is a story about a displaced bourgeoisie living in cramped quarters. Accordingly the film does without establishing shots; in cramped quarters you are always bumping into details and can never stand back and survey the space you inhabit. *In the Mood for Love* has a pervasive quality of memory, of nostalgia, of the way you recollect things in bits and pieces and keep returning to the same ones and omitting the rest. "He remembers those vanished years," a title reads at the end. "As though looking through a dusty window pane . . . everything he sees is blurred and indistinct." But the film is not narrated by Mo-wan and does not stick to his point of view. It combines the subjective coloring of remembrance with grounding in a concrete social reality. Wong declared his intention "to re-create the actuality . . . to say something about daily life then."[76]

The repeated, waltz-accompanied images of Maggie Cheung in entrancing slow motion heighten her sinuous beauty and deportment, and make her indelibly captivating. Even when just going to the noodle shop nearby for food to take out—which she often does, for her husband is often away—Li-zhen likes to look good and dress up. She wears one elegant, colorful cheongsam dress after another. We are drawn into, as a reviewer notes, "an almost narcotically tactile world of textures and surfaces, lovingly noticed and brilliantly realised."[77] At the noodle shop, or on the way there or the way back, Li-zhen and Mo-wan often cross paths, for his wife is often gone too. They come to realize that her husband and his wife are having an affair. They see more and more of each other—more than once they get caught in the rain and take shelter together, more than once they spend the night together—but they don't want to imitate their unfaithful spouses. They may or may not have sex—the film is so elliptical that we can't be sure—but they do fall in love.

Li-zhen and Mo-wan playact what they imagine happened in the affair between their spouses—who are almost always kept off screen—or what they imagine would happen if she confronted her disloyal husband. Wong brings about a momentary confusion of mimicry with reality, so that the playacting seems at first to be actually happening between Li-zhen and Mo-wan. Their developing romance is thus seen as a kind of doubling of their adulterous spouses. According to Peter Brunette, the doubling of the two couples, the way one love story leads to another, "sheds new light on the nature of subjectivity" and raises the question whether "we ever have the possibility of saying things to each other that aren't already lines of dialogue, scripted by our culture or society." In his deconstructive reading, "virtually all of the emotions in this film are prerehearsed or 'quoted.'"[78] But who would ever suppose that falling in love is something incomparable and unprecedented? That an emotion such as love depends on the conventions and constructions of a culture and society doesn't mean that it can't be genuine. And the other couple whose story Li-zhen and Mo-wan rehearse is no model for their own story but more like a shadow they disclaim. Their sense of their difference from a love affair they deem unworthy never slackens, which is why they hold back from committing adultery themselves.

The fragmentation and repetition, the slow-motion waltz, the Nat King Cole songs in accented Spanish popular in Hong Kong at the time, the then fashionable cheongsam dresses, the trips to and from the noodle shop, the hazy atmosphere of confined interiors and rainy streets, the oblique or obstructed views down corridors or through windows or mirrors, the pieces of things past recurring like a dream— this story, the romance of two displaced persons become neighbors in Hong Kong, is not so much told as itself displaced onto its details, its aspects, its ambiance, synecdoche and metonymy not merely embellishing but taking over the narrative. Adherents of psychoanalysis will call such displacement "fetishistic."

Freud's theory of fetishism goes like this: the little boy believes that his mother has a penis, and when he sees that she has none he regards her as castrated, which inspires such fear of his own castration that he displaces the perceived wound onto an adjacent object that in his mind fills in for the missing penis—panties the mother wears, fur resembling her pubic hair, feet or shoes encountered while peering up her skirt—a fetish object enabling the boy, and later the man, to disavow a lack he can't bear to face. A fetishist is a patho-logical case, a man (presumably never a woman) able to reach sexual satisfaction only through an object taking the place of a person; but psychoanalysis blurs the line between psychopathology and every-day life. The concept of disavowal—holding on to a belief in spite of knowledge to the contrary—surely applies to many everyday situa-tions, though the far-fetched theory of the little boy and his castrated mother may well not. What about the everyday situation of watching a movie? Psychoanalytic film theorists have proposed that the illusion of reality on the screen is like the mother's absent penis, that view-ers cling to their belief in a movie's reality and can't face the fact that there's nothing there but insubstantial images. And what would the fetish be that enables such disavowal? For Christian Metz it is cine-matic technique, connoisseurship of film artistry, and for Laura Mul-vey it is primarily the erotic image of woman. Beauty, whether artistic or feminine, they alike take as the fetish through which the beholder forgets the absence of reality. The problem with this fetish theorizing isn't just that we all know that a movie is not real; it's that nothing like castration anxiety attaches to the knowledge. Back in childhood we all had fun playing games of make-believe.

Marx's notion of fetishism, though sometimes conflated with Freud's, is very different. Whereas the Freudian fetish disavows an imagined lack, the fetishism of commodities explicated by Marx dis-sembles the actual human labor that goes into them. *In the Mood for Love* portrays a consumer bourgeoisie: look at all the pretty dresses Li-zhen wears, almost like a fashion show. But the acquisitions the characters talk about, rice cookers, handbags, neckties, bought abroad by Li-zhen's husband or Mo-wan's wife on their business trips, have a tawdry association, an odor of adultery—Li-zhen's husband buys handbags for his wife and his mistress and for the wife and mistress of his wife's boss—and play no part in the film's beauty. Li-zhen's dresses are not only part of her beauty but part of her dignity and part of what distinguishes her and Mo-wan from the meretricious society their spouses represent. Pretty dresses may be fetishized commodi-ties in Marx's sense, but Wong treats them as cherished memories, and he seems to be making a distinction between the two.

Is it fetishistic, in Freud's sense, to cherish the clothes that your beloved used to wear? Is it fetishistic to remember the noodle shop where your paths would cross, the rain that would bring you together, the song that was playing on a jukebox while you were sharing a meal? Is it fetishistic to be captivated by a characteristic way of walk-ing, of turning the head, of inhabiting the body? It is certainly not pathological. Love thrives on details, cherished particularities. If such details and particularities are displacements, postponements, avoidances of the feared imagined wound, does this mean that *wham bam thank you ma'am* is the real thing?

Love also thrives on impediments and prohibitions; lovers long for each other when something obstructs their union, when some force of circumstance keeps them apart. One reason for the decline of love stories in recent times is the lowering of barriers, the loosening of norms. In the days when adultery was a grave sin we got great stories of adulterous love, *Tristan and Iseult, Anna Karenina, Day of Wrath*—stories of conflict between forbidden passion and the social norm forbidding it, a norm transgressed yet nonetheless binding. (When adultery was a grave sin we could also laugh at it, but bedroom farce has declined along with tragic tales of infidelity.) Adultery between Li-zhen and Mo-wan would have been no real transgression and no great love story. In the milieu they live in, their two spouses and her boss get away with adultery without much problem, but Li-zhen and Mo-wan have too much integrity for that and take their sentiments, the pain that marital betrayal has caused them as well as their feelings for each other, too seriously. The impediment to their love is not a loosened social norm against adultery but their personal enforcement of that norm, their own unshakable sense that love is a serious matter not to be lightly entered into. They conduct something like an old-fashioned courtship of the kind that postpones sex until marriage, but they are already married, and not to each other, so for them sex is to be postponed indefinitely.

Hence the very sexy suspension of sex, the mood for love that hovers in the air and never dissipates, the sustained displacement of erotic feeling—call it fetishistic if you must—onto that "almost narcotically tactile world of textures and surfaces." *In the Mood for Love* is not *Brief Encounter*; it is not a moralistic story of adulterous love nobly renounced in deference to the sanctity of marriage. Li-zhen and Mo-wan aren't renouncing sex to preserve either his marriage, which breaks up anyhow, or hers, which seems to endure but not thanks to any sacrificial nobility or marital sanctity. They would make love if they felt ready for it, if it felt right for them, and perhaps they do in the end—"I don't want to go home tonight," she says to him as they ride in a cab and hold hands—and we may even wonder whether her child is his.

"Quizás, quizás, quizás," we hear Nat King Cole singing on the soundtrack: perhaps, perhaps, perhaps. Mo-wan goes off to Singapore, and Li-zhen follows him there, sneaks into his place when he's out, getting a whiff of him and giving him one of her, calls him but keeps silent when he comes to the phone, and leaves town without seeing him. A few years later she returns to Hong Kong with her child, and he returns too and learns that she has moved back where she used to live, but they never see each other again. Wong likes to rework the script as he goes along, and these characters, he said, were in many ways reconceived during the filming, but one thing he knew from the start was that they would not end up together. Why not? Because this is a film about the promise rather than the fulfillment of love, the promise of happiness that for Stendhal defined beauty.

Wong designed *In the Mood for Love* "to be like chamber music . . . something very intimate, in an enclosed environment," but at the end he "thought we should provide another perspective . . . something with histories and a more spiritual side."[79] So he closes by opening the enclosure with a newsreel of De Gaulle's official visit to Cambodia in 1966, which we may surmise Mo-wan is covering in his capacity as a journalist, followed by a scene at the ancient Cambodian temples of Angkor Wat, to which Mo-wan pays his own personal visit. There he whispers a secret into a hole in a temple wall that will purportedly keep it forever. What can it be? That he will always love Li-zhen? That they consummated their love, that they begot a child? Brunette takes this coda to mean that we are to regard the story *sub specie aeternitatis*, that its "context has transcended the merely social to become the universal."[80] But under the aspect of eternity, with a sense of love's eternal transience, is the way we usually would regard a story of love lost and nostalgically recollected. The newsreel of De Gaulle's visit serves as a sudden reminder that this story belongs in a particular time and place. The Angkor Wat temples that offer spiritual solace for human suffering are old but not eternal, and have themselves suffered not only the effects of time but the injuries of history; we may recall in particular the damage from the war being fought in neighboring Vietnam when De Gaulle visited Cambodia and soon to be extended there. Maybe love never lasts except in memory, but this coda suggests that we mustn't forget the specific historical circumstances in which this memorable love didn't last.

Tragic Narration

Pity and fear, Aristotle says, are the chief emotions aroused in tragedy. They are also the chief emotions aroused in melodrama. In Greek tragedy there are no villains—the hero contends against the gods and inevitably loses—but in melodrama there usually are. "Pity for the 'hero' is the less impressive half of melodrama," Eric Bentley maintains. "The other and more impressive half is fear of the villain."[81] Pity is the sentimental side of melodrama, the tears we cry for wronged Anna or sacrificial Stella, the nostalgia for Li-zhen and

Mo-wan's lost love—the feminine side, if you will, and to deem it the weaker side bespeaks a masculine bias. *Stella Dallas* and *In the Mood for Love* are so much melodramas of pity that they do without villains, and they are no weaker for that. In *Way Down East* the pitiable heroine cuts a much stronger figure than the villain, whom we fear much less than we fear the storm standing in for the gods. Melodrama can get far largely on pity. But of course it can make heavy play of fear, as in horror movies, film noir, action thrillers, gangster films, and other forms of what (without drawing too sharp a gender line) you could call male melodrama.

Crime melodramas can side with the law or with the lawbreaker (or a bit of both), so that the criminal can be the villain or the hero (or a bit of both). In the classic gangster films of the early 1930s (*Little Caesar, The Public Enemy, Scarface*), the gangster is a tragic hero, utterly driven to succeed in the land of opportunity yet doomed to fail, his career "a steady upward progress followed by a very precipitate fall," as Robert Warshow convincingly argues:

> In the opening scene of *Scarface*, we are shown a successful man; we know he is successful because he has just given a party of opulent proportions and because he is called Big Louie. Through some monstrous lack of caution, he permits himself to be alone for a few moments. We understand from this immediately that he is about to be killed. No convention of the gangster film is more strongly established than this: it is dangerous to be alone. And yet the very conditions of success make it impossible not to be alone, for success is always the establishment of an *individual* pre-eminence that must be imposed on others, in whom it automatically arouses hatred. . . . The gangster's whole life is an effort to assert himself as an individual, to draw himself out of the crowd, and he always dies *because* he is an individual. . . . At bottom, the gangster is doomed because he is under the obligation to succeed.[82]

The gangster film has evolved over the years—in *The Godfather* Vito and Michael Corleone are killers never killed, never brought down from the top they ruthlessly reach—but it has kept to the governing trope of business as crime and crime as the drive for success.

The gangster genre first flourished in the days before the Production Code. The gangster hero is a bad guy, but a hero must enlist our sympathy even so, which became harder to manage under the moralistic Code. Though gangster movies were still made, including some good ones, it wasn't until after the Code's repeal that the genre had a second flourishing with *The Godfather* and its successors. There have always been complaints that the gangster film glorifies violence and—because it tends to draw its characters from among immigrants or the marginalized aspiring to make a place for themselves—that it puts ethnic or racial groups in a bad light. Trying to forestall such objections, the 1932 *Scarface*, which revels in the brazen animality of its hero and is all the more gripping for it, carries an opening disclaimer ("This picture is an indictment of gang rule in America") and has a scene with decent, hardworking Italian Americans protesting that the gangsters getting attention give them a bad name. The black gangster films that have come out in recent years have met with similar objections to their portrayal of violence and of African Americans as violent.

Even if horrifying, the movie gangster's violence is usually exciting—exciting enough to foster identification (not unmixed, but still identification) with the hero and his criminal rise in life. *Menace II Society* (1993, directed by the Hughes brothers, Albert and Allen, and written by them and Tyger Williams, all three in their early twenties at the time) is a black gangster movie that departs in some significant ways from established generic practice, and it portrays violence with revulsion and dismay admitting no excitement. It opens with a shock of senseless murder. In a precredit sequence, two young black men, Caine (Tyrin Turner) and his friend, O-Dog (Larenz Tate), go into a grocery store to buy beer and make the Korean merchant and his wife nervous. O-Dog takes offense, pulls out a gun, and promptly kills the man behind the counter and then the screaming woman, fear of violence bringing on violence at the ready, robbery not the motive but merely an addition after the fact. As the two young men rush out, we hear Caine's voice-over narration: "Went into the store just to get a beer. Came out an accessory to murder and armed robbery. It was funny like that in the hood sometimes. You never knew what was going to happen or when. After that, I knew it was gonna be a long summer." This comes as a surprise, narration in the past tense heard over action of aggressive immediacy, reflective comment voiced on the heels of reckless crime. Heard off and on all through the movie, Caine's narration is another divergence from the gangster genre, in which first-person voice-over is not a usual device as it is in film noir. The movie gangster is a man of action, not of reflection.

If the traditional gangster hero rises before his fall, yet another way in which *Menace II Society* breaks with generic convention is that its young black gangsters never rise, never get anywhere, as Stanley Crouch points out:

> In *Public Enemy*, *Scarface*, *Little Caesar*, *The Godfather*, and *GoodFellas*, the criminals aspire to some sort of quality beyond good suits and flashy

cars. They go to elegant clubs, wear tuxedos, become equestrians, attend the opera, dine in five-star restaurants, own grand pianos, drink champagne, and so on, trying their best to achieve aristocratic position, however poorly they succeed. The criminals of *Menace II Society* have no aspirations beyond jewelry and cars. They murder and sell drugs but spend their time in squat project apartments, drink beer, smoke reefers, shoot dice, almost always eat fast food, and sit up watching television. In place of having grand pianos, they carry boom boxes. There is no society beyond the one they grew up in.[83]

If we identify with the energy of the traditional gangster, the exciting criminality by which he rises in life, then violence in *Menace II Society* is not only stripped of excitement but even of purpose—so much criminality, so little rise in life. What, if anything, are we then to identify with? The consciousness speaking to us in voice-over, for one thing.

From the killings at the Korean store, we go back in time to the Watts riots of 1965, which the film presents as an originary event. From Caine's first person we shift to the impersonal voices of news announcers and watch, as if on an old TV set, pixelated newsreel footage of the police and the National Guard suppressing the street revolt with clubs, guns, even tanks, like an occupying army, a brutal military presence relentlessly beating down the population of South Central L.A. For the remainder of the film the police mostly stay in the background. "The occupying fascist army within lower-class black communities," according to Crouch, "is not, as the radical rhetoric would have it, the police but black street criminals like O-Dog."[84] Maybe so, but who set the pattern, the mode of operation? The film puts it to us right at the start that the primal occupying army, the model for social interactions adopted by the likes of O-Dog, is the police. The racial subjugation, the violence inflicted on African Americans by the ruling powers, has taught the young black criminals in *Menace II Society* how to relate to one another and to everyone around them. They call each other "nigger" all the time—and not only blacks. Anyone they have or would gain power over, they characterize that way. O-Dog leans over the Korean merchant's dead body and calls him "nigger." Dominance through violence, racist violence, is the only authority, the only hierarchy, they know.

"When the riots stopped, the drugs started," says Caine in voice-over, and a title tells us we are moving on to Watts in the late 1970s. Now we see Caine as a little boy in his parents' house. This sequence is done in a stylized, phantasmagoric fashion that evokes the unreality induced by drugs—drugs that started after the riots stopped, drugs bespeaking a violence turned inward, against oneself and one's own people. Imbuing these phantasmagoric images are blue and red tones recurring throughout in similarly stylized interior scenes. Interiors are predominant in *Menace II Society* ("Everything is closed in, the world almost a succession of apartment and automobile interiors," Crouch writes. "The claustrophobic mood rarely lets up and much of the menace comes from explosive personalities moving through small places"),[85] and in these confining interiors, which breathe an atmosphere of drugs and crime, the predominant colors are blue and red. The significance of this blue and red becomes clear later on, when Caine and O-Dog attempt to steal a car at a parking garage. Before they are able to make off with it, two police cars arrive—police cars with flashing blue and red lights. Caine is captured, and when he is interrogated at the police station, the camera, in a striking maneuver, repeatedly circles the table where he sits across from the police officer. As the camera goes around and around, we see blue windows with bars on one side of the table and red windows with bars on the other side. Blue and red prison windows: this scene recalls the stylized look and closed-in mood of the drug-colored interiors, yet here the colors, and the sense of circumscription enhanced by the circling camera, belong not to the black gangsters but to the police, the originary occupying army, the blue and red of drugged criminality identified with the flashing blue and red of police cars.

The interrogation scene gets nowhere. The police officer suspects Caine of complicity in the incident at the Korean store, but O-Dog snatched the surveillance tape, and without it, as Caine explains in voice-over, the police lack proof and have to let him go. What, then, is the point of this extended scene that does little to advance the story? It is a symbolic point, symbolic not only in the blue-and-red connection between gangsters and police but also, I take it, symbolic in the way that, just as the camera keeps circling the room during an interrogation that amounts to nothing, so the young black criminals keep going around in circles, circles of destruction mostly visited on one another and amounting to nothing. These gangsters do little to advance themselves; they are gangsters without a story.

The story of the classic gangster is a parable of ambition, ambition in a society that divides the world into winners and losers, and proclaims that anyone can be a winner. Antisocial though he is, the gangster acts on the beliefs of his society, the ideology of individual success and equal opportunity his tragic story gives the lie to. It's a different story with Vito and Michael Corleone, but if they are successful killers, successful businessmen, no would-be winners destined to be losers, neither are they individuals acting on their own. The success they represent is that of the family, the organization, the corporation. *The Godfather* tells a truly patriarchal story, with the mantle of power passed on from the father to the son. The classic gangster's story can be described as the son's revolt against the father, certainly a masculinist—the gun is the phallus—but not exactly a patriarchal story. In the tribal model Freud proposes in *Totem and Taboo*, the sons kill the father, but they continue to worship him as a totem that symbolizes their own patriarchal rule. In the gangster movie, the son kills the father but is in turn killed before he has a chance to establish his own patriarchal line. The gangster remains the son and dies as the son; he never gets to assume the mantle of the father, never sets up the patriarchal totem. The gangsters in *Menace II Society* are all very young, the implication being that black criminals in the streets of South Central L.A. don't get to be much older: before long they'll all be in jail or dead. They are sons without a father who kill one another.

Here is Roland Barthes on narrative and Oedipus:

> Death of the Father would deprive literature of many of its pleasures. If there is no longer a Father, why tell stories? Doesn't every narrative lead back to Oedipus? Isn't storytelling always a way of searching for one's origin, speaking one's conflicts with the Law, entering into the dialectic of tenderness and hatred? Today, we dismiss Oedipus and narrative at one and the same time: we no longer love, we no longer fear, we no longer narrate. As fiction, Oedipus was at least good for something: to make good novels, to tell good stories (this is written after having seen Murnau's *City Girl*).[86]

If storytelling is always searching for an origin, why can't that lead to the mother as well as the father? I'm not sure Barthes is saying anything other than that, under patriarchy, stories have a likely patriarchal bent. In *Menace II Society* the brutally masculinist gangster story (the worst insult in these black criminals' vocabulary isn't "nigger" but "bitch": "Bitch-ass trick," says O-Dog as he kicks the dead body of a man he killed for offering to suck his dick) gets nowhere, but another story can be discerned alongside it, a patriarchal story struggling to be born.

A gangster with no story, no rise before the fall, is no tragic hero. *Menace II Society* doubles the protagonist into Caine and O-Dog—Jekyll and Hyde, you could say—which doesn't mean a simple partition between good and evil: Jekyll has the evil Hyde in him as Caine has O-Dog, the vicious criminal caught up in the vicious circles of violence, the gangster with no story. But Caine gets himself a story that may get him somewhere, a story of fathers and sons, surrogate fathers and sons.

In *Little Caesar*, *Scarface*, and *The Public Enemy*, the gangster has a sidekick, and Caine and O-Dog are similarly paired. But the classic gangster is more ruthless than his sidekick—his pushing to the limit in the drive for success is what makes him the hero—and *Menace II Society* reverses that. More than Caine, who describes him in voice-over as "the craziest nigger alive, America's nightmare," O-Dog is like the classic gangster. And he is beautiful, with something of the dancer about him, an energy and elegance of the gutter that reminds you a little bit of James Cagney (who was a dancer and brought that quality to his tough-guy roles) as Tom Powers in *The Public Enemy*. The beauty and energy and grace of Cagney in motion draw us to the gangster hero in spite of his savagery and make us appreciate his undismissible human vitality. Tom Powers's beauty suggests a promise, a potential, in the rebellious son, the street kid fighting for his life, and that sense of promise and potential gone terribly wrong lends him tragic stature. No such thing with O-Dog. His beauty represents not a potential but a temptation—the temptation of violence for its own sake, leading nowhere but to its own pleasures in a kind of aestheticism of violence. He likes nothing better than the image of his murderous self caught on the surveillance tape, which he watches over and over again.

Caine's father, stuck in that miasma of drugs and crime and soon to meet his death, can pass on nothing to his son. But Caine's not much older friend, Parnell, serves as a father figure to the little boy and teaches him how to use a gun. Years later, with Parnell in jail, his son, Anthony, learns from Caine, just out of high school, how to use a gun. The phallus is thereby passed on from Parnell to Caine to Anthony, a masculinist though not as yet a patriarchal line. A true patriarch, even if not a father figure able to teach Caine much, is the pious grandfather in whose upright middle-class home he lives and who at one point, standing at the door, asks him gravely, "Hey, do you care whether you live or die?" "I don't know," Caine replies. He starts to care whether he lives or dies through his relationship with Anthony and with the little boy's mother, Ronnie (Jada Pinkett), a young woman who offers Caine his best chance at patriarchy. *Menace II Society* draws a tacit yet crucial distinction between the masculinist crime story, which amounts to nothing, and the patriarchal love story that may amount to something.

Ronnie wants nothing to do with the phallic gun passed on from Parnell to Caine to Anthony, the gun that represents the violence of the son rather than a genuine patriarchal line. She cares for Caine and he reciprocates the feeling, with some reluctance because he thinks of her as Parnell's woman. An Oedipal triangle: Parnell was a father figure to Caine, and now Caine not only becomes a father figure to Parnell's son but takes over Parnell's place as the man in Ronnie's life.

The son's desire for the mother, his aspiration to patriarchy, threatens to come into Oedipal conflict with the father. But when Ronnie and Caine visit Parnell in jail, he gives his blessing to their love; the father relinquishes the mother to the son. This twist on the Oedipal story disarms the son's violence. The gun can be put away; the father does not have to be killed for the son to assume his place. Psychoanalysis talks about the positive and the negative Oedipus complex—the positive being the son's desire for the mother, the negative the law of the father forbidding the son's desire—but Parnell's twist on Oedipus makes the father's law positive. The father allows the son's desire, grants him the phallus that would possess the mother and thereby takes away the gun that would kill the father. Not the gun but its removal makes for patriarchy in *Menace II Society*. Ronnie cannot take the gun away from Anthony; only Caine can. Only the father can take the gun away from the son, as Parnell does from Caine by consenting to his romance with Ronnie. With him by her side, him as a father to her son, she wants to leave South Central L.A. behind and move to Atlanta. It would seem that Caine's alternative story is headed for a happy ending.

Why does Ronnie need Caine? Why doesn't she just leave him behind and take off with her son for a better future? Because her son needs Caine. This is a gangster movie, a story of sons, and the moral of the story is that the sons need fathers. *Menace II Society* calls for black patriarchy as a counter to the self-destructive rule of the gun among the boys in the hood. Liberals often say that the lack of proper black fathers is a hangover from the past, a legacy of slavery, which is not wrong but takes the lack as a cultural matter and supposes black culture to be separate and self-contained, when in fact it is bound up with American culture and society at large. This movie makes us see how the enduring subjugation of African Americans perpetuates that patriarchal lack in the present.

It is as a father that Caine could have acquitted himself, and it is because he falters as a father that he comes to a bad end. He seduces a young woman named Ilena and makes her pregnant, and when she calls to tell him he brusquely dismisses her: "You're man enough to take a life," she says before he hangs up, "you ain't man enough to take care of one?" A male cousin of Ilena's comes to see him in her behalf, and Caine, the gangster in him banishing the father, attacks the cousin savagely and goes on kicking him when he lies on the ground. Retaliation ensues in full-blown gangster fashion. As Ronnie and Caine are packing the car for their departure, the aggrieved cousin and his friends, armed with guns, drive by the house and shoot and shoot. Caine's life is taken in revenge for the life he would not take care of—though before dying he saves little Anthony, the life he would take care of, from the bullets whizzing by. It's a gangster-movie ending, but if the classic gangster dies on account of inordinate ambition, Caine dies by reason of insufficient responsibility as a father. His hope was in his reaching for patriarchy, his death in his falling short of it.

Ronnie and her son survive and perhaps will find a better future in Atlanta. Caine and his friend Sharif are killed, but O-Dog is still standing. Why? We know the police have gotten hold of the surveillance tape and will catch him soon enough, but why have him survive the final onslaught? Why let Hyde live as Jekyll dies? Because O-Dog epitomizes the gangster with no story, the violence that goes nowhere. Caine has acquired a story and dies as a tragic hero after all. Had O-Dog been killed beside him, something of the better man's tragedy would have rubbed off on the bad man.

Not only has Caine acquired a story, he has the ability to tell it. If his narration surprises us when we first hear it, if it strikes us as coming from a different place, a place of awareness removed from the purposelessness of the action, it surprises us even more at the end. As Caine lies dying on the sidewalk, we hear him speaking on the sound-track: "After stomping Ilena's cousin like that, I knew I was going to have to deal with that fool some day." Cut to a black screen, then to a flashback shot of Caine kicking Ilena's cousin, and from here until the end, Caine's narration proceeds over a series of flashback shots punctuated by black screens signifying death. The flashback shots are his life flashing before him, the narration his unuttered dying words: "Damn! I never thought he'd come back like this, blasting. Like I said, it was funny like that in the hood sometimes. You never knew what was going to happen, or when." These repeated words from the preamble link the end to the beginning, and it becomes clear that we are retroactively to take the entire first-person voice-over as spoken from the beginning by the dying Caine at the end. The reflective tone of the narration, which has seemed at odds with the action, finally makes sense when we understand that all along we have been hearing the hero's retrospective account at the point of his death. The dead man's narration in Sunset Boulevard (1950) has been proposed as a precedent. But in Sunset Boulevard we know from the start that the narrator is dead—we see his corpse floating in a swimming pool as we hear his voice-over—and the effect is ironic, facetious, a kind of noir comedy. In Menace II Society we only find out at the end that these are a dying man's words, and the effect is tragic.

Can there be tragedy in the first person, in the protagonist's first person? Tragedy calls for our identification with the hero, our pity and fear, but it also calls for a larger perspective—a chorus, in ancient times. We must take a certain distance from the protagonist, if for no other reason than to see how tall he or she stands and how far she or he falls, and the first person puts us too close. No man is a hero to his valet, and no man can be a tragic hero in his own account. *Menace II Society* is an exception to this rule—maybe the exception that proves the rule. Most of the action we see is violence without a story. It is chiefly through the voice-over narration, thoughtful while the action is unthinking, aware of consequences while the action is heedless of consequences, that the film puts together a story. And so it is primarily through his first-person narration that Caine gets to be a tragic hero.

As the fatally wounded hero tells us again that "it was funny like that in the hood sometimes," the flashback images with black screens between show us Parnell teaching little Caine and then Caine teaching little Anthony how to use a gun, Caine and O-Dog at a playful moment, O-Dog being pulled into a police car with flashing blue and red lights. "I'd done too much to turn back, and I'd done too much to go on," the narration continues. "My grandpa asked me one time, do I care whether I live or die," we hear as we flash back to Caine and Anthony on the sidewalk and to Caine kissing Ronnie, two images of the potential family shortly before the burst of gunfire. "Yeah, I do," he answers his grandfather now, over a black screen. "And now it's too late," he adds over another black screen, preceded by a flashback to the stricken Caine rushing to save the endangered Anthony and followed by the closing image of guns firing from a car. Then, over a final black, the end credits unroll.

Woe is me, cries the hero at the suspended moment of his death. In opera, an art form of suspended moments, this would have been an aria sung at the finish. At the finish of *Menace II Society* Caine's voice-over speaks to us less as a narration, an account of events, than as a dramatic soliloquy, the tragic hero's soliloquy expressing his consciousness of his fate. And we may look back on the whole film and construe the first-person voice-over less as a narration than as a soliloquy spoken by the hero at the moment of death and resonating all through the story, the exception proving the rule that tragedy cannot be narrated in the first person. And the first person, the consciousness it expresses, here invests the hero with tragic stature. His disavowal of fatherhood gets him killed before his capacity for it finds fruition, yet his ability to tell the story makes him a kind of father after all, for the consciousness he has gained is something he can pass on to the future.

The Personified Camera

The family is moving out of town, and from the car driving away, the mother looks back at the house they're leaving behind. "The only way to be happy is to love," she says in voice-over. "Unless you love . . . your life will flash by." On her backward glance we cut to her point of view, and through the car's rear window, we see the pale green two-story home receding down the quiet street. Then, unpredictably, we cut inside the empty house and, through the middle one of its three tall bay windows, past a green tree overhanging the road, see the car disappearing into the distance. The home returns the mother's gaze; in a kind of shot/reverse shot, the glance of farewell is reciprocal. This occurs toward the end of Terrence Malick's *The Tree of Life* (2011), which centers on a family in a Texas town in the 1950s. The use of voice-over is characteristic of Malick; no other filmmaker has been so devoted to the device. Also characteristic is the personified yet unascribed perspective, the sense we get in the empty house of seeing through the eyes of someone unseen, some house spirit watching the car go.

Malick's first movie, *Badlands* (1973), is narrated by a girl of fifteen, Holly (Sissy Spacek). She and her dog are in her wrought-iron bed as she starts telling the story: "My mother died of pneumonia when I was just a kid. My father kept their wedding cake in the freezer for ten whole years. After the funeral he gave it to the yard man. He tried to act cheerful, but he could never be consoled by the little stranger he found in his house." Wherever there is discrepancy between a narrator and the implied author, there is always irony. In Holly's case, some take this irony as an invitation to feel superior to a benighted girl, but the condescension or even scorn toward her that they would impute to the author is their own. Holly's adolescent sensibility, her forlorn romantic fantasies, her reliance on trite embellishments and her reluctance to go into unpleasant things, her desire to tell the truth and still acquit herself as best she can for her part in what she knows to be a frightful tale—all this the author renders with sympathetic accuracy. Malick has compared Holly to Nancy Drew or Tom Sawyer as an "innocent abroad."[87] *Badlands* was loosely based on the actual case of Charles Starkweather, who went on a killing spree in Nebraska in the late 1950s together with his teenage girlfriend, Caril Ann Fugate. In the movie Holly meets Kit (Martin Sheen) in a South Dakota town: "Little did I realize," she tells us over the image of her twirling her baton on the street, "that what began in the alleys and back ways of this quiet town would end in the badlands of Montana."

When her father (Warren Oates) finds out she's been seeing a young man "ten years older than me and . . . from the wrong side of the tracks, so called," he punishes her by killing her dog and having her take extra music lessons. At the redbrick music school she looks out of a Palladian window whose tripartite design—two smaller windows at each side of an arched central one—is amplified in the tripartite composition of the image, with two more windows on opposite sides of the wide screen accompanying the conjoined three at the center; little Holly seems to be held prisoner by traditional architecture. This image of confinement dissolves to an open field where Kit has gone to speak to her father, who is at work painting a billboard. An advertisement for feed and grain, the billboard depicts a farm in bright colors, green most of all, with assorted plants and animals, gabled roofs under a pretty sky; a square hole at the bottom of the unfinished picture lets the actual sky show through, no less pretty in its deeper shade of blue, though the expanse of land under it lacks the lustrous green of cultivation. Holly's father flatly tells Kit he doesn't want him around, and as the young man takes his leave, we cut to a distant long shot of the painter and his billboard, now dwarfed and decentered against the big sky. It feels as if the landscape were inspecting the image on the billboard, as if the world in its uncontainable vastness were finding the human attempt to represent it wanting. And Malick would not exempt his own attempt. His images may be more realistic than the painter's billboard, but he invites us to consider whether they're really so different from it, to imagine how they too would be dwarfed and decentered when set against the real thing.

Visually as well as verbally Malick is an exacting craftsman. And verbally as well as visually he liberates his films from the tyranny of the plotline. Voice-over is the device he uses to embroider events with musings and reflections and also to fill in narrative gaps, releasing the images from their usual subordination to the story so that they can flourish in splendid autonomy. Few scenes in *Days of Heaven* (1978) are allowed to unfold for long or to reach any dramatic resolution. Instead we get bits and pieces of scenes arranged into a mosaic of shifting impressions. A train crossing a high bridge near the beginning, with nothing but a blue sky and white clouds in the background, seems headed for heaven; yet in a minute the narrator brings up the flames of hell. This is a film of continual interruptions, breaks in perspective and mood. One moment we may respond to the grandeur of nature, the next to the arduous labor of migrant farmhands, then to the characters' personal feelings, their romantic yearning or petty scheming; then a sudden circumstantial detail will cut a scene short so that it amounts to no more than a glimpse. As the drama escalates, a flying circus with clowns and a belly dancer descends from the sky; as love seems about to prevail, hate furiously takes over and a plague of locusts inflicts rampant destruction.

"This farmer, he didn't know when he first saw her or what it was about her that caught his eye. Maybe it was the way the wind blew through her hair." Again in *Days of Heaven* a young girl narrates, this time an even younger one called Linda (Linda Manz), here telling us about the rich farmer (Sam Shepard) and his burgeoning love for Abby (Brooke Adams). The time is the early twentieth century, the place a farm in the Texas panhandle where Abby and her lover, Bill (Richard Gere), are migrant workers who came on the train together with Linda, who is his little sister. Because people will talk, Abby passes for his sister too, and the farmer accordingly courts her. Having overheard a doctor say that the farmer hasn't long to live ("Maybe a year"), Bill prods her to marry a man he sees as their chance to rise in life. The film's central drama, or melodrama, concerns this triangle of Bill, Abby, and the farmer, with Linda as an observer: "This farmer, he had a big spread and a lot of money. . . . Wasn't no harm in him. You'd give him a flower, he'd keep it forever."

There may be no harm in the farmer, but his farmhands get low pay for long hours of hard work. Bill may be mean in trying to take advantage of the farmer's love for Abby, but he loves her too, and "he was tired," as Linda explains, "of living like the rest of them, nosing around like a pig in a gutter. He wasn't in the mood no more. He figured there must be something wrong with them, the way they always got no luck." *Days of Heaven* deals with the tangled interplay between the personal and the social, the attempt to manage the social through the personal, the typically American ambition to become a winner, to lift yourself out of the group and leave all those losers behind. But unlike a John Ford or a Jean Renoir—whose *Toni* also tells a story of tragic love among migrant workers—Malick conveys scant sense of the group, the living relationships, concordant or discordant, that bind people together. Like the outlaw couple in *Badlands*, the characters in *Days of Heaven* are alienated from a human community that seems hardly to exist at all.

The frontier in Westerns is the scene of history, the landscape that saw the founding of the American nation. While people and even towns may look small against the awesome natural setting, they play a part on that epic stage, which lends them dignity and in turn acquires human significance. The landscape in *Days of Heaven* is surpassingly beautiful—Néstor Almendros deserved his Oscar for the cinematography—but human things look out of place in it, whether the transient, oppressed farmhands or the farmer's lofty Victorian house, sitting alone like some presumptuous ornament plumped in the middle of a vast field. Here people are inconsonant figures amid the elemental majesty of a landscape standing apart from history, beyond human ken.

"I think the devil was on the farm," Linda comments in voice-over as the farmer's suspicions that his wife is not Bill's sister grow. When the locusts arrive, the fire used to combat them spreads through the farm like the flames of hell Linda spoke of. Isn't she an uneducated child mouthing superstitious notions she's picked up from those around her? Isn't her narration to be taken ironically? Yes, but it was the author, not the character, who set up a parallel between the triangle of Bill, Abby, and the farmer and the biblical story of Abram and Sarai's sojourn in Egypt, where they passed for brother and sister; when Pharaoh took the fair Sarai into his house, "the Lord plagued Pharaoh and his house with great plagues because of Sarai Abram's wife" (Genesis 12:17). What this parallel means isn't clear—it makes most sense as an ironic way of registering the difference between modernity and biblical antiquity—but clearly the author intended it. The wrath of God is unmistakable in the flames that engulf the personal drama just as it nears a resolution with Abby's emergent love for the farmer and Bill's imminent departure. Violent death ensues for both men. Divine punishment seems extravagantly out of proportion to ordinary human sins. The mixture of melodrama, epic of the land, and religious allegory doesn't quite come off.

Malick didn't make another movie for twenty years. He was part of what is often seen as the generation of the 1970s, a transitional decade when American filmmakers enjoyed unusual artistic freedom after the collapse of the old studio system and before the reassertion of commercial Hollywood that began with *Jaws* and *Star Wars*. During his long absence Malick became something of a legend, and so much prestige accrued to the reclusive director that virtually every able-bodied male actor in Hollywood wanted to play soldier for him when he returned to make a war movie, *The Thin Red Line* (1998), which he adapted from James Jones's novel about the battle of Guadalcanal.

A predatory crocodile slides and slowly sinks into green water to the sound of an ominously sustained musical chord. Then, over images of a jungle, with sunbeams peering through thick foliage, an unidentified voice asks in a Southern accent, "What's this war in the heart of nature? Why does nature vie with itself, the land contend with the sea? Is there an avenging power in nature? Not one power, but two?" So starts *The Thin Red Line*. Presumably that killer crocodile symbolizes all the killing in war, which the film portrays "without qualification," according to Leo Bersani and Ulysse Dutoit, "as a massive manifestation of human evil, and the only question asked about it is how it got into the world. Any historical answer to the question is simply ignored."[88] But to ignore history and see war in the heart of nature is to see it as inevitable, irremediable, however deplorable you find it to be. Is that the view Malick takes? He may pay little attention to the historical context and consequence of the battle he depicts—you wouldn't know from his movie that it was the first major Allied offensive in the Pacific war—but this doesn't mean he imputes it to some evil power transcending history. The crocodile, though frightening, is surely not evil, nor does the voice say it is. And in any case we mustn't assume that a character's voice-over speaks for the author.

In this movie several characters speak in voice-over. Whose voice is it that speaks of war in nature, not one power but two? It's the first and the last voice we hear, the most prominent and the hardest to identify. Almost all commentators have attributed it to Private Witt (Jim Caviezel), who is a Southerner and a leading character, but to my ears the voice doesn't sound like his. The subtitles on a DVD of the film (an option provided for the hard of hearing and useful for the hard to understand) attribute it to a minor character, a private named Train who is also a Southerner, and that seems right. A more recent DVD approved by the director has no subtitles; I guess Malick didn't want them because they would make it too easy to tell one voice from another.

Voice-over, which is how a movie can take us inside a character's head, is here a way of connecting one character with another. Here, much more than in *Days of Heaven,* Malick gives us a sense of the group, the soldiers in C Company—C for Charlie—sent to fight the Japanese on the island of Guadalcanal. They are a disparate group, lacking in the patriotic spirit and soldierly solidarity usual in war movies. They face death together in the greenest of battlefields, but the fear visible on their faces isolates more than it unites. One soldier keeps the fear at bay through his love for his remembered wife, the cherished images of her he summons to mind, a private haven of past marital bliss far removed from the deathly present. An ambitious colonel (Nick Nolte) clashes with a humane captain but proves himself right by victory in battle. Witt dreams of a life close to nature among the Melanesian islanders, while Sergeant Welsh (Sean Penn) expresses the view that each man should look out for himself, had better make himself an island. And yet a sense of connection among these men comes across, owing in no small measure to the collectivity of voices, inner voices linking together soldiers outwardly at odds, voices confusable with one another because the soldiers are in some way at one, if not in their views, then in their contradictions. The hardened colonel's voice-over reveals a man as afraid as the rest of them: "The closer you are to Caesar, the greater the fear." And near the end, passing by the graves of soldiers, Welsh gainsays in voice-over his professed cynicism and egoism: "If I never meet you in this life, let me feel the lack. A glance from your eyes, and my life will be yours."

When the men of Charlie Company arrive in Guadalcanal, the camera advances through a field of green grasses, with trees in the background and blue mountains beyond. It feels as if we were one of the advancing soldiers, any one of them, for the traveling shot goes on for a while before a cut retroactively identifies the soldier whose point of view we've been sharing. The camera has built into it the perspective of an individual observer; the conventional point-of-view shot personifies that perspective by ascribing it to a character in the story. *The Thin Red Line* often personifies the camera while leaving the ascription of point of view dangling, which has the effect of identifying the unidentified individual observer with the soldiers as a group. Neither assuming authorial omniscience—in this film, as Michel Chion notes, "there are no shots, or very few, that are not at the level of the mud, the water, the ground, the human being in the grass"[89]—nor limiting us to one character's consciousness, Malick instead sets up a play of consciousnesses, making us feel that the camera's perspective could belong to any one of them.

Moving the camera can serve to personify it by having it represent the way things appear to a person looking around or moving through space. From the grassy field the soldiers proceed to a rain forest, and there too the camera moves like one of their number, looking up at the sunlight shining through the tall fronded trees. "Who are you to live in all these many forms?" asks the Southern voice of Private Train. Cut to a pair of bright-colored parrots, and then to a stand of bamboo, where the camera's skyward look tilts down to soldiers making their way through the thicket of thin trees. "You're death that captures all," Train continues. "You, too, are the source of all that's going to be born." While it is understandable that many would mistake this voice for Witt's, it is fitting that a voice so difficult to identify should be heard over images that seem to be taking the perspective of an unidentified soldier. And it is striking that before long Train's voice is heard, ruminating on "courage, the contented heart," over flashback images in the mind of the soldier remembering his wife— one man's inner thoughts, another's visual memories. "Maybe all men got one big soul," Witt wonders later on—this is his voice-over for sure, heard as he looks at the wounded in battle, the blood in the water—"all faces of the same man, one big self."

Malick studied philosophy, taught it at M.I.T. for a year before taking up the movies, and translated Heidegger's *The Essence of Reasons*. In the wake of one world war Heidegger pondered the meaning of death, and it makes sense to consider how his philosophy may have informed Malick's picture of another world war. I'm not sure that Kaja Silverman understands Heidegger very well—I'm not sure I do—but I think she's right to point out that the philosopher stresses the individuating effect of death on human beings, while the filmmaker lays more emphasis on death as something we have in common not only with one another but with the rest of creation.[90] Dying is one half of war; the other half is killing. Many of the men of Charlie Company die in the extended fight to capture a hill from the enemy, but those who reach the top proceed to kill, and kill rampantly, horribly. It is then, during the massacre of the defeated Japanese, that Train is moved to ask, "This great evil, where's it come from? How'd it steal into the world? What seed, what root did it grow from? Who's doing this? Who's killing us?" It's curious that Train asks who's killing us when his fellow soldiers are doing the killing. Is it because he knows them, knows they're not evil men, though they are perpetrating this great evil? He's identifying with the killed, identifying the killers with the killed. The suggestion, borne out by the images, is that men kill in war out of fear of being killed, that the fear of death made acute by the experience of war leads in turn to the inflicting of death.

The frightening crocodile, symbol of Train's Manichean war in the heart of nature, is caught by the soldiers and tied up; in nature, though maybe not in human war, the fear of impending death can be subdued. This initiates a series of reversals, contravened views. The man clinging to memories of his beloved wife receives a letter from her telling him that she has fallen in love with another man and asking for a divorce: "Oh, my friend of all those shining years, help me leave you." Witt looks again at the Melanesians he idealized ("I seen another world") and now finds contention, pain, human skulls inside their huts. Love will not save you from death, may not even last you for long in this life; the Melanesians are not the sweetness and light you dream of. Yet the images of the man and his wife in their shining years, of Witt immersed with the islanders in their idyllic clear waters, embody longings impossible to dispel. They're not false images, they're an aspect of the truth; if not the answer, they're part of the question.

Fear is as central to James Jones's novel as to Malick's movie, the fear all soldiers feel and each in his own way tries to deal with. Unlike the novel, however—and like Faulkner's *As I Lay Dying* or *Absalom, Absalom!*—the movie gives the characters worldviews, not just sentiments and opinions but whole philosophies of life. These mostly unschooled, regionally accented, often ungrammatical and inconsistent philosophies, which some critics snobbishly belittle, the movie presents as a kind of eloquent colloquial poetry we are to take quite seriously: living in the world, facing death in it, surely qualifies a human being to express a worldview. Introducing his translation, Malick writes that the world, in Heidegger's sense, "is not the 'totality of things' but that in terms of which we understand them, that which gives them measure and purpose and validity in our schemes." He adds that we "share certain notions about the measure and purpose and validity of things," but "sometimes we do not, or do not seem to, share such notions."[91] In *The Thin Red Line* the soldiers put forward several such notions, which they may or may not share among themselves and which we may or may not share with them. A movie constructs a world, gives the things it depicts measure and purpose and validity in its schemes, but *The Thin Red Line* offers various worldviews without deciding for us which serves best to understand things.

Near the beginning Witt recalls his mother's death: "I asked her if she was afraid. She just shook her head. I was afraid to touch the death I seen in her. I heard people talk about immortality, but I ain't seen it. I wondered how it'd be when I died. . . . I just hope I can meet it the same way she did, with the same calm. 'Cause that's where it's hidden, the immortality I hadn't seen." Witt does come to meet his death with something of the same calm. Because he sacrifices himself for his fellow soldiers he has been construed as a Christ figure; because he makes his death his own he can also be seen as an existential hero. Both readings see him as the exception that sets the rule, the one soldier whose story really matters. Those who attribute Train's voice-over to Witt suppose that at the end Witt speaks from beyond the grave, having presumably attained immortality. But on the boat carrying the men of Charlie Company out of Guadalcanal, Train talks to another soldier just before he speaks in voice-over, and now it should be easier to identify his voice: "Darkness and light, strife and love. Are they the workings of one mind, the features of the same face? Oh, my soul, let me be in you now. Look out through my eyes. Look out at the things you made, all things shining." This is an ordinary man speaking, almost anonymous, neither Christlike nor a hero who has transcended fear and embraced his own death. Some movies arrange the meaning of things around a central character, but not this one.

Jump Cuts

Although earlier examples can be adduced, I believe the term "jump cut" was first applied to Godard's *Breathless* (1960). As Patricia (Jean Seberg) rides in a car with Michel (Jean-Paul Belmondo), cuts skipping forward in time keep returning to her back profile, seen from the same angle at different points along the ride. These cuts jump because, with so much staying the same, the sudden changes in the background, the light, the position of her head, are made all the more manifest. Cuts from one actor, one detail, one scene to another may be abrupt but do not jump that way. What makes a jump cut jump is the very continuity setting off the discontinuity. Often any abrupt cut is called a jump cut, but only a cut that maintains enough sameness for the difference to jump on the screen should be so called. Abrupt cuts abound in *Days of Heaven*, but only in Malick's recent work—availing himself of digital editing, as some have noted—does he put jump cuts to salient, systematic use.

In *The Thin Red Line* Malick uses jump cuts when depicting the memories of the soldier who recalls his wife. Take the flashback that, as he advances up a grassy hill on a lone reconnaissance mission, transports us to the couple in their bedroom, where gossamer curtains blowing in the breeze let in golden sunlight. The jump cuts that punctuate the scene find sameness and continuity above all in the wife's face glowing with desire, now on one side of the screen, now on the other, now gazing at her husband, now in his caressing hands, now tightly beside his face with her eyes closed and her arms hugging his back. If in *Breathless* the successive jump cuts on Patricia's back profile express obsessive fixation amid incessant motion—the man on the run stuck on the American girl in Paris—here we have a similarly expressed fixation on a woman whose jumpily reiterated image seems continually at risk of slipping away. Right after the lovemaking in the golden bedroom the wife turns up in the distance, wading in the vast blue ocean that separates her from her husband and inviting him to come join her there.

In *The Tree of Life*, which took three years to edit, jump cuts multiply and enter into intricate shot arrangements. At the start the mother as a little girl looks out of a window; there is a jump cut to a somewhat different angle—which has the effect of insisting on the image—as we hear her adult voice: "The nuns taught us there are two ways through life, the way of nature" (we see the little girl holding a lamb in her arms) "and the way of grace" (we see a field of sunflowers out of Dovzhenko's *Earth*). We may think of sunflowers as nature and tenderness to baby animals as grace, but Malick seems to be proposing the opposite, or suggesting that the line between nature and grace may not be so easy to draw. "Grace doesn't try to please itself," the mother's voice-over continues. "Accepts being slighted, forgotten, disliked. Accepts insults and injuries." Fade to the adult mother (Jessica Chastain) swinging on a swing, her shadow joining the shadow of trees on the green lawn, the camera swinging back with her and then forward—until a jump cut suddenly shifts to a boy now on the swing, the mother and a dog beside him. Cut to the father (Brad Pitt) and two other boys inside the house; jump cut to the mother bringing food to the table, where she and her husband and their three boys now sit. "Nature only wants to please itself," her voice-over resumes. "Get others to please it too. Likes to lord it over them, to have its own way. It finds reasons to be unhappy when all the world is shining around it, when love is smiling through all things." In this dichotomy—which is the nuns', the mother's, not necessarily the author's—the father represents the way of nature and the mother the way of grace, of love smiling through all things.

"They taught us," she goes on, "that no one who loves the way of grace ever comes to a bad end"—and we cut to her point of view on one of her boys, the one who will die young. Cut to water falling down a steep waterfall, then to a view of the sun and the sky through the spreading branches of a big tree: "I will be true to you," she says, "whatever comes." In the next image, from years later, what comes is a man delivering a telegram with the news of her son's death. Two successive jump cuts mirror her startled response, and an abrupt cut to the father at work interrupts her sobbing and transforms it into the deafening sound of an aircraft motor roaring as he picks up the phone on which, we infer, she has called him with the news. Distraught, she walks down the street with her arms crossed, and the camera moves alongside her and then turns around to face her, letting us glimpse the father following her. She turns away from the camera to face him, but a jump cut puts us right back in front of her. Her distress is palpable, something that must inescapably be confronted. Inside the house—not the same house where we saw the family at table a minute earlier but a better-appointed later residence—she walks past her dead son's room, but the camera goes in and takes a look at his paintbrushes and his guitar from a personified mobile perspective that could perhaps be hers at some other time she now remembers. Then, through the open window blinds, we see the postman on his daily round. He isn't the man who delivered the telegram, but he does call him to mind and thereby situates inconsolable sorrow in the context of everyday life and its cyclical time.

The Tree of Life is Malick's first portrayal of everyday life, a family melodrama without much drama, as if the unremarkable conflicts and muted apprehensions of family life had all along harbored the tragedy announced in that initial telegram. "The whole film might be a poem," Geoffrey O'Brien writes, "of deep grief diffused over a life-time. . . . The effect is of seeing a memory staged, indelible in the realism of its details but edited and compressed over time. . . . The world as processed by the mind, with finally only the bright bits magnetized by emotion remaining to flash against darkness."[92] The oldest boy,

Jack (played as a boy by Hunter McCracken and as an adult by Sean Penn), can be seen as an autobiographical figure: Malick was himself the oldest of three boys growing up in 1950s Texas, and a few years later one of his little brothers died young, apparently by suicide. Is Jack, then, the central consciousness, the recollecting mind? Maybe, but *The Tree of Life* does not, unlike *The Thin Red Line*, stay with the point of view of "the human being in the grass." It ranges grandiosely, cosmically, over sunflowers and dinosaurs, days and eons, primordial life and human birth, children playing and cells pulsating, fiery stars and interstellar space—like the eye of God, you could say, but perhaps more like a prayer to God in the form of images, a prayer for the lost brother that can, after all, be ascribed to Jack's consciousness.

The story of the Texas childhood, as typical as it is specific—the sweet mother, the also sweet yet sad-eyed younger brother, the frustrated authoritarian father, the woman next door who attracts Jack's gaze as she hangs the laundry and whose nightgown the boy steals from her bedroom in a fit of displaced Oedipal desire, the family Studebaker he wishes at one moment would crush the hated father working under the car—is peculiarly affecting for being perfectly commonplace. It is the heart of the movie, and through the telling of it, the flashing bits magnetized by emotion, the boy Jack is the protagonist and principal witness as the adult Jack may be the mind sorting it out.

At the end, after the departure from the childhood home, the adult Jack follows the boy Jack onto a beach where he finds his family, including his lost brother, as they were when he was a boy, together with many others, some of them recognizable from his past. As this glimpse of heaven winds to a finish, just before Jack and his mother say good-bye to his lost brother, a black mask invoking theater, reiterated by a jump cut, sinks into the water, telling us that the show is over: *La commedia è finita*. I thought of the ending of Fellini's *8½*, which brings all the characters together in a fantasy circus show. *8½* is a comedy, and *The Tree of Life* is not, but its ending, though an exalted affair quite unlike a circus show, is still declared as fantasy, imagination, artifice. Art is in the end the path to the lost brother, the way through which he can be regained. Thus the author, the artist, is deeply identified with Jack. Art as the way of grace: sunflowers are nature, but Dovzhenko's sunflowers are art, and now they return for a curtain call.

Like his camera movements, and often jointly with them, Malick's jump cuts personify the camera. Personified camera movement imitates a human gaze moving through space; Malick's jump cuts imitate the mind's eye looking back in time. How do we remember things? How do they come back to us? Not as dramatic scenes but as retrieved moments, not in cohesive narrative sequence but in bits and pieces. We remember places, the context but not so much the story; we remember faces, the expression but not so much the event. We remember moments and details, parts more than wholes, and try as we may to fit parts into wholes, discontinuities keep breaking continuities, moments and details keep coming back to us as images in their own right, with their own light, a little different each time as they shift in the mind, now the mother on the family swing, now the brother in her stead. The jump cut is the device Malick uses to evoke this process of recollection: the soldier's memory of his wife in *The Thin Red Line*, Jack's memory of his childhood in *The Tree of Life*, the memory of the wonder of love in *To the Wonder* (2012).

Lovers on a train—unnamed until the end credits, they are Marina (Olga Kurylenko) and Neil (Ben Affleck)—open *To the Wonder*. "Newborn," she says in subtitled French voice-over. "I open my eyes. I melt . . . I fall into the flame." She gushes like that much of the time. Malick, as always with his voice-overs, keeps a certain ironic distance but assumes no superiority. Homespun digital images—shot, as we soon see, by Neil on his cell phone—shakily register the first rush of his and Marina's love, and announce from the outset that this film— otherwise shot in luminous 35 millimeter by Emmanuel Lubezki, Malick's cinematographer since *The New World* (2005)—is to be in the mode of personal memory.

If you didn't like *The Tree of Life* you wouldn't like *To the Wonder*, but even ardent admirers of the former have been cool to the latter. All through his career Malick has aroused divided responses, but in the case of *To the Wonder* critics were overwhelmingly negative. I was moved and amazed by it. I imagine it embarrasses people to see love depicted so earnestly, and to see it connected with a sense of the divine. Romantic elation and religious devotion haven't been much in fashion of late, let alone a link between the two. The wonder that is love is explicitly identified with the abbey of Mont Saint-Michel on the coast of Normandy. The film's two most vivid characters, and its two principal voice-over speakers, are a woman rapturously in love, Marina, and a Catholic priest struggling to retain his faith, Father Quintana (Javier Bardem).

Marina and Neil fall in love during his visit to France. From their driving together down a Parisian street we jump cut to their approaching Mont Saint-Michel in their car. "We climbed the steps," she begins saying in voice-over as they ascend toward the abbey, and after an inserted shot of their hands clasping, she finishes the sentence as they arrive at the cloister: "to the Wonder." The tide is coming in as they leave, and the muddy sand around the abbey gives way under their feet, suggesting that their romance does not rest on solid ground. Cut to a view out of a high window in a Parisian apartment, where Marina's ten-year-old daughter asks her why she is unhappy. The question surprises us—so far Marina has been all smiles—and we realize how little we know of the story, how elliptical these glimpses of the past are. Having just found out that Marina has a daughter, we now learn that Neil is returning to the United States and isn't proposing marriage. "I don't expect anything," Marina tells him. "Just to go a little of our way together." And the three go together to Oklahoma.

The Oklahoma we see in this film does not suffer by comparison with France. In its own way it looks beautiful—not only the prairie but even the supermarket where Neil, Marina, and her daughter shop, even the housing subdivision where they live. Malick seems to believe, like Plato, that things are most themselves at their most beautiful. And like Godard, he avoids the lamps and reflectors usually used to light movie scenes and cultivates the beauty of natural light. While cleaning the stained-glass windows in the Oklahoma town's Catholic church, the white-haired, bearded black janitor speaks in tongues to Father Quintana for a quick moment—so convincingly that I think he must be an actual person, not a performer—and, putting his hand on the stained glass, says: "I can feel the warmth of the light, brother. That's spiritual, you know. I'm feeling more than just natural light." And he adds, as both he and the priest put their hands on the glass: "I can almost touch the light, coming right from the sky." Malick wants us to feel the light, to feel that this scene was shot with natural light coming right from the sky, and to feel in that light something spiritual.

"I've been thinking what to do with my future," muses Linda at one point in *Days of Heaven*. "I could be a mud doctor, checking out the earth, underneath." That's what Neil is in *To the Wonder*, a mud doctor, an engineer checking out the Oklahoma earth and water, testing for oil pollution. Like the spongy ground around Mont Saint-Michel, the endangered Oklahoma soil is both actual and metaphorical. In a ditch, on a river shore, Neil finds pollution. As the waters run broader and deeper in successive images, Marina's voice asks: "What is this love that loves us? That comes from nowhere. From all around." Her lyrical question accompanies ironically lyrical images of flowing waters shining in the sun, beautiful yet polluted. The irony lends her question a metaphysical implication: how can love shine in a tainted, a fallen world? Father Quintana wrestles with a related worry, a persistent feeling of God's withdrawal from him: "Intensely I seek you. My soul thirsts for you. Exhausted. Will you be like a stream that dries up?" He doesn't answer when a woman bangs on the door. She is a haggard addict who may want money for a fix, one of the poor he ministers to but doesn't love: "My heart is cold. Hard." His priestly duties bring him into contact with the needy, the imprisoned, the frail, and the maimed, images of human imperfection, the imperfections that make it hard to love people. Evidently actual unfortunates, Malick photographs them with his abiding sense of beauty, not prettifying misery but regarding them in the light of love, which despite all doubts can be seen to shine in our fallen world. "Show me how to love you," Marina says. "Show us how to seek you," the priest says. Not just the wonder but the difficulty of love is the theme of *To the Wonder*.

Marina is a dancer, and Olga Kurylenko plays her in a kind of incessant dance. Like the mother in *The Tree of Life*, another figure of love, she keeps gamboling and twirling about, the way of grace forever in motion. Some find her irritating, and she's meant to be a bit much. We can understand both Neil's enchantment with her and his reluctance to marry her. She ends up alone—alone as the one who, though she has her downs, comes closest to the wonder, the one who best understands love as a divine gift and rises to it even without a ground to support her. Largely a solo performance with only the camera as her partner, her dancing manifests an incontrovertible energy of body and soul. But it is continually being interrupted, broken down into fragments. It represents not the actuality but the memory of love. In no other film are jump cuts more deftly managed and combined with camera movements to achieve the effect of a retrospective gaze, a mind's eye reaching into the past.

If the whole film is a montage of memory fragments—"a kind of unframed flashback," as Peter Bradshaw puts it, "not a narrative so much as remembered feelings, glimpses and moments . . . dreamily extended to epiphany length"[93]—whose memory are we seeing staged? Like *The Tree of Life*, *To the Wonder* seems to be partly autobiographical, and like Jack, Neil may be taken as Malick's surrogate. We stay with him when Marina, her tourist visa expiring, returns to France with her daughter. We see him on the sidewalk watching them drive away, jump cut inside the house to a camera movement following him out into the yard, jump cut closer to him as he looks at the departing car in the distance, jump cut back inside the house to his lone dark figure silhouetted against the external light. We see him at work inspecting places that have suffered oil damage and get glimpses of him with Marina that can only be memories flashing through his mind. We also see him with another woman, Jane (Rachel McAdams), but then Marina speaks in voice-over about Jane and addresses him: "You told me about her. . . . Someone you'd known in your youth." Even after Marina has gone, when the images we see appear to represent Neil's consciousness, we hear her voice. Once again Malick gives us a play of consciousnesses. The memory fragments sometimes seem to belong to one character, sometimes to another, but overall are best ascribed to an indeterminate, floating subjectivity. An objective account transcending individual sentiments in favor of social and material realities was the point of the Soviet montage style—the dazzlingly omnipresent camera in Vertov, the elaborate, disjunctive syntax of images in Eisenstein, the poetic parallel cutting in Dovzhenko. But Malick's montage of recollections, whether of the wife in *The Thin Red Line*, the Texas childhood in *The Tree of Life*, or just about anything in *To the Wonder*, assembles keenly personal pieces of experience. Yet the fragmentary and elliptical rendering attains a kind of universality precisely because so much of the story is left out, giving us space to project onto Marina and Neil's intense, failed romance our own memories of intense, failed romances.

Crosscutting

S tormy Monday (the title comes from the song: "They call it stormy Monday, but Tuesday is just as bad") begins with a red sports car at a gas station. This was Mike Figgis's first movie (1988), set in Newcastle at the time of Reagan and Thatcher, a film noir of sorts with a political edge. It is night, and from the red sports car, now driving along a highway, we cut to a young woman, Kate (Melanie Griffith), asleep in bed. An intricate pattern of crosscutting is taking shape. We see an architectural model of a city and notice a bridge with a high arch reaching across it; later on we find out that this model of Newcastle belongs to Cosmo (Tommy Lee Jones), an unscrupulous American entrepreneur who would like the city itself to belong to him. Cut to the red car, where we see two men in the front seat; it transpires that these are thugs working for Cosmo and headed for Newcastle. Cut to Kate asleep. Cut to the city itself, the real arched bridge, as the day dawns—the stormy Monday of the title (but Tuesday is just as bad). Cut to the red car on the road; an accident has occurred, and the car gets caught in a traffic jam. Cut to an alarm radio going off, to wake up Kate, we may think, but in the next shot, lying in bed, we see a young man, Brendan (Sean Bean). Now the film cuts back and forth between Brendan and Kate getting up in the morning of this stormy Monday. Although Kate and Brendan are apart from each other, each unknown to the other, they and the details of their awakening are run together on the screen. Crosscutting between them makes a comparison and promises a conjunction. It draws a parallel between the two young risers, both lone outsiders in the city (Kate from Minnesota, Brendan from Ireland) and both working class (he's looking for a job, she's employed as a waitress but also works for Cosmo, and this morning receives a phone call summoning her to that corrupt work); and it anticipates their meeting, their actually coming together.

Crosscutting was the principal invention of Griffith's inventive years at Biograph, the form of editing he used most assiduously and developed most systematically, his preferred method of arranging shots into a sequence enacting a story. Rather than cutting *within* a scene, to a closer view or a different angle, he would much more often cut *between* scenes, from one place to another, from one strand of action to another and back again. Griffith explored both the comparative (as in *A Corner in Wheat*, where the parallel strands of action never meet) and the conjunctive possibilities of crosscutting. In the 1910 *Country Doctor*, for example, he cuts back and forth between the doctor's own daughter and another little girl who has also fallen ill, which serves to bring forward not only the similarity between the two sick girls but also the difference between the doctor's prosperous household and the other girl's poorer circumstances. Besides this parallel and contrast, this drawing of comparisons, Griffith's crosscutting builds up here the suspense of conjunction: will the doctor be able to go back and forth between his own house and the other girl's so that he may succeed in treating both girls and effecting their cure? In *The Country Doctor* the doctor succeeds in curing the other girl, but his own daughter dies. More characteristically, however, Griffith's crosscutting reaches a happy conjunction, as in his famous last-minute rescues, of which the prototype was the 1909 *Lonely Villa*: the mother and children are threatened by intruding bandits; the father comes to the rescue of the imperiled home and gets there just in time. The suspense of conjunction—of disjunction working its way toward conjunction—usually carries with it a promise of felicitous resolution, a reassurance that what lies apart will come together.

It is often said that film is an art of fragments. Griffith's innovations in the technique of film editing were instrumental in that fragmentation. The space of a painting stands whole before our eyes. So does the space of a theater stage—and Aristotle prescribes that the action enacted on it be "whole and complete, with a beginning, a middle, and an end." But in a film, after Griffith started breaking down scenes into shots, with the camera now here and now there, now closer and now farther away, what stands before our eyes at any moment is only a fragment, only a detail of an implied space extending unseen beyond the frame. Space and time are broken into pieces on the screen. It can also be said that the fragmentation of film reflects and expresses the fragmentation of modern life. A movie is broken into pieces as our experience is broken into pieces. The father in *The Lonely Villa* is away from home as our fathers are so often away from home; the villa is lonely and imperiled as our homes are so often lonely, isolated from a sustaining community, and thereby imperiled. The cuts punctuating a movie are, then, breaks articulating what in our lives is already broken. Our actions can no longer be expected to unfold whole and complete before our eyes. "Maryland train derailment delays terrorism trial at Guantanamo": when I saw this headline running across the bottom of my television screen, the abrupt juxtaposition of two places far away from each other seemed to me almost surreal.[94] But ours is a world of faraway connections, the Maryland story being bound up with the Guantánamo story; best to tell the two stories together and keep cutting from one place to the other and back again.

From the collages of cubism to the found objects and incongruous juxtapositions of dada and surrealism to the discontinuities and interruptions of Brecht's epic theater, the fragment, the broken form, has been characteristic of much modern art. Yet in some manner art must achieve order and coherence; fragmentation calls for a countervailing pull toward some form of integration. "While life will never let one have anything both ways," Eric Bentley remarks, "it is the mission of art to do just that."[95] And that's just what film does with broken and cohesive form. A cut at once interrupts and connects, breaks off something and links it to something else, thereby having it both ways: the break that links, the fragments of modern life pieced together on the screen. Conjunctive crosscutting, which began with Griffith's last-minute rescues and is still going strong, takes the form of a rupture anxiously looking forward to its mending. Film is able to combine the fragmentation of a modern art with the completion of a classical art.

Often it is love that comes to the rescue and mends the rupture. Crosscutting between Kate and Brendan in *Stormy Monday* creates the expectation that their lonely paths will cross and join in a love story. Their paths indeed cross more than once during that day. The first time they meet, at a shopping mall where she has been buying clothes for the job with Cosmo and is coming down an escalator, they literally bump into each other and fall to the floor, she on top of him. They are evidently falling in love, though not at first bump. Only after another chance encounter, when he goes to eat that evening at the restaurant where she waits on tables, does their romance start to blossom. Figgis wittily plays with the boy-meets-girl convention, but he takes it seriously, and the romance between Kate and Brendan carries unusual conviction as a kind of life raft in the shipwreck of modern life. Their antagonist is Cosmo, the capitalist as gangster, no tragic hero this time but the chief villain, the corrupter in chief, the public enemy that leaves no privacy untouched.

Love as the rescuer from alienation comes to a dead end in *Leaving Las Vegas*, yet retains its romantic glow. Made on a shoestring from a novel by a suicide, this 1995 film has been Figgis's most celebrated work. A hopeless alcoholic goes to die in Las Vegas and there meets a prostitute—boy meets girl taken to a terminal extreme, a romance with nowhere to go but still a romance. Detractors of this film object to the romanticism, which they see as a falsification of the hopelessness. But *Leaving Las Vegas* is no less hopeless for being romantic and no less romantic for being hopeless. Therein it finds its poise and its beauty.

A cut cuts both ways. It divides and it joins; it joins and it divides. Taking apart and bringing together, it may take apart yet promise to bring together, and it may bring together yet threaten to take apart. Kate's and Brendan's are not the only paths that cross at the restaurant in *Stormy Monday*. The red sports car has arrived in Newcastle and parks on the street outside, and the two thugs working for Cosmo come in to have a meal. The crosscutting that brings Kate and Brendan together also involves the violence that may take them apart. The red car that started the film and got the crosscutting going represents that violence. At the restaurant, Brendan, who has found employment at a neighboring jazz club, overhears the thugs talking about the job they've come to do, the violence being planned against the owner of the jazz club to force its sale to Cosmo. After Brendan alerts his boss, the thugs are foiled, and his boss rewards him by forcing them to sell their sports car to Brendan for one pound. But even in Brendan's possession the car remains the vehicle of violence, and at the film's end a planted time bomb meant for Kate and Brendan kills two friends who happen to borrow the car.

Not only the vehicle of violence in the story the film tells, the red car may be taken to represent the violence in the crosscutting itself, in the brisk fragmentation by which the film tells the story. Certainly the crosscutting does not cease once Kate and Brendan are together. If earlier it promised their union, now it threatens something worse than their separation. Bruised after an encounter with Cosmo's hirelings, Kate and Brendan make tender love—tender both from pain and from love—and the film breaks this sweet scene by crosscutting it with a brash parade out in the street, part of the Cosmo-orchestrated America Week in Newcastle, and then with the parade on a television screen, being watched by someone who is setting up the bomb for the car. The cuts breaking the space of love point to the site of violence. A cut does a kind of violence, the sharper the cut the more palpable the violence. It is not coincidental that masters of film violence such as Griffith and Eisenstein, Kurosawa and Peckinpah, are also masters of film cutting. *Stormy Monday* may not be in their league, but few recent movies have so cannily placed themselves in that nexus of cutting and violence.

Crosscutting is one way to tell a story on the screen. There are other ways. A film may stay in one place for some time and enact something like a scene in a stage play; it may then use a "master shot" encompassing the whole area, the stage where the action takes place, and serving to situate the shots of details, all the closer views and angles and reverse angles, within that circumscribed space. Or a film may stay with a character and follow that character around, a restriction not to one place but to one consciousness, the point of view of one person within the story. This is Hitchcock's method in films like *The 39 Steps* or *North by Northwest* or the first halves of *Vertigo* and *Psycho* (*Rear Window* stays in one place and with one consciousness). *Stormy Monday* could have chosen to stay with Kate, showing us things only as she comes to them, letting us know only what she knows, limiting us to her perspective and perceptions. Crosscutting implies a governing intelligence that knows, not necessarily everything—"omniscience" is an overused word—but things beyond what any of the characters knows. We know about Kate before Brendan is aware of her and about Brendan before Kate is aware of him; we know about the red sports car before either Kate or Brendan is aware of it. The arranging intelligence that starts the film with the red car knows that this car will play a central part in the story and that the film will end with it, with its going up in flames intended to kill Brendan and Kate. The car may represent the threat of violence but there is a certain reassurance in that representation, for it implies that the maker of this film, the arranger of this crosscutting, is in control of that violence.

Split Space, Unbroken Time

The first movies were brief and proceeded without cuts. Film editing, as Charles Musser has argued,[96] in effect began with the projectionist whose task it was to string together short movies of different sorts, to arrange in some suitable order a variety picture show. Edwin S. Porter was such a projectionist, and as a pioneering director he kept faith with the projectionist's editing, the assembling of discrete, heterogeneous, uninterrupted views. In *The Life of an American Fireman* (1903) Porter depicts the climactic rescue both from inside and outside the house on fire. But he did not cut back and forth between the two viewpoints as Griffith in a few years would have done. Rather, he showed the whole scene twice over, first from inside a room where a woman and her child are in danger, and then from the street outside, where the firemen have arrived and one of them climbs a ladder to the rescue. With Porter the inside and the outside remain separate, as if two different observers were giving us two different accounts of the same event. With Griffith's crosscutting the camera can switch at will from here to there and back again, so that we get the sense of a single observer, an eye somehow endowed with the capacity to see what goes on in two places at once. Porter was a compiler of views brought together after the fact. The view from inside knows nothing about the view to come from outside; the view from outside knows nothing about the view just seen from inside. What Griffith put in place was a single commanding eye, an overseeing intelligence bringing this into view while keeping that in mind, then switching to that in relation to this and to the anticipated next thing.

The single eye that Griffith established has governed movies down to this day. Its reach, its prerogatives, its limitations, may vary from one movie to another, or even from one moment to the next, but all the same that single eye frames our view and gives us our perspective at every point, the eye through which we see everything that is made visible on the screen. Sometimes filmmakers have called into question the authority of that eye, the convention investing it with the ability to pick out for us at each moment just what we should see. But like the theatrical convention marking out the stage as a space of performance apart from the audience, the rule of that eye is a basic convention of the medium, amenable to variation, susceptible to challenge, yet almost never overthrown.

Sometimes a scene is filmed with more than one camera, but the different views, integrated in the editing, will give the impression of a single comprehensive eye. What about documentaries, which often assemble found footage, old pictures, bits of bygone newsreels, images from here and there mixed in with talking heads? Unlike the variety show mounted by early projectionists, documentary filmmakers put together an argument, an account and an interpretation of the facts, so that the variegated images are cut up into pieces and harnessed to a rhetorical or narrative logic that usually finds expression in an accompanying voice-over commentary—an authoritative voice, even if not an eye, behind all the heterogeneous views.

Superimposition, double exposure, two images appearing one over the other on the screen, would seem to break the single-eye convention. But most often this device serves to create an otherworldly illusion, with one of the images regarded as real, the other as phantasmal, and the two coalescing into a single view of a ghost-inhabited scene. Avant-garde films lay bare the device, however, and superimpose images without fostering the illusion of their merging into one. No film has made better or bolder use of superimposition than Ernie Gehr's *Still* (1969–71). And yet in its own minimalist way it decidedly keeps to the single eye. For the duration of *Still*—nearly an hour—the camera stands still. We look out a window at a stretch of a New York street, the people coming and going, the traffic passing by, but the eye registering this movement never itself moves. We see the street in winter, we see the coming of spring and the onset of summer, but as time passes and the seasons grow cold and warm, the space we watch on the screen stays in place. We get a double vision of the street, two images layered in double exposure, which gives rise to a pattern of interlacement, shifting transparency and opacity; but both images frame exactly the same section of space from the same fixed viewing position. There is no otherworldly illusion in *Still*. Everything we see belongs in this world, everything recognizably part of actual street life. And with no mobility between here and there, there is only here, though not only now, for the two superimposed images represent two different times, now and then, The only ghosts are those of memory, of history. Stuck in one place, the single eye of Gehr's camera has the ability to apprehend at once two moments in time.

Movies have on occasion split the screen into two or more images—as when Doris Day and Rock Hudson, sharing a party line in *Pillow Talk* (1959), appear on opposite halves of a divided wide screen—but rarely as anything more than a short break from the single eye. The three screens in Abel Gance's *Napoleon* (1927) only materialize at the finale, and even then mainly serve to give us a compound panoramic view rather than a split into separate images. *Chelsea Girls* (1967) puts two images side by side on the screen for over three hours, but rather than telling a story it paints a series of portraits, and rather than two different viewpoints it presents two different subjects at once, both exposed to the same unblinking eye, the impassive yet implacable stare of Andy Warhol's camera. The sole narrative film I know that splits the screen all the way through is Mike Figgis's *Timecode* (2000).

The screen in *Timecode* is split down and across the middle into four equal smaller screens. At the start we see, on the lower left quadrant, a monitor divided into four little quadrants displaying images from a building's surveillance cameras; in the first of many self-referential gestures, the film compares itself to the eyes of surveillance that are a fixture of our society. *Timecode* uses four eyes to survey its characters, four video cameras not fixed like those in a building but highly mobile, and able to run without interruption for an hour and a half—which is how long the film runs, without cuts or shot changes of any sort on any of its four screens. Having split its space, *Timecode* lets its time flow unbroken. It leaves the crosscutting up to us, to our own shifts of attention from one smaller screen to another within the movie screen. Well, not entirely up to us: Figgis has arranged the sound mix so as to direct our attention by playing up or playing down the sound we hear at different points from the different screens within the screen. But at every point we still have the choice to look at any of the four screens, or at two of them back and forth, or at all four at once. It can truly be said that no two spectators of *Timecode* will see the same movie, that no one will see the same movie twice, and that each of us watching just one of the possible movies unfolding before our eyes will miss much of what there is to see. This bothers some—they don't like to miss anything—but I'm with those who enjoy their freedom from the rule of the single eye deciding for us what we are to see.

Usually the actors in a movie play to the camera. Jean Renoir preferred to have the actors play to one another and move in and out of view without regard for the convention of the eye that always sees the significant thing, the eye for whose benefit everything is being staged. Other directors such as Robert Altman and John Cassavetes encourage the actors to play their parts in their own unrehearsed way, with the camera following rather than governing the moves of their performance, and the film thus becoming less like a staged fiction and more like a documentary whose camera, not knowing in advance what people are going to do, keeps up with them as best it can. The four cameras in *Timecode* follow actors allowed latitude for improvisation, and follow them in their own unbroken time—often called "real" time, though it's not the time of real life but the time of dramatic performance. Even with only one camera, giving the actors freer rein, giving them autonomy from the camera's dominance, tends to create a polyphony, to use a musical term applied by Mikhail Bakhtin in his book on Dostoevsky to the kind of novel that allows other voices autonomy from the author's.[97] Novels are strictly sequential, as words are; we may keep other voices in mind, but we can hear only one at a time. Music, as Mozart said, has the advantage over speech, and opera over spoken drama, of being able to orchestrate several voices that we hear at once. Movies usually proceed in strict sequence, one thing at a time, but even a single camera can show us several things going on at once, and with four cameras the polyphonic possibilities are multiplied.

As in Griffith, in *Timecode* the fragments come together. The polyphony makes a unity. The four cameras track not separate but interweaving and often intersecting stories, which add up to one story unfolding on four screens at once. While enjoying freedom to improvise, the actors were required to conform to the narrative framework Figgis provided, demanding the exact synchronization of the four screens. During the film, set in earthquake-prone L.A., four earthquakes occur, each on all four screens at precisely the same time, as if the earth were trembling in order to have the actors synchronize their watches. The telephone served Griffith in *The Lonely Villa* to establish

synchronicity between the parallel strands of action; from her threatened home the wife reaches her husband over the telephone with a
call for help before the bandits cut the line. That line of connection
was useful for orienting audiences just getting used to crosscutting.
In *The Lonedale Operator* and *The Girl and Her Trust* (1912) the telegraph
served a similar synchronizing purpose. Those were the quick connections the world could make between one place and another in the
early twentieth century, the synchronicity it could establish across
a distance. *Timecode* inhabits the world of the cell phone, which all
the characters carry and on which they keep calling one another, a
world of telecommunications where simultaneity is far more intricate and pervasive. If crosscutting synchronizes the consecutive,
Timecode establishes synchronicity in simultaneity, different pieces of
space sharing the same time side by side much as places geographi-
cally apart become conjoined in a world increasingly interconnected.
Crosscutting arranges a looser concurrency between things it shows
one at a time, one after the other. Able to abridge or stretch time in
the cutting room, it does not require the kind of precise synchronization *Timecode* sets up between four screens on which we see at once
what is happening at once.

Most of the action takes place in and around the offices of an
independent movie company, Red Mullet, which, in another self-
referential gesture, is the name of the company that has produced
several of Figgis's movies, including this one. At one point in the
film, Cherine (Leslie Mann), an actress who just had a screen test
at Red Mullet, is on the street outside and asks for a light from Lauren (Jeanne Tripplehorn), a wealthy woman who is in her limousine
waiting for her live-in lover, Rose (Salma Hayek), an aspiring actress
who hopes to have a screen test at Red Mullet and who, as Lauren
suspects, is cheating on her. Lauren and Cherine have never crossed
paths before and probably never will again; nothing happens when
they do, other than the lowering of a car window and the lighting of
a cigarette, yet something about their momentary encounter, enacted
on the upper two screen quadrants, arrests the attention. If this were
a normal movie and there had been crosscutting between them, their
encounter would have been anticipated; as it is, it strikes us, like
other occasions when the paths of *Timecode*'s numerous characters
cross, and like few such crossings in other movies, as truly a chance
encounter. On the upper left, the quarter screen where she has been
from the beginning, we see Lauren inside her limousine, and Cherine
comes into view on the left through the open window; on the upper
right we are with Cherine outside the limousine, and Lauren comes
into view on the right through the open window. We get, complete
with the conventional symmetry, a kind of shot/reverse shot on two

screens simultaneously. In a normal shot/reverse shot two characters facing each other are shown alternately, each from the other's side. Here the shot and the reverse shot are shown side by side. As in Porter's *American Fireman*, a view from inside and another from outside stand here as two separate reports on the scene, two different viewpoints not made to interlock but set next to each other, not joined together for us but there for us to join them. Cutting back and forth between shot and reverse shot, as a normal film would have done, conveys a sense of deliberation, an encounter the film has arranged and measured. Here the feeling—and there is a peculiar thrill to it, a surprise and a delight arising from the sight of order that seems to be taking shape spontaneously before our eyes—is of a *found* shot/reverse shot, a chance encounter we encounter by chance.

The four main characters in *Timecode* are Lauren and Rose and another troubled couple, Alex (Stellan Skarsgård) and Emma (Saffron Burrows). Emma is the first character we see, relating a dream at a session with her therapist shown on the upper right, the quarter screen assigned to her for the most part as the upper left is to Lauren. Emma's dream was about Alex bleeding "an awful lot of blood coming from this tiny little cut. And the tissues I was laying down weren't . . . weren't soaking it up." Rather like the red car in *Stormy Monday*, this dream at the outset of *Timecode* is a prefiguration of violence to come. It foreshadows Alex's death at the end, when he does indeed bleed profusely from a bullet wound inflicted by Lauren, who, having confirmed her suspicions and found out that Rose has been having an affair with Alex, walks into the conference room at Red Mullet, points a gun at him in front of everybody, and proceeds to shoot him. But *Stormy Monday* builds up through crosscutting the red car's prefiguration of violence, whereas *Timecode* invests the foreshadowing dream with little sense of fatality. Emma speaks softly and haltingly, and in the initial confusion of adjusting to four screens at once we may easily miss what she's saying; even if we hear it, or overhear it, we have no reminders of it until Alex lies bleeding on the floor at the end. The sense is of contingency rather than necessity, not violence impending but violence just happening in the course of things. Why the foreshadowing, then? Even while cultivating chance, Figgis makes us aware of design, the calculation behind this contingency. In *Stormy Monday* we are certainly aware of design, but we are caught up in it as something like inexorable fate, the red car as the vehicle of inescapable violence. Because it makes us see the calculation even in contingency, not the designs of fate but the designs of fiction, of art, *Timecode* gives us a heightened sense of artifice.

The artifice of a screen divided into four declares itself, and the self-referential gestures keep reminding us that it's only a movie we're watching. The boldest of these, and the funniest, occurs in the conference room before Lauren's entrance interrupts a meeting at which a young woman named Ana Pauls (Mia Maestro) has been making a pitch to Red Mullet executives for a new kind of film she wants them to produce. She speaks with the self-assured affectation of the resolutely trendy:

> My film has the necessity, the urge, to go beyond the paradigm of collage. Montage has created a fake reality. . . . Eisenstein and Vertov . . . created the so-called Soviet montage. . . . At that time that was a vanguard. It's not that any more. The capitalistic system that we are living in has absorbed all the innovations, all the vanguards. It's time to move forward, to move beyond . . . It's time to go back to Leibniz and his monadology. . . . My film will be an unmade film . . . a film with not one single cut, no editing, real time. . . . Imagine four cameras displayed in sync. Imagine a situationistic type of play, a Guy Debord type of play. . . . Each of these four cameras will follow a character. . . .

The film she's proposing, in terms that make Alex laugh irrepressibly, is of course the film we're watching. Alex has been drinking all day, and after emerging from sex with Rose behind the screen during a screening, he had to be forced to attend the meeting. "Most pretentious crap I've ever heard," he mutters drunkenly yet aptly. Ana keeps her poise, however, and says she looks forward to working with such an honest man, while for his part he seems amenable to her project until Lauren walks in with a gun and gives things another turn. *Timecode* is a movie capable of laughing at its own pretensions even when nearing a bloody denouement.

It implicates itself in its satire of indie films. Its lightheartedness, its sense of humor about itself along with its characters, has led critics to make light of this daring as well as endearing film. Daring is supposed to be for the avant-garde, endearing for the popular movie that aims to please, but *Timecode* manages a blend of both. One critic who appreciates this is A. O. Scott in the *New York Times*: "It's amazing to see a film so brazenly experimental, so committed to reflecting on the circumstances and techniques of its making, that is at the same time so intent upon delivering old-fashioned cinematic pleasures like humor and pathos, character and plot." Scott notes that the mixture of humor and pathos amounts to a mixture of genres, that the characters' "entwined destinies send this satire staggering toward the precipice of tragedy" or at least melodrama: "Maybe, like Paul Thomas Anderson's *Magnolia*, another recent film to forsake the discipline of montage for the reckless freedom of the long take, *Timecode* offers nothing more than melodrama in the end."[98] Melodrama it is in both cases, and that's not necessarily a lesser thing. Mixing humor and pathos, even mixing genres, may be old-fashioned, but *Timecode* goes further. Its doing away with the single eye selecting things for our attention, and also with editing, a chief cinematic means of interpreting things for us, has the effect of leaving open, undecided, whether we are to take what unfolds on its four screens as humor or pathos, farce or melodrama, satire or tragedy.

Alongside the social satire, this film has much of the bedroom farce. Alex is married to Emma and having an affair with Rose, who is living with Lauren, who points a gun at Alex while, on another screen, Emma almost has a fling with Cherine. We may laugh at Alex as least as hard as he laughs at Ana. We may laugh when, as he lies on the floor dying and Ana hangs over him with her video camera, his cell phone rings one last time. It is Emma, who had told him she was leaving him and now, unaware of his situation, is calling to tell him that she loves him. He replies that he loves her too and wants to see her that night, and he dies on a pool of blood while talking on his cell phone about reserving a table at a nice restaurant. We may laugh at the drunk, sentimental, manipulative Alex, who gets what he has coming to him; we may laugh at Lauren the jealous lover and at Emma the enabling wife. But these characters aren't played for laughs. They're played realistically, with emotional conviction; they suffer and we may suffer with them. Comedy and melodrama are not so far apart. Both are, for one thing, genres that often rely on coincidence, chance encounters that seem chancier on the four screens synchronized in unbroken time. The ambiguity of not knowing whether to laugh or cry can be just the response a work seeks from us, the response we should be having; but *Timecode* doesn't so much elicit responses as make them possible, available to us. It compounds the ambiguity: we don't even know whether we should know whether to laugh or cry.

After proposing to update Leibniz's *Monadology*, Ana drops yet another name in her pitch and brings up Borges's "The Aleph," which she describes as the story of a young man and an old man who come to realize they are the same person. "It would be beautiful," she says, if the characters separately followed by the four cameras "are exactly the same person." Leibniz's monads are atomized individuals that know nothing of one another yet are all in perfect accordance, what the philosopher calls preestablished harmony. For Ana this seems to translate into the sameness of different characters. Utterly separate yet exactly the same—not a bad way to characterize so many of the individuals in our society. The four screens in *Timecode* let us see at once the separation and the sameness.

P. T. Anderson's *Magnolia* (1999) is also about separation and sameness. It is about unhappy families. Tolstoy thinks that happy families are all alike. In our society we have come to believe that unhappy families are all alike too. Although *Magnolia* favors long takes as well as fluid, extended, even meandering camera movements, the basic principle of its construction is parallel editing, crosscutting from one to another of several stories. At times the stories intersect, but the crosscutting is not arranged to lead up to their points of intersection so that, as in *Timecode*, these seem surprising, fortuitous. The crosscutting in *Magnolia* is almost exclusively comparative rather than conjunctive. It draws parallels between the separate stories to make us see what they all have in common as stories of child abuse: unhappy families are all alike because they all involve the parental abuse of children. Each of the stories in *Magnolia* would tend to tragedy if told on its own, but when they are all told together and seen to be essentially the same story, they tend to comedy. Tragedy deals in singularity, comedy in commonality, in community. A flaw that sets an individual apart is tragic; a flaw that brings people together is in the spirit of comedy. *Timecode* may be funnier, but *Magnolia* is more of a comedy—a melodrama oriented toward comedy—because its crosscutting asserts the commonality of its characters, the shared flaw that should bring them together. And yet because its crosscutting merely draws parallels between them and leaves their actual coming together to chance, merely asserts commonality without leading to community, *Magnolia* must fall short of the comedy it aspires to. Its most arresting moment comes about when it contrives to have all its disparate characters impossibly singing together the same song—doing in barefaced fiction what they should be doing in reality, tragic characters in search of a comedy, a community they lack. *Magnolia* never gives up the search. It remains hopeful down to the lovely last shot, in which the most damaged of its abused characters, like Cabiria at the end of Fellini's film, shyly turns her gaze to meet the camera's and begins to smile.

Like the crosscutting in *Magnolia*, the divided image in *Timecode* is a vehicle of comparison. Things set side by side invite us to look for similarities between them, and Figgis mobilizes the comparative geometry of the quartered screen. We may get four close-ups at once, even a four-way zoom into tight close-ups of four pairs of women's eyes. At one point we may notice that as Emma on the upper right is leaving her therapy session and going into a mirrored elevator that doubles her worried face, Cherine on the lower left is leaving her screen test and then goes into a mirrored bathroom to snort cocaine with the security guard at Red Mullet. Parallels multiply, surprising congruencies, unexpected dovetailings, matches and mismatches, ironic contrasts. We see how these disparate characters rhyme with one another, chime in with one another—how these monads all wrapped up in themselves, even if they're not in the preestablished harmony of Leibniz's philosophy, even if they're not the same person of Ana's pitch, have more correlations and correspondences with one another than they'd ever imagine.

After Alex dies on the lower right, that quarter screen fades out to black. Soon the upper left fades out too. That leaves, diagonally across from each other, Emma on the upper right, which from the beginning has been her quarter screen, and Lauren on the lower left, which was not where she started but where she came in with the gun. Having just talked to Alex, Emma is walking along the street, while Lauren, having just shot Alex, has walked out into the street, and in each case the camera frames the woman in close three-quarters view and follows her steadily from the front. The visual parallel is palpable. Between the two women an identification is being made whose implications we're left to ponder. They're both betrayed women. We could say that Emma is well rid of Alex and Lauren well rid of Rose. We could even say that, in ridding her of Alex, the jealous Lauren did for the enabling Emma what she couldn't bring herself to do. They were both wronged by Alex. Yet they are not united in sisterhood. The monads may be in harmony, but they walk alone.

Displeasure

"What I want," a young Luis Buñuel announced to the audience at an early screening of his first film, *Un Chien andalou* (1929), "is for you not to like the film. . . . I'd be sorry if it pleased you."[99] The opening scene, which culminates in the famous close-up of a straight-edge razor being drawn through a woman's eyeball, is often taken as the epitome of cinema's potential to do violence to its audience. The suasions of rhetoric, the effects of art on the observer, are of course achieved by inflicting pain as well as eliciting pleasure, by aggression as well as ingratiation. Horror movies frighten us; violent thrillers agitate us; sentimental stories make us cry. Suffering is often part of our enjoyment—within limits, however. We are not to be so displeased that we are not pleased. Buñuel deliberately goes beyond the limits of permissible displeasure. And so, in his own way, does Austrian filmmaker Michael Haneke.

Funny Games (1997) is a violent melodrama about a respectable family set upon by nasty criminals, much as in *The Desperate Hours* (1955) or *Cape Fear* (1962). (Both these films were remade in the 1990s, by Michael Cimino and Martin Scorsese respectively; Haneke himself remade *Funny Games* in Hollywood in 2007.) The difference is that the criminals in *The Desperate Hours* or *Cape Fear* have a motive for assaulting the family, whereas in *Funny Games* they terrorize for the sake of it, which, Haneke implies, is the real motive for this kind of picture: to terrorize an audience that enjoys being terrorized. Yet he makes sure that his own movie offers us no such enjoyment. The family in *Funny Games*—husband, wife, and small son—arrive, sailboat in tow, at their gated lakeside summer house, where their dog is waiting for them. A chubby young man comes to the door, tells the wife he's staying with a neighbor, and asks to borrow four eggs, which he then clumsily drops on the floor. He asks for four more, and as she reluctantly complies he drops her cell phone in the kitchen sink. He leaves but promptly returns with another young man, slim and slick and clearly the leader of the pair. Nothing like the lowlifes in *The Desperate Hours* or *Cape Fear*, these well-bred young men seem to belong in this wealthy milieu—which is why the wife lets them in the house in the first place and why, even after she senses that something is wrong and tells them to get out, the husband hesitates for a fatal moment and allows them to gain control of the situation. It transpires that the slim young man, who has noticed a splendid set of golf clubs and asked if he could try one out on the lawn, has used it to kill the dog. As the wife looks for the dog, he stands in the near foreground, back to the camera, in soft focus, calling out "cold" or "warm," and then comes into sharp focus as he turns to the camera and winks at the audience.

An actor looking into the lens is not so unusual a breach, such an unconventional gesture, as some suppose; it breaks the fourth wall, we say, but it could be argued that in films there is no fourth wall, or else every reverse angle would be breaking it. Neither is it strange for a melodrama to enlist our complicity with the villain; from Dr. Mabuse to the femme fatale in film noir to Norman Bates, it is typically the villain who drives the story forward. The young man's wink merely makes this explicit. Later on, when the wife manages to get hold of a gun and shoots the chubby young man, the slim one regains control by using a remote control to wind back the images on the screen, so that the scene can be redone according to his intentions. This time the wife is rendered unable to retaliate against his partner. Manifestly it is the villain here who is writing the script.

Haneke does want to teach us a lesson, though, to call us to task for our complicity with villains and our enjoyment of screen violence. He recalls in an interview that the audience at Cannes cheered when the wife killed the chubby villain—the only moment of graphically depicted violence in the movie, and the only instance in which the violence doesn't go in the other direction—but fell silent after the rewinding and revising of the scene because they understood that they had been manipulated into applauding murder. Let's not forget, though, that this woman has seen her family brutalized, her dog and her little boy killed, and that her husband is next in line; she has tried to escape but was captured and brought back to the house and is now being forced to say a prayer to procure for her husband a quicker, less excruciating death. What's wrong with cheering when she picks up a rifle and shoots her tormentor?

Behind the villain stands the author, and directors such as Hitchcock and Fritz Lang declare their complicity, their identification, with their villains. Like the author, the audience in melodrama identifies with both good and evil. But in *Funny Games* Haneke makes the bad guys so repellent—motiveless, affectedly polite, affectlessly vicious— that we can't even love to hate them, can only recoil from the complicity they solicit. And the victim family, who would normally have been the good guys, Haneke makes unappealing and incapable of fighting back, their gated self-satisfaction turning into equally gated self-pity, so that our identification with them is held in check—though it is at the ready, as the audience reaction to the wife's retaliation demonstrates. Haneke erases that moment because he would have us refuse identification with violence of any kind, and we are more tempted to identify with justifiable than with unjustifiable violence.

Why was Gus Van Sant's remake of *Psycho* so bad when it so closely followed the original? The answer lies not least with the actors: Anne Heche and Vince Vaughn are no match for Janet Leigh and Anthony Perkins. Haneke's American remake of *Funny Games*, even closer to the original movie in story and shot arrangement, is also inferior, and again the actors are a primary reason. The villains aren't quite right in their social demeanor. *Funny Games* is a story of violence not intruding from without but rather erupting from within an affluent class that is more precisely observed in the Austrian than in the American version. And Naomi Watts and Tim Roth, two talented actors, render the wife and husband more sympathetic, more endearing, than they are in the Austrian version. Why should it be detrimental that the good guys are easier for us to identify with? Because our identification with them as individuals blurs the focus on social class.

Funny Games isn't just a critique of screen violence and its audience but a disquieting picture of the violence fostered by insulated privilege. When the family first arrives at the house and the gate mechanically closes behind them, Haneke holds the image for a long, ominous moment, conveying a sense that the gate meant to protect them actually entraps them in their own defended privacy. They're all on their own, too fenced in to get out, too sheltered inside to get help from outside, the cell phone—their sole connection to the out-side world—drowned in the kitchen sink. This is the ultimate bour-geois nightmare.

At the start of *71 Fragments of a Chronology of Chance* (1994), a screen title tells us that on December 23, 1993, a nineteen-year-old student killed three people in a bank in Vienna, then shot himself. The ensuing fragments of Viennese life give us glimpses of different stories, some in the news on television, others taken without expla-nation from everyday existence: a migrant boy wandering the streets; an edgy young man now contemplating jumping out of a window, now strenuously playing ping-pong with a machine; an old man living alone, having a protracted and uneasy phone conversation with his daughter; a couple contacting the migrant boy after they see him on television; another couple eating at home in silence until the husband mutters to his wife that he loves her and she asks him if he's drunk. The incessant crosscutting from one fragment to another makes no clear connection between them—code unknown, to invoke the title of a later Haneke film that crosscuts in a similar manner—yet we expect the pieces to come together in some way to throw light on the story of the killing spree. It's the edgy young man who eventu-ally goes berserk at the bank, but couldn't it just as well have been the old man estranged from his daughter, who works at the bank, or the man, drunk or not, who loves his wife and is a bank guard? As it is usually told, the story of a mass killer treats him as a singular case and focuses on his individual psychopathology, but by decentering the story Haneke suggests that the pathology could be anyone's, that any of us could break under everyday stress. The film is a depiction not of individual but social pathology.

On the day before Christmas, the edgy young man, whose car is running on empty, stops at a gas station but is short of money and has his card refused. He is sent to the bank across the street, but its cash machine is out of order, and when he tries to jump the line at the teller's window by explaining that he's holding things up at the gas station, he's not only rebuffed by the teller but beaten up by an irate customer. This sounds like farce, which is often crueler, more violent than melodrama. Farce gives us the outlet of laughter as melodrama gives us that of tears, but Haneke lets us neither laugh nor cry, allows us no outlet, no satisfaction. His comedy has a rigorous, grim detach-ment. The three people the young man kills at the bank are the old man, the bank guard, and the woman taking care of the migrant boy, whom she has left waiting for her in her car.

Benny's Video (1992) begins with a videotape of the slaughter of a pig, which is then rewound and replayed in slow motion. This is a video Benny has made, and he watches it again and again. Benny (played by Arno Frisch, later the slim villain in *Funny Games*) is a spoiled teenage boy who looks at the world through the lens of video. Even the view out the window in his gadget-filled room he watches on a video monitor. Outside a video store he frequents he picks up a girl and takes her to his room, where he shows her the video of the pig and brings out the butcher's gun, which he has stolen. He kills her with the gun. Whether he had planned to do so all along or not isn't clear; nor is it clear, when he shows his video of the murder to his parents, whether he is confessing out of remorse or spite, whether he wants to be punished or to punish them, or whether he just needs their help to dispose of the body. Haneke doesn't probe the psychology of his characters. In any case Benny's parents decide to cover up his crime. Otherwise his life would be ruined, they decide, and so would their own good name. They think he's asleep in his room, but it turns out that the indefatigable video maker has slyly recorded their conversation. He leaves for a week in Egypt with his mother—a trip mostly spent either videotaping or watching television—while his father cleans up the mess at home. On his return, Benny denounces his parents to the police; he hands over the video he made of their conversation, on which they are heard plotting to cut up the girl's body into pieces small enough to flush down the drain without leaving a trace.

This could be black comedy, after the manner of Buñuel's *Él* (1953) or *The Criminal Life of Archibaldo de la Cruz* (1955). Archibaldo is, like Benny, a well-heeled aesthete of violence. Francisco in *Él* is a perfect Christian gentleman and a paranoid monster, a paranoid monster because a perfect Christian gentleman; his insanity, like Benny's, or like the mass killer's in *71 Fragments*, is very much a product of his society. Comedy deals in commonality. While detached enough to make us laugh, it tells us that we're all in this together. We laugh at Francisco and are taken aback by him, but we identify with him nonetheless—Buñuel does too—as a disturbingly recognizable version of ourselves: we're all in this together, this state of affairs so awful we can only laugh. In a way Haneke identifies with Benny, a protagonist he stays with throughout and whose videos he incorporates into his film, though the rough homemade video images are distinct from his own polished film images. When the boy turns his parents in to the police, surely the director endorses this twist toward justice? The killing of the girl is strictly revolting, and no less so for being kept out of view. Haneke may refrain from graphic violence, may switch to Benny's oblique video of the scene, but the girl's screams alone are upsetting in the extreme. Haneke has little apparent sense of humor, but he has an appalled sense of commonality: we're all in this together, this state of affairs awful beyond the blackest comedy.

Caché (*Hidden*, 2005) also begins with a video, though for a while we don't know it. On a Parisian back street, the camera gazes fixedly at a house situated among taller buildings and obscured by a leafy tree in the garden. The credits appear in small letters as if being typed on a computer screen. The stationary image continues unperturbed. This is a nice, quiet neighborhood. A man walks by, a woman comes out of the house, a cyclist turns into the street. Then we hear voices on the soundtrack. "Where was it?" a man asks. "In a plastic bag on the porch," a woman answers. They are Georges (Daniel Auteuil) and Anne (Juliette Binoche)—Georges and Anne, Georg and Anna, George and Ann are names Haneke likes to give his couples—and they are inside their house watching a videotape taken of the outside of the house. This is the very footage we have been watching and, to our surprise, see revealed as video when Georges and Anne fast-forward it and horizontal scan lines appear across the screen. In *Caché*, Haneke does not make it easy to distinguish between his own images and those on videotape—he used a high-definition digital camera for both—or between images of reality and images in the mind. Where the image comes from is an issue he thematizes and has us ponder. Where the videos come from—someone is recording them and leaving them at Georges and Anne's door—is the central mystery in the film.

It is night, and we see the house from the same fixed viewpoint in the street. This, we suspect, could be another video. The lights of a car being parked behind the camera shine into the dark image and cast long shadows, perhaps of the camera itself. The car belongs to Georges, who at length comes into view as he walks toward the house and enters it. As Thomas Elsaesser points out, Haneke draws attention in unusual ways to the implied space behind the camera.[100] He thereby raises the question of agency: who or what is behind what appears on the screen? Cut to a well-lit close-up of Georges facing the camera, an image coming from somewhere else: Georges hosting a literary talk show on television. After the show Anne tells him over the phone that they have received, wrapped in a childish drawing of a face spewing blood, another videotape, which we now see being rewound—more scan lines across the screen—as they watch it on his return home. It's the footage of their house at night we saw a few moments before. Cut to another night image, but one we cannot place in relation to anything we've seen so far: a frightened Arab boy looking out of a window in our direction and wiping blood from his mouth. This, we later infer, is an image from Georges's childhood. Haneke seems to be suggesting that our inner images get mixed up with the outer images we keep receiving.

"What's wrong?" Anne asks as they watch the tape. "Nothing,"

Georges says after a pause. "You want to call the police?" "Yes. . . . No. I don't know. Let me see the drawing again." At work he receives a postcard bearing another childishly drawn figure spewing blood. The tapes are inducing paranoia—someone out there is watching—but the drawings are stirring up something hidden within. The couple go to the police station but leave dissatisfied and irritated. Georges walks ahead of Anne into the street, where a passing cyclist almost hits him. He yells at the cyclist, a young black man, who yells back at him with equal vehemence. This "raises the spectre of racism," Catherine Wheatley writes in her monograph on the film, and she thinks Anne settles the matter "with a measure of temperance": both men were at fault; neither one was looking.[101] Georges and Anne are educated, enlightened, surely not personally racist. Yet the specter is not dispelled. In this overwrought altercation there is a palpable undercurrent of racial tension that excludes no one.

The next tape left at the door, again inside a childish drawing—blood now issues from a dead rooster's neck—is not of the house in Paris but shot through the windshield of a car driving to the farmhouse where Georges grew up and his old mother still lives. He goes to visit her but says nothing about the worrisome tapes, though he tells her that he dreamed about Majid, an Algerian boy who lived on the farm when Georges was a boy and whom his parents wanted to adopt. And that night, sleeping at his old home, Georges has a dream about Majid, who is the boy bleeding in the night unaccountably introduced earlier. In the dream Majid kills a rooster with an ax and, with the ax in his hands and the rooster's blood on his face, advances toward little Georges menacingly until the screen goes dark. Another tape arrives: after a car journey through city streets, the camera enters a dim hallway and stops at the door of the low-rent apartment where Majid now lives. Georges follows the tape's path to Majid's place and there encounters a mild-mannered, downtrodden man who, when Georges rudely accuses him of sending the tapes, gently denies having anything to do with it. Georges lies to his wife afterward; nobody was in, the apartment seemed unoccupied. He withholds from Anne what the bloody drawings suggest to him. He's not a man to talk about the guilty past.

The next and final tape, sent not only to the couple but to an executive at the television station, is a record of the encounter in Majid's apartment and of Majid crying after Georges left. Georges is now called on to tell Anne the truth about Majid, whose parents worked on the family farm and never came back from a demonstration in Paris during the Algerian war: "October 17, 1961. Enough said. Papon. The police massacre. They drowned about two hundred Arabs in the Seine." It annoyed little Georges that his parents were planning to adopt the orphaned Arab boy, and he tried to dissuade them by telling lies he tells Anne he doesn't remember but in fact, of course, does. These are the images that haunt him in the night: he had told his parents that Majid was coughing up blood, then misled him into killing the rooster. The upshot was that his parents sent Majid away. He finally admits these things only after he visits the apartment a second time, when—a gush of blood again—Majid cuts his own throat in front of him.

From place to place, Parisian house to farmhouse to rented apartment, the videotapes in *Caché* trace the narrative path; like the villain in a melodrama, they drive the story forward. For some the film is all about the fear of surveillance, but if that is so, then surveillance is a villain that Haneke identifies with. Most strikingly in the opening image and twice again subsequently, he identifies his camera with the anonymous video maker's by having what seems to be the one turn out to be the other. After the daytime and nighttime videos of Georges and Anne's house, any time we return to a stationary view of the house from the street we feel as if we were spying through a surveillance camera. Spying on what? The view from the street is perfectly public; it sees nothing that is not there for everyone to see. Only the bourgeois obsession with privacy makes this public gaze threatening. Only if you have something to hide inside are you frightened of the view from outside.

He was only six years old at the time, Georges pleads, what he did was normal. He may be arguing in bad faith, but he's right. That, for Haneke, is the worst thing about it—that it would be normal for a little boy to do what Georges did. And it is normal, too, for a grown man to keep his feelings of guilt to himself—normal, that is, for the bourgeoisie, a class without much sense of community. At the time what he did to Majid wasn't traumatic for little Georges, Haneke has explained. It becomes traumatic once Georges is an adult because he doesn't want to admit his guilt. He tersely mentions 1961, Papon, the Arabs drowned in the Seine, assuming that nothing more need be said about that atrocity, but about his own small atrocity he resists saying anything. And the French as a whole have resisted saying anything about the police massacre—the fascistic Maurice Papon was the Paris police chief—of peaceful Algerian demonstrators that took place on October 17, 1961. Georges's personal guilty secret is the nation's guilty secret.

The whodunit mystery of the videotapes is never solved. How can it be, when the filmmaker's camera has from the start been working in alliance with the culprit's video camera to uncover a different culprit? The film concludes with two extended stationary long shots that look like surveillance videos. The first seems to be a dream—Georges has taken sleeping pills and gone to bed early—though we don't imagine dreams taking the form of stationary long shots. We see the farmhouse, chickens in the yard; a green car from an earlier era pulls up. The view is distant, but we can make out clearly enough that the car is from the orphanage and that it has come to pick up Majid. Georges's parents stand motionless as Majid tries to escape and is seized; then they go back into the house as he is driven away, calling after them. Georges is absent from the dream. He carries the burden of guilt, but in the end it was up to his parents to rescind their benevolent gesture and shut the door on the Arab boy. Again, the racial tension spares no one.

The final shot is a static view, from across the street, of the entrance to the school attended by Georges and Anne's twelve-year-old son, Pierrot. There are a lot of people in the shot: parents waiting, students coming out of the doors, standing or sitting on the steps, and we might not notice Pierrot among them or, entering the frame and looking for him, Majid's somewhat older son. We haven't seen the two meet before, but now they talk at the foot of the steps. We can't hear what they're saying. Were they behind the videotapes? Many critics have seen *Caché* as a puzzle film. Some have proposed that the final shot belongs not at the end but at the beginning of the story and shows the two boys plotting the harassment of Pierrot's parents. Others have seen hope in the ending, with the two sons friends, overcoming the animosity between their fathers. Yet the mood is unsettling, not reassuring. This is another public view from which something private is hidden. If the previous shot looked back at the past with regret, this one looks to the future with apprehension.

The White Ribbon (2009) has a subtitle: "A German Children's Story." It takes place in a village in northern Germany shortly before World War I, so far the only Haneke film set in the past and the only one shot in black-and-white, which better evokes the period. It is narrated in voice-over by an old man, the village schoolteacher recollecting the story many years later, and although what we see departs from his perspective, showing things he could only imagine, and continually shifts from one part of the story to another, having him as narrator serves to dramatize the limits to our knowledge. We never quite find out what went on in the strange events being related.

The narrator thinks it all began when the local doctor was riding home one day and his horse tripped on a wire that had been strung between two trees, an act of malice that seriously injures him. Then the wife of a farmer is killed while working in unsafe conditions for the local baron. One of the farmer's sons decapitates the cabbages in the baron's patch with his scythe; after that, no one in his family can find work, and the farmer hangs himself. The baron's little blond son is abducted and cruelly caned, not by anyone in the farmer's family but by persons unknown, presumably the same persons who injured the doctor and who later burn down the baron's barn and abduct another child, the village midwife's son, who has Down syndrome and gets even crueler treatment. The baron, the rich exploiter nobody likes, could have been the villain here; so could the doctor, who humiliates the midwife when he breaks off his affair with her and sexually abuses his adolescent daughter; and so could the puritanical village pastor, a harsh disciplinarian who canes his children, giving them advance notice so that they suffer in the meantime, and who makes them wear white ribbons as a mark of sin, a reminder that they have strayed from purity.

In this village, even the children could be villains. Already at the time of the doctor's fall from his horse, the way several kids banded together around Klara, the oldest of the pastor's children, seemed odd to the narrator. Her brother, Martin, was also part of the children's group that increasingly aroused his suspicions—though after the doctor skipped town and the midwife borrowed a bicycle to go to the police and was never seen again, village gossip blamed the two of them for the unexplained crimes. It is understandable that Klara and Martin would resent their father and revolt against his authority, as it is understandable that the farmer's son would wreck the baron's cabbage patch. But even against reprehensible authority, as Haneke shows, protest can shade into malice, revolt can darken into viciousness. Nietzsche despises the politics of rancor, not because rancor cannot be justified but because, no matter where it comes from, rancor is bad for the soul. That's what *The White Ribbon* is about: revolt poisoned by rancor the village children harbor. At one point Klara kills a pet parakeet with her father's scissors and leaves it on his desk, evil authority breeding evil in its rebel offspring. These aren't just kids imitating their parents, beating as they are beaten, which would mean more of the same. They are subversives fighting the bad with the bad and portending worse. This is the Nazi generation, as Haneke has noted: two decades later, by which time these children would have been adults, Hitler, himself a son in revolt against the father, rose to power. Yet the film doesn't spell out the Nazi connection and should not be reduced to that. It is a broader parable, warning against rancor as a political force.

The schoolteacher narrator has a sweetheart, an angel in this village of the damned, and their story of young love is like nothing else in Haneke, except maybe for *Amour* (2012), which tells a story of old love. This time Georges and Anne (Jean-Louis Trintignant and Emmanuelle Riva) are retired music teachers in their eighties, and their love story has not only lasted through their long marriage but also has a happy ending of sorts. The film begins, however, with the police breaking down the door to their apartment in a frontal shot from inside that makes it look as if they are coming toward us, intruding on our space. There is an odd detail: a window is open in the entrance hall of the apartment, which is otherwise shut tight. Inside, the police discover Anne's rotting corpse, dressed up in bridal white and decked out with flower petals, lying on her bed. After this preamble, which is also an ending, the film retrospectively tells the couple's story.

Returning from a concert given by one of her pupils, Anne and Georges find that someone has tried to break into their apartment. Georges tells her how pretty she looks and how proud she should be of her pupil's success, but she isn't soothed and can't sleep. At breakfast the next morning she suddenly becomes numb and blankly unresponsive to her husband. He applies a wet towel to her face, forgetting to turn off the water as he hurries to get help. But then, off screen, the sound of the water stops. "You left the tap running," she chides him, remembering nothing of her lapse. She has had a stroke, apparently brought on by her anxiety the night before. The threatened privacy of the bourgeoisie is a theme as central to *Amour* as it is to *Caché* or *Funny Games*.

Once the couple has returned from their musical evening out, the last they are to enjoy, we remain inside the apartment until the end. Yet even though we are cooped up with them in their private space, we remain detached. Like Antonioni, a filmmaker he admires, Haneke puts us in the position not of an intimate but of a stranger who knows only what can be gathered from appearances, fragments of narrative that are sometimes attentively drawn out, sometimes elliptically cut short. The couple's daughter (Isabelle Huppert) comes to visit, and as she talks to her father we realize that some time has passed. Anne, after her stroke, has been in the hospital for an operation that has failed. She returns to the apartment in a wheelchair and asks Georges to promise never to take her back to the hospital. He keeps his promise. Anne is increasingly unwilling to receive visitors, to let them see her in her worsening condition, and even fends off her daughter. This story of love, face-to-face with death, is also a story of isolation.

Like the couples in *Funny Games* and *Caché*—like Haneke and most of his audience too—Georges and Anne are members of the comfortable, cultivated bourgeoisie. They find themselves entrapped in an apartment that is just what they have wanted all their lives. And we are entrapped with them, and shocked each time the film skips forward without warning to a further stage in her deterioration. An "unflinching portrait of an elderly couple and the ravages of time" is how one reviewer describes the movie,[102] in which there is no villain, nobody is at fault, and grief is a natural inevitability. Yes, but this is nature as we have domesticated it in our culture. Who among us would not want to live in such a nice apartment? And even if we have children, even if we have a loving partner, who among us does not fear the dire eventualities of lonely old age? When Anne has trouble swallowing and spits out the water Georges makes her drink, to his own surprise he gives her a hard slap. And finally, out of love and pity and despair, he kills her, suddenly suffocating her in her bed. It is another bourgeois nightmare.

I mentioned a happy ending. Earlier in the film a pigeon flies in through the window in the entrance hall, and Georges helps it fly out. After he kills Anne, it flies in again, but this time Georges gets up from his writing, shuts the window and captures the pigeon in a blanket. He writes that he let the pigeon go, but we never see him do it. He stays alone in the apartment. From his bed he hears the sound of water off screen: Anne is there, washing the dishes in the kitchen. I'm almost finished, she says, put on your shoes if you want. She puts on her coat and reminds him to take his as she opens the door of the apartment and they go out for the evening. The shot is held after they leave. No doubt this is a dream, but it suggests something like their entering the afterlife together. When asked to comment on the pigeon, Haneke observed that they often fly into Parisian apartments. But this one might represent the freedom from confinement that Georges refuses following his wife's death, then accepts in his dream. Perhaps he flew out of the window, now open again, as the police noticed when they broke in.

The Devil's Point of View

An image of waltzing couples haunts Hitchcock's *Shadow of a Doubt* (1943). It's an image of old-world elegance and romance. It belongs nowhere in the world of the film, yet it keeps impinging on it. Where does it come from? It seems to come from the past, but a past that never was, a fantasy of bygone glamour, an unattainable yet persistent dream. It's an image that floats on the screen, fluidly dissolving in and out of view, a construct of the imagination unmoored from reality. The waltzing couples in their old-fashioned fancy dress turn and turn, impeccably, incessantly, with something of the clockwork quality of figurines on a revolving table, but figurines uncannily animated and aggrandized, glamorous ghosts dancing without end in the circles of the mind.

What does this image mean? For some the meaning is all in the music, in the strains of the "Merry Widow Waltz" accompanying the dancing couples and pointing to the fact that one of the two main characters, the worldly, shady uncle visiting his family in sunny Santa Rosa, California, is the so-called Merry Widow murderer sought by the police. According to Mladen Dolar, "one has to consider the couples as the images in a rebus: if we concentrate on the images, on the ornate visual presentation, we will never find the answer, which lies only in words—here in the title of the operetta from which the waltz is taken."[103] But that answer, which we are virtually given from the start—when we see the uncle in a shabby room in Philadelphia, a pile of money beside him, two detectives after him—does not dispel the haunting image of the waltzing couples and the mesmeric mystery it evokes.

The waltzers are the film's initial image, seen under the credits, and they recur, briefly yet arrestingly, several times later on. They are photographed from a rather low angle, as if someone were looking up to them. Though set apart from the rest of the film as credit sequences usually are, they keep going after the credits are finished, and, like dancing angels hovering above a fallen world, they lingeringly dissolve into a panning shot along a river on the run-down outskirts of Philadelphia, where the story begins. These lofty romantic angels make three other intrusions into the world of the film, each at a key point in the story.

Angels dancing, a fallen world—this sounds rather metaphysical. Hitchcock has often been interpreted in such terms, as have stories of mystery and suspense more generally. But the metaphysical does not exclude the social. *Shadow of a Doubt* may be construed allegorically, but the allegory has social texture and specificity. Raymond Durgnat sees the waltzing couples as something from the Gilded Age and the run-down outskirts as representing the Depression. The Depression was barely over at the time the film was made, and the impoverished middle class would look back to the Gilded Age as a "dream of bourgeois splendor."[104]

Together with *Strangers on a Train* (1951), *Shadow of a Doubt* is Hitchcock's most sustained treatment of a theme that preoccupied him throughout his career, a theme rooted in romanticism and Gothic melodrama: the doppelgänger, the alter ego, the double. "Everything in this film depends on the principle of rhyme," Eric Rohmer and Claude Chabrol write of *Shadow of a Doubt*. "There is probably not one moment in it that does not somewhere have its double, its reflection. Or, if you prefer, let us say with François Truffaut . . . that *Shadow of a Doubt* is based on the number two."[105] The film has two main characters, two detectives in Philadelphia, two detectives in Santa Rosa, two suspects who could be the Merry Widow murderer, two church scenes, two family meals, two scenes in the garage, two attempted

killings in the family home—and, among other doublings, two opening sequences, the first in Philadelphia, the second in Santa Rosa, the
first introducing Uncle Charlie (Joseph Cotten), the second his niece,
Charlie (Teresa Wright), who was named after him and who, when
he comes to Santa Rosa, tells him that the two of them are "sort of
like twins," which we knew already, from their neatly parallel intro-
ductions in the twin beginnings.

The principle of rhyme, deployed by Hitchcock with what Durgnat
calls "his virtuoso sense of form as meaning,"[106] establishes the doubling of the two Charlies in this double beginning. The camera proceeds in each case from an overview of the location to a tilted shot of
the window of each Charlie's room to a traveling shot approaching
each Charlie as he or she lies in bed in the daytime, each awake and
dressed, supine and pensive, and then to a profile shot of each Charlie, seen in the foreground as he or she talks with someone standing at the door (the rooming-house landlady in Uncle Charlie's case,
young Charlie's father in her case). Some have stressed the opposition between the two Charlies, who may be taken as small town versus big city, innocence versus corruption, good versus evil. Form as
meaning: each of the two profile shots is the reverse of the other—we
see Uncle Charlie's left profile screen right and young Charlie's right
profile screen left—which suggests that the two are opposites. But
the two traveling shots are not reversed, each advancing from right
to left on the screen in its movement toward the recumbent figure.
And the insistent visual rhyming bespeaks twinning. If the uncle is
evil and the niece good, we may surmise that good and evil are twins,
reflections of each other.

No less striking than the differences are the similarities, the congruencies between the two Charlies. The uncle sends a telegram to his
family announcing his coming to Santa Rosa just as the niece decides
to send him a telegram asking him to come. There is something
beyond the ties of family that binds this uncle and niece together.
Let me mention two overlooked points of analogy between them.
If Uncle Charlie is indifferent to the money on his bedside table,
some of which has fallen on the floor, young Charlie too cares little
about money, as she chidingly tells her father, who works in a bank
and takes money to be the likely cause of her worries. If the uncle's
cigar has often been noted as a phallic symbol, few have noticed the
bedpost, somewhat out of focus but placed in the foreground, surely
deliberately, so that it seems to rise out of the niece's crotch like
a phallus symbolizing, in contrast to her emasculated father—who
stands in the place of the landlady in the corresponding shot of the
uncle—young Charlie's mettle, her spirit. Sometimes a cigar is just
a cigar; sometimes a bedpost is just a bedpost. But Hitchcock is a

calculating filmmaker, and *Shadow of a Doubt* is a film suffused with sexuality.

The Philadelphia beginning lets us know that Charles is a criminal. The law is after him; two policemen have come to the rooming house and await him in the street outside. He looks at them from his window and mutters to himself, "What do you know? You're bluffing. You've nothing on me." He goes outside, walks right past them, and manages to elude their pursuit. We don't know what this man has done, but we know that he has done something bad. Yet when the film moves to Santa Rosa—where it stays through to the end—for a long stretch we view Uncle Charlie not as someone we know to be a criminal but much as young Charlie views him: a man of the world who brings sophistication and excitement to the uneventful small town. Though there is a shadow of a doubt, we want Uncle Charlie to be if not exactly innocent, then at least someone who isn't so bad, who maybe did something wrong but we hope will turn out to be all right. Which is to say that for much of the film we are in denial; we disavow what we know. That's where Hitchcock puts us. *Shadow of a Doubt* is, among other things, a film about denial, disavowal of the undeniable.

When Charles looks out of his upstairs window at the two policemen down in the street, the camera assumes his point of view, as it does again when he goes down to the front door and looks at the two men standing at a corner, and again when he draws closer, and again as he strides toward them and the camera tracks with him and gives us a tracking point-of-view shot through his eyes. But as he walks past them the point of view switches. We stay with the two detectives as Charles turns the corner and recedes into the background; they start following him and we stay in place as they recede. Cut to an overhead long shot of a stretch of urban wasteland where we see the tiny figures of the man pursued and his two pursuers. This is the kind of commanding high view that strikes us as authorial, godlike. Cut to another godlike perspective on another barren stretch, but now the two pursuers have lost their quarry, and the man pursued is nowhere to be seen until, in a stunning move, "a gesture whose audacity matches Charles's own," as William Rothman notes, "the camera twists elegantly to the left, spanning this cityscape and finally settling on Charles himself, in profile . . . survey[ing] the scene with amusement and contempt as he puffs on his cigar."[107] Hitchcock takes us by surprise and switches the point of view back to Charles, whom we would have thought to be somewhere down there but find right here, up above, puffing on the cigar that symbolizes his potency and assuming the commanding high view as his own. We associate that view with the author, and the author associates it with Charles, in a poised and daring gesture of identification with this poised and daring villain. The godlike perspective is revealed to be the point of view of the devil.

The authorial high view that becomes identified with the villain occurs in other Hitchcock films. In *The Birds* (1963) there is the broad aerial vista of Bodega Bay under attack by birds, a vista that at first seems godlike, far above everything, but then starts being invaded by birds in the sky. Hitchcock likes to mix anxiety and humor, and here a stroke of wit brings on a shudder of terror as we realize that the fearsome birds rightfully command this commanding bird's-eye view. In *Psycho* (1960), as the detective walks upstairs in the Bates house, there are two successive cuts that do something remarkable. First, as William S. Pechter describes it, "Hitchcock shifts abruptly to the remote impersonality of an overhead angle; the very ultimate in aplomb; managing, thereby, not only to analyze and anatomize the action with an almost scientific, cool precision, but, almost inexplicably, succeeding in making it incalculably more terrifying as well. For, in classic nightmare fashion, the overhead perspective has the effect of showing you everything and yet revealing nothing; the essential secret is left more unknowable than ever."[108] Then, as a figure we take to be Norman Bates's mother briskly comes out of a room onto the landing, wielding a knife, and attacks the detective at the top of the stairs, Hitchcock cuts from high above to a close view, also from above, of the detective's bleeding face, with his widened eyes looking straight into the camera—a view maintained on the screen as the detective falls backward down the stairs, flailing his arms and gaping aghast at his killer, whose face we don't see but whose implacably descending perspective we share. The detective's gaze into the camera puts us in the place of the killer close above him all the way to the bottom. This isn't exactly a point-of-view shot. For that there must be a preceding—or an ensuing, and usually both a preceding and an ensuing—shot of the character whose perspective the camera is adopting. Here Hitchcock cuts directly from the overhead authorial perspective to the overhead point of view of the killer, which, as Slavoj Žižek has discussed,[109] makes a startling identification between the godlike author and the satanic, faceless killer.

Hitchcock's identification with his villains may be understood simply as an acknowledgment of the villain's agency in getting the plot going and of the author's agency behind the villain's. The villain is a surrogate for the author, the one who really gets the plot going, who unleashes the birds on Bodega Bay and sets Norman Bates on his psychotic path and Uncle Charlie on his murderous career and his fateful visit to Santa Rosa. But the godlike author who created these devils could have chosen to remain outside his creation, and Hitchcock instead makes his presence felt—his presence and his complicity with the evil that motors his plots.

No other director is present in the film in the way Hitchcock is. I don't just mean his signature cameo appearances, though these indicate how his presence is felt in the film as a whole. No other director could appear on the screen as himself, for everyone in the audience to spot and recognize, without disrupting the illusion, without intruding like a foreign body in the world of the film. Significantly, in his one attempt at realism, *The Wrong Man* (1956), Hitchcock chose not to appear except in a preamble, because his appearance in the midst of the story would have disturbed the illusion of reality. This tells us what kind of illusion Hitchcock usually creates—not the illusion of reality but the illusion we enter into knowingly, in a spirit of play, without quite suspending our disbelief. The kind of relationship he establishes with his audience—and he's nothing if not a director of audiences—asks us to recognize his authorial presence, his agency in making this movie we're watching. His characteristic rapport with us calls for our awareness that he's in control, that we are in his hands, at the mercy of his manipulation. We willingly consent, we are complicit, with the director, with the villain—at the end of *Psycho*, as Žižek observes, Norman's grinning death's-head look into the camera directly addresses us and makes us his accomplices[110]—and we are to own up to our complicity as Hitchcock owns up to his.

Rohmer and Chabrol attach much importance to Hitchcock's Catholicism and offer a theological reading of his films—though we may agree with Pechter that "there is clearly not a trace of actual religious feeling in them."[111] Žižek in his Lacanian fashion basically accepts the Catholic—or more precisely Jansenist, which isn't far from Protestant—construction of "Hitchcock's universe" as the domain of a *Dieu obscur*, a cruel and inscrutable God bestowing grace or inflicting misfortune arbitrarily, without discernible correspondence to a person's character or deeds.[112] In such a universe we are at the mercy of a ruling deity who may be good, but as Žižek says, is not easy to distinguish from the devil.[113] And, he continues, "it is ultimately Hitchcock himself who, in his relationship with the viewer, assumes the paradoxical role of a 'benevolent evil God,' pulling the strings and playing games with the public. That is to say, Hitchcock as *auteur* is a kind of diminished, 'aestheticized' mirror-image of the unfathomable and self-willed Creator."[114] Who would so usurp the role of God? Who would pull the strings and play games and take such wicked pleasure in it? Who else but the devil?

Allegorical Dimensions

The Wrong Man accords perfectly with the notion that a cruel and arbitrary deity rules over the universe: the protagonist is a good man who finds himself in bad trouble for nothing he has done. Yet the Hitchcockian edge is missing from this film, which has its admirers but failed with the public and has never won much critical favor. What's wrong with *The Wrong Man*, Žižek argues, is that here Hitchcock steps aside and lets God do his inscrutable will in God's world, the world of our reality. The characteristic Hitchcock universe is not God's world but Hitchcock's, the world of a movie over which the godlike director is seen to preside. "What *The Wrong Man* lacks," Žižek elaborates, "is the *allegorical* dimension"—by which he means that, as he sees it, a Hitchcock movie is essentially about itself, an "allegory of its own process of enunciation," its real theme being the transaction between the director and the viewer. "One is even tempted to say that Hitchcock's films ultimately contain only two subject positions, that of the director and that of the viewer."[115] One might propose, then, that such dual protagonists in Hitchcock as Uncle Charlie and young Charlie, or Norman and Marion in *Psycho*, or Bruno and Guy in *Strangers on a Train*, stand for the director and the viewer. What Žižek calls the Hitchcockian allegory[116]—which he considers modernist, self-referential, as opposed to traditional allegory, which refers meaning somewhere beyond the work—lies in the way the characters and incidents serve to stage and signify the director's relationship with his audience.

But a Hitchcock movie isn't merely about the director and the audience. Žižek's own reading of *Psycho* takes the film as a parable of American life, with the Bates Motel, built in a nondescript modern style, standing for the present and the adjacent Gothic house for the past—architectural symbolism is part of Hitchcock's Gothic inheritance—and Norman's psychotic split for the breach between present and past in a society incapable of relating them. The shift from Marion's story to Norman's, the terrible narrative rupture effected by the shower murder, represents for Žižek the point when "American alienation (financial insecurity, fear of the police, desperate pursuit of a piece of happiness—in short, the *hysteria* of everyday capitalist life) is confronted with its *psychotic* reverse: the nightmarish world of pathological crime."[117] Surely this is an allegorical reading in the traditional mode. The self-referential allegory—modernist, if you will—combines in Hitchcock with the traditional kind. An emphasis on Hitchcock as auteur tends to neglect the generic character of his movies, which are thrillers, mysteries, suspense stories, in the line of popular expressionism. At once intensifying and generalizing, dealing in emotions and at the same time in abstractions, expressionism is fundamentally allegorical.

The cinematic language of expressionism, the play of light and shadow, the studio-constructed ambiance of anxiety, was developed in Weimar Germany. *The Cabinet of Dr. Caligari* (1919) translated the World War I it closely followed into an allegorical horror tale, with the demonic doctor as a figure of insane authority and the somnambulist made murderous under his spell as a figure of death, of all the young men sent to kill and be killed in the war. Hitchcock owes an evident debt to Weimar cinema. His first completed picture as director, *The Pleasure Garden* (1925), was filmed in Germany, and while working at U.F.A. he visited F. W. Murnau on the set of the soon-to-be-famous *Der Letzte Mann* (*The Last Laugh*, 1924) and has acknowledged his influence. An interesting parallel can be drawn between *Shadow of a Doubt* and Murnau's *Nosferatu* (1922), the first movie adaptation of Bram Stoker's Gothic novel *Dracula* (1897). While Count Dracula may be construed as a figure of wicked sexuality threatening Victorian womanhood, the vampire in *Nosferatu* is not suave or seductive but a death's-headed monster whose bite, unlike Dracula's, kills his victims rather than turning them into vampires themselves. Nosferatu is, like the somnambulist in *Caligari*, a figure of impending death. In the novel Dracula's opponent is a scientist, a figure of reason, Professor Van Helsing, but in Murnau's film the professor plays a minor part, and the character who confronts the vampire is a courageous young wife. Science can postpone but not conquer death; the wife bravely embraces her death as part of her humanity, makes it her own, and thereby conquers not the actual fact but the frightening specter of death.[118] In the central pairing of a young woman and a fiend lies the most remarkable similarity between *Nosferatu* and *Shadow of a Doubt*.

Like the two Charlies, the heroic wife and the horrific vampire, even as they stand in opposition to each other, are linked together by a mysterious bond. From far away the wife somehow has the power to stop the vampire's deathly advance on her husband, and Murnau cuts back and forth between the awakening wife in her Baltic hometown and the vampire in his Transylvanian castle, her extended arms and intent gaze reaching out toward the left of the screen, his head turned to look behind him toward the right, as if he were glancing back at her, as if this were a shot/reverse shot and the two were preternaturally facing each other across the distance. "Do you believe in telepathy?" young Charlie asks at the telegraph office where she has gone to send her uncle a telegram and finds that one from him has just arrived. In *Nosferatu* there seems to be a similar telepathic connection between the young woman and the fiend. The wife waits by the sea for her husband's return from Transylvania, but, as she couldn't know except through a paranormal intuition, it's the vampire, not her husband, who's coming by sea.

For some the doubles in *Nosferatu* are the vampire and the husband. At first the film centers on the husband, whom we follow in his trip to Transylvania and his encounter with the vampire, but he collapses into utter helplessness when death stares him in the face, and the film switches to the wife, who distantly yet powerfully takes over and faces down the vampire. At that crucial moment it becomes manifest that this is between her and the vampire, and from then on the husband recedes into a relatively minor role as one of several characters whose attitudes toward death are seen to be inadequate—inauthentic, as Heidegger would put it (*Being and Time* came out in 1927, five years after *Nosferatu*, but Heidegger's ideas had earlier begun to circulate in Germany); the wife is the authentic existential hero. Every duality in *Shadow of a Doubt*, Mladen Dolar argues, involves a third.[119] An example he gives is Emma (Patricia Collinge), young Charlie's mother and Uncle Charlie's sister, who named her daughter after her brother and who loves him beyond a sister's love as her daughter loves him beyond a niece's love, the mother's desire "now delegated to the daughter marked by his name. . . . The mother is thus in the position of the third in the relationship Charlie–Charlie."[120] Also in the position of third party to that duality is the detective, one of the two in Santa Rosa, who falls in love with young Charlie and makes Uncle Charlie apprehensive about his investigation of him and jealous about his courtship of her. The husband in *Nosferatu* may be reckoned a similar third party to the wife–vampire duality.

Shadow of a Doubt recalls *Nosferatu* in other ways besides the woman–fiend duality. Just as the vampire and his attendant plague-carrying rats travel from the spooky Carpathians to the ordinary Baltic town, so the sinister Uncle Charlie comes to a small town that epitomizes placid normality. The sunlit site of the familiar is in each case struck by the frightful. *Dracula* also moves from a remote setting to a familiar one, but Murnau's treatment of space and actual locations in *Nosferatu* (a far cry from the distorted sets of *Caligari*) conveys an arresting sense of a natural world where death inheres. After the vampire arrives in town bringing the plague with him, the phantasmal monster vanishes from sight, and to all appearances we witness a natural calamity. Hitchcock, by inclination a studio director—better to keep things under control—went out on location for *Shadow of a Doubt* as he had rarely done before, and he gives us a vividly rendered Santa Rosa. Both Hitchcock's film and Murnau's depict the passage of anxiety into the heart of everyday life.

Lying in bed during the day, Uncle Charlie seems inert when we first see him, but he suddenly grows alert when the landlady pulls down the shade and his face is covered in shadow. "He awakens to darkness like a vampire," Rothman observes. "The idea that Charles is a kind of vampire runs through the film."[121] Yes, but what kind? Sexy like Dracula and death dealing like Nosferatu, he seduces and strangles rich widows. If not money, which apparently doesn't matter to him so much, what drives him to murder? Those strangulations occurred before the film begins; we see his murderousness in action when he directs it at young Charlie, and then it is mixed up with the love they harbor for each other. In connection with this film Hitchcock mentioned Oscar Wilde on killing the thing you love.[122] Are the widows Charles killed perhaps associated, in the recesses of his mind, with his older sister, Emma, who was like a mother to him when he was a child ("We were so close growing up," she tearfully reminisces), so that he enacts a version of the Oedipus complex by repeatedly killing his mother (like some suave forerunner of Norman Bates)? And the mother's desire has been transferred to the daughter, whom he repeatedly tries to kill and who ends up killing him as the wife in Nosferatu kills the vampire. I read Nosferatu as an allegory of the human confrontation with death. What about Shadow of a Doubt?

Uncle Charlie arrives in Santa Rosa with presents for the family, and he has something special for his niece Charlie. But at first she declines: "It would spoil things if you should give me anything." "You're a strange girl, Charlie. Why would it spoil things?" he asks. "Because we're not just an uncle and a niece," she replies. "I know you. . . . I have the feeling that inside you somewhere there's something nobody knows about . . . something secret and wonderful and— I'll find it out." "It's not good to find out too much, Charlie." "But we're sort of like twins, don't you see? We have to know." "Give me your hand, Charlie"—and now the shot/reverse shot alternating between them changes to a symmetrical two-shot. His present for her is a splendid emerald ring. With an air of ceremony he takes her hand and, the camera drawing closer as he draws her closer, puts his ring on her finger just as if he were giving her an engagement ring. The two Charlies, Rothman comments, "are now betrothed."[123]

But their betrothal is tainted. When her uncle prompts her to behold the fine piece of jewelry he has given her, she notices a detail that had escaped him. There is a rather faded inscription on the ring: T.S. from B.M. He wants to return the ring and have the inscription removed, but she likes it that way: "Someone else was probably happy with this ring." Her uncle doesn't look happy, though. And at this point the image of the couples dancing to the "Merry Widow Waltz," unseen since the credits, dissolves onto the screen over the subdued, somber Uncle Charlie, which intimates that this may be an image, and a sound, in his mind. But now, as if uncle and niece were again in telepathic touch, the sound of the "Merry Widow Waltz" comes into young Charlie's mind. She doesn't know what it is, but she starts humming the tune and can't get it out of her head. Intending to mislead, her uncle says it's the "Blue Danube" waltz, and he knocks over a glass to cut her short when she's about to say the right name. The emerald ring belongs in the world of romance evoked by the waltzing couples, but it holds a secret that taints the romance between uncle and niece. His gift to her will spoil everything, just as she thought it would.

What taints the romance between uncle and niece? The "something secret and wonderful" she was sure she would find out turns out to be something awful: the initials inscribed on the ring prove that her uncle is the Merry Widow murderer. But even if he were not a murderer, a romance between an uncle and a niece nonetheless carries the taint of incest. Doubles of the same gender are the more common—Jekyll and Hyde, the student of Prague and his reflection, Jane Eyre and the madwoman in the attic, the good Maria and her evil mechanical replica in Lang's *Metropolis* (1927), or, in Hitchcock's films, Guy and Bruno in *Strangers on a Train*, the dual Kim Novak character in *Vertigo* (1958). Doubling between a man and a woman usually, in the Gothic tradition, has to do with the fear of incest—the brother and sister in Poe's "The Fall of the House of Usher," Norman Bates and his mother in *Psycho*. And incest marks the twinship of the two Charlies in *Shadow of a Doubt*. Murder is a metaphor for what really taints the uncle's engagement ring on the niece's finger.

Incest is not a subject that, under the Hollywood Production Code, a movie could have dealt with directly. But murder is always okay, and Hitchcock, through the conventions of the murder mystery, deals with incest allegorically. Merely a rebus as far as the murder mystery is concerned, the waltzing couples make more sense and take on larger resonance as a symbol of the romance between uncle and niece, secret and wonderful yet frightening and forbidden. The denial in which we find ourselves in *Shadow of a Doubt*, the disavowal of what we ought to know, also makes more sense with regard to incest, which families are often unwilling to recognize even though it happens right in their midst. Such denial seems to have kept even critics aware of the curious close bond between uncle and niece from looking into it as an incestuous bond.[124]

Hitchcock's films are psychological, but more in a symbolic than in a realistic way. His characters are not rounded individuals whose minds he probes. (When he attempts such a probing, as with the psychiatrist's speech at the conclusion of *Psycho*, the result is simplistic and unconvincing.) Like Jekyll and Hyde, like Norman Bates and his mother, Charlie and Charlie are Gothic doubles, generic rather than realistic characters. But if classic Hollywood had a way with genre, it was in no small part owing to the peculiar capacity of movie actors, whose bodily traits gain distinctive presence on the screen, to invest generic characters with individuality and reality. Like John Ford or Howard Hawks or Frank Capra, Hitchcock was an excellent director of actors in that mode poised between the generic and general and the individual and particular. The performances of Janet Leigh and Anthony Perkins in *Psycho*, of Ingrid Bergman, Cary Grant, and Claude Rains in *Notorious* (1946), of Teresa Wright, Joseph Cotten, and Patricia Collinge in *Shadow of a Doubt*, attest to it.

The incestuous Charlie–Charlie duality is compounded and complicated by the analogous relationship between Charles and Emma. "For the reunion of brother and sister," Robin Wood writes, "Hitchcock gives us an image (Emmy poised left of screen, arrested in mid-movement, Charlie right, under trees and sunshine) that iconographically evokes the reunion of lovers (Charlie wants to see Emmy again as she was when she was 'the prettiest girl on the block')."[125] Near the end, at a party celebrating her brother, Emma cries in front of everybody when Charles suddenly announces his departure from town, and her tears are mirrored in her daughter's tears for her. Emma—Hitchcock's most memorable portrayal of a mother, done when his own mother, also called Emma, had just died—is her daughter's double both because she shares with her the object of desire, the incestuous love handed down from the past, and because she represents the future, the life of paltry domesticity that lies ahead for young Charlie in the small town.

The detective in love with young Charlie is another variation on the incest theme. He sees her as the nice girl next door and sees himself as the nice boy next door. He talks to her about how similar the two of them are, how they both come from average families, how average families are the best. The two are like brother and sister, but this is incest without erotic spark, incest as the reassurance of the familiar—which, here as in *Nosferatu*, is shown to be a false reassurance. The detective proposes marriage to young Charlie. There are many marriages such as he proposes, like with like, no romance, no glamour, no waltzing couples. She gives him no answer. And she can't reach him on the telephone when she needs help, nor does any telepathic communication bring him to her side. Young Charlie must face her uncle, as the wife in *Nosferatu* faces the vampire, all by herself.

Joe and Herb are a running joke in the film, young Charlie's father and his neighbor talking about murder all the time. This is of course ironic, two clowns obsessed with murder stories and unaware of the real murderer in the house. But it's also Hitchcock's joke on us in the audience, who sit there watching a murder story, and on himself, who concocted it for us. The murderer in the house isn't real. This, Hitch-cock reminds us—as he liked to remind actors he thought were tak-ing things too seriously—is only a movie. On another level, though, the movie can be taken quite seriously, and by playfully reminding us that the murder story is only a fiction while still arousing in us real emotion, Hitchcock points us to what's really in the house, which the murder story stands for.

Walking by within earshot of the two Charlies, Joe and Herb discuss the news that the police have solved the case of the Merry Widow murderer and found the culprit to be a man in the east acci-dentally killed while trying to escape. Only the two Charlies know the truth. They alone share the secret that he is the true murderer—or, taking murder to signify incest, that he is her true love. Only she now stands in the way of his official exculpation, only her knowledge, the shared secret knowledge binding them together and locking them in conflict. She doesn't expose him because she fears it would break her mother—which can be understood either way, as exposure of the murderer or of the incestuous love. If in the murder story she, rather than any of the policemen, is the detective who solves the crime, in the incest allegory she, as well as her mother, partakes of the guilt her uncle represents.

Now the uncle attempts to kill the niece who could send him to the electric chair. Regrettably, according to Wood, this "turn[s] the film's most complex and ambivalently viewed figure (Uncle Charlie) into a mere monster for the last third."[126] According to Rothman, Uncle Charlie may just mean to scare young Charlie, who has given him back his ring and wants him to leave Santa Rosa, so that she will let him stay and come to terms with him and their feelings for each other.[127] But the murderer means to murder. Only at the allegorical level, with murder construed as incest, can it be said that his trying to kill her bespeaks a threatened and threatening love. At this level it is significant that, when he first contemplates killing her and makes a strangling gesture with his hands, he looks at her out the win-dow—he commands a high view, but his phallic cigar slips from his contorted fingers—while in the garden below she meets the detective positioning himself as a rival for her affections. The detective, now off duty, free of worry about a case he thinks closed, proposes to her in the garage, which is where one of her uncle's attempts on her life takes place.

Uncle Charlie is staying upstairs in young Charlie's room, an architectural symbol of their twinship. That he stay there was her idea, her father tells him on his arrival at the house, and supersti-tiously warns him not to put his hat on the bed; but after Joe leaves the room Charles takes a flower from a vase to adorn his lapel, looks out the window—as if to satisfy himself that the high view is his— and, the camera panning in complicity with his gesture, defiantly tosses his hat onto his niece's bed. The liberties he takes in her room smack of sexual liberties with her. Now she wants him out of there, but she no longer has the evidence of his guilt, the incriminating ring she returned to him, and in order to force him out, she must find that ring symbolic of their betrothal somewhere in that room symbolic of their intimacy.

When she comes downstairs wearing the ring, her uncle is raising his glass for a toast. This is the party in his honor, following a lecture he gave in town. She didn't go to the lecture, having just survived the car fumes in the garage by which she knows he tried to kill her; she stayed home and retrieved the ring, her weapon against him, which she brandishes at his party. We see her from his point of view as she makes her entrance down the stairs, her eyes on him, so that she looks right at the camera, which mimics his attention and moves in close to the accusatory ring he notices on her finger—whereupon he relinquishes the toast he was about to propose and instead raises his glass for "a farewell toast. . . . Tomorrow I must leave Santa Rosa." But that's only the murder story. The incest allegory lends quite another dimension to the scene. She comes down wearing his ring, and he raises his glass when she makes her entrance, just as if this were their engagement party.

"The stage is set," as Rothman interprets the scene, "for Charles to toast Charlie as his intended bride," and she in kind, "radiant, a vision of beauty," descends into the party "dressed as a promised bride" who seems to be "offering herself to him" in a way that "inscribes a pledge as well as an ultimatum. . . . She wears Charles's ring and vows her faithfulness to him, on the condition that he depart."[128] His farewell toast may then be construed as his acceptance of her terms, both erotic and chaste, and dealing in one stroke with both his amorous and his murderous aspect: you can have me, so long as you go away. But the murderer would go away simply on account of the evidence she has against him—no need to offer herself to him and vow faithfulness—and in any case he doesn't accept her terms. She knows too much about him. As he departs he makes one last attempt to kill her. And as for the amorous uncle, Rothman comes short of recognizing either that this is incest—he never uses the word—or that this is allegory, with the murder story and the incest theme as literal and figurative levels of meaning. Young Charlie is complicit with Uncle Charlie both in the murder story (Durgnat, who doesn't take the incest very seriously, says that "the young, idealistic American girl is, by her collusion, already, in moral equivalent, keeper of a gigolo and accomplice after the fact"[129]) and in the incest allegory, but she's complicit on two different levels. And the ring as evidence of murder and as symbol of the amorous pairing between uncle and niece works on two different levels. The niece may be pushing away both the murderous and the amorous uncle, but the ring she flaunts on her finger as he raises his glass means one thing to the murderer and another to the lover.

Seeing their uncle off, young Charlie and her two younger siblings accompany him aboard the train he's taking out of town, and he keeps her with him after her siblings have left and the train has started going. The murderer means to murder. "For the first time," as Rothman notes, "he allows himself to be viewed without his mask; he appears as a monstrous figure"—shades of Nosferatu—"condemned to haunt the earth and to represent death."[130] As the train gains speed, he holds her by an opened door, his strangling hand over her mouth, the two locked together in what at moments resembles a "conventional Hollywood image of a lovers' clinch,"[131] the camera tilting down to their intertwined legs, which move around as if doing the steps of a dance, as if the uncle and niece were waltzing together at death's edge.[132] The waltzing couples dissolve onto the screen for their final appearance when Uncle Charlie falls to his death. Whether he slipped or she pushed him is hard to tell.

He never intended to kill her, Rothman suggests, but to have her kill him.[133] Already at the start, when he lies recumbent and listless in his seedy room, Uncle Charlie is a man visibly tired of life. Young Charlie also lies recumbent when we first see her, but she's dissatisfied rather than listless. She wants something better from life; she's reaching out for something wonderful that she thinks he represents. She's animated by her dreams, while his seem spent. If the waltzing couples are an image the uncle and niece share in their minds, they share it from opposite perspectives. He has been through that dream of glamour and romance and come out the other end, having decided that, as he tells her after she finds out his secret, "The world's a hell." Stories of the double often end in suicide. It's fitting that the jaded uncle, despairing of life, would have his double, the spirited niece who bears his name, put an end to it all for him.

The Garden of Eden

Making the amorous uncle into a murderous monster aggrandizes the fear of incest into a confrontation with evil. This is melodrama. But even if the Hollywood censorship and his own talent had allowed it, I wouldn't have wanted Hitchcock to paint a more realistic picture of a family corroded by incest. "All the irony of the situation stemmed from her deep love for her uncle," the director notes. "The girl will be in love with her Uncle Charlie for the rest of her life."[134] If depicted in a more realistic way, such incestuous love would come across as unpalatable, unclean. Melodrama lets us cheer for young Charlie, lets her be a heroine, lets the movie develop the romance of a girl who seeks more from life than the confinements and conventionalities of a small town. A disreputable but popular genre— disreputable because popular, snobbishly regarded as inferior even though it has produced its share of the superior—melodrama doesn't exclude realism but gives freer rein to romance and allegory.

Along with the incest allegory, *Shadow of a Doubt* enacts an allegory of good and evil, of the knowledge of good and evil acquired from forbidden fruit. The two, good and evil, niece and uncle, are, as she tells him, "like twins" who "have to know." She learns his terrible secret in that repository of knowledge, the public library in town. Suspecting he was trying to hide something when, in a game he played with her younger sister, he tore and folded a page of the daily newspaper, she hurries to the library to track down that page. She gets there a little after closing time, 9 PM, but the librarian lets her in and turns on a light for her. On the page she finds a story about the Merry Widow murderer, and the story mentions the names of one of the strangled widows and her late husband. The initials match the T.S. and B.M. inscribed on the emerald ring.

From a close-up of the ring, which young Charlie takes off and inspects, the camera now rises to an extreme high angle in a crane shot as striking, an authorial move as assertive, as the panning shot near the start that surprisingly identified the godlike perspective with the devil. Again godlike, this craning high angle responds to the girl's coming to know the truth about her uncle, but it detaches itself from the character down below: the commanding view belongs to the author alone, not to the young sleuth distraught at her discovery and casting a long shadow amid the library's shadows, as if the ring incriminating her uncle had brought out her own dark side. The godlike perspective is commonly called omniscient, all-knowing, but at this moment of knowledge, the shadows evoke a sense of mystery. The waltzing couples now appear, superimposed first over young Charlie, dwarfed in the view from far above as she gloomily leaves the library, and then over Uncle Charlie at the house, reading a newspaper as she just did—which again insinuates that the recurrent dancers may be a mental image telepathically shared between uncle and niece. Although the mystery of the Merry Widow waltzers would now seem solved, nevertheless it lingers and even deepens. In the panning shot that revealed the high-placed Uncle Charlie coolly looking down at his baffled pursuers, there was as well, combined with the posture of knowledge, a sense of mystery about this man, his misdeeds and his motives. Mystery may come from lack of knowledge, but with greater knowledge comes deeper mystery.

Shadow of a Doubt can be read as a parable of the Garden of Eden, with Uncle Charlie as the devil, Santa Rosa as paradise—though paradise from the devil's point of view looks rather comical and confining—and the godlike high angle as the tree of knowledge. Biting into the fruit of that tree doesn't mean knowledge but merely the wish, the will to know, the presumption to probe into the unknown, the reaching for rather than the gaining of knowledge—hence the high angle fraught with mystery, not an all-knowing perspective but a recognition that you never know. "You think you know something, don't you? You think you're the clever little girl who knows something," the uncle tells the niece when she gives him back his ring. "Do you know the world is a foul sty? Do you know if you ripped the fronts of houses, you'd find swine?" Even as he tries to keep her from knowing his secret, he represents for her the temptation of knowledge, knowledge of the wide and risky world, the knowledge of good and evil associated with the devil. To rise to the high angle of knowledge is to fall from grace; Uncle Charlie is the fallen angel who assumes a godlike posture. Hitchcock's knowing camera cannot identify itself with God but only with the devil.

Home after her visit to the library, young Charlie hears her mother humming the "Merry Widow Waltz" and asks her to stop—she wants to get that tune out of her head. Though nothing paranormal got it into Emma's head, the hummed waltz signifies the mother's implication in the incestuous family romance. But Emma doesn't know, and her innocence in paradise sets her apart from her daughter, the clever girl who knows something. Except for the two Charlies, all the inhabitants of Santa Rosa are portrayed more or less humorously, which is how Uncle Charlie sees them. ("The whole world is a joke to me," he says when his malicious humor embarrasses his brother-in-law at the bank.) But the film can't be said to adopt Uncle Charlie's point of view; rather than the central consciousness, he's more like the central mystery. The point of view is closer to young Charlie's as we grow suspicious with her, find out with her about her uncle, fear him with her; and she, though never malicious, may well be amused by people in the small town she would transcend. She's enough like her uncle to look askance at paradise.

Yet the high angle of knowledge, associated with Uncle Charlie from the beginning and often given to him, is withheld from young Charlie. When the uncle and niece hear about the police's conclusion that the Merry Widow murderer has been killed in the east, the camera follows the gleeful Uncle Charlie ("I think I'm going to get ready for dinner. I'm hungry. I can eat a good dinner today") briskly up the stairs, and when he pauses at the top and turns around to look at the niece who knows better, we get a high-angle point-of-view shot through his eyes as the two Charlies stare at each other and she looks right at the camera. It is a shared moment of knowledge—she knows, he knows that she knows, she knows that he knows she knows—but the high angle of knowledge belongs to the uncle. Standing at the door, the sun behind her, young Charlie casts a long shadow here as at the library, a shadow that doubles her, suggesting that there are two sides to her nature, sunny and dark, good and evil, the side that opposes her uncle and the side complicit with him, the side that stands in his way and the side vulnerable to him. But it is from the uncle's high angle that we see the niece's two sides.

When Uncle Charlie and the rest of the family have gone off to his lecture, young Charlie, alone in the house, tries unsuccessfully to reach the detective, and the camera twice dissolves to successively higher angles and then pans to the view from the top of the stairs, the uncle's high angle in his absence. This feels as if the author were directing young Charlie to give up on the detective and assume the high angle vacated by her uncle. Seen from that angle of knowledge, the author's knowledge but not yet hers, she goes upstairs to look for the ring in her uncle's—and her—room. Cut to the view from the top of the stairs later in the evening, an empty view until the door opens and the family and the guests coming to the party arrive from the lecture. Having found the ring that gives her the upper hand, young Charlie is ready to descend the stairs and confront her uncle. Now, we would expect, is her moment to assume the high angle. On her way downstairs she must of course start there, at the top, but Hitchcock doesn't give us her view from that angle. The author declines to put her in the symbolic position of knowledge, as if she still hadn't earned it.

She attains the high angle of knowledge only at the end, and then it is Uncle Charlie the devil, here completing his surrogacy for the author identified with him, who puts her in that position as he's about to throw her off the train. Only then do we get a high-angle point-of-view shot from her perspective, and what she sees—and we through her horrified eyes—is a quickening, dizzying blur of railroad tracks, the least omniscient of high angles. The high angle in Hitchcock may be knowing but is always unsettling, an angle we assume at our risk. Here, as in *Vertigo*, or when the detective in *Psycho* falls down the stairs facing his killer, it is vertiginous. It is a view of the abyss, comparable to the view, from the wife's window in *Nosferatu*, of a procession of coffins down in the street coming out of the distance and steadily, irremediably advancing toward the viewer. But if the wife in *Nosferatu* confronts the death we all face, young Charlie faces murder at the hands of the uncle she loves. Unlike Dracula, Nosferatu is not evil—he personifies death as a natural fact we human beings fear because we are aware of our own inevitable end—but Uncle Charlie personifies evil, whether it stems from murder, incest, or both. Young Charlie's view from the accelerating train finally brings her to the knowledge of evil, the undiminished apprehension of the world as a hell.

Yet the niece survives the encounter with the uncle who drops his mask and reveals himself as a monster. Her confrontation is not as final as the wife's with Nosferatu. Knowledge in the story of the Garden of Eden is knowledge of good *and* evil—no knowledge of evil without knowledge of good. Young Charlie has her dark side, whether in the murder story (her willingness to cover up for a murderer and let him get away, free to murder again, and her own capacity to kill, though she can't be blamed for killing him in self-defense) or in the incest allegory (her dark desire for her uncle, though she recoils from his predatory amorousness when she becomes aware of what he's up to). Still, whatever her shadows, she is good, and better for her knowledge. Others besides Hitchcock have taken the devil's side in his rebellion against a God who would forbid us to know. Young Charlie is not the devil, but she is his double, and a rebel. "Uncle Charlie loved his niece," Hitchcock told Truffaut, "but not as much as she loved him."[135] "If equal affection cannot be," to quote from W. H. Auden's poem about looking up at the stars, "Let the more loving one be me."[136] Young Charlie is the more loving one, and in the end better not only for her knowledge but also for her love of her uncle, tainted yet true. Hitchcock rightly undercuts the conventional resolution in which she would have found love with the nice average detective. She's too good—good in significant part because she knows evil—for him.

An Eve without an Adam and restless in paradise, young Charlie has dreams of glamour and romance beyond the small town, and she learns—this is her uncle's teaching, the devil's knowledge—that with the glamour and romance comes evil. She finds out the world's a hell, but she also knows that's not all it is. Maybe she'll always love her Uncle Charlie; certainly she'll never forget him. But the presence of evil in the world shouldn't deter her from pursuing life's possibilities, though along that pursuit she should keep aware of that presence. This is her uncle's gift to her. Like *Nosferatu*, *Shadow of a Doubt* is the story of a coming to fearsome yet brave consciousness of what it means to be human in the world.

Melodrama and Comedy

At an academic conference on film melodrama,[137] many loudly objected to a clip from what seemed to them like a horror movie. Melodrama, they insisted, is the genre of pathos, of tears, not fear. But fear of the villain, including the monster in a horror movie, is for Bentley the strongest emotion in melodrama. Pathos is one of three modes of persuasion, three main ways for a speaker to appeal to an audience, set forth in Aristotle's *Rhetoric*. Logos persuades by reason, argument; ethos persuades by character, the speaker's personal credibility; and pathos persuades by arousing the audience's emotions. That, however, means any emotions rhetorically serviceable, love and hate, anger and desire, shame and envy, pity and fear. Maybe you can define melodrama by the effect of pathos, but you can't confine pathos to the effect of tears. The amplified emotions of melodrama range more widely. *Shadow of a Doubt* is both a crime melodrama and a family melodrama, a love-and-death melodrama like *Vertigo* and a Gothic melodrama bordering on a horror movie like *Psycho*. It mixes genres, you could say, or you could say that it shows how various a genre melodrama is. In an article from 1936 Hitchcock maintains that the Victorian theater he grew up with put on either melodramas or comedies, with the only difference between the serious dramas favored by sophisticates and the popular melodramas they disdained was the price of a seat, and he proudly declared himself a maker of melodramas.[138]

This chapter began by considering how melodrama stands between tragedy and comedy. Hitchcock's melodramas—*The 39 Steps*, *The Lady Vanishes*, *Rear Window*, *North by Northwest*, *Psycho*—typically have an admixture of comedy. People who laugh at old melodramas they feel superior to may not realize that the genre often contains an element of comedy put there on purpose. Villainy can have something funny about it even as we fear it, something intentionally lighthearted. Comparing the villainy in two of Shakespeare's plays, Bentley regards Richard III as a villain of melodrama and Iago in *Othello* as a villain of tragedy: "Richard III's wickedness is always, in some degree, 'for fun'; Iago's is 'for real.'"[139] In some degree, the critic says; the line between melodramatic "for fun" and tragic "for real" cannot be drawn so clearly. Hitchcock's movies are by and large for fun, but in some unsettling degree they are for real.

At the melodrama conference some suggested that there is a deep structure to the genre, a common underlying pattern presumably discernible beneath the variety of surface. What this deep structure might be remained nebulous, however. Perhaps there is an archetypal plot for tragedy or for comedy, but not, I think, for melodrama. The plot about the virtuous heroine and the wicked villain can be seen to derive from New Comedy. Even *Stella Dallas* can be seen as a version of New Comedy, with Stella's daughter and the rich boyfriend she finally marries as the young lovers and Stella as the blocking figure who removes herself to bring on the happy ending. The ending is not exactly happy, of course, but it is still the marriage ending of comedy. In a review of Woody Allen's *Blue Jasmine* (2013), Michael Wood faults the film for mixing "the structure and narrative causality of comedy and the doomed tempo of melodrama: plot by Molière, let's say, mood by some awkward disciple of Dostoevsky."[140] But *Blue Jasmine* is as awkward in its plot as in its mood. The problem is not that comedy and melodrama don't mix but that the film lacks the skill and conviction to mix them. Comedy and melodrama often manage narrative structure and causality in similar ways, and moreover they share a tendency to disregard causality—which is a way of managing it—and rely on coincidence. Melodrama is, according to Dictionary.com, "a dramatic form that does not observe the laws of cause and effect," and that applies just as well to the twists and flukes of comedy.

The plot of Pedro Almodóvar's *Women on the Verge of a Nervous Breakdown* (1988) relies so much on coincidence that it virtually makes it its structuring principle. Pepa (Carmen Maura) is being abandoned by her lover, Iván—they are both actors, and each is seen dubbing into Spanish the "Lie to me" scene from *Johnny Guitar*—and is desperately trying to reach him before he leaves town with another woman. It's by sheer coincidence that his stuttering son, Carlos (Antonio Banderas), whom Pepa knew nothing about until that very day and who happens to be looking for a place to rent, turns up in her Madrid penthouse together with his prim girlfriend. It's by sheer coincidence that the feminist lawyer Pepa consults on behalf of Candela, a friend who has unwittingly become involved with Shiite terrorists, turns out to be the woman Iván is leaving town with. It's by sheer coincidence that the plane the terrorists intend to hijack that evening is the one Iván and the lawyer are taking to Stockholm.

The abandoned and acutely distressed Pepa, who could well have been a subject of melodrama, is here a subject of farce. *Women on the Verge*, though some have taken it as an unstable mixture of genres, brilliantly and consistently plays as farce. Almodóvar likes to remind us that we are watching a movie. In his far-fetched plots, his overt camera maneuvers, his penchant for what academics call intertextuality—besides the explicit reference to *Johnny Guitar*, here he makes allusions to several Hitchcock movies—he may be reckoned a postmodern parodist. But a work such as *Women on the Verge* can also be placed in the long comedic tradition of manifest artifice. At the airport Pepa saves Iván's life, and the man she has been seeking all day now mellifluously approaches her; but by this point she has lost interest in reconciliation, and she gladly lets him go with the lawyer. The strenuous farce she has lived through seems to have set her free, to have finally released her from her anxious fixation on the man who abandoned her. Like the audience, the protagonist herself has undergone catharsis in the manner of comedy.

The Flower of My Secret (1995) is another Almodóvar movie with an abandoned woman as protagonist. Leo Macías (Marisa Paredes) is a successful writer of *novelas rosas*, romance novels, "rose-colored" women's fiction she concocts under the pen name of Amanda Gris (an author she herself utterly disparages in a newspaper article she writes under a different pseudonym). Unhappy with her husband, an army officer she ardently loves but seldom sees—and who she comes to learn has been having an affair with her best friend—Leo has lately been finding it hard to manage the rose color she is under contract to produce and instead gives her publisher a novel inadmissibly dark. Although Leo is another woman on the verge of a nervous breakdown, *The Flower of My Secret* is no strenuous farce. It is deftly poised between comedy and two kinds of melodrama, two colors of sentimental fiction, pink and black. We may not cry for Leo, but neither do we laugh at her; we only smile at the recognition that her distress, which she takes to be so black that she almost kills herself, is merely a darkish shade of pink. (Let it be noted that Gris is Spanish for gray.) And unlike Amanda Gris's latest novel, Almodóvar's film manages a happy ending—not swooningly romantic but satisfyingly affectionate, maybe not the ending for a *novela rosa* but befitting a wise and sensible comedy.

Leo is portrayed with a sympathy and subtlety, an emotional depth, never before seen in Almodóvar, who was a little embarrassed to admit to an interviewer that he had gained maturity.[141] His earlier movies were "pulpy, campy and gleefully overwrought," A. O. Scott notes in the *New York Times*, but *The Flower of My Secret* "marked . . . a new direction, as if Mr. Almodóvar, starting from a parodic, camp sensibility, had found his way back to the full, theatrical emotionalism that camp feeds upon and travesties."[142] Camp is not necessarily travesty, however, and the more mature Almodóvar still refrains from full emotionalism, still retains a cool irony of self-conscious artifice and a distinct even if more nuanced quality of camp. Leo's change from romantic pink to jarring black—reality is like that, she contends, whereupon her irate publisher cries out that reality should be banned—is taken by Daniel Mendelsohn to mirror Almodóvar's

own change.[143] But for Mendelsohn this change means the eschew-
ing of melodrama, a genre he deems so far removed from reality in
its excess and exaggeration that Almodóvar, having mocked it in the
brazen campy manner of his younger days, can only leave it behind
in his mature work: if you don't like it, it's melodrama, and if you do
like it, it can't be melodrama. Melodrama it is all the same, more or
less excessive, more or less emotional, always in the vicinity of comedy, never without connection to reality.

"Firmly grounded in reality": so Mendelsohn describes the film
he's not alone in considering Almodóvar's best, *All About My Mother*
(1999). It is the story of a single mother, Manuela (Cecilia Roth), a
nurse at a Madrid hospital who oversees the donation of organs for
transplantation to the ailing, and who (after a turn of events lifted
from Cassavetes's *Opening Night*) herself donates her teenage son's
heart. On his birthday she takes him to a performance of *A Streetcar
Named Desire*, and the boy, seeking the autograph of the lead actress,
Huma Rojo (Marisa Paredes), runs in the rainy night toward the car
driving her away and is hit by another car and killed. Manuela now
goes to Barcelona in quest of her son's father, whom the boy never
knew and she has long lost touch with. She looks for the missing
father among prostitutes and there finds an old friend, Agrado (Anto-
nia San Juan). Like the father, now called Lola, Agrado (a name that
translates as agreeableness, pleasingness) is a transsexual who had
breasts implanted and still has a penis, which she finds good for ply-
ing her trade. Manuela nurses the battered Agrado. Throughout the
movie, you could say, she transplants her mothering heart to one
recipient after another. She and Agrado call on a young nun engaged
in charitable work with prostitutes, Rosa (Penélope Cruz), who, it
transpires, was impregnated by Lola and infected with AIDS. Seeing
that Rosa is estranged from her mother, Manuela mothers her. She
also serves as personal assistant, nurse, and mother of sorts to the
brittle Huma Rojo, who turns up in Barcelona with the *Streetcar* production and her drug-addicted actress girlfriend. Huma weeps when
she hears about the boy killed in headlong pursuit of her and gives
him posthumously the autograph he never got in life. Rosa and Lola
both die, but their baby, though born with their disease, is miraculously cured, a boy Manuela happily adopts as her son, as if her own
lost son had come back to life. Is this, we may ask, realism? Isn't it
the ultimate maternal melodrama?

It's a crazy story, so much so that if you recount it, Almodóvar
notes in an interview, it sounds like a screwball comedy, but he did
not have it played that way. He sought "a very sober tone" in his
work with the actors, "something absolutely true and serious."[144] For

all the comedic or melodramatic coincidences and improbabilities in the plot, the film does gain grounding in reality through the conviction carried by the performances. Death and sadness figure here as never in screwball comedy, yet a comedic spirit makes itself felt. At one point Agrado—who, as the director said, turns the movie into a comedy whenever she appears, and who embodies its spirit perhaps more than any other character—reads aloud Blanche's line from *Streetcar* about cruelty being an unforgivable thing. Nobody is cruel in *All About My Mother*, and everybody is forgiven. Tragedy deals with the unforgivable, comedy with things we can forgive.

At the start of *Volver* (2006) women busily clean and embellish their family tombstones at a provincial cemetery. The breeze agitates the graveside flowers—the reputedly discomposing wind that blows in La Mancha, land of Don Quixote and his windmills and birthplace of Pedro Almodóvar—but the women go about their work with a diligence and efficiency accustomed to the wind and unperturbed by the adjacency to death. Like *All About My Mother*, this film portrays what Almodóvar has called women's natural solidarity. From *The Flower of My Secret* it takes the plot of Leo's rejected dark novel, in which a mother comes home from her work as a cleaning woman, finds that her husband has been killed by her daughter, whom he tried to rape, and hides his body in a restaurant freezer next door. In *Volver* this plot is doubled by another, which involves the mother, Raimunda (Penélope Cruz), and *her* mother, Irene (Carmen Maura)—two mothers and two daughters, and in both cases a sexually abusive father who ends up killed.

Raimunda the cleaning woman is among the women cleaning tombs; Almodóvar pays his respects to the cleaning done by women. It's her mother and father's grave that Raimunda cleans; they died together in a fire, or so she thinks. She now lives in Madrid, and with her daughter and sister she is visiting her hometown in La Mancha for the day. After the cemetery she and her companions go see her mother's sister, a senile old aunt living alone and managing mysteriously well by herself; people in this small town believe her dead sister has come back as a house ghost (*volver* means "come back"), but the aunt, whose mind is in the past, maintains that Irene is alive and living with her, and she turns out to be right.

Back in Madrid Raimunda learns that her husband, who sits drinking beer and watching a soccer game on television, has been fired from his job, and after work the next day she finds her daughter waiting for her at the bus stop, rain-soaked and hardly able to speak. Her husband lies dead on the kitchen floor. The girl explains that he drunkenly assaulted her and she tried to fend him off with the knife that killed him. The cleaning woman proceeds to clean up the mess. It reminded me of Norman Bates cleaning up the bloody mess in the bathroom after the shower murder in *Psycho*; like Hitchcock, Almodóvar observes with cool detachment the patterns, the geometry of cleaning, but his detachment, unlike Hitchcock's, mirrors the character's, the way Raimunda cleans up this mess as adeptly as she would any other. White, textured paper towels she lays out on the floor flatly fill the screen—Almodóvar punctuates his films with such frontal, screen-flattening geometric configurations—and grow gradually redder and redder, darker and darker as they sop up the dead man's blood. The director calls attention to his artifice, his way with the tools of his trade, and at the same time to the cleaning woman's proficiency, her way with the tools of her trade.

Before Raimunda can dispose of her husband's body, the doorbell rings. It's a neighbor who has come to give her the keys to his restaurant, which he wants to sell, so that she will show it to prospective buyers while he's out of town. Then the phone rings, as if signaling that we mustn't forget the other part of the plot. It's her sister, Sole, calling her with the news that their old aunt has died. Sole assumes they would go together to La Mancha for the funeral, but Raimunda, much as she loved her aunt, says she can't possibly go. Now, late at night, with nobody else around, she and her daughter carry the dead body to the restaurant next door she has keys to. Sole drives by herself to the La Mancha town, where the first thing she encounters is the ghost of her mother; and when she returns to Madrid she hears a banging in the trunk of her car and her mother's voice asking to be let out. This ghost story has a shading of comedy, however; Irene stuck in the trunk of her daughter's car doesn't so much bring on a shudder as a smile. A knock on the restaurant door surprises Raimunda, who is taking a look at the body she hid in the freezer the night before, but when she finds that a man wants to arrange lunch for a film crew shooting in the vicinity, she readily agrees to provide food for thirty at a place that isn't hers. She enlists the help of women friends and cooks and runs a restaurant with her usual competence and self-possession; a true working-class heroine, Penélope Cruz's Raimunda commands our sympathy as well as our admiration. We might think—and for a little while Almodóvar does nothing to keep us from thinking—that she will serve her dead husband to the film crew for lunch, but Raimunda and the movie portraying her are both too humane, too generous in spirit for that. *Volver* is no revenge tragedy but something more like a comedy of reconciliation.

The principal reconciliation occurs between Irene and Raimunda, who has long harbored an unspoken enmity toward her mother and felt closer to her aunt, after whom she named her daughter, Paula. Irene comes to Madrid with Sole, her other daughter, and stays with her and helps her with the beauty parlor she runs at home. Soon enough Paula finds out that her aunt's helper is her grandmother, but the secret is kept from Raimunda, though she thinks she recognizes the smell of her mother's farts in the bathroom and the four women laugh together, including Irene, who remains hidden under the bed through this overt moment of comedy. When at length Raimunda discovers her mother's presence, Irene tells her she has come back to ask her forgiveness, and Raimunda runs away with Paula as if scared of ghosts. Out in the street she has second thoughts, and her daughter urges her to turn right back and talk to her mother without delay. This is shrewd plotting on Almodóvar's part; almost anyone else would have had Raimunda either stay and talk or run away and delay talking, but having her run away and turn right back succinctly expresses both her fear and her spunk. It plays up her double doubling with her mother on one hand—she comes back to her mother just as her mother has come back to her—and on the other hand with her daughter, who accompanies her flight and encourages her return and who in significant measure has herself repeated her mother's story.

"You're not a ghost, are you? You're not dead?" From the start of her talk with her mother, whom everyone else seems to take as a ghost, practical, hardheaded Raimunda wants to set things straight. Likewise *Volver* brings the ostensible ghost story down to earth in the debunking manner of comedy. Yet the debunked ghost story becomes if anything more far-fetched and melodramatic when stripped of otherworldly trappings. Irene wasn't killed in a fire together with her husband, as everyone thought; she killed the continually unfaithful husband she found in bed with another woman by setting the place on fire while the lovers slept, as she tells Raimunda when the two finally get to talk. It seems fitting that mother and daughter have their talk not inside but outside, during an evening stroll around the Madrid neighborhood, for their family secrets are not a merely private but a broader social matter. The usual ways of rendering a conversation on the screen are the two-shot and the shot/reverse shot, and here Almodóvar uses traveling two-shots for the most part, saving the shot/reverse shot, and giving it special emphasis with nearly frontal close-ups of each woman, for the climactic moment when Irene confesses that she had not known until her sister apprised her that her husband sexually abused and impregnated Raimunda. "I hated you for not noticing," the daughter admits with tears in her eyes, and she was quite right to feel that way, the mother admits in turn. It was on the day Irene learned about her daughter's abuse that she took fiery revenge, and rather than being arrested for her crime, she was mistaken for a ghost when she came back to look after her senile sister. But the revenge tragedy lies in the past; forgiveness and reconciliation are now the chief concern. Almodóvar at his best can blend melodrama and comedy indissolubly.

CODA

OF IDENTIFICATION

Notions and Kinds of Identification

Why are we afraid at a horror movie when we know we're in no danger? We aren't actually afraid, says the philosopher Kendall Walton, because by definition fear is something we feel only when we are in danger or think we are. Walton offers this as a typical audience response:

> Charles is watching a horror movie about a terrible green slime. He cringes in his seat as the slime oozes slowly but relentlessly over the earth, destroying everything in its path. Soon a greasy head emerges from the undulating mass, and two beady eyes fix on the camera. The slime, picking up speed, oozes on a new course straight toward the viewers. Charles emits a shriek and clutches desperately at his chair. Afterwards, still shaken, he confesses that he was "terrified" of the slime.[1]

But horror movie viewers, as Walton makes clear, don't believe or even half believe they face any danger; Charles is well aware that the terrifying slime is a fiction. So it can't be real fear he feels, the argument goes, but what Walton calls make-believe fear. Walton misrepresents, however, the way horror movies work on the audience. No screen monster would threaten the viewer directly like that green slime headed straight toward Charles. A horror movie wouldn't be very frightening if it simply depicted a monster coming in our direction. It has to have a story and characters imperiled within the story, so that the monster threatening them makes us afraid on their account. It is our identification with them that brings on our fear.

Two different questions arise. One is the question of fiction and our emotional response to it. To answer this question Walton proposes his theory of mimesis as make-believe, fiction as a game that uses props—by which he means not just stage props but performing actors, painted likenesses, written descriptions, anything serving to embody the imagination—in the same way that children use snowmen or toy trucks or rag dolls in games of make-believe. Another question is that of our capacity to feel for or with others, which is certainly not confined to fiction. Actual images of a tsunami striking a coastal village can elicit our fear as much as any monster, our fear not for ourselves but for others in whose place we put ourselves.

We call that identification. It is a word that academic film theory of the 1970s and 1980s used in a specialized way, essentially to mean that the viewer is locked in a subject position, "sutured" into the film. Those who repudiate the theory would often repudiate the word too. I use it in this book much as people ordinarily use it. Let me point out that games of make-believe are games of identification: children identify toy trucks with real trucks and rag dolls with babies, and their emotional investment in the game starts there. Likewise, we identify actors with the characters they play, and our emotional identification with stage or screen characters rests on their identification with the actors who play them. We wouldn't identify ourselves with Sam Spade if we didn't identify Humphrey Bogart with Sam Spade in the first place. Am I using the word in different senses? Maybe, but they are surely interrelated senses.

Empathy and sympathy are often distinguished, even opposed. Empathy is feeling what someone else feels, identity of feeling, identification. Sympathy responds to others but comes short of such identity. When we speak of empathy, however, we mean only an *approximate* identity of feeling. If we insisted on an exact identity we would find precious few cases of it. Our sympathy for another person involves our feeling, to some degree, in some manner, what we imagine the other person is feeling. The line between empathy and sympathy is not easy to draw, and especially not in the midst of emotion. Aristotle says that tragedy moves the audience to fear and pity: fear is empathic, pity sympathetic, two emotions bound up together in our response to tragedy, two forms of identification often almost indistinguishable.

Freud never claimed to have an adequate theory of identification, but he does seem to distinguish it from sympathy:

Supposing, for instance, that one of the girls in a boarding school has had a letter from someone with whom she is secretly in love which arouses her jealousy, and that she reacts to it with a fit of hysterics; then some of her friends who know about it will catch the fit, as we say, by mental infection. The mechanism is that of identification based upon the possibility or desire of putting oneself in the same situation. The other girls would like to have a secret love affair too, and under the influence of a sense of guilt they also accept the suffering involved in it. It would be wrong to suppose that they take on the symptom out of sympathy. On the contrary, the sympathy only arises out of the identification. . . . One ego has perceived a significant analogy with another upon one point—in our example upon openness to a similar emotion; an identification is thereupon constructed on this point.[2]

Freud relegates sympathy to a side effect. It's one of the nobler emotions, and he tends to stress the pettier or baser ones in his analysis of human motives. At all events, identification is for him no passing feeling but "an emotional tie with another person" that by way of analogy bears on one's sense of identity, as when a little boy identifies with his father, "would like to grow like him and be like him, and take his place everywhere. We may say simply that he takes his father as his ideal."[3] The wish for a love affair that Freud considers the point of identification between the other girls and the letter recipient is a more enduring emotional tie than sympathy for a fit of jealousy. Note that this tie, however enduring, is based on one point of analogy alone, a partial rather than a full identification. Note also that the girls identify with a situation—being in love, having a love affair—rather than a person. Freud is right about both the partial and the situational aspects of identification.

Some have tried to disprove the whole notion of identification by arguing that if we identified with the characters in a horror movie, when the monster comes, we would fear for our lives and run out of the theater. I have argued that if we didn't identify with them we wouldn't be scared at all, for we know we are perfectly safe sitting in the theater. Identification is always partial: you are still you even as you imagine yourself in someone else's place. We are scared at a horror movie because to some extent we identify with the characters; we don't run out of the theater because we don't fully identify with them. Another objection to the idea of identification points out that our feelings in response to a character are often at palpable variance with the character's own feelings, as happens in a horror movie when a character is smilingly unaware of the lurking monster while we shudder in fear. In such a case we identify not with the person but with the situation: we imagine ourselves not in the person's consciousness but in the person's circumstances.

Finding that "the ordinary notion of identification is peculiarly loose and unarticulated," Richard Wollheim favors the psychoanalytic notion, which seems, however, not to apply so well to our involvement with fictive characters: "When Freud talks of identification, he is, of course, thinking not of some transient mental phenomenon; something which could, in a theatre, at moments of high dramatic intensity, as when Gloucester is blinded, or Bérénice parts from her lovers, strike the audience: but, rather, of something that constitutes a pattern of emotion and behaviour."[4] Our identification with a character may last beyond such moments of intensity and may even, like a boy's with his father, inspire us to emulate the hero of a play or movie; but it can never have the defining effect on our self-identity that the boy's identification has on his. Or that, in Freud's account, Leonardo da Vinci's identification with his mother had on his. Or that, in Lacan's account, identification with the image in the mirror has on the child's nascent identity. Our temporary emotional ties with fictive characters are incapable of such shaping consequence. This is not to belittle the identifications that art brings about, but to warn against taking too far as their model psychoanalytic notions.

Whatever the validity of Lacan's theory of a mirror stage formative of the child's self-identity, Lacanian film theory is wrong to presume that the transient and variable experience of watching a movie can be similarly formative, determinative. While it is true that we always sit in front of the screen and always identify with the camera—that is, we put ourselves in its place and see what it sees—nothing warrants the conclusion that we are stuck in a subject position fixed in advance and always the same. Let me enlist against Lacanian film theory the words of one of its founders, Christian Metz, regarding the "permanent play of identification without which there would be no social life (thus, the simplest conversation presupposes the alternation of the *I* and the *you*, hence the aptitude of the two interlocutors for a mutual and reversible identification)."[5] The simplest alternation of shot and reverse shot on the screen affords two different subject positions. If having a conversation requires a mutual identification—you have to put yourself enough in the other person's place for you to understand another subject position—watching a movie entails a play of identification apt to shift and complicate and multiply.

Our identification with the camera is for Metz primary. Though indeed this is a fundamental convention of film—we are to look with the camera, to identify our eyes with it—nevertheless it is but a partial identification. A character opens the refrigerator door, and in the next shot we find ourselves looking out from inside the refrigerator.

We don't imagine ourselves there in the cold, squeezed amid the milk and juice bottles; we make a merely visual identification with the disembodied perspective. The camera's viewing position is often similarly disembodied; in a crane shot we don't imagine ourselves up in a crane moving through the air. And when a point-of-view shot attributes the camera's perspective to a character in the scene, our identification need go no further than a momentary viewing position: we don't necessarily take the character's side or share the character's sentiments. As Berys Gaut says, "The reaction shot is more important than the point-of-view shot in mobilizing affective and empathic identification."[6] Looking through a character's eyes, even though it puts us visually in his or her place, is less conducive to our putting ourselves in his or her place emotionally than looking at a character's face. In identifying with the camera, however, we identify not only with the visual perspective in each image but with the governing intelligence we sense behind the arrangement of images. We identify, that is, with the image maker, the implied author, which to some extent we must do in order to follow a film, just as we must identify with another person in order to engage in conversation. Our identification with characters is always part of a larger play of identification.

All through the first forty minutes of *Psycho* (1960) we are with Marion Crane (Janet Leigh). As she steals money from her employer and skips town, the narrative moves with her, is identified with her. We in the audience identify ourselves with her in various ways Gaut distinguishes: perceptually (we often see what she sees), epistemically (we know no more than she knows), motivationally (we imagine wanting what she wants, though we may not approve of her conduct), affectively and empathically (we imagine feeling what she feels and to greater or lesser extent we feel it).[7] And yet the experience of *Psycho* is somehow cool and detached. Even as we are with Marion in a state of tension and apprehension, we also identify with the author, the Hitchcock we imagine slyly smiling while the character and the viewer suffer. We willingly submit to his manipulation, knowingly put ourselves in his hands, and in that way identify ourselves with him. The master of suspense keeps his distance from his characters, and though we are more involved with them than he seems to be, at the same time we stand back with him. Aesthetic experience always combines some measure of involvement with some measure of distance.

In the name of aesthetic distance Theodor Adorno consigns identification to the philistines: "Aesthetic experience first of all places a distance between the observer and the object. This is part of the idea of disinterested contemplation. Philistines are people whose relationship to works of art is determined by the extent to which they can somehow place themselves in the position of the persons who appear there. All branches of the culture industry are based on this tendency and encourage their customers in it."[8] Adorno's disdain for our sentimental investment in fictive characters, his haughty insistence that art should be kept apart from life, epitomizes what may be called the aesthetic objection to identification. Brecht, too, advocates distance, but not exactly aesthetic distance, not disinterested contemplation. His alienation effect fosters in the audience an *interested* detachment, a weighing of art against the concerns of life. Then there is the antiaesthetic, the postmodern objection to identification, which regards it, along with all aesthetic illusion, as a seductive deception in line with the ruling ideology, and prescribes for art the task of critique. But art cannot live by critique alone, cannot do without identification and illusion, which can have on the audience an eye-opening, liberating effect. Aesthetic experience has the capacity to break norms as well as to create or confirm them, argues Hans Robert Jauss, and he sees identification as central to the effects of art, "aesthetic distance and identification [being] by no means mutually exclusive."[9]

If Gaut looks at the cause, the common ground we have with a character, Jauss looks at the effect of identification on us. If Gaut classifies identifications according to different aspects of a character on which they can be based—perceptual, affective, epistemic—Jauss, a founder of response theory, takes as his criterion for classification different responses to a character the audience can have—admiring, sympathetic, cathartic. Following Aristotle and Northrop Frye, Jauss considers the standing of characters in relation to the audience, whether they are better, worse, or at the same level; we admire those better than we are and sympathize with those similar to us. Like the boy taking his father as his model, the admiring audience looks up to the hero, and in the Christian tradition saints and martyrs would be taken as exemplary figures to be emulated. With the rise of the middle class and of a genre like melodrama, the sympathetic audience relates to characters of its own sort, at its own level. Admiration and sympathy, whether for Oedipus or Stella Dallas, of course often go together. Another of Jauss's categories is associative identification, which occurs when the audience feels itself part of a ritual or ceremony or game, a collective action that seems to embrace us so that we identify not with a person but with a group we join or want to join, the kind of identification we have with the revolutionary sailors in *Battleship Potemkin*. Ironic identification is what Flaubert in *Madame Bovary* or Brecht with his alienation effect brings about. Jauss describes it as the negation of identification, but nothing can be negated that is not there in the first place.

We may identify with a character's perception or situation, action or emotion. We may be stirred to high esteem or fellow feeling for the character or gain cathartic composure or ironic distance. Jauss talks about our identification with heroes, but we identify with other characters too, including villains (who appeal to our wicked side, our antisocial wishes, our will to power). And usually we identify not just with a person but with something he or she represents socially or morally or politically. Our attachment to characters always entails identifications of other kinds.

The Projectionist

In *Sherlock Junior* (1924) Buster Keaton is a movie projectionist who also wants to be a detective. Most of all he wants to impress the girl he loves. When her father's watch is stolen, however, Keaton not only fails to find the thief but is himself accused of the theft and told never to come to the house again, so he dejectedly returns to the projection booth. Unaware that the girl, who loves him too, has solved the crime for him—the culprit is his rival for her affections—he starts projecting a movie, falls asleep, and dreams of the movie he's projecting. Through the eyes of his dreaming self we watch, on the screen within the screen, the girl in the movie turn into his girl, the villain in the movie turn into his rival, and the father in the movie turn into her father. He identifies the persons in the movie with the persons in his life. *Sherlock Junior* is a comedy of identification.

The dreaming projectionist now wants to enter the screen within the screen. First the villain throws him out, and then, in a famous sequence, the movie keeps cutting from place to place, and the disconcerted intruder again and again finds himself suddenly elsewhere. It's as if Keaton had stepped into a film directed by D. W. Griffith and didn't like it. In his own films Keaton the director cuts sparingly and allows Keaton the actor ample unbroken space for his performance. Here the actor plays a viewer trying to project himself into the movie before him, and the successive cutaways disrupt not only the actor's performance but the viewer's involvement. Keaton is always an outsider seeking and never quite gaining a place in the world he inhabits—a world recognizably real yet inalterably strange.[10] This hallucinatory sequence suggests that the viewer of a movie is likewise an outsider seeking and never quite gaining a place in the projected world.

Now, however, the camera moves closer, and the smaller screen within the screen enlarges to fill the screen. The world of the movie Keaton is projecting wholly takes over, and just as he identifies the depicted characters with persons in his life, so he can now identify himself with the hero of the movie, the great detective, Sherlock

Junior. The projectionist who wanted to be a detective now imagines himself as a surpassing one: Sherlock Junior is Keaton's look-alike, his dashing screen double. It is an admiring identification. Rather than Freudian or Lacanian notions, we might more aptly invoke Melanie Klein's concept of *projective* identification, the imaginary projection onto another person of some part of the self.[11] The boy's identification with his father Freud considers *introjective*, the father as an ideal the boy takes into himself. Keaton's identification with Sherlock Junior is a projection of a fantasy he entertains of himself onto a character in a movie. Kleinian projective identification may help explain why we so often identify with heroes or heroines unattainably superior to us, stronger or cleverer or better looking than we could ever hope to be, and how we contrariwise identify with villains we hate but onto whom we project bad parts of ourselves.

As Sherlock Junior, Keaton does amazing things. From the roof of a house he jumps onto a tall railroad barrier that descends and deposits him in the backseat of the open convertible being driven by the villain in the street below—a feat utterly dreamlike yet visibly real, for, as usual with Keaton, he actually performed it and shows us his performance in an uninterrupted long shot. Keaton almost never gives himself close-ups, which tend to ask for a sympathetic rather than an admiring identification such as his long shots elicit. Still, his comedy blends the real with the unreal, the physical with the otherworldly, admiration with disbelief. We never lose sight of the improbability, the contrivance of the actions, nowhere more manifestly than in a ceaselessly astonishing sequence in which he rides on the handlebars of a motorcycle, all the while unaware that the driver has fallen off. When eventually Keaton looks back and sees that no one behind him has steered him through this perilous course miraculously negotiated at the mercy of happenstance, he is struck with terror. The shaky moving camera enhances the alarmed urgency. In a rare moment in Keaton's work he glances right at us in the audience. He glances, you could say, at his viewing, dreaming double, at the projectionist identified with him who now feels the terror of recognizing that the great detective hero has been protected by the artifice of fiction and in reality would have been as helpless as anybody.

Like other Keaton comedies—*Our Hospitality, The General, Steamboat Bill Jr.*—*Sherlock Junior* is a parody of an action melodrama, a parody exquisitely poised between thrills and laughs, a sublime balance of dream and reality. The feats of the action hero, which of course are always improbable, Keaton makes at once comically far-fetched and surprisingly convincing. *Sherlock Junior* parodies both the hero's improbable actions and the viewer's admiring identification.

The projectionist awakens from his dream and, framed by the window of the projection booth, looks out at the screen within the screen. Rather than an equation, these doubled frames within the frame propose a comparison with a difference. On the screen before him Keaton is disappointed to see not his dream of himself and his girl but the couple in the movie. He looks toward the camera but not at the viewer. It is characteristic of Keaton to ignore the audience— he's not soliciting our sympathy or complicity—and look right past the camera at something in the world around him claiming his attention. Now his girl comes into the projection booth and apologizes for having suspected him of the theft. She offers him a romantic happy ending, but how is he to proceed? He looks to the lovers in the movie for instruction in the ways of romance. Many of us have done that. The man in the movie kisses the woman's hands and puts a ring on her finger, and Keaton follows suit. The man in the movie kisses the woman on the lips, and Keaton shyly follows suit. Again we alternate between his looking out from within the frame of the booth window and the screen within the screen he's looking at—again, a comparison with a difference, just what identification is. His identification now is not projective but introjective. He's trying to take into himself the model of movie romance and succeeding pretty well until, after the kiss on the lips, the movie fades out to the couple later on with their two babies. *Sherlock Junior* then fades out on Keaton scratching his head in puzzlement.

NOTES

Preface

1. Immanuel Kant, "On a Supposed Right to Lie from Benevolent Motives" (1797), in *The Critique of Practical Reason and Other Writings in Moral Philosophy*, ed. and trans. Lewis White Beck (Chicago: University of Chicago Press, 1949), 346–50.

2. Horace, *Ars Poetica*, https://www.poetryfoundation.org/articles/69381 /ars-poetica.

Introduction

1. Jacqueline Lichtenstein, *The Color of Eloquence: Rhetoric and Painting in the French Classical Age*, trans. Emily McVarish (Berkeley: University of California Press, 1993), 236.

2. Lichtenstein, *Color of Eloquence*, 93

3. Lichtenstein, *Color of Eloquence*, 76, translation slightly modified.

4. Lichtenstein, *Color of Eloquence*, 76.

5. Northrop Frye, *Anatomy of Criticism: Four Essays* (Princeton, N.J.: Princeton University Press, 1971), 44.

6. Frye, *Anatomy of Criticism*, 166.

7. I owe to my friend and colleague William Park the suggestion that Judge Priest is the wise old man of romance. With regard to *The Tempest*, Frye brings up the Old Comedy of Aristophanes: "In the figure of Prospero we have one of the few approaches to the Aristophanic technique of having the whole comic action projected by a central character" (*Anatomy of Criticism*, 44). Old Comedy is in what Frye calls the "high mimetic" mode, in which the hero is superior to the rest of us. Like most comedy, *Judge Priest* is in the "low mimetic" mode, in which "the hero is one of us: we respond to a sense of his common humanity, and demand from the poet the same canons of probability that we find in our own experience" (34). But perhaps, like Prospero, Judge

Priest could be related to Old Comedy. Since he is a leader, a kind of Southern aristocrat, it wouldn't be implausible to construe him as a figure superior to the rest of us but assuming in his style of rhetoric, in his whole manner, the posture of being one of us.

8. Frye, *Anatomy of Criticism*, 163.

9. Joseph McBride, *Searching for John Ford* (New York: St. Martin's Press, 2001), 210.

10. McBride, *Searching for John Ford*, 210.

11. Kenneth Burke, *A Rhetoric of Motives* (1950; reprint, Berkeley: University of California Press, 1969), xiv.

12. For the concept of the implied author, see Wayne C. Booth, *The Rhetoric of Fiction*, 2nd ed. (Chicago: University of Chicago Press, 1983), 67–77.

13. McBride, *Searching for John Ford*, 211.

14. Editors of *Cahiers du cinéma*, "John Ford's *Young Mr. Lincoln*," first published in *Cahiers du cinéma*, no. 223 (1970), translation published in *Screen* 13, no. 3 (1972), and reprinted in, among other places, *Movies and Methods*, ed. Bill Nichols (Berkeley: University of California Press, 1976), 1:493–529. For the future perfect tense, see especially 503–4.

15. Geoffrey O'Brien, "Hero in Waiting," in the booklet accompanying the Criterion Collection DVD of *Young Mr. Lincoln* (2006), 4–5.

16. Translating this into the politics of 1939, the *Cahiers* editors supposed that the film was endorsing the Republicans, the party of Lincoln—which didn't exist in 1832, when he was with the Whigs, but which succeeded the Whigs later on and whose first elected president he was—against the Democrats, the party of Jackson and Franklin Roosevelt. But Lincoln should not be taken to represent the Republicans of 1939. In the rhetoric of the New Deal, Roosevelt identified himself with both Jackson and Lincoln.

17. O'Brien, "Hero in Waiting," 6.

18. Sergei Eisenstein, "Mr. Lincoln by Mr. Ford," reprinted in the booklet accompanying the Criterion Collection DVD of *Young Mr. Lincoln*, 14.

19. Eisenstein, "Mr. Lincoln by Mr. Ford."

20. Editors of *Cahiers du cinéma*, "John Ford's *Young Mr. Lincoln*," 512.

21. Editors of *Cahiers du cinéma*, "John Ford's *Young Mr. Lincoln*," 512.

22. Robert G. Dickson, "Kenneth Macgowan," in *Films in Review*, October 1963, qtd. in Editors of *Cahiers du cinéma*, "John Ford's *Young Mr. Lincoln*," 500.

23. C. Vann Woodward, "The Populist Heritage and the Intellectual," in *The Burden of Southern History*, 3rd ed. (Baton Rouge: Louisiana State University Press, 1993), 156–57.

24. Editors of *Cahiers du cinéma*, "John Ford's *Young Mr. Lincoln*," 515.

25. I owe this insight to Diane Stevenson, who knows a lot about American humor.

26. Editors of *Cahiers du cinéma*, "John Ford's *Young Mr. Lincoln*," 505.

27. Editors of *Cahiers du cinéma*, "John Ford's *Young Mr. Lincoln*," 523.

28. Vernon Young, "Long Voyage Home with John Ford," in *On Film: Unpopular Essays on a Popular Art* (Chicago: Quadrangle Books, 1972), 88–94.

29. "Straub and Huillet on Filmmakers They Like and Related Matters," in *The Cinema of Jean-Marie Straub and Danièle Huillet*, ed. Jonathan Rosenbaum, booklet for a retrospective at Film at the Public (New York City, November 2–14, 1982), 6.

30. For a discussion of the ending of *Fort Apache* and of Straub's work in lifelong collaboration with Danièle Huillet, see Gilberto Perez, *The Material Ghost: Films and Their Medium* (Baltimore, Md.: Johns Hopkins University Press, 1998), 247–51 and 283–335.

31. Quoted in Tag Gallagher, *John Ford: The Man and His Films* (Berkeley: University of California Press, 1986), 246.

32. Peter Bogdanovich, *John Ford* (Berkeley: University of California Press, 1978), 86.

33. Gallagher, *John Ford*, 253.

34. Kenneth Burke, *A Grammar of Motives* (1945; reprint, Berkeley: University of California Press, 1969), xv–xxiii and 3–20.

35. Frederick Jackson Turner, *The Frontier in American History* (New York: Holt, 1962).

36. William S. Pechter, *Twenty-Four Times a Second* (New York: Harper & Row, 1971), 228.

37. Pechter, *Twenty-Four Times a Second*, 226. For Pechter, *Liberty Valance* "is a sporadically imagined work; passages which are fully realized artistically alternating with others which merely point sketchily to what they might have been, with another cast, perhaps, or another budget, or in another time." I am arguing that the alienation effect is calculated.

38. Pechter, *Twenty-Four Times a Second*, 234.

39. The Western, Robert Warshow notes, "offers a serious orientation to the problem of violence such as can be found almost nowhere else in our culture." The Westerner is a "man who wears a gun on his thigh. The gun tells us that he lives in a world of violence, and even that he 'believes in violence.' But the drama is one of self-restraint: the moment of violence must come in its own time and according to its special laws, or else it is valueless." Warshow, *The Immediate Experience* (New York: Atheneum, 1979), 151, 153.

40. Robert B. Pippin, *Hollywood Westerns and American Myth: The Importance of Howard Hawks and John Ford for Political Philosophy* (New Haven, Conn.: Yale University Press, 2010), 85.

41. Pippin, *Hollywood Westerns*, 162.

42. Pippin, *Hollywood Westerns*, 63, 65.

43. Pippin, *Hollywood Westerns*, 8.

44. Thomas Schatz, "*Stagecoach* and Hollywood's A-Western Renaissance," in *John Ford's "Stagecoach,"* ed. Barry Keith Grant (Cambridge: Cambridge University Press, 2003), 22, 23, 36.

45. See the discussion of Ringo and Dallas in Gaylyn Studlar, "'Be a Proud, Glorifed Dreg': Class, Gender, and Frontier Democracy in *Stagecoach*," in Grant, *John Ford's "Stagecoach,"* 132–57.

46. Quoted in Pechter, *Twenty-Four Times a Second*, 226.

47. Jacques Rancière, *Disagreement: Politics and Philosophy*, trans. Julie Rose (Minneapolis: University of Minnesota Press, 1999), 34.

48. Diane Stevenson, "The Mixture of Genres in Two Films by Howard Hawks," *Film International* 7, no. 6 (2009): 24–31.

49. James Harvey, *Romantic Comedy in Hollywood, from Lubitsch to Sturges* (New York: Knopf, 1987), 469.

50. Pippin, *Hollywood Westerns*, 40, 53.

51. Pippin, *Hollywood Westerns*, 133.

52. Pippin, *Hollywood Westerns*, 87, 94.

53. Pippin, *Hollywood Westerns*, 89, 93.

54. Quoted in Antoine de Baecque and Serge Toubiana, *Truffaut: A Biography* (New York: Knopf, 1999), 300.

55. Robert B. Pippin, *Hollywood Westerns and American Myth: The Importance of Howard Hawks and John Ford for Political Philosophy* (New Haven, Conn.: Yale University Press, 2010), 134–35.

56. Peter Stowell, *John Ford* (Boston: Twayne, 1986), 139–40.

57. Diane Stevenson, "Race in John Ford's *The Searchers*," paper presented at the Film and Literature Conference, Florida State University, Tallahassee, January 1998; and "Why Are Scar's Eyes Blue? Race in John Ford's *The Searchers*," paper presented at the Society for Cinema and Media Studies Conference, Minneapolis, March 2003. Scar's blue eyes of course belong to a white actor, Henry Brandon, who plays Quanah Parker in another Ford Western, *Two Rode Together* (1961)—which confirms the link between Quanah Parker and Scar.

58. "Ethan hates Scar because he hates himself," Stowell maintains; "he must kill Scar to exorcise the guilt he himself bears. For, unconsciously, Ethan wished to commit Scar's crimes, killing his brother and raping his sister-in-law. Scar, as the name suggests, is Ethan's mark of Cain." Stowell, *John Ford*, 135. Other commentators (Pippin among them) concur with this reading. That Ethan hates himself is a plausible surmise. But that he hates himself for loving his brother's wife, that he would harbor a wish to kill his brother and rape Martha, is mere speculation. Ford refrains from probing into Ethan's mind: too much individual psychology gets in the way of telling a national story.

59. Pechter, *Twenty-Four Times a Second*, 232.

60. McBride, *Searching for John Ford*, 498.

61. I am indebted to Diane Stevenson for this characterization of *High Noon*, which she sees as basically a Gothic story in which the return of the bad guys on the hero's wedding day is the return of the repressed—the violence

the hero vows to renounce by marrying a Quaker—and the woman who pre-
cipitates the crisis also resolves it with her own violence.

    62. McBride, *Searching for John Ford*, 333, 498.

I. Cinematic Tropes

    1. Richard A. Lanham, *A Handlist of Rhetorical Terms*, 2nd ed. (Berkeley: University of California Press, 1991), 154–55.

    2. Warshow, *Immediate Experience*, 207.

    3. Warshow, *Immediate Experience*, 223–24.

    4. Walter Kerr, *The Silent Clowns* (New York: Knopf, 1975), 347.

    5. "Two Aspects of Language and Two Types of Aphasic Disturbances" originally appeared as the second part of a book Jakobson wrote with Morris Halle, *Fundamentals of Language* (The Hague: Mouton, 1956). It is reprinted in Roman Jakobson, *Language in Literature*, ed. Krystyna Pomorska and Stephen Rudy (Cambridge, Mass.: Harvard University Press, 1987), 95–114.

    6. Jakobson, "Two Aspects of Language," 99.

    7. I. A. Richards, *The Philosophy of Rhetoric* (New York: Oxford University Press, 1965), 96ff.

    8. Aristotle, *The Rhetoric and the Poetics*, with *Rhetoric* trans. W. Rhys Roberts and *Poetics* trans. Ingram Bywater (New York: Modern Library, 1954), *Rhetoric*, III, 1406b, 173.

    9. Instancing "such motion pictures as those of Charlie Chaplin and Eisenstein," Jakobson speaks of a "metaphoric montage with its lap dissolves—the filmic similes" ("Two Aspects of Language," 111). But dissolves, though they have sometimes served as transitions of comparison, never acquired a set meaning as the equivalent of *like* or *as*. More often they are used as markers of the passage of time. As for subsuming simile under metaphor, Aristotle already did that while drawing the distinction between them: "The Simile also is a metaphor; the difference is but slight." Aristotle, *Rhetoric*, III, 1406b.

    10. Fritz Lang's *Metropolis* (1927) is all about the opposition between the organic and the mechanical. The machines relentlessly dehumanize the workers, whom the good human Maria would redeem and the bad mechanical Maria would doom; mechanical time, as symbolized by an outsize clock whose hands a worker must keep turning by hand one way and the other through an interminable ten-hour shift, exacts an onerous toll on human time. The solution the film proposes rests on an organic model of human society: "The mediator between the head and the hands must be the heart." That is, the rulers stay at the top and the workers at the bottom, only the head that rules should be kinder and gentler to the hands that work. Organic models of society are often hierarchical and conservative in some such manner. Taking issue with the view of Vertov as a champion of the machine in art and society,

Malcolm Turvey has argued that, rather than the machine, Vertov's model for the new Soviet society was the organism. But for Vertov, the machine was an instrument of liberation—not, as with Lang, of oppression—and the equality of parts working together in the ensemble of a machine surely provides a better model for an egalitarian society than the head and the hands and the heart. In any case, the opposition between the organic and the mechanical, which Turvey posits, implies a derogation of the mechanical quite foreign to Vertov. Turvey, "Vertov: Between the Organism and the Machine," *October* 121 (2007): 5–18.

11. Brian Vickers, *In Defence of Rhetoric* (Oxford: Clarendon Press, 1997), 445.

12. Jakobson, "Two Aspects of Language," 111.

13. Jakobson, "Two Aspects of Language," 111.

14. This was the order in which Giambattista Vico thought the tropes came into being: first metaphor, which for him is "the most luminous and therefore the most necessary and frequent" and "is most praised when it gives sense and passion to insensate things"; then synecdoche and metonymy, which "give names to things from the most particular and the most sensible ideas"; and finally irony, which "could not have begun until the period of reflection, because it is fashioned of falsehood by dint of a reflection which wears the mask of truth." Vico, *The New Science of Giambattista Vico*, 3rd ed., trans. T. G. Bergin and M. H. Fisch (Garden City, N.Y.: Anchor Books, 1961), 87–91.

15. Kenneth Burke, "Four Master Tropes," appendix to *Grammar of Motives*, 503–17.

16. Vico, *New Science*, 89.

17. Burke, "Four Master Tropes," 508.

18. Jakobson, "Two Aspects of Language," 113.

19. Burke, "Four Master Tropes," 503.

20. Lanham, *Handlist of Rhetorical Terms*, 148.

21. Kenneth Burke, *The Philosophy of Literary Form*, 3rd ed. (Berkeley: University of California Press, 1973), 26. It should be noted that Burke defines synecdoche in broader terms than part and whole, so that it encroaches on the traditional domain of metonymy: "the container for the thing contained, the cause for the effect, the effect for the cause, etc."

22. Burke, "Four Master Tropes," 508. As regards artistic representation, Burke adds: "There is also a sense in which the well-formed work of art is internally synecdochic, as the beginning of a drama contains its close or the close sums up the beginning, the parts all thus being consubstantially related." With drama as his model—his synecdoche—for art as a whole, Burke here makes generally the same point I made specifically about film as a medium of details arranged into an unfolding plot. All "well-formed" art may be "internally synecdochic," but film, an art bound to particulars, is particularly so.

23. Peter Burke, *The Fabrication of Louis XIV* (New Haven, Conn.: Yale University Press, 1992), 26.

24. Siegfried Kracauer, *Theory of Film: The Redemption of Physical Reality* (New York: Oxford University Press, 1965), 47–48.

25. V. I. Pudovkin, *Film Technique and Film Acting*, trans. Ivor Montagu (New York: Grove Press, 1970), 168.

26. Béla Balázs, *The Theory of the Film: Character and Growth of a New Art*, trans. Edith Bone (New York: Dover, 1970), 61.

27. Noa Steimatsky, *On the Face of Film* (New York: Oxford University Press, forthcoming).

28. David Bordwell, "The Movie Looks Back at Us," David Bordwell's Website on Cinema, April 1, 2009, http://www.davidbordwell.net/.

29. In her monograph on the film, Laura Mulvey notes this transition and remarks that the poster of Susan "can only be seen by the audience" and so "sets up a complicity between screen and spectator." Mulvey, *Citizen Kane* (London: BFI, 1992), 24.

30. Quoted in James Harvey, *Movie Love in the Fifties* (New York: Knopf, 2001), 300.

31. Harvey, *Movie Love*, 300.

32. Harvey, *Movie Love*, 300.

33. Andrew Sarris, *"You Ain't Heard Nothing Yet": The American Talking Film: History and Memory, 1927–1949* (New York: Oxford University Press, 1998), 292.

34. For a discussion of a scene in Robert Flaherty's *Moana* (1926) that arouses and satisfies our curiosity with a similar move from parts to a revealed whole, see Perez, *Material Ghost*, 53–55.

35. P. E. Salles Gomes, *Jean Vigo* (Berkeley: University of California Press, 1971), 62.

36. P. Adams Sitney, "The Rhetoric of Robert Bresson," in *The Essential Cinema*, ed. Sitney (New York: Anthology Film Archives and New York University Press, 1975), 196–97.

37. Northrop Frye, "The Argument of Comedy," in *Shakespeare: An Anthology of Criticism and Theory, 1945–2000*, ed. Russ McDonald (Malden, Mass.: Blackwell, 2004), 96ff.

38. Stanley Cavell, *Pursuits of Happiness: The Hollywood Comedy of Remarriage* (Cambridge, Mass.: Harvard University Press, 1981), 100. Cavell argues that "the genre of remarriage [which includes such movies as *It Happened One Night*, *The Awful Truth*, *Bringing Up Baby*, *The Philadelphia Story*, and *The Lady Eve*] is an inheritor of the preoccupations and discoveries of Shakespearean romantic comedy" (1), and one of the generic features he traces back to Shakespeare is "the action's moving from a starting place of impasse to a place Frye calls 'the green world,' a place in which perspective and renewal are to be achieved" (49). In this respect, however, he thinks *It Happened One Night* is an exception: it "has no such settled place; instead what happens takes place 'on the road'

. . . there is nothing that corresponds to the feature of 'the green world'" (29, 105). But isn't the road on which Ellie and Peter travel the site of perspective and renewal? And that moonlit night, that sparkling stream, that bed of hay—what is that whole pastoral scene if not a "green world"? Cavell's own description of the scene suggests as much: "What happened one night is that the man took the woman to his island . . . and they and the moon and the landscape all become one, as movingly a part of something big and marvelous as any expressionist painterly composition by a movie camera can achieve" (100). No other of these remarriage comedies exhibits as much feeling for nature and its renewing powers as does *It Happened One Night*.

39. Leon Wieseltier, "*Shoah*," in *Claude Lanzmann's "Shoah": Key Essays*, ed. Stuart Liebman (New York: Oxford University Press, 2007), 90.

40. Timothy Garton Ash, "The Life of Death," in Liebman, *Claude Lanzmann's "Shoah*," 136.

41. Radio interview on the *Leonard Lopate Show* (WNYC, December 10, 2010).

42. Quoted in Dominick LaCapra, "Lanzmann's *Shoah*: 'Here There Is No Why,'" in Liebman, *Claude Lanzmann's "Shoah*," 220.

43. Gertrud Koch, "The Aesthetic Transformation of the Image of the Unimaginable," in Liebman, *Claude Lanzmann's "Shoah*," 129.

44. Claude Lanzmann, "Site and Speech: An Interview with Claude Lanzmann about *Shoah*," conducted by Marc Chevrie and Hervé Le Roux, in Liebman, *Claude Lanzmann's "Shoah*," 38.

45. Lanzmann, "Site and Speech," 45.

46. Dai Vaughan, *For Documentary: Twelve Essays* (Berkeley: University of California Press, 1999), 58.

47. Lanzmann, "Site and Speech," 44.

48. Lanzmann, "Site and Speech," 42–43.

49. Quoted in LaCapra, "Lanzmann's *Shoah*," 192.

50. Phillip Lopate, "Night and Fog," in the booklet accompanying the Criterion Collection DVD of *Night and Fog* (2003).

51. Claude Lanzmann, "Hier ist kein Warum," in Liebman, *Claude Lanzmann's "Shoah*," 51–52.

52. Jan Karski, "*Shoah*," in Liebman, *Claude Lanzmann's "Shoah*," 172, 174.

53. Pauline Kael, *Hooked* (New York: Dutton, 1989), 88.

54. Synecdoche, *pars pro toto*, is for Eisenstein "the most typical example of a thinking form from the arsenal of early thought processes. . . . At that stage of non-differentiated thinking the part *is* at one and the same time also the whole." Here he is concerned with establishing a correspondence between "early thought processes" or "sensual thinking" or "inner speech" (as opposed to logical thinking or articulated speech) and the methods of art. Sergei Eisenstein, *Film Form: Essays in Film Theory*, ed. and trans. Jay Leyda (New York: Harcourt, Brace, 1949), 132–34.

55. Eisenstein, *Film Form*, 238. Eisenstein is pointing out the difference

between the close-up as used by Griffith and American filmmakers after him and as used in his own work and that of other Soviet filmmakers.

56. It's significant that, as the sailors seize the doctor and drag him to his watery fate, Eisenstein links him with another ideologist: the priest. It's curious, however, that we never get to see the fate of the captain, the man who really holds the power on the ship. He orders the shooting of the sailors under the tarpaulin, but after the mutiny breaks out, we lose sight of him in the confusion.

57. Eisenstein, *Film Form*, 175.

58. "Like the jerking woman at the beginning of the sequence, they are quasi-diegetic," David Bordwell writes. But the woman hit by the Cossacks as they start firing on the people, though shown in abrupt, successive close-ups not clearly placed in the space of the Odessa steps—the diegesis—is evidently part of the crowd gathered there and is a synecdoche for the whole crowd suddenly under attack from the Cossacks. The stone lions may be supposed to lie somewhere in the neighborhood of the Odessa steps—they are actually at a palace in Alupka, a Crimean city—but their manifestly fabricated motion removes them from reality and makes them purely symbolic. Bordwell, *The Cinema of Eisenstein* (Cambridge, Mass.: Harvard University Press, 1993), 76–77.

59. Bordwell, *Cinema of Eisenstein*, 78.

60. Otto Karl Werckmeister, *Icons of the Left* (Chicago: University of Chicago Press, 1999), 45.

61. "The Ship of State" is the title of an anonymous political poem from the fifteenth century. In his book on allegory, Angus Fletcher quotes that poem and comments that "the traditional analogy of ship to state . . . can be traced at least as far back as Plato's *Republic*" and "is a commonplace for Quintilian and reappears as a standard example in rhetoric texts." Fletcher, *Allegory: The Theory of a Symbolic Mode* (Ithaca, N.Y.: Cornell University Press, 1964), 77.

62. Originally *Potemkin* carried an epigraph from Trotsky: "The spirit of insurrection hovered over the Russian land. Some enormous and mysterious process was taking place in countless hearts. The individual was dissolving in the mass, and the mass was dissolving in the outburst." That fit in better with the shots of the sea and breaking waves that open the film, but after Trotsky's fall from power, the Lenin epigraph took its place: "Revolution is war . . . the only legitimate, reasonable, just, really great war." Werckmeister cites both epigraphs and remarks that "Trotsky's sense of revolution as a socially indeterminate mass movement" gave way to "Lenin's principles about the military preconditions of revolution," and that the Lenin epigraph, together with his statement on "revolutionary armed forces" at the film's close, "proclaimed world revolution to be a global warfare led by Soviet power." Werckmeister has a point, but his critique of *Potemkin* as an icon of the left makes the film out to be more militaristic than it really is. The replacement of the Trotsky

epigraph doesn't change the depiction of the sailors' mutiny as a mass move-ment, a popular outburst, a revolt against oppression collectively undertaken in a spirit of equality and fraternity. Werckmeister, *Icons of the Left*, 46–47.

63. Sergei Eisenstein, "Constanța (Whither *The Battleship Potemkin*)," in *Writings, 1922–34*, ed. and trans. Richard Taylor (Bloomington: Indiana University Press, 1988), 1:67.

64. Eisenstein, "Constanța," 1:67.

65. Quintilian, *The Orator's Education*, ed. and trans. Donald A. Russell (Cambridge, Mass.: Harvard University Press, 2001), 8.6.44 (3:451).

66. Siegfried Kracauer, *From Caligari to Hitler: A Psychological History of the German Film* (Princeton, N.J.: Princeton University Press, 1947), 61–76. Kra-cauer drew on Janowitz's unpublished account of the making of the film, written in exile two decades later. For portions of Janowitz's text, see Hans Janowitz, "*Caligari*—The Story of a Famous Story (Excerpts)," in *The Cabinet of Dr. Caligari: Texts, Contexts, Histories*, ed. Mike Budd (New Brunswick, N.J.: Rutgers University Press, 1990), 221–39.

67. Lotte H. Eisner, *The Haunted Screen: Expressionism in the German Cinema and the Influence of Max Reinhardt*, trans. Roger Greaves (Berkeley: University of California Press, 1969), 110. When seeking a permit for his fairground side-show, Caligari feels humiliated by the town clerk and subsequently has him killed—the somnambulist's first victim. This suggests that the mountebank's petty resentment of authority lies behind the doctor's insane authority.

68. See Anton Kaes, *Shell Shock Cinema: Weimar Culture and the Wounds of War* (Princeton, N.J.: Princeton University Press, 2009), 46–54.

69. Janowitz, "*Caligari*—The Story of a Famous Story (Excerpts)," 224.

70. Kracauer, *From Caligari to Hitler*, 66–67. Among the papers of Werner Krauss, who played Dr. Caligari, an early version of the screenplay was dis-covered that already has Francis as narrator. For some this calls into question Janowitz's account of the unwelcome addition of a framing prologue and epi-logue; but in the discovered version there is only a prologue, and the narrating Francis is sane, not out of his mind as he's found to be in the finished film. See Mike Budd, "The Moments of *Caligari*," in Budd, *Cabinet of Dr. Caligari*, 28–29. Budd thinks that Janowitz and Kracauer objected to the unreliable narrator because they would have wanted the film to be "realistic," but *Caligari*, with or without a narrator, could never have been that.

71. Walter Benjamin, *The Origin of German Tragic Drama*, trans. John Osborne (London: NLB, 1977), 233.

72. Fletcher, *Allegory*, 81–83.

73. Quoted in Fletcher, *Allegory*, 16–17.

74. Fletcher, *Allegory*, 40–41.

75. For an interpretation of *Nosferatu* as an allegory of death, see Perez, *Material Ghost*, 123–48.

76. Kracauer, *From Caligari to Hitler*, 220.

77. Kracauer, *From Caligari to Hitler*, 221.

78. Eric Rhode, *Tower of Babel: Speculations on the Cinema* (London: Weidenfeld and Nicolson, 1966), 98, 100.

79. Rhode, *Tower of Babel*, 86.

80. This section is indebted to Diane Stevenson's paper, "The Ethics of War and Its Transformation in the Movies," presented at the MLA Convention, Washington, D.C., December 2005.

81. Erich Auerbach, "Figura," trans. Ralph Manheim, in *Scenes from the Drama of European Literature* (Minneapolis: University of Minnesota Press, 1984), 29. Auerbach considers another aspect of *figura*: "Beside the opposition between *figura* and fulfillment or truth, there appears another, between *figura* and *historia*; *historia* or *littera* is the literal sense or the event related; *figura* is the same literal meaning or event in reference to the fulfillment cloaked in it, and this fulfillment itself is *veritas*, so that *figura* becomes a middle term between *littera-historia* and *veritas*. In this connection *figura* is roughly equivalent to *spiritus* or *intellectus spiritalis*, sometimes replaced by *figuralitas*" (47). In his introduction to the fiftieth anniversary edition of Auerbach's *Mimesis* (Princeton, N.J.: Princeton University Press, 2003), Edward W. Said stresses this "more interesting sense" of *figura* as a middle term between history and truth, as "the intellectual and spiritual energy that does the actual connecting between past and present, history and Christian truth, which is so essential to interpretation" (xxi–xxii).

82. Auerbach, "Figura," 66.

83. Auerbach, "Figura," 67–68.

84. Auerbach, "Figura," 71.

85. Auerbach, "Figura," 72.

86. Fredric Jameson, "Third-World Literature in the Era of Multinational Capitalism," *Social Text* 15 (1986): 85–86.

87. James Leahy, "Ceddo," *Senses of Cinema*, no. 33 (2004), http://sensesof cinema.com/.

88. Philip Rosen, *Change Mummified: Cinema, Historicity, Theory* (Minneapolis: University of Minnesota Press, 2001), 286.

89. For this distinction, see Claudio Guillén, "Algunas literariedades de *Cien años de soledad*," in *Cien años de soledad*, by Gabriel García Márquez, commemorative ed. (Madrid: Real Academia Española, 2007), xcviii–ciii; and Ramon Fernandez, "The Method of Balzac: The Recital, and the Aesthetics of the Novel," in *Messages*, trans. Montgomery Belgion (New York: Harcourt, Brace, 1927), 59–88.

90. Serge Daney, "Ceddo," *Cahiers du cinéma* 304 (1979): 51–53; an English translation can be found at http://home.earthlink.net/~steevee/ Daney_ceddo.html.

91. Daney, in "Ceddo," makes the same point in his review: "This is the music that the *ceddo* people and their children will make later, elsewhere. . . . The music is a future past, *it will have been*."

92. David Murphy, "An African Brecht," *New Left Review* 16 (2002): 126.

93. Rosen, *Change Mummified*, 296.

94. Rosen, *Change Mummified*, 265.

95. Quoted in Leahy, "*Ceddo.*"

96. See Robert N. Bellah, "Civil Religion in America," *Daedalus* 96, no. 1 (1967): 1–21.

97. A kiss was inserted in this scene against Ford's wishes.

98. Cavell, *Pursuits of Happiness*, 81.

99. Cavell, *Pursuits of Happiness*, 82–83. *It Happened One Night* came out early in 1934, and the Production Code did not go into effect until a little later. But this does not invalidate Cavell's reading of the blanket as a trope for the movie screen under a censorship that, even if not yet in place, the filmmakers well knew soon would be.

100. Cavell, *Pursuits of Happiness*, 107–8.

101. Cavell, *Pursuits of Happiness*, 109.

102. William Empson, *Seven Types of Ambiguity* (New York: New Directions, 1966), 23–24.

103. David Bordwell, "Pierced by Poetry," David Bordwell's Website on Cinema, May 13, 2009, http://www.davidbordwell.net/.

104. Bordwell, "Pierced by Poetry."

105. James Harvey, *Romantic Comedy in Hollywood, from Lubitsch to Sturges* (New York: Knopf, 1987), 114–15.

106. Phillip Drummond, "Textual Space in *Un Chien andalou,*" *Screen* 18, no. 3 (1977): 55–119.

107. Quoted in J. Francisco Aranda, *Luis Buñuel: Biografía crítica* (Barcelona: Editorial Lumen, 1969), 87.

108. Aristotle, *Poetics*, chapters VI.13 and XI.6, trans. S. H. Butcher (New York: Hill & Wang, 1961), 63, 73.

109. Aristotle, *Rhetoric*, III, 1412a, Roberts translation, 191–92.

110. Aristotle, *Rhetoric*, III, 1410b, Roberts translation, 187.

111. Noël Burch, *Theory of Film Practice*, trans. Helen R. Lane (New York: Praeger, 1973), 123–26. Burch compares Georges Franju's *Le Sang des bêtes* (1949) with *Un Chien andalou* and maintains that, unlike Franju's slaughterhouse documentary, whose "entire rhythm . . . is based on a succession of painful shocks," Buñuel's film relies on the initial shock alone (126). But a rhythm of aggression, successive shocks in the wake of the initial one, is just what *Un Chien andalou* enacts.

112. Linda Williams, *Figures of Desire: A Theory and Analysis of Surrealist Film* (Berkeley: University of California Press, 1992), 64, 72–73.

113. Williams, *Figures of Desire*, 82.

114. Jeff Smith made this remark after a talk on *Un Chien andalou* I gave at Washington University in St. Louis in January 2001.

115. Luis Buñuel, "Notes on the Making of *Un Chien andalou,*" qtd. in Phil Powrie, "Masculinity in the Shadow of the Slashed Eye: Surrealist Film Criticism at the Crossroads," *Screen* 39, no. 2 (1998): 156.

116. Williams, *Figures of Desire*, 69–72.

117. According to Buñuel, "Beatriz could be the Magdalene and Andara would be a feminine version of St. Peter (for example: Peter pulls out the sword when Christ is arrested; Andara hits a guard when Nazarín is arrested)" (my translation). This is from his interviews with José de la Colina and Tomás Pérez Turrent that appear in *Luis Buñuel: Prohibido asomarse al interior* (México: Joaquín Mortiz/Planeta, 1986), 122.

118. Pechter, *Twenty-Four Times a Second*, 219.

119. Frye, *Anatomy of Criticism*, 210.

120. Frye, *Anatomy of Criticism*, 215–16.

121. Frye, *Anatomy of Criticism*, 237.

122. Quintilian, *Orator's Education*, 9.2.44 (4:59).

123. Burke, "Four Master Tropes," 503.

124. Jean Renoir, *My Life and My Films*, trans. Norman Denny (New York: Atheneum, 1974), 154.

125. Renoir, *My Life and My Films*, 154–55.

126. Christopher Faulkner makes much the same point: "The immigrant is *déraciné*, dispossessed; his expectation of happiness is brilliantly commented upon at the opening of the film with the shock-cut from the sound of the men singing of their hopes in the railway compartment as the open sea passes by the window to the dissonant shriek of the train as we see it thundering across the trestle from a low angle. 'Do you think we'll be happy?' one of the newcomers asks on the road into town, only to be answered by a pan up to the empty web of steel and concrete over which the train has just passed. . . . The same trestle that will figure in the film's conclusion, and we should remember it as the film's principal reference for an industrial way of life from which these people are also alienated." Faulkner, *The Social Cinema of Jean Renoir* (Princeton, N.J.: Princeton University Press, 1986), 49.

127. William Rothman, *The "I" of the Camera: Essays in Film Criticism, History, and Aesthetics* (Cambridge: Cambridge University Press, 1988), 127–28.

128. Faulkner, *Social Cinema*, 44.

129. Cited in Giorgio Agamben, *Profanations*, trans. Jeff Fort (New York: Zone Books, 2007), 40.

130. Acín and his wife were put to death by pro-Franco forces during the Spanish civil war. As Buñuel told the story, Acín's wife was captured and threatened with execution unless her husband gave himself up, and when he did, they were both executed. Buñuel, *Luis Buñuel*, 36.

131. Octavio Paz, "El poeta Buñuel," in *Las Peras del Olmo* (Mexico City: Imprenta Universitaria, 1957), 229 (my translation).

132. For a related discussion of *Land without Bread*, see Perez, *Material Ghost*, 43–45.

133. Jean-André Fieschi brings up the marginal puff of smoke in his entry on Buñuel in *Cinema: A Critical Dictionary*, ed. Richard Roud (New York: Viking, 1980), 1:173. Buñuel said that he shot the goat with a revolver and

noticed afterward that the puff of smoke was visible in the image (*Luis Buñuel*, 36). But he chose to keep the telltale image in the film: it was his final—even if not his original—intention to show on the screen the sign that the goat was actually shot down.

134. Bill Nichols, *Introduction to Documentary* (Bloomington: Indiana University Press, 2001), 6–8.

135. Frye writes that "whenever a reader is not sure what the author's attitude is or what his own is supposed to be, we have irony." Frye, *Anatomy of Criticism*, 223.

136. Frye, *Anatomy of Criticism*, 41.

137. Frye, *Anatomy of Criticism*, 34.

138. Roland Barthes, "The Discourse of History," in *The Rustle of Language*, trans. Richard Howard (New York: Hill & Wang, 1986), 131–32.

139. Frye, *Anatomy of Criticism*, 40.

140. Wayne C. Booth, *A Rhetoric of Irony* (Chicago: University of Chicago Press, 1974), 240–45.

141. Robin Wood, "Two Films by Michael Cimino," in *Hollywood from Vietnam to Reagan* (New York: Columbia University Press, 1986), 270.

142. Wood, "Two Films by Michael Cimino," 274.

143. Quoted by Penelope Houston in "The Figure in the Carpet," *Sight and Sound* 32, no. 4 (1963): 164.

144. Pauline Kael, "*The Deer Hunter*: The God-Bless-America Symphony," in *For Keeps* (New York: Plume, 1996), 801–2.

145. Roland Barthes, "The Reality Effect," in *The Rustle of Language*, 141–48.

146. Barthes, "Reality Effect," 146.

147. Quoted by Gérard Genette in *Narrative Discourse Revisited*, trans. Jane E. Lewin (Ithaca, N.Y.: Cornell University Press, 1988), 47. In connection with what he calls the "mimetic illusion," Genette brings up Barthes and others who have stressed the role of unnecessary details in realistic representation.

148. On both Renoir and Rossellini, the first critic to read is André Bazin. See in particular Bazin, "The French Renoir," in *Jean Renoir*, ed. François Truffaut, trans. W. W. Halsey II and William H. Simon (New York: Simon & Schuster, 1973), 74–91; and "An Aesthetic of Reality: Cinematic Realism and the Italian School of the Liberation," in *What Is Cinema?*, trans. Hugh Gray (Berkeley: University of California Press, 1971), 2:16–40.

149. Kael, "*Deer Hunter*," 801–2.

150. Wood, "Two Films by Michael Cimino," 283.

151. Robin Wood, *Hollywood from Vietnam to Reagan . . . and Beyond* (New York: Columbia University Press, 2003), 254.

152. Wood, "Two Films by Michael Cimino," 284.

153. Kael, "*Deer Hunter*," 803.

154. Kael, "*Deer Hunter*," 804–5.

Notes to Cinematic Tropes

369

155. Kael, "Deer Hunter," 803. Kael's language in her description of this scene ("virgin mountain," "male choir in the sky") is colored by her view that Cimino "can't resist eroticizing the hunt—it's a sexual surrogate, a man's man wedding."

156. Wood, "Two Films by Michael Cimino," 285.

157. Kael, "Deer Hunter," 803–4.

158. Kael, "Deer Hunter," 805.

159. Sylvia Shin Huey Chong, "Restaging the War: The Deer Hunter and the Primal Scene of Violence," Cinema Journal 44, no. 2 (2005): 89–106.

160. Aristotle, Nicomachean Ethics, III, 6–7.

161. To call a work "self-reflexive" is redundant, though one may call it "self-reflective," reflecting on itself.

162. See Raymond Williams, "Metropolitan Perceptions and the Emergence of Modernism," in The Politics of Modernism, ed. Tony Pinkney (London: Verso, 1989), 37–48.

163. For the founding exposition of apparatus theory, see Jean-Louis Baudry, "Ideological Effects of the Basic Cinematographic Apparatus," trans. Alan Williams, Film Quarterly 28, no. 2 (1974–75): 39–47.

164. Reflexivity in Max Ophuls's Letter from an Unknown Woman (1948) serves to uphold illusion rather than to dispel it. The unknown woman is Lisa (Joan Fontaine), and her letter, which we hear in voice-over narration, is addressed to the man she has always loved, Stefan (Louis Jourdan), a concert pianist and inveterate womanizer who has forgotten their unforgettable evening together. On that romantic occasion, Lisa and Stefan go to an amusement park in the winter—the better to imagine it in the spring—and watch painted scenery rolling by their window in a simulated train ride that offers paying costumers the illusion of traveling in exotic lands. "Lisa describes to Stefan the workings of her imagination," writes Charles Affron; "the mechanical, illusionistic scene-changing procedures (the Venetian panorama rolls to its conclusion, the Swiss one replaces it when an old man operates a set of levers and gears) are meticulously revealed." Affron, Cinema and Sentiment (Chicago: University of Chicago Press, 1982), 102–3. Calling attention to the machinery of illusion, the levers and gears of a moving picture, Ophuls draws a reflexive parallel with the movies and implies that the Vienna around 1900 depicted in his mise-en-scène is just such an illusory exotic land. Lisa's love for Stefan is an illusion, an adolescent crush sustained all her life; but she knows it is an illusion, knows full well by the time she writes her letter that the Stefan she loves exists only in her mind. Yet she loves him still, as she loves the spring she imagines in the winter; she still cherishes the romantic dream that has given her life meaning. As Ophuls declares his own artifice, he also makes clear Lisa's awareness of her own attachment to illusion. His reflexivity might be seen as ironic detachment, but it is more like identification with her undeceived romantic illusionism.

165. Harold Bloom, "*The Fatal Glass of Beer*: W. C. Fields as Master of the Aesthetics of Being Outraged," in *The Movie That Changed My Life*, ed. David Rosenberg (New York: Penguin Books, 1993), 154.

166. Warshow adds that "it is significant of the character of this movie, and to some extent, perhaps, of Chaplin's personal character, that one should feel that he does not always understand the implications of his work." Warshow, *Immediate Experience*, 212.

167. Warshow, *Immediate Experience*, 213.

168. The notion of "serious parody" is set forth by Giorgio Agamben in an essay on parody and Elsa Morante in *Profanations*, 37–51. For parody "without the satirical impulse, without laughter," Fredric Jameson has proposed that we use the term "pastiche," but his notion of pastiche is confined to postmodernism, and he seems to think that parody has no other object than the individual author, the idiosyncratic style. Jameson, "Postmodernism and Consumer Society," in *The Anti-Aesthetic: Essays on Postmodern Culture*, ed. Hal Foster (Seattle: Bay Press, 1983), 113–14. For another postmodern take on parody as not necessarily comical, see Linda Hutcheon, *A Theory of Parody: The Teachings of Twentieth-Century Art Forms* (Urbana: University of Illinois Press, 2000).

169. P. Adams Sitney, *Visionary Film: The American Avant-Garde*, 2nd ed. (New York: Oxford University Press, 1979), 371.

170. For a related discussion of Godard, see Perez, *Material Ghost*, 336–66.

171. Novalis, *Philosophical Writings*, ed. and trans. Margaret Mahony Stoljar (New York: Sunny Press, 1997), 41.

172. Pauline Kael, *Kiss Kiss Bang Bang* (Boston: Little, Brown, 1968), 112.

173. Kael, *Kiss Kiss Bang Bang*, 113.

174. Agamben, *Profanations*, 40.

175. Eisenstein, *Film Form*, 16.

176. Alexander Dovzhenko, "Autobiography," in *Alexander Dovzhenko: The Poet as Filmmaker*, ed. and trans. Marco Carynnyk (Cambridge, Mass.: MIT Press, 1973), 14.

177. Eisenstein, "The Montage of Attractions," in *Writings, 1922–34*, 1:33–38. See also "The Montage of Film Attractions," 1:39–58. Tom Gunning borrows the term "attractions" for his theory of early cinema. Tom Gunning, "The Cinema of Attraction: Early Film, Its Spectator, and the Avant-Garde," in *Film and Theory: An Anthology*, ed. Robert Stam and Toby Miller (Oxford: Blackwell, 2000), 229–35.

178. Quoted in Jay Leyda, *Kino: A History of the Russian and Soviet Film* (New York: Collier Books, 1973), 243–44.

179. Ray Uzwyshyn, "*Zvenyhora* (1928): Ethnographic Modernism," http://rayuzwyshyn.net/dovzhenko/Zvenyhora.htm.

180. Uzwyshyn, "*Zvenyhora* (1928)."

181. Ray Uzwyshyn, "*Arsenal* (1929): Ukraine in Revolution," http://rayuzwyshyn.net/dovzhenko/Arsenal.htm.

182. For a discussion of *Earth* and its treatment of cinematic space, see Perez, *Material Ghost*, 161–92.

183. Bertolt Brecht, "The Modern Theatre Is the Epic Theatre," in *Brecht on Theatre: The Development of an Aesthetic*, ed. and trans. John Willett (New York: Hill & Wang, 1964), 37. Playwright David Edgar holds that Brecht's "major legacy" in the theater can be "encapsulated in the slogan 'each scene for itself.'" Edgar, "Each Scene for Itself," *London Review of Books* 21, no. 5 (1999): 26.

184. Bertolt Brecht, "A Short Organum for the Theatre," in *Brecht on Theatre*, 201.

185. André Bazin, "Le Réalisme cinématographique et l'école italienne de la libération," in *Qu'est-ce que le cinéma?*, vol. 4, *Une esthétique de la réalité: Le néo-réalisme* (Paris: Editions du Cerf, 1962), 31–32 (my translation). For Hugh Gray's translation, see Bazin, *What Is Cinema?*, 2:35–36.

186. Brecht, "Short Organum," 201.

187. Salles Gomes, *Jean Vigo*, 106.

188. Salles Gomes, *Jean Vigo*, 109.

189. Lindsay Anderson, "*L'Atalante*, the Forgotten Masterpiece," in *Never Apologise: The Collected Writings*, ed. Paul Ryan (London: Plexus, 2004), 531.

190. Quoted in Salles Gomes, *Jean Vigo*, 143.

191. I borrow the title "Black Sheep" from Dana Stevens's review of *Killer of Sheep* from *Slate*, http://www.slate.com/.

192. Andrew O'Hehir, "*Killer of Sheep*," Salon, March 30, 2007, https://www.salon.com/.

193. Charles Burnett talking to Nelson Kim, "Burnett, Charles," May 2003, http://sensesofcinema.com/.

194. J. Hoberman, "L.A. Story," *Village Voice*, March 20, 2007.

195. Armond White, "*Killer of Sheep*," in *The A List: The National Society of Film Critics' 100 Essential Films*, ed. Jay Carr (Cambridge, Mass.: Da Capo Press, 2002), 160.

196. Interview with Kiarostami in Mehrnaz Saeed-Vafa and Jonathan Rosenbaum, *Abbas Kiarostami* (Urbana: University of Illinois Press, 2003), 107.

197. For a discussion of *Close-up* and of Kiarostami's modernism in relation to his realism, see Perez, *Material Ghost*, 260–72.

198. Hamid Dabashi, *Close Up: Iranian Cinema, Past, Present, and Future* (London: Verso, 2001).

199. This is Kiarostami's account in the interview with him in the Criterion DVD of *Close-up* (2010).

200. Jean-Luc Godard, *Godard on Godard*, ed. Jean Narboni and Tom Milne (New York: Viking, 1972), 181.

II. Melodrama and Film Technique

1. My older colleague was Francis Randall, who taught history at Sarah Lawrence College for many years.

2. See Cavell, *Pursuits of Happiness,* and *Contesting Tears: The Hollywood Melodrama of the Unknown Woman* (Chicago: University of Chicago Press, 1996).

3. Peter Brooks, *The Melodramatic Imagination: Balzac, Henry James, Melodrama, and the Mode of Excess* (New Haven, Conn.: Yale University Press, 1976), 14. In Thomas Elsaesser's account, melodrama preceded the revolution and declined in the aftermath: "Paradoxically, the French Revolution failed to produce a new form of social drama or tragedy. The Restoration stage (when theaters in Paris were specially licensed to play 'melodramas') trivialised the form by using melodramatic plots in exotic settings, and providing escapist entertainment with little social relevance. The plays warmed up the standard motif of 18th-century French fiction and drama, that of innocence persecuted and virtue rewarded, and the conventions of melodrama functioned in their most barren form as the mechanics of pure suspense. . . . The sudden reversals of fortune, the intrusion of chance and coincidence had originally pointed to the arbitrary way feudal institutions could ruin the individual unprotected by civil rights and liberties. . . . Now, with the bourgeoisie triumphant, this form of drama lost its subversive charge and functioned more as a means of consolidating an as yet weak and incoherent ideological position. Whereas the prerevolutionary melodramas had often ended tragically, those of the Restoration had happy endings, they reconciled the suffering individual to his social position." Elsaesser, "Tales of Sound and Fury: Observations on the Family Melodrama," in *Imitations of Life: A Reader of Film and Television Melodrama,* ed. Marcia Landy (Detroit: Wayne State University Press, 1991), 71.

4. John G. Cawelti, "The Evolution of Social Melodrama," in Landy, *Imitations of Life,* 33–34.

5. A. Nicholas Vardac, *Stage to Screen: Theatrical Method from Garrick to Griffith* (Cambridge, Mass.: Harvard University Press, 1949). See also Ben Brewster and Lea Jacobs, *Theater to Cinema: Stage Pictorialism and the Early Feature Film* (New York: Oxford University Press, 1997).

6. In *The English Stage* (1897), A. Filon characterizes melodrama in this way: "When dealing with Irving, I asked the question, so often discussed, whether we go to the theater to see a representation of life, or to forget life and seek relief from it. Melodrama solves this question and shows that both theories are right, by giving satisfaction to both desires, in that it offers the extreme of realism in scenery and language together with the most uncommon sentiments and events." Quoted in Elsaesser, "Tales of Sound and Fury," 89.

7. "It is the ability to show real sleigh rides and spacious barn dances, to place Gish and Barthelmess in a real blizzard, and on a real river as the winter

ice breaks, that gives the film an insuperable advantage over the stage. What-ever reservations one entertains about the motives and psychology of these characters, whatever strain has been placed on credibility by the coincidences on which the story so heavily depends, they are (almost literally) blown away by the storm sequence, so powerfully is it presented." Richard Schickel, *D. W. Griffith: An American Life* (New York: Simon & Schuster, 1984), qtd. in Linda Williams, "Melodrama Revised," in *Refiguring American Film Genres*, ed. Nick Browne (Berkeley: University of California Press, 1998), 68.

8. Stanley Kauffmann, "Way Down East," in *Living Images: Film Comment and Criticism* (New York: Harper & Row, 1975), 284.

9. Peter Brooks, *The Melodramatic Imagination: Balzac, Henry James, Melo-drama, and the Mode of Excess* (New Haven, Conn.: Yale University Press, 1995).

10. Barthes, "Reality Effect," 141–48.

11. Brooks, *Melodramatic Imagination*, 148.

12. Williams, "Melodrama Revised," 42.

13. Kauffmann, "Way Down East," 282. The Hollywood Production Code may have demanded earthly justice, but that doesn't mean that the form of melodrama does.

14. Williams, "Melodrama Revised," 61, 65.

15. Williams, "Melodrama Revised," 68–69.

16. Williams, "Melodrama Revised," 61.

17. Renoir, *My Life and My Films*, 45.

18. Laura Mulvey has a chapter on "Close-ups and Commodities" in *Fetishism and Curiosity* (London: BFI, 1996), but she mainly deals with the glamorous image of the female body and the male anxieties she takes it to guard against, and she doesn't say much about the close-up as such.

19. For a related discussion of Griffith's close-ups in comparison with Dreyer's and Godard's, see Perez, *Material Ghost*, 349–51.

20. Balázs, *Theory of the Film*, 62–63.

21. Quoted from the *New York Dramatic Mirror*, December 25, 1909, in George C. Pratt, ed., *Spellbound in Darkness: Readings in the History and Criticism of the Silent Film* (Rochester, N.Y.: University of Rochester Press, 1966), 61.

22. "In *A Corner in Wheat* it is these contrasts," Tom Gunning writes, "that form the center of the film, substituting a paradigmatic axis of compar-ison for the syntagmatic axis of story development." Gunning, *D. W. Griffith and the Origins of American Narrative Film: The Early Years at Biograph* (Urbana: University of Illinois Press, 1991), 241.

23. Pratt, *Spellbound in Darkness*, 61. Pratt corrects the misapprehension that *A Corner in Wheat* was based on Frank Norris's novel *The Pit*.

24. Alfred Kazin, *On Native Grounds: An Interpretation of Modern American Prose Literature* (New York: Reynal & Hitchcock, 1942), 100.

25. Quoted in Gunning, *D. W. Griffith*, 249.

26. Gunning, *D. W. Griffith*, 248–49.

27. Quoted in Herman G. Weinberg, *Saint Cinema: Writings on the Film, 1929–1970* (New York: Dover, 1973), 139.

28. E. M. Forster, *Aspects of the Novel* (New York: Harcourt Brace, 1927), 67–78.

29. Forster, *Aspects of the Novel*, 78.

30. Eric Bentley, *The Life of the Drama* (New York: Atheneum, 1964), 166–68.

31. Kazin, *On Native Grounds*, 101–2.

32. Frank Norris, "Zola as a Romantic Writer," in *Frank Norris: Novels and Essays*, ed. Donald Pizer (New York: Library of America, 1986), 1106–7.

33. Kazin, *On Native Grounds*, 102.

34. Frank Norris, *McTeague: A Story of San Francisco*, in *Frank Norris: Novels and Essays*, 303.

35. Norris, *McTeague*, 411.

36. André Bazin, "The Evolution of Film Language," in *The New Wave*, ed. Peter Graham (Garden City, N.Y.: Doubleday, 1968), 30–31.

37. Fereydoun Hoveyda and Jacques Rivette, "Entretien avec Roberto Rossellini," *Cahiers du cinéma* 94 (1959).

38. Warshow, *Immediate Experience*, 251.

39. Penelope Houston, *The Contemporary Cinema* (Baltimore, Md.: Penguin Books, 1963), 22.

40. Tag Gallagher, *The Adventures of Roberto Rossellini* (New York: Da Capo Press, 1998), 205.

41. I lifted this sentence from my discussion of Rossellini in Perez, *Material Ghost*, 41.

42. Warshow, *Immediate Experience*, 256.

43. Gallagher, *Adventures of Roberto Rossellini*, 145.

44. Gallagher, *Adventures of Roberto Rossellini*, 257.

45. André Bazin, *What Is Cinema?*, 2:98 (translation modified).

46. Bentley, *Life of the Drama*, 205.

47. Eric Bentley, *In Search of Theater* (New York: Knopf, 1953), 158.

48. Cavell, *Contesting Tears*.

49. Linda Williams, "'Something Else Besides a Mother': *Stella Dallas* and the Maternal Melodrama," *Cinema Journal* 24, no. 1 (1984): 2–27. E. Ann Kaplan replied in *Cinema Journal* 24, no. 2 (1985): 40–43. Further installments of the debate appeared in *Cinema Journal* 25, no. 1 (1985): 50–54; and no. 4 (1986): 44–53. See also E. Ann Kaplan, "The Case of the Missing Mother: Patriarchy and the Maternal in Vidor's *Stella Dallas*," *Heresies* 4, no. 4 (1983): 81–85.

50. Williams, "Something Else Besides a Mother," 2.

51. Edmund Wilson, "The Ambiguity of Henry James," in *The Triple Thinkers: Twelve Essays on Literary Subjects* (New York: Oxford University Press, 1963), 88–132.

52. Cavell, *Contesting Tears*, 204.

53. Affron, *Cinema and Sentiment*, 72–74.

54. Harvey, *Romantic Comedy*, 560–61.

55. Williams, "Melodrama Revised," 45.

56. Cavell, *Contesting Tears*, 200–201.

57. Cavell, *Contesting Tears*, 201–2.

58. Cavell, *Contesting Tears*, 203.

59. Cavell, *Contesting Tears*, 202.

60. Rothman, *"I" of the Camera*, 86.

61. Rothman, *"I" of the Camera*, 86–87.

62. Rothman, *"I" of the Camera*, 91.

63. Cavell, *Contesting Tears*, 219.

64. Benjamin, *Origin of German Tragic Drama*, 107–8, 109–10.

65. Godard made this statement ("Les travellings sont affaire de morale") in a roundtable discussion of *Hiroshima mon amour* in *Cahiers du cinéma* 97 (1959).

66. Bruce Bennett, "Following the Camera with Japan's Greatest Storyteller," *New York Sun*, September 8, 2006, https://www.nysun.com/.

67. Dudley Andrew, "The Passion of Identification in the Late Films of Kenji Mizoguchi," in *Film in the Aura of Art* (Princeton, N.J.: Princeton University Press, 1984), 178.

68. Quoted in Daniel Morgan, "Max Ophuls and the Limits of Virtuosity: On the Aesthetics and Ethics of Camera Movement," *Critical Inquiry* 38, no. 1 (2011): 132.

69. Morgan, "Max Ophuls," 131.

70. Morgan, "Max Ophuls," 140.

71. Morgan, "Max Ophuls," 140.

72. Harvey, *Movie Love*, 228.

73. Harvey, *Movie Love*, 228.

74. Quoted in Susan White, *The Cinema of Max Ophuls: Magisterial Vision and the Figure of Woman* (New York: Columbia University Press, 1995), 263.

75. Noël Burch, *To the Distant Observer: Form and Meaning in the Japanese Cinema* (Berkeley: University of California Press, 1979), 229. Burch greatly admires the earlier, purer Mizoguchi but misguidedly slights the director's later work.

76. Quoted in Peter Brunette, *Wong Kar-wai* (Urbana: University of Illinois Press, 2005), 86.

77. Peter Bradshaw, review of Wong Kar-wai, *In the Mood for Love* (2000), *Guardian*, October 26, 2000, https://www.theguardian.com/.

78. Brunette, *Wong Kar-wai*, 96.

79. Quoted in Brunette, *Wong Kar-wai*, 100.

80. Brunette, *Wong Kar-wai*, 100–101.

81. Eric Bentley, *Life of the Drama*, 200.

82. Warshow, *Immediate Experience*, 132–33.

83. Stanley Crouch, "Menace II Society," in *The All-American Skin Game, or The Decoy of Race* (New York: Vintage Books, 1997), 219.

84. Crouch, "Menace II Society," 219.

85. Crouch, "Menace II Society," 218.

86. Roland Barthes, *The Pleasure of the Text*, trans. Richard Miller (New York: Hill & Wang, 1975), 47.

87. Beverly Walker, "Malick on Badlands," *Sight and Sound* 44, no. 2 (1975): 82.

88. Leo Bersani and Ulysse Dutoit, *Forms of Being: Cinema, Aesthetics, Subjectivity* (London: BFI, 2004), 129–31.

89. Michel Chion, *The Thin Red Line*, trans. Trista Selous (London: BFI, 2004), 38.

90. Kaja Silverman, "All Things Shining," in *Flesh of My Flesh* (Stanford, Calif.: Stanford University Press, 2009), 110–13.

91. Quoted in Richard Neer, "Terrence Malick's New World," Nonsite .org, June 12, 2011, http://nonsite.org/issues/issue-2/terrence-malicks-new -world.

92. Geoffrey O'Brien, "The Variety of Movie Experience," *New York Review of Books* 58, no. 12 (2011), https://www.nybooks.com/.

93. Peter Bradshaw, review of Terrence Malick, *To the Wonder* (2012), *Guardian*, February 21, 2013, https://www.theguardian.com/.

94. This news ticker appeared on CNN on August 22, 2012; David Ariosto, "Maryland Train Derailment Delays Terrorism Trial at Guantanamo," CNN, August 22, 2012, https://edition.cnn.com/.

95. Eric Bentley, *Life of the Drama*, 179.

96. Charles Musser, *Before the Nickelodeon: Edwin S. Porter and the Edison Manufacturing Company* (Berkeley: University of California Press, 1991).

97. Mikhail Bakhtin, *Problems of Dostoevsky's Poetics*, ed. and trans. Caryl Emerson (Minneapolis: University of Minnesota Press, 1984).

98. A. O. Scott, "Film Review: A Digital Prism Refracts Reality," *New York Times*, April 28, 2000, https://www.nytimes.com/.

99. Quoted in Aranda, *Luis Buñuel*, 86 (my translation).

100. Thomas Elsaesser, "Performative Self-Contradictions: Michael Haneke's Mind Games," in *A Companion to Michael Haneke*, ed. Roy Grundmann (Oxford: Wiley-Blackwell, 2010), 65–66.

101. Catherine Wheatley, *Caché (Hidden)* (London: BFI, 2011), 31.

102. Caitlin Hughes, "NYFF: Haneke's 'Amour' Is a Brilliant, Unflinching Portrait of an Elderly Couple and the Ravages of Time," Film School Rejects, October 6, 2012, https://filmschoolrejects.com/.

103. Mladen Dolar, "Hitchcock's Objects," in *Everything You Always Wanted to Know about Lacan (But Were Afraid to Ask Hitchcock)*, ed. Slavoj Žižek (London: Verso, 1992), 34.

104. Raymond Durgnat, *The Strange Case of Alfred Hitchcock* (Cambridge, Mass.: MIT Press, 1974), 185.

105. Eric Rohmer and Claude Chabrol, *Hitchcock: The First Forty-Four Films*, trans. Stanley Hochman (New York: Ungar, 1979), 72.

106. Durgnat, *Strange Case of Alfred Hitchcock*, 185.

107. William Rothman, *Hitchcock—The Murderous Gaze* (Cambridge, Mass.: Harvard University Press, 1982), 183.

108. Pechter, *Twenty-Four Times a Second*, 182.

109. Slavoj Žižek, "'In His Bold Gaze My Ruin Is Writ Large,'" in Žižek, *Everything You Always Wanted to Know*, 247–52.

110. Žižek, "In His Bold Gaze," 244–45.

111. Pechter, *Twenty-Four Times a Second*, 178.

112. Žižek, "In His Bold Gaze," 211–16.

113. "Indeed, only a thin line separates this notion of '*Dieu obscur*' from the Sadeian notion of the 'Supreme-Being-of-Evil.'" Žižek, "In His Bold Gaze," 215.

114. Žižek, "In His Bold Gaze," 215–16.

115. Žižek, "In His Bold Gaze," 218. Žižek draws on Fredric Jameson's account of Rothman's *Hitchcock*. See Jameson, "Allegorizing Hitchcock," in *Signatures of the Visible* (New York: Routledge, 1990), 99–127.

116. Žižek, "In His Bold Gaze."

117. Žižek, "In His Bold Gaze," 227.

118. For a fuller interpretation of *Nosferatu* as an allegory of death, see Perez, *Material Ghost*, 123–48.

119. Dolar, "Hitchcock's Objects," 33–39.

120. Dolar, "Hitchcock's Objects," 37.

121. Rothman, *Hitchcock*, 182.

122. François Truffaut, *Hitchcock*, rev. ed. (New York: Simon & Schuster, 1984), 153.

123. Rothman, *Hitchcock*, 192.

124. Robin Wood is an exception to this disavowal. "The key to Hitchcock's films is less suspense than sexuality," Wood argues. "In *Shadow of a Doubt* it is above all sexuality that cracks apart the family facade. As far as the Hays code permitted, a double incest theme runs through the film: Uncle Charlie and Emmy, Uncle Charlie and Young Charlie. Necessarily, this is expressed through images and motifs, never becoming verbally explicit." Wood, *Hitchcock's Films Revisited* (New York: Columbia University Press, 1989), 300.

125. Wood, *Hitchcock's Films Revisited*, 300.

126. Wood, *Hitchcock's Films Revisited*, 219.

127. Rothman, *Hitchcock*, 227–28.

128. Rothman, *Hitchcock*, 232–33.

129. Durgnat, *Strange Case of Alfred Hitchcock*, 182–83.

130. Rothman, *Hitchcock*, 237.

131. Rothman, *Hitchcock*, 238.

132. I owe this observation to my student William Parker Marshall, who made it in class.

133. Rothman, *Hitchcock*, 240–42.

134. Truffaut, *Hitchcock*, 155.

135. Truffaut, *Hitchcock*, 153.

136. W. H. Auden, "The More Loving One," in *Collected Poems*, ed. Edward Mendelson (New York: Random House, 1976), 445.

137. Academic conference on Film Melodrama, Columbia University and New York University, New York, February 28 to March 2, 2013.

138. Alfred Hitchcock, "Why I Make Melodramas" (1936), cited by Linda Williams in her keynote address at the Film Melodrama conference, http://www.labyrinth.net.au/~muffin/melodramas.html.

139. Bentley, *Life of the Drama*, 267.

140. Michael Wood, "At the Movies," *London Review of Books* 35, no. 20 (2013), https://www.lrb.co.uk/.

141. Pedro Almodóvar, *Almodóvar on Almodóvar*, ed. Frédéric Strauss, rev. ed. (London: Faber & Faber, 2006), 155.

142. A. O. Scott, "FILM; The Track of a Teardrop, a Filmmaker's Path," *New York Times*, November 17, 2002, https://www.nytimes.com/.

143. Daniel Mendelsohn, "The Women of Pedro Almodóvar," *New York Review of Books* 54, no. 3 (2007), https://www.nybooks.com/.

144. Pedro Almodóvar, interview with Annette Insdorf in the Columbia TriStar DVD of *All About My Mother* (2000).

Coda

1. Kendall L. Walton, *Mimesis as Make-believe: On the Foundations of the Representational Arts* (Cambridge, Mass.: Harvard University Press, 1990), 196.

2. Sigmund Freud, *Group Psychology and the Analysis of the Ego*, trans. James Strachey (New York: Bantam, 1965), 49.

3. Freud, *Group Psychology*, 46.

4. Richard Wollheim, "Imagination and Identification," in *On Art and the Mind* (Cambridge, Mass.: Harvard University Press, 1974), 73–74.

5. Christian Metz, *The Imaginary Signifier: Psychoanalysis and the Cinema*, trans. Celia Britton, Annwyl Williams, Ben Brewster, and Alfred Guzzetti (Bloomington: Indiana University Press, 1982), 32.

6. Berys Gaut, "Identification and Emotion in Narrative Film," in *Passionate Views: Film, Cognition, and Emotion*, ed. Carl Plantinga and Greg M. Smith (Baltimore, Md.: Johns Hopkins University Press, 1999), 210.

7. Gaut, "Identification and Emotion," 204–5.

8. Theodor W. Adorno, *Ästhetische Theorie* (Frankfurt am Main: Suhrkamp, 1971), 514, qtd. in Hans Robert Jauss, "Levels of Identification of Hero

and Audience," trans. Benjamin and Helga Bennett, *New Literary History* 5, no. 2 (1974): 284–85.

9. Jauss, "Levels of Identification," 286.

10. For an account of Keaton's distinctive kind of comedy, see Perez, *Material Ghost*, 92–122.

11. See Melanie Klein, "Notes on Some Schizoid Mechanisms" and "On Identification," in *Envy and Gratitude and Other Works, 1946–1963* (New York: Free Press, 1975), 1–24, 141–75.

INDEX

Acín, Ramón, 140; death of, 367n130
actors: autonomy of, 301; glances of,
  214; Hitchcock's direction of, 329
Adams, Brooke: in *Days of Heaven*, 282
Adams, Eddie: *Saigon Execution*, 157
"Adios" (song), 228
Adorno, Theodor: on identification,
  349–50
adultery: in literature, 269; melodrama of, 249; in Mizoguchi's work,
  252; in Wong's work, 266–69
aesthetics, xix; effect on norms, 350;
  as ethics, 168; of identification, 349;
  of melodrama, 204; postmodern,
  62; of violence, 276
Affleck, Ben: in *To the Wonder*, 291
Affron, Charles, 369n164; on *Stella
  Dallas*, 241
Africa, patriarchy of, 112
Agamben, Giorgio: on parody, 170,
  370n168
alienation, Brechtian, 164, 169, 177–
  78, 230, 350
allegory: binary oppositions in, 100;
  character embodying, 98; Christian,
  97, 131–32; of *Divine Comedy*, 106;
  Eisenstein's use of, 95, 98, 112–13;
  etymology of, 97; expressionist,
  100–101, 124; as extended metaphor, 95; and extended synechdoche, 95–99; figural mode of, 105,
  106; Ford's use of, 31, 39, 113, 115;

Freud on, 98; of human finitude,
  118; Ophuls's use of, 259, 261;
  political, 102, 103; self-referential,
  117, 324; subjectivity in, 124, 155;
  surrealist, 124; of time, 120–21;
  urban versus rural, 100; of violence,
  31, 155–56; in the West, 106–7
allegory, national, 39, 106–8, 176; of
  Third World, 113; of United States,
  113
Allen, Woody: addresses to audience,
  164; *Blue Jasmine*, 338
Almendros, Néstor, 282
Almodóvar, Pedro: comedy/melo-
  drama blend in, 344; emotionalism
  of, 339; on female solidarity, 341
  All About My Mother: comedy of,
  341; melodrama of, 340
  The Flower of My Secret: camp in, 339;
  melodrama of, 339, 340
  Volver: artifice in, 342; close-ups
  of, 343; comedy of, 342, 343;
  detachment in, 342; ghosts of,
  342, 343; murder in, 341–42,
  343; traveling two-shots of, 343
  *Women on the Verge of a Nervous Break-
  down*: artifice in, 339; Hitchcock
  reference in, 338
Altman, Robert: actors' autonomy
  under, 301
"Amor de Medianoche" (song), 228
Anderson, Lindsay: *Magnolia*, 44, 182

Ciceronian rhetoric, 18; as theater, 27

populism: of 1890s, 23; of Gilded Age, 25–26; of New Deal, 23; Will Rogers's, 13

Porter, Edwin S.: *The Life of an American Fireman,* multiple perspective of, 202, 298–99

Prado, Pérez: in *Aventurera,* 227

Pratt, George, 209, 373n23

prefiguration, 105–13; in Dante, 105–6; Old Testament, 105; pagan, 105. *See also figurae futurorum*

Prince Potemkin (armored cruiser): in Constanța, 94; sailors' mutiny aboard, 92, 93, 94–95

prose, invention of, 170

Prouty, Olive Higgins: *Stella Dallas,* 237–39, 240, 243, 247

The Public Enemy, 276

Pudovkin, V. I.: *Film technique and Film Acting,* 64

Queen Christina (1933), close-up of, 65

Quintilian: on allegory, 135; on irony, 135; on metaphor, 95; ship of state metaphor, 95, 363n61; on synechdoche, 63

Rabal, Francisco: in *Nazarín,* 130

racism: of *The Searchers,* 40–43; in Westerns, 39–43

Radziwilowicz, Jerzy, 171

Rancière, Jacques, 34; on police logic, 36

Raritan, Perez's work in, xii

rationality, human, xvii

Ray, Satyajit: *Pather Panchali,* 66–68; circular imagery of, 67–68; close-ups of, 67; dramatic irony of, 139–40; emergent life imagery, 67; identification in, 140; soundtrack of, 139; synechdoche of, 68

realism: artifice and, 180; conviction through, 150; ellipsis in, 194; excess in, 203; in fiction, 169; Hitchcock's, 323; idealization and, 153; identification in, 150; irony

and, 134–35; melodrama and, 202–4, 211, 333, 372n6; metonymy in, 98, 135, 179; as modern invention, 137; montage of attractions and, 173; open synechdoche and, 150–52, 179; opposition to classicism, 180, 203; photographers', 224–27; as principle of representation, 204; reality resistant to, 152; rhetoric of, 59, 135; Rossellini's, 224–27; search for meaning in, 151–52; social issues in, 206

Red Mullet (production company), 302

reflexivity, 369n164; of art, 161–62; avant-garde, 161, 162; comedy and, 161–66; definition of, 161; ironic, 164; of parody, 163; in rhetoric, 162

Reggiani, Serge, 74

Renner, Jeremy: in *The Hurt Locker,* 159

Renoir, Jean: on Griffith, 207; realism of, 152; and single-eye convention, 301; work with Becker, 75

The Rules of the Game, 226; as comedy, 134–35; irony in, 135, 138; realism of, 134

Toni, 136–38; bridge motif of, 136–37; camera work of, 136–37; closing sequence of, 138; direct sound of, 136, 137; immigrants of, 136–38, 282, 367n126; irony in, 138; modernity in, 136–37; naturalism of, 137; peasant tradition in, 136; realism of, 138; setting of, 136; song in, 136, 137–38; source for, 136

repetition, emphasis through, 86

Resnais, Alain: *Night and Fog,* 87

Restoration, melodrama of, 372n3

reverse angles, 213–16, 229; actors' glance in, 214; conventions of, 216; Griffith's, 214; in identification, 216; space in, 214; Stroheim's, 214–16, 221–22, 223

rhetoric: boundaries in, 133; comedy and, 7–10; decorum in, 166–67; effect on audience, 158; identification in, xx–xxi; of melodrama, 202,

109, 116; illusion in, 108; individual and group in, 109; Islam in, 108, 109–11; national allegory in, 107–8; past and present in, 111–12; peasant and aristocracy in, 110–12; personification in, 108, 111, 112; rhetorical gesture of, 110; slavery in, 109–10; soundtrack of, 109, 111, 365n91
Xala, 107
senex iratus (New Comedy), 7, 8
Sepehri, Sohrab: "Where Is the Friend's House?," 192
Sevilla, Ninón, 231; in *Aventurera*, 227, 228–29
Shakespeare, William: romantic comedy of, 361n38; villains of, 337. Works: *King Lear*, 135; *Othello*, 337; *Richard III*, 337; *Romeo and Juliet*, 75; *The Tempest*, 8, 355n7
Shaw, Bernard: *Pygmalion*, 212
Sheen, Martin: in *Badlands*, 280
Shepard, Sam: in *Days of Heaven*, 282
Shimizu, Hiroshi: style of, 121
  Mr. Thank You, 121–25; axial movement in, 121, 123; bus trope of, 122; as comedy, 124; community in, 122, 123–24; love story of, 122, 124; prologue of, 121; space and time in, 122; tracking shots of, 121–23; voice-over narrative of, 124
"The Ship of State" (poem), 363n61
Shirley, Anne: in *Stella Dallas*, 238
Signoret, Simone: in *Casque d'or*, 74
Silverman, Kaja, 286
simile: subsumed under metaphor, 57, 259n9; tenor and vehicle in, 57
Sirk, Douglas: melodramas of, 167; on Stanwyck, 242
Sitney, P. Adams, 76
Skarsgård, Stellan: in *Timecode*, 303
Smith, Jeff, 128
society: organic models of, 259n10; as theater, 135
Socrates, Aristophanes' depiction of, 163

Spacek, Sissy: in *Badlands*, 280
speech disorders, 56–57
Spielberg, Steven: anti-intellectualism of, 104
  Saving Private Ryan, 103–5; historical allegory of, 104; rifle metaphors of, 103; unworthy enemy synechdoche of, 104
  Schindler's List, 87, 88
Srebnik, Simon: survival of Holocaust, 83–84, 85–86
Stanwyck, Barbara, 232; in *The Bitter Tea of General Yen*, 242; in *Stella Dallas*, 239, 242–43, 245–48
Starkweather, Charles, 280
Star Wars, 283
Steimatsky, Noa, 65
Stella Dallas (1925), 240–41, 244; abandonment in, 245
Stella Dallas (1937): ambiguity of, 236–49; appearances in, 239, 241–42; audience of, 243; authorial intention in, 243; camera movement in, 253; camera's agency in, 249; class in, 236, 238–48; decorum in, 241–42; divided perspective of, 246–47; *Doña Bárbara* and, 232; female spectator of, 237; feminist debates over, 236, 374n49; free indirect style of, 243; identification in, 350; as melodrama, 199, 271; modes of display in, 241; motherhood in, 238, 248; movie spectator trope of, 240, 241; multiple identifications in, 246; as New Comedy, 333; pathos of, 244, 247; performance in, 245–46, 248–49; points of view in, 237–39, 246, 248; sacrifice in, 237, 238; social embarrassment in, 249–47; source for, 237–39; spectators of, 246–47, 248; as tragedy, 244; tragic heroine of, 249; vulgarity in, 238; wedding scene, 247–48
Stendhal, on beauty, 270
Stevenson, Diane: on Hawks, 36; on *High Noon*, 358n61; on naturalism,

Gilberto Perez (1943–2015) was professor of film studies at Sarah Lawrence College, where he held the Noble Foundation Chair in Art and Cultural History. He was a film critic for the *Yale Review*, and the writer of numerous articles for *Cineaste*, *Hudson Review*, *London Review of Books*, *The Nation*, *New York Times*, *Raritan*, and *Sight and Sound*.

James Harvey is a film critic, essayist, playwright, and author of numerous books on film, including *Watching Them Be: Star Presence on the Screen from Garbo to Balthazar*.

Diane Stevenson is author of the poetry collection *The Beauty Shop Monologues, Ocean Springs, Mississippi, 1962*. She and Gilberto Perez were married for twenty-eight years.